Entrepreneurship and
Small Business

Entrepreneurship
and
Small Business

PAUL BURNS

palgrave

First published 2001 by
PALGRAVE
Houndmills, Basingstoke, Hampshire RG21 6XS and
175 Fifth Avenue, New York, N.Y. 10010
Companies and representatives throughout the world

PALGRAVE is the new global academic imprint of
St. Martin's Press LLC Scholarly and Reference Division and
Palgrave Publishers Ltd (formerly Macmillan Press Ltd).

ISBN 0–333–91473–2 hardback
ISBN 0–333–91474–0 paperback

This book is printed on paper suitable for recycling and made from fully managed and sustained forest sources.

A catalogue record for this book is available from the British Library.

Library of Congress Cataloging-in-Publication Data

Burns, Paul, 1949–
    Entrepreneurship and small business / Paul Burns.
        p. cm.
    Includes bibliographical references and index.
    ISBN 0–333–91473–2 (cloth)
    1. Small business—Study and teaching. 2. Small business—Management—Study and teaching. 3. Entrepreneurship—Study and teaching. 4. Business education. 5. Small business—Case studies. 6. Entrepreneurship—Case studies. I. Title

HD2341 .B873 2001
658.02′2—dc21   2001040653

Copy-edited and typeset by Povey–Edmondson
Tavistock and Rochdale, England

10   9   8   7   6   5   4   3   2
10 09 08 07 06 05 04 03 02

Printed and bound in Great Britain by
Antony Rowe Ltd, Chippenham, Wiltshire

To my wife, Jean

Contents

TC = FC + VC

lab +

Sale −

List of Tables

List of Figures

Mini cases: the businesses

Business references also appear in the text. For these, see the Index.

Mini cases: the entrepreneurs

References to entrepreneurs also appear in the text. For these, see the Index.

Preface

This book is about the dominant form of business on this planet – the small firm. It looks at how firms develop from start-up, sometimes to grow, sometimes to fail, but mainly to stagnate. It looks at their contribution to society. It looks at their defining characteristics – how they are not just scaled-down versions of large firms. It looks at how they go about business and the problems they face. It looks at family firms and the added complexity this brings.

The book is also about owner-managers and, most interesting of all, entrepreneurs. It is about what motivates them to do what they do – their personal and family influences. It is about how they go about the task of management – making decisions, balancing risk and return – and how they are different to managers in large firms. It is about how they must develop and change as the firm grows. It is about how certain defining characteristics they possess shape and define the business they run – for good or ill.

This book is also a 'how-to-do-it' text, synthesising good management practice for entrepreneurs involved in start-ups and growing firms. It is informed by research and based on thirty years experience of working with small firms and small firm advisors. Management in small firms is a holistic activity, so the skills developed include marketing, accounting, finance, people management and strategy development. Over 100 mini case studies are linked to the main text to illustrate how the concepts are actually used in small, growing and successful firms. Stories of success – and failure – are what makes the study of entrepreneurship and small business so interesting. The book also contains signposts – including websites – that enable students to get practical help and advice as well as access to up-to-date research and information. There are recommended books for further reading in selected areas and recommended journals for further research.

The major challenge facing Business Schools today is how to encourage and develop the entrepreneurial skills of students. This book is designed to address this issue. It is written to motivate students at the same time as providing frameworks to nurture these precious skills in a systematic way. There is also a chapter on the most interesting entrepreneurial development of the moment – e-business.

The book contains extensive teaching materials. Each chapter has essays and discussion topics as well as practical exercises and assignments. However, entrepreneurship is essentially a practical activity so there are a series of business ideas and start-up activities that lead to the development of a start-up business plan. There is also a series of activities that enable a growth audit to be undertaken on an existing firm. These are supported by pro formas and checklists. There is also a pro forma business plan with examples from retail, service and manufacturing businesses.

COURSES USING THE BOOK

The book is written for a range of undergraduate and postgraduate courses with the aim of fostering entrepreneurial talent and developing entrepreneurial skills:

1 First-year undergraduate business studies skill-development courses. Relevant chapters are designed to act as a holistic introduction to the topic of business studies in the practical context of a business start-up project.

2 Third-year undergraduate and postgraduate business studies skill-development courses. These develop the themes to a greater depth by looking at growth as well as start-up and can be used by students who have previously studied business by skimming early skills-based chapters. Students can undertake the start-up project or the business growth audit. For students who have previously studied business and management, an entrepreneurship course typically aims to integrate and apply most of the functional areas they have previously studied and give it a practical focus.

3 Third-year undergraduate and postgraduate specialist courses on entrepreneurship and small business (including MBA). Students can use the book to study this topic in its own right – reviewing research and developing their understanding of the sector. They can rely simply on the essays and discussion topics or exercises and activities, or alternatively undertake the business growth audit. For these students, the entrepreneurship course still aims to integrate and apply the functional areas they have previously studied and provide a practical focus, albeit at a higher level, but also to give them an insight into the study of entrepreneurship and small business in its own right.

It would be nice to think that students would find this book sufficiently interesting to read it all but, given the pressure of time and the different skills and backgrounds of these groups, it is more realistic to think that they will dip into it where they find it relevant to their course. The table below attempts to signpost which chapters are most relevant to these three groups.

Chapter	Pathway 1	Pathway 2	Pathway 3
1	☆☆☆	☆☆☆	☆☆☆
2	☆☆☆	☆☆☆	☆☆☆
3	☆☆☆	☆☆☆	☆☆☆
4	☆☆☆	☆☆☆	☆☆☆
5	☆☆☆	☆	☆
6	☆☆☆	☆	☆
7	☆☆	☆☆	☆☆
8	☆☆☆	☆☆☆	☆
9	☆	☆☆☆	☆☆☆
10		☆☆☆	☆
11		☆☆☆	☆
12	☆☆	☆☆	☆☆☆
13			☆☆☆
14		☆	☆☆☆

Key: ☆☆☆ Core, essential reading
☆☆ Relevant and of interest, but not essential
☆ Dip into as required depending on interest and/or skill level

Students will find many of the accounting concepts in Chapters 6 and 11 difficult to grasp; since many courses may wish to omit some of this material, the more technical aspects have been relegated to appendices in these chapters.

VISITORS AND CASES

Courses on entrepreneurship are greatly enriched by visiting speakers, particularly the entrepreneurs themselves. They can tell students what it is really like and often have some wonderful 'derring-do' stories to tell. I shall never forget the incredulity of an MBA class at Cranfield as they were told how a Rolls Royce-driving entrepreneur, who left school at the age of 16, made his first million selling meat from open markets across the south-east of England. And there was the time Anita Roddick said she would never hire anybody from a Business School. That went down well. My experience is that these talks are normally the highlight of the course. No matter how good the teacher, there is no substitute for the real thing – somebody who did it. Cases can help develop skills and illustrate important points in a practical context. Unfortunately the entrepreneur is such a vital part of the entrepreneurial business that, without access to them in person or through a video, they can seem a little flat.

LEARNING OUTCOMES AND REFERENCES FOR CHAPTERS

Each chapter has clear learning outcomes. This assumes that students will undertake relevant discussions, essays, assignments and exercises. Each chapter has full journal and chapter references as well as a list of relevant websites to visit. There is also a short list of selected readings, websites and recommended small business journals at the back of the book.

CASES AND SUMMARIES

The book has over 100 mini cases linked to relevant parts of the text. These are intended to illustrate the points being made and to show that theory normally does reflect the practical reality of small business management. The summary at the end of each chapter ties the cases into the main points being made in that chapter.

DISCUSSION AND ESSAY TOPICS

Each chapter has topics for group discussion or essay writing, which can be used as a basis for tutorials. They are designed to make students think about the text material and develop their critical understanding of it and what it means in the real world. The summaries and discussion topics help students discriminate between main and supporting points and provide mechanisms for self-teaching.

EXERCISES AND ASSIGNMENTS

Alongside these are exercises and assignments, which additionally involve doing something, in the main further research. This research is often desk-based – including visits to websites – but some of the most popular assignments, in my experience, involve students going out to do things – such as interviewing entrepreneurs. In relevant chapters there are financial exercises for which model answers are provided at the end of each chapter. There are also quizzes to help students monitor their understanding of the chapters.

ENTREPRENEURSHIP EXERCISES

At the end of the book there are exercises to help students evaluate whether they really might have what it takes to become an entrepreneur and set up their own business, to help them plan to set up the business and to evaluate whether a business has growth potential. This is split into three parts.

The dream

These exercises allow the student to evaluate whether they have what it takes to be an entrepreneur as well as think through the consequences of becoming self-employed. These five exercises can be undertaken after Chapter 2.

Start-up

Central to any entrepreneurship course ought to be a practical project, the most commonly used being the business start-up. This is normally assessed by the development of a business plan. Ideally students should be asked to prepare a plan on an idea of their own that they think has some commercial potential. Preparing the plan forces them to be creative and entrepreneurial. It also takes them beyond the ideas stage and forces them to crystallise the ideas, write them down and show how they can be made to happen. This is not only creative, but also an excellent management discipline. It integrates all the functional areas of management that are too often taught separately.

By working through the 16 exercises students can develop this project from the ideas stage into a complete business plan. Extensive use is made of pro formas and worksheets to develop students' practical skills. Working either individually or in groups, these exercises can be undertaken as relevant chapters are completed. I normally ask students to present their plan either to fellow students or to an invited panel.

Start-up exercise

Chapter	Exercises	Topics
4	1–3	Business ideas
5	4–9	Feasibility: customer and benefit analysis, market research, break-even, resources
6	10–11	Profit and cash-flow evaluation
8	12–15	Business plan
12	16	Obtaining finance

Growth audit

An alternative activity, suited better to older, more experienced students, is to write a report on the growth prospects of a small firm. This involves them going out and actually talking to entrepreneurs, finding out what small firms really are like. It gets them to apply theories and concepts to a real situation. If undertaken by mature MBA students, it can often provide the entrepreneur with an invaluable outside view on how their business is doing. Running a small firm can certainly be a lonely, insular affair. This sort of project also provides a much needed link between university or college and the small business community.

The 10-part exercise involves students undertaking a growth audit on an existing business. This can be undertaken individually, but my experience is that it is best undertaken in small groups. The exercises can also be undertaken as relevant chapters are completed. Because many students may not have much business experience, extensive use is made of checklists and worksheets to help students undertake the audit. Sometimes student reports can provide a basis for case study development. Sometimes the personal links they develop open up research opportunities.

Growth audit exercise

Chapter	Exercises	Checklist/activity
9	1–2	Personal qualities of the owner-manager
		The management team
10	3–6	The product-market offering
		The competitive environment
		Financial performance
11	7–10	Evaluation of growth options

In the final analysis, any course on entrepreneurship must challenge students to think entrepreneurially. It must make them aware of opportunities in the marketplace and generate a 'can-do' mentality. It must empower them and convince them that they can shape their own destinies. It must make them realise how important the entrepreneur is to the small firm and to society as a whole. It must make them realise how business problems do not come in neatly labelled boxes reflecting the way the subject is taught. But, most of all, it must be interesting and fun.

ADDITIONAL TEACHING MATERIALS

The website accompanying this book contains additional teaching materials including suggested course outlines, additional cases (with teaching notes) and overhead slides. It also contains a complete copy of the Entrepreneurship Exercises, which form the cornerstone of this book. These can all be accessed and downloaded free by instructors.

KEY AND COGNITIVE SKILLS FOR THE COURSE

Having completed a course in entrepreneurship and small business using this book, with the seminar discussion topics, exercises and activities designed around it, a student should have developed a number of important skills:

- Information interpretation, critical analysis and evaluation skills;
- Data analysis and interpretation skills;
- Problem identification and solving skills;
- ICT skills, in particular the use of the internet;
- Independent and/or team working skills;
- Writing and presentation skills.

LEARNING OUTCOMES FOR THE COURSE

In the same way, on completing such a course, depending on which pathway they took, a student should:

1 Have a clear understanding of the environment in which small firms operate and how it impacts on them;
2 Have a clear understanding of how small firms develop, grow and, in particular, how the role of the entrepreneur changes;
3 Have a clear understanding of the nature of entrepreneurship;
4 Have a sound knowledge of the functional areas of management that are necessary to start-up and grow a business;
5 Have a sound knowledge of the sources of information and advice that are available to help in the start-up and growth of a business;
6 Have a sound knowledge of the sources of finance that are available for start-ups and growth businesses;
7 Have the ability to carry out the preparatory work necessary to develop a business idea, draw up a business plan and present it to a provider of finance;
8 Have the ability to implement, operate and monitor the execution of the plan;
9 Have an ability to set up the appropriate information systems to control a start-up business;
10 Have a clear understanding of the growth strategies available to small firms and their pros and cons;
11 Have an ability to undertake a growth audit and evaluate the potential of that firm to grow;
12 Have a clear understanding of the exit options available to entrepreneurs and their pros and cons;
13 Have developed a range of applied management skills in a holistic way.

I also hope that any entrepreneur using this book would have a better chance of success!

Acknowledgements

This book really is the accumulation of thirty years of experience of working with small firms. The first acknowledgement must therefore be to the hundreds of small firms that I have been able to work with in that period – to the millionaire successes, the failures and the lifestyle business. They have helped me to understand the problems and issues they face, to see the patterns and make the generalisations. They are an inspiration. Thanks also to the students at South Bank, Cranfield and Warwick Universities who have spurred me to develop the teaching materials and who have helped test them.

I am used to collaborating on writing projects and this is the first book I have written completely on my own. I wrote my first book and a number of subsequent ones with Jim Dewhurst. Sadly he died a couple of years ago. I learnt a lot about writing from Jim. He is missed.

Over the past few years I have worked extensively with partners in Grant Thornton, probably the leading UK accountants working with small firms. I have learnt enormously from their experience and much of the content of this book has been developed with their help and support. Thanks particularly to Andrew Godfrey, Bill Blythe, Mike Saville and David White and all the staff at their excellent training centre at Bradenham Manor.

Thanks to Peter Jennings at Southampton University for invaluable comments on an early draft. Hopefully the final book is much improved.

Finally, thanks to my wife Jean for her patience and understanding during the project and her help with proof reading the final manuscript.

David and Goliath

Contents

Learning outcomes

By the end of this chapter you should:

- Understand why small firms and entrepreneurs are the focus of so much interest;
- Understand the meaning of the terms entrepreneur and owner-manager and why they are different;
- Understand the statistical definition of small firms and appreciate their special characteristics;
- Understand the relationship between small firms and entrepreneurship;
- Appreciate the size and other characteristics of the UK small firms sector compared to other countries and the significant contribution it makes to the economy;
- Appreciate the influences on the growth of the small firm sector.

The stuff of dreams

There is nothing new in life. As we enter the third millennium, small firms, new firms and entrepreneurialism have become the focus of business interest. These are the by-words of business, the latest fashion in the fashionable world of business education. They provide the glamour pages for the business press with 'against-all-odds' start-up stories and biographies of millionaire entrepreneurs guaranteed to sell well.

Entrepreneurs have become the stuff of legends, 'economic heroes' (Cannon, 1991) increasingly held in high esteem and held up as role models to be emulated. They are often said to embody many ephemeral qualities – freedom of spirit, creativity, vision, zeal. Like Bill Gates, they have the courage and self-belief to turn their dreams into realities. They see an opportunity, commercialise it and in the process create jobs from which the rest of society benefits. They become rich and society benefits. Or so the story goes.

Yet take time to get a perspective on this. Just a century ago, as we entered the twentieth century, the focus was on big. Big was beautiful and size really mattered. Big was respectable, it was political-establishment. Big was the future. It offered economies of scale; mass production that brought well-being, if not wealth, to the masses. It was how the Western democracies would keep the common man, not only in food, shelter and life's necessities, but also in his place. It even spawned its own professional elite – managers. Whilst this has been a fundamental activity throughout history, the recognition and study of it as a discipline and profession is a thoroughly modern, twentieth century phenom-enon. Harvard Business School awarded its first Masters degree in the discipline in 1910. And all of this was based upon the best practices in large corporations. Business Schools have reflected the wider establishment view and traditionally eschewed the arts of running a small business and largely ignored the skills of entrepreneurialism (Crainer and Dearlove, 1998).

But have small firms, like David, suddenly triumphed over the Goliath of large firms? In fact small firms, new firms and entrepreneurs never went away. And in the later part of the last century reality began to dawn. In 1973 E. F. Schumacher, in his somewhat romantic book *Small is Beautiful* asserted that giant organisations and increased specialisation resulted in economic inefficiency, environmental pollution and inhumane working conditions and proposed a system of intermediate technology based on smaller working units. Others began to doubt even the hard-nosed economic orthodoxy. In 1983 Jim Dewhurst wrote:

> In all the short history of modern business there is nothing so strange as this. On the one hand we have the traditional belief in the rightness and power of size. Rationalisation, standardisation and concentration are the watchwords. Economies of scale rule the industrial world. And in the UK we have gone further along this road of concentration than any other country in the world. Yet this predilection for economic orthodoxy has not brought us economic success. (Dewhurst and Burns, 1983)

The reality is that large firms were not so much the future of business but the natural consequence of businesses being set up by entrepreneurs and then growing. Unfortunately, like many things in life, they have a natural life expectancy and prolonging this is not always beneficial – to the firm or to society. According to Arie de Geus (1997) large organisations have proved amazingly inept at survival. He quoted a Dutch survey showing the average corporate life expectancy in Japan and Europe was 12.5 years. 'The average life expectancy of a multinational corporation – the Fortune 500 or equivalent – is between 40 and 50 years.' The reality is that large companies die young, or at least their ownership changes fairly quickly.

In the last twenty years we have come to realise that new firms have done more to create wealth than firms at any time before them – ever! Ninety-five per cent of the wealth of the USA has been created since 1980. By 1997, one in every three households in the USA – 37 per cent or 35 million households – had at least one person who was involved in a primary role in a new or emerging business (*Economic News*, 1997).

When Bill Gates founded Microsoft, IBM dominated the computer market with over 70 per cent of the market and more cash on its balance sheet than the sales of the rest of the industry. Yet by the late 1980s it was under attack from Apple, Lotus Development Corp., Dell and Gateway 2000. Its stock market valuation plummeted and the workforce was slashed by half. Also over the last twenty

Founded in the late 1970s by **Bill Gates**, **Microsoft** is one of the outstanding business success stories of a generation. In 1980 it had a turnover of $8 million from only 38 employees. By 1997 turnover was $6.5 billion, it had 21 000 employees and a stockmarket valuation of $151.4 billion and was the sixth largest public company in the world. This compared to IBM's market valuation of only $89.6 billion.

. . . to be continued

years people have begun to appreciate the sheer proportion of firms that can be described as small – by any definition, in any country. Small firms, virtually no matter how they are defined, make up at least 95 per cent of enterprises in the European Community. At the same time, their contribution to the economies of their countries began to be appreciated. It was David Birch (1979) who, arguably, started this process with his seminal research which showed that 81.5 per cent of net new jobs in the USA, between 1969–76, were created by small firms (under 500 employees). The general pattern has been repeated yearly. Small, growing firms have outstripped large ones in terms of job generation, year after year. At times when larger companies retrenched, smaller firms continued to offer job opportunities. It has been estimated that in the USA small firms now generate 50 per cent of GDP and over 50 per cent of exports now come from firms employing less than 20 people. In 1996 there were some 3.5 million start-ups.

Europe lags a little behind the USA. Nevertheless, in the UK small firms generate 62 per cent of employment. In the EU, overall, it is 66 per cent. In the UK small firms generate over 25 per cent of GDP. By just about any measure the contribution small firms make to the economy is increasing and their importance is now fully recognised.

As the pace of change in just about every aspect of our life accelerates, small firms seem more able to cope than large. Start-ups are on the increase across the world. Big firms are slimming down or deconstructing – becoming many small firms – because this is the only way they can cope with the pace of change and remain responsive to changes in the market. The entrepreneur has been recognised as a vital part of the process of economic wealth generation.

This book looks at a range of things that make up this whole romanticised, but blurred, vision – entrepreneurs and small business. It looks at entrepreneurs. Who are they? Are they born rather than developed? What do they do? What is their link with the process of innovation, so loved by governments in most countries? Can entrepreneurs manage large firms or do they have to change as the business grows? Are entrepreneurs any different to managers or leaders? Are they any different to owner-managers? Are they any different to managers of small firms generally?

The book looks at small firms. Are all small firms the same? Are owner-managed small firms really different to any others? What are the skills you need to manage a small firm and a growing firm? What are the particular problems small firms face and how can they be overcome?

The book looks at start-ups and growing firms. How does the start-up happen? Are some people more likely to start up a business than others? What are the qualities and skills required to ensure a successful start-up? How do you pull together the necessary resources? What sectors do small firms have the best chances in? What marketing strategies should they use? Are growth businesses different in any way from the 'normal' small firm? Are the particular problems they face as they grow predictable and how can they be overcome? How should growth be financed? What skills are needed to grow the firm? Are there business strategies that are more likely to work than others? Can you spot 'winners'?

The book also looks at family firms and the social role they play within the family structure. Does being a family firm make any difference to how they operate? How do they deal with the succession from one owner-manager to another? Are the particular problems they face predictable and how can they be overcome?

With over twenty years of research into entrepreneurship and small business there are answers to many of these questions. This book will take a conceptual perspective to develop a theoretical framework for understanding the area and, based on this, move forward to show how many of these concepts may be operationalised and developed into practical help in successfully launching and growing a business. But first, what are the dreams and what is the reality about entrepreneurship and small business?

One reason why dreams are difficult to come to terms with is because the visions within them are continually changing. In this way they defy definition. So, to enable us to examine the reality more closely we need to define some of the terms we are using.

Entrepreneurs

There is no universally accepted definition of the term entrepreneur. The *Oxford English Dictionary* defines an entrepreneur as 'a person who attempts to profit by risk and initiative'. This definition emphasises that entrepreneurs exercise a high degree of initiative and are willing to take a high degree of risk. But it covers a wide range of occupations, including that of a paid assassin. No wonder there is an old adage that if you scratch an entrepreneur you will find a 'spiv'. The difference is more than just one of legality. Therefore a question you might ask is how do they do it?

Back in 1800, Jean-Baptist Say, the French economist usually credited with inventing the word said; 'entrepreneurs shift economic resources from an area of lower productivity into an area of higher productivity and greater yield'. In other words entrepreneurs create value by exploiting some form of change, for example in technology, materials, prices or demographics. We call this process innovation and this is an essential tool for entrepreneurs. We shall examine it in greater detail in Chapter 3. Entrepreneurs, therefore, create new demand or find new ways of exploiting existing markets. They identify a commercial opportunity and then exploit it.

Central to all of this is change. Change causes disequilibrium in markets out of which come the commercial opportunities that entrepreneurs thrive upon. To them change creates opportunities that they can exploit. Sometimes they initiate the change themselves – they innovate in some way. Other times they exploit change created by the external environment. Often in doing so they destroy the established order and complacency of existing social and economic systems.

Richard Branson is probably the best known entrepreneur in Britain today and his name is closely associated with all the many businesses that carry the **Virgin** brand name. He is outward-going and an excellent self-publicist. He has been called an 'adventurer', taking risks that few others would contemplate. This shows itself in his personal life with his transatlantic powerboating and round-the-world ballooning exploits as well as in his business life where he has challenged established firms like British Airways and Coca-Cola.

Now over 50 years old, his business life started as an 18-year-old schoolboy when he launched *Student* magazine, selling advertising space from a phone booth. He started selling mail-order records but soon decided he needed a retail site. Because it could not be let, he got his first store, above a shoe shop on London's Oxford Street, rent free on the grounds that it would generate more customers for the shoe shop. It was a great success and Richard next branched into the music business with Virgin Records.

Since those early days the Virgin brand has found its way onto aircraft, trains, cola, vodka, mobile phone, cinemas, a radio station, financial services and most recently the internet. In 1986 Virgin was floated but later reprivatised because Richard did not like to be accountable for his actions to institutional shareholders. In 1999 a 49% stake in the airline was sold to Singapore Airlines. Today Virgin describes itself as a 'branded venture capital company', having created over 200 businesses.

. . . to be continued

How entrepreneurs manage and deal with change is central to their character and essential if they are to be successful. Most 'ordinary people' find change threatening. Entrepreneurs welcome it because it creates opportunities that can be exploited and often create it through innovation.

Another key feature of the entrepreneur is their willingness to accept risk and uncertainty. In part this is simply the consequence of their eagerness to exploit change. However, the scale of uncertainty they are willing to accept is altogether different to that of other managers. This high degree of uncertainty they are willing to accept reflects itself in the risks they take for the business and for themselves.

It is no wonder that entrepreneurship has been described as 'a slippery concept . . . not easy to work into a formal analysis because it is so closely associated with the temperament or personal qualities of individuals' (Penrose, 1959). We shall examine it in more detail in the next chapter where we attempt to differentiate them from others by their character traits. We shall also address the question of whether entrepreneurs are born or made.

Notice in these definitions that there is no mention of small firms. Indeed, Richard Branson, surely a successful entrepreneur in his own right, said

I am often asked what it is to be an 'entrepreneur' and there is no simple answer. It is clear that successful entrepreneurs are vital for a healthy, vibrant and competitive economy. If you look around you, most of the largest companies have their foundations in one or two individuals who have the determination to turn a vision into reality (Anderson, 1995).

Anita Roddick may have just retired as Chairman of what is now an international public company, but when she opened the first, tiny **Body Shop** in a cobbled back street in Brighton, England in 1976 the roof leaked and the ugly unpainted walls were covered with green garden lattice primarily because it was cheap. The shop had lots of pine shelves but stocked only about a dozen inexpensive, natural cosmetics, herbal creams and shampoos, so pot plants were placed between the products.

Anita was the daughter of Italian immigrants who settled in the small town of Littlehampton and ran the Clifton Cafe. Originally a teacher, she spent some time travelling around the world before returning to England where she met her husband, Gordon. They originally wanted to travel around the world together and then open a pineapple plantation but first the arrival of one and then a second child forced them to change plans. Instead they opened a restaurant and later a small hotel in Littlehampton. About a month after they opened the first shop Gordon left to ride a horse across the Americas from Buenos Aires to New York. He did not get very far because within a few months it was obvious that Body Shop was going to be an enormous success.

Now the Roddicks rank among the top 100 richest people in the UK and are no longer actively involved with Body Shop. They started-up a business that became a multinational enterprise with a life of its own and harvested the fruits of their hard work. They have come a long way from that first small shop in Brighton.

. . . to be continued

The point is that an entrepreneur is defined by their actions, not by the size of organisation they happen to work within. Any manager can be entrepreneurial. The manager of a small firm may not be an entrepreneur – an important distinction that is often missed in the literature. Equally entrepreneurs can exist within large firms, even ones that they did not set up themselves, and how large firms encourage and deal with this is an important issue for them.

Combining these definitions and elements of character gives us a good definition for this elusive term:

> *Entrepreneurs use innovation to exploit or create change and opportunity for the purpose of making profit. They do this by shifting economic resources from an area of lower productivity into an area of higher productivity and greater yield, accepting a high degree of risk and uncertainty in doing so.*

Owner-managers

You do not have to own a firm to manage it. However, some managers do own the firms they manage and these make up the majority of managers of small firms. These are owner-managers. Sole traders are owner-managers. Limited companies, however, have share capital and must have two shareholders. The term owner-manager, therefore, needs further refinement. An obvious one would be that to qualify as an owner-manager requires ownership (or beneficially ownership) of over 50 per cent of the share capital, thereby controlling the business.

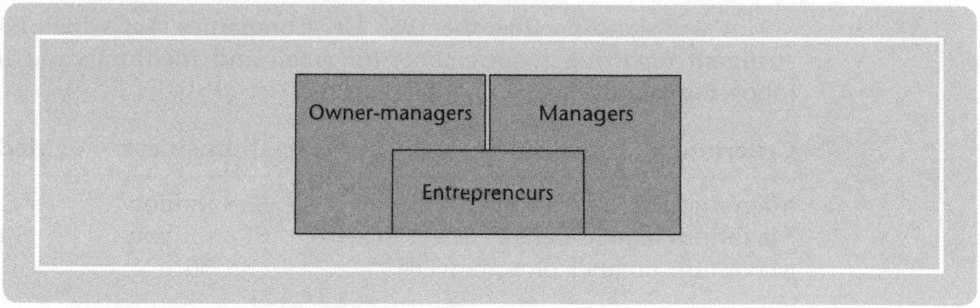

Figure 1.1 Managers, owner-managers and entrepreneurs

These definitions are, however, restrictive. For example, if a company is owned equally by two managers they would not be called owner-managers. Would this be any different if it were a partnership? Many people would call the managers in both situations owner-managers. But where does this dilution begin and end? How many managers do you need to own part of the business before they cease being called owner-managers? Are all the employees of the John Lewis Partnership owner-managers? The real issue is not ownership, but control. Owner-managers significantly control the operations of their firm on a day-to-day basis. Notice, however, that this is a question of judgement and therefore this term, as with the term entrepreneur, is likely to be used very loosely.

Notice also that, using these definitions, owner-managers need not be entrepreneurs. Indeed, most owner-managers are not entrepreneurial. This book argues that entrepreneurs can be described in terms of their character and judged by their actions and one of the major defining factors between them and owner-managers is the degree of innovation they practice.

Many managers of small firms do not own or control the firm they are employed by. The firm is controlled by its larger, parent company. The manager is therefore not an owner-manager. Paradoxically, however, they might be an entrepreneur, depending on the way they act. Figure 1.1 shows these relationships. Managers are different people to owner-managers, but both can be entrepreneurs.

Small firms

As with the other terms, there is no uniformly acceptable definition of a small firm. Back in 1971, what is usually held to be a definitive report on the state of small business in Britain at the time, the Bolton Report (Bolton, 1971), made heavy weather of providing a statistical definition. Recognising that one definition would not cover industries as divergent as manufacturing and service, it used eight definitions for various industry groups. These ranged from under 200 employees for manufacturing firms to over £50 000 turnover (in 1971) for retailing, and up to five vehicles or less for road transport. So many definitions clearly cause practical problems. What is more, definitions based on financial criteria suffer from inherent problems related to inflation and currency translation.

Not withstanding this, the 1985 UK Companies Act which has special less-stringent reporting requirements for small and medium-sized firms, uses the following definitions:

Criterion	Small business	Medium business
Maximum annual turnover	£2.8 million	£11.2 million
Maximum annual balance sheet total	£1.4 million	£5.6 million
Maximum number of employees	50	250

The European Commission has coined the term 'small and medium enterprise' (SME) and in 1996 defined them as organisations employing fewer than 250 people. This is disaggregated into three parts and, to qualify as a SME, both the employee and the independence criteria must be satisfied plus either the turnover or balance sheet criteria:

Criterion	Micro business	Small business	Medium business
Maximum number of employees	9	49	249
Maximum annual turnover	–	7 million euros	40 million euros
Maximum annual balance sheet total (total assets)	–	5 million euros	27 million euros
Maximum % owned by one, or jointly by several, enterprise(s) not satisfying the same criteria	–	25%	25%

Despite the independence criteria, SMEs could still include organisations managed by non-owner-managers. Even so, some of them may be entrepreneurs. We are still, therefore, left with our three groups – managers of small firms, owner-managers and entrepreneurs – without any clear delineation. However, it is likely to be true that the smaller the firm, particularly the owner-managed firm, the more important the personality and influence of the manager, be they entrepreneurial or not.

Being a small firm is not just about size, defined in simple statistical terms. Small firms also have important defining characteristics. The same Bolton Committee described a small firm as satisfying three criteria, all of which defy practical statistical application:

1 *Market influence* In economic terms, the small firm has a small share of the market. Therefore it is not large enough to influence the prices or national quantities of the good or service that it provides. Unfortunately, two fundamental problems arise with this, firstly with the definition of market and secondly with the ability of the small firm to influence price and the quantity sold in that market. Many of the most successful small firms operate in market niches so slim that they dominate that market segment, with no clear competition, and they can and do influence both price and quantity sold. In that respect Bolton's definition looks naïve and dated and was probably influenced by the economists' definition of perfect competition. It is certainly not one that I or most entrepreneurs would agree with.

2   *Independence*   The small firm is independent in the sense that it does not form part of a larger enterprise and that the owner-managers are free from outside control in taking their principle decisions. This means that only owner-managed firms are considered small firms. This is clearly unsatisfactory if you believe, as I do, that there are certain specific characteristics about managing a small firm that mark it out as different from a large one.

3   *Personal influence*   The small firm is managed in a personalised way and not through the medium of a formalised management structure. This person is involved in all aspects of the management of the business and is involved in all major decision making. Frequently there is little devolution or delegation of authority.

Small firms start to make managerial appointments when they have some 10–20 employees and at this point they start to take on the appearance of more formal structures (Atkinson and Meager, 1994). Nevertheless, this third point is the key to a definition of the real small firm – the real small firm, the one with potential, the one that economists cannot understand, the one that is so different to the large firm. Essentially the real small firm can be described as having *two arms two legs and a giant ego*, in other words it is an extension of a person, be they owner-manager or entrepreneur. The personality of the manager is imprinted on the way it operates and the personal risks they and their family face, if the firm fails, influences how business decisions are made.

Why small firms are different

Small firms are not just scaled down versions of large ones. They go about their business in a number of fundamentally different ways. The key to understanding how a particular small firm goes about management and why and how decisions are made is to understand the personality of the owner-manager. Their personality and their behavioural characteristics will strongly influence this. More than large firms, small firms are social entities that revolve around personal relationships. They approach risk and uncertainty in a particular way that sometimes may seem far from rational, which explains why they are so little understood by economists.

There are a number of other characteristics that are typical of small firms and underline their different approach to management and business. The first is that they are typically short of cash. They cannot raise capital in the same way that a large company can. This has major strategic implications. Firstly, it constrains the strategies that they can adopt. For example, they cannot afford to adopt expensive advertising and promotion campaigns, so instead the manager develops close relationships with customers and prospective customers, investing their time rather than money. Secondly, it dictates that business decisions must have a quick pay-off and therefore decision making is short-term. For a growing business it means that raising finance becomes a major strategic issue and relationships with financing institutions such as banks and venture capitalists can become a major resource issue.

The second characteristic is that small firms are likely to operate in a single market, or a limited range of markets, probably offering a limited range of products or services. This means that their scope of operations is, or at least should be, limited. In that sense they face fewer strategic issues than larger firms and often business strategy is synonymous with marketing strategy. However, unlike large firms, they find it difficult to diversify their business risk, which is another reason they find it hard to raise finance.

Related to this is the characteristic that most small firms are overreliant on a small number of customers. This means that they are particularly vulnerable to losing any one customer and the effect on the firm of such a loss will be disproportionately large. This is yet another reason why they are riskier than large firms and find difficulty raising finance.

The final characteristic is the effect of scale on the economics of the business and how that translates into financial evaluation and decision-making. Most Business Finance textbooks are written with large companies in mind; consequently, whilst the principles they espouse are sound, the examples they use and generalisations that result are not. For example, taking on an additional member of staff for a small firm is a major strategic decision involving relatively large sums of money that represent a step increase in their fixed costs. Consequently they are reluctant to do so unless absolutely necessary. Yet in most Business Finance textbooks wage costs are treated as a variable cost, a view that can only be justified when there are a large number of staff. As we shall see later in this book, this error can lead to quite incorrect business decisions being made. It is little wonder that managers of small firms have little faith in professional advisors and accountants. Banks have for some time realised that traditional financial analysis says little about the health of the small firm and have started to broaden their approach.

These characteristics start to combine to distinguish small firms from large ones on a basis other than scale. Wynarczyk *et al.* (1993), strongly influenced by Casson (1982), argue that the much greater role played by uncertainty, innovation and firm evolution is the real defining characteristic of small firms. Small firms face more uncertain markets than large firms. They have a limited customer base and often cannot influence price. The owner-manager's own aspirations and motivations may also be uncertain. The effect of this high degree of uncertainty is to force decision-making to become short-term. Small firms also innovate in a particular way that we shall explore in a subsequent chapter, that makes them different to large firms. The final distinguishing characteristic is evolution – the recognition that the nature, style and functions of management change considerably as the small firm grows and evolves. Once more, we shall explore this in detail in a subsequent chapter, in particular looking at the 'stage theories' of how firms grow.

Lifestyle and growth firms

Small firms and entrepreneurship have often been linked together in a very loose fashion. They are broadly overlapping sets. As Storey and Sykes (1996) explained,

the small firm is less concerned with formal systems and its decision-making process will be more judgemental, involving fewer individuals, and can therefore be quicker. It can be much more responsive to changes in the marketplace but, conversely, is much less able to influence such developments. Hence the small firm is likely to adjust more quickly than the large firm to situations of market disequilibrium and, in these senses, embodies the characteristics of the classic entrepreneur.

However, this is a question of scale and, just as it was necessary to distinguish between owner-managers and entrepreneurs, it might be useful to distinguish between two categories of small firms:

1 *Lifestyle firms*   These are businesses that are set up primarily to undertake an activity that the owner-manager enjoys or gets some comfort from whilst also providing an adequate income, for example craft-based businesses. They are not set up to grow and, therefore, once a level of activity that provides the adequate income is reached, management becomes routine and tactical. There is probably little thought about strategic management unless things start to go wrong, and the most likely thing to go wrong is that the market changes without the owner-manager realising it. These firms are rarely managed by entrepreneurs and if they are, the entrepreneur will be extremely frustrated. Most owner-managed firms fall into this category. Many are sole-traders (un-incorporated businesses). However, a lifestyle business can change, if the owner-manager's motivations change, and they have the entrepreneurial qualities to see it through.

2 *Growth firms*   These are set up with the intention of growth, usually by entrepreneurs. Occasionally a lifestyle business can turn into a growth business unintentionally. However, if the manager does not have entrepreneurial characteristics they are unlikely to succeed in the long run. Rapid growth is risky and creates major problems that must be addressed within very short time frames. Effective strategic management is vital if the firm is to succeed, indeed possibly survive. Not withstanding this, these firms will face numerous problems and crises as they grow, some of which are predictable, others that are not. This is the classic entrepreneurial firm so beloved by the financial press.

It is important to realise that the small firm sector is far from homogenous. Consider issues of size and age of business, sector, location, growth and decline, economic and market conditions. What is more, the people that manage them are many and varied. You do not have to own a small firm to manage it and you

---

In the late 1980s **Julian Lever** and **Tim Slade** were looking for ways to finance their lifestyle as 'ski-bums' in the French Alps. They travelled the world financed by selling printed T-shirts out of rucksacks. In 1993 they decided to open a clothes shop in London's Fulham Road selling a range of high quality sports clothing. Named after a famous down-hill run in Val d'Isère, **Fat Face** really took off selling both to fashion conscious young people and a 'niche' technical market.

In 1995 sales were £760 000. By 1999 this had grown to over £7 million and Fat Face were number 53 in the *Sunday Times* Fast Track 100 British companies. The firm had made the transition from lifestyle to growth business.

. . . to be continued

certainly do not have to be an entrepreneur. Consider also issues of age, sex, ethnicity, social origins, family relationships and then you start to realise the scale of the complexity.

Generalisations about small firms and the people that manage them are therefore just that . . . vast generalisations that are supposed to cover what makes up some 95 per cent of firms in most countries. Small firms are not homogeneous but, notwithstanding this, let us try to paint a broad picture of their nature and role in the UK.

Small firms in the UK

Over the last century, until the 1960s, the UK saw a decrease in the importance of small firms, measured in terms of their share of manufacturing employment and output. The proportion of the UK labour force classified as self-employed was at its lowest point in the 1960s. It was no wonder that the Bolton Committee (*op. cit.*) set up in the late 1960s to investigate the role of small firms in the economy, concluded that 'the small firm sector was in a state of long-term decline, both in size and its share of economic activity'. From the 1970s the situation has been reversed. Since then small firms have increased in importance, measured in terms of their share of manufacturing employment and output. The number of small firms continues to rise, as does the number of people classified as self-employed. In 1979 there were only 2.4 million SMEs in the UK. By 1999 this had grown to 3.67 million. The number has remained approximately constant since 1994. This growth in numbers had two main causes; the shift from manufacturing to services, and structural changes within companies, such as downsizing and contracting out. Even within manufacturing, SME's share of employment increased substantially in the 1970s and 1980s, reversing the trend of earlier decades.

SMEs now generate over a quarter of UK GDP. As can be seen from Table 1.1, they generate some 55 per cent of employment with micro and small businesses generating 44 per cent. The trends are all upwards. Small firms are increasing in their importance to the UK economy. Most of the growth in the business population between 1998 and 1999 was in the 1–4 employee size. Nevertheless, most small firms in the UK remain very small. Only some 1.6 million are registered for value added tax (VAT) as their turnover is too low. As you can see from Table 1.1:

● 63% – 2.3 million – are sole traders or partnerships with no employees (almost a quarter of these are in the building trade).
● 95% have fewer than 10 employees – micro businesses – and they generate 30% of employment.
● 99% have fewer than 50 employees and they generate 44% of employment.

Put in another way, only some 24 000 firms are medium-sized, with 50–299 employees, and less than 7000 are large, with over 250 employees.

The share of employment provided by SMEs varies widely from sector to sector. In construction some 84 per cent of employment was within SMEs in 1999 while in the finance sector it was only 21 per cent. Of the 2.3 million enterprises with no employees, 24 per cent were in the construction sector and 18 per cent in

Table 1.1 Number of businesses, employment and employees, by size of business, UK 1999

Size	Number			Percentage		
Number of employees	Businesses (000s)	Employment (000s)	Turnover (£ millions)	Businesses (%)	Employment (%)	Turnover (%)
0	2 324	2 708	90 463	63.2	12.5	4.7
1–4	964	2 395	221 986	26.2	11.0	11.4
5–9	202	1 459	123 029	5.5	6.7	6.3
10–19	109	1 533	149 451	3.0	7.1	7.7
20–49	47	1 462	147 505	1.3	6.7	7.6
50–99	14	1 011	102 860	0.4	4.7	5.3
100–199	8	1 131	116 638	0.2	5.2	6.0
200–249	2	349	38 633	–	1.6	2.0
250–499	3	1 121	149 275	0.1	5.2	7.7
500+	4	8 576	804 039	0.1	39.4	41.4
All	3 677	21 746	1 943 880	100.0	100.0	100.0

Sources: Small and Medium-sized Enterprise Statistics for the UK, 1999; Small Firms Statistics Unit, Department of Trade and Industry, August 2000.

'business related services'. As you would expect, only 3 per cent of employment in the electricity, gas and water supply sector was provided by SMEs, whilst 84 per cent of education employment was within SMEs – a sector rarely considered.

Information about VAT registrations and deregistrations is usually accepted as giving the best guide to patterns of change in the small-firm sector – levels of entrepreneurship and the health of the business population. They are widely used in regional and local economic planning. The net change in business stocks is a particularly important figure. In 1999 this increased by 6400 (Table 1.2), representing the difference between registrations (down 4 per cent to 178 500) and deregistrations (up 10 per cent to 172 000), taking the stock of registered enterprises to 1.66 million at the end of the year. The net gain shows a rise in total business stocks for the fourth consecutive year. In 1999 there were 38 registrations and 37 deregistrations for every 10 000 adults in the UK.

The net change in stock tends to be highly related to the state of the economy. Small firms are particularly vulnerable to economic changes because of their often precarious financing situation. In times when the economy is in recession there tends to be a net decrease in the stock of businesses and vice versa. So, the 1980s saw a large increase in the stock of registered companies, whereas the stock decreased between 1991 and 1995.

The VAT statistics show that the most dangerous time for a new business is in its first three years of existence. Almost 50 per cent of businesses will cease trading within that period. This does not, of course, mean that the closures represent failure in terms of leaving creditors and unpaid debts. Most are simply wound down. Businesses that cease trading do so for a number of reasons. Some will close because the business ceases to be lucrative. Others because of the death or retirement of the proprietor, or changes in their personal motivations and aspirations. Some will simply close to move onto other, more lucrative opportunities. This 'churning effect' of small firms closing and opening is part

Table 1.2 Business stocks, start-ups and closures – VAT registrations and deregistrations, UK 1995–99

	1995	1996	1997	1998	1999
Stocks (000s)					
Start-year stock of registered enterprises	1629.3	1600.1	1603.2	1621.3	1651.7
Net change in stock	−9.2	+3.1	+18.1	+30.4	+6.4
End-year stock of registered enterprises	1600.1	1603.2	1621.3	1651.7	1658.1
Registrations					
Number	163.9	168.2	182.6	186.3	178.5
Rate per 10 000 people age 16+	35	36	39	40	38
Deregistrations					
Number	173.2	165.1	164.5	155.9	172.0
Rate per 10 000 people aged 16+	37	35	35	33	37

Sources: Business Start-ups and Closures: VAT registrations and deregistrations in 1999; Small Firms Statistics Unit, Department of Trade and Industry, August 2000.

of the dynamism of the sector as they respond to changing opportunities in the market place and is why the net change in the stock of businesses is more important than the individual number of failures.

In 1999 the stock of manufacturing businesses continued to decline in the UK for the sixth consecutive year. With a net decrease of 4600 firms, fewer than 10 per cent of small firms are now in manufacturing – an indication of a rapidly changing economy. By way of contrast, with a net increase of 18 100 firms, business services (which include consultancy, legal, accounting and computer services) continue to increase year-on-year. One in four of VAT registrations were in the business services sector during 1993–99. Service businesses are, of course, easier to set up, they require less capital and often less expertise. But also today's markets offer more lucrative service rather than product-based opportunities.

In 1999 registrations outnumbered deregistrations in every region of the England other than Yorkshire and Humber, where there was a net loss of 700 businesses, the East Midlands with a net loss of 200, and the North East with a net loss of 100. There was also a net loss in Scotland (500), Wales (700) and Northern Ireland (100). By way of contrast, the largest net gains were in London (4600) and in the South East of England (2400) – indicating a consistent trend. Regions with consistently high registrations tend to have high deregistration rates. This reflects the short life-span of many businesses.

SMEs tend to have lower productivity than large firms, even in the same industry. Firms with fewer than 200 employees had 55 per cent of the productivity (measured in value added per employee) of firms with 1000 or more employees. In the computer and office machinery sectors SME productivity is only a third of that of larger firms. These differences are largely because of lower capital backing.

SMEs vary widely in the resources they allocate to innovation. Of SMEs with over 20 employees, about one in ten spends 10 per cent or more of turnover on new product or process development. However, one-third of manufacturing SMEs spend nothing at all.

Stories of successful entrepreneurs always make good reading. And successful entrepreneurs have been with us for many, many years in Britain. One – **Joseph Bamford** – died in 2001. Joseph Cyril Bamford gave his initials to the ubiquitous yellow hydraulic excavator and digger seen on just about every building site or road works – the **JCB**. In fact JCB became one of the few postwar British industrial success stories. By the time of his death the company employed over 4500 people across three continents and had a turnover of £833 million. Over 70% of JCB production is for overseas markets.

Joseph Bamford came from a prosperous Staffordshire engineering family which had been making agricultural equipment since mid-Victorian times. When he returned to civilian life after the Second World War he decided to start up on his own doing what he knew best. Starting his business with only an electric welder he bought for £2.50, he started producing tipping farm trailers from a garage in Uttoxeter, using materials from old air-raid shelters. These sold well, but in 1948 he decided to branch out into hydraulic equipment and, in 1953, went into partnership to produce a range of earth-moving machines before eventually coming up with the famous backhoe loader that combined the two functions of excavator and shovel that became the visual embodiment of the initials JCB.

Joseph Bamford was a paternalistic employer, who provided a social club and a fishing lake next to his factory in Rochester. He ran a tight ship but rewarded effort. He also knew how to get PR. In 1964, when he famously paid his workers £250 000 in bonuses because the company's turnover had topped £8 million, he personally handed out the bonus to each employee standing on the first farm tractor he had designed in 1947.

Joseph Bamford made JCB into one of the most successful privately owned companies in Britain. Eventually the company diversified from his central control into a group of several operating companies. He gave up his chairmanship of the group in 1975, handing it over to his eldest son, now Sir Anthony Bamford, and retired to Montreux, Switzerland where he enjoyed yacht designing and landscape gardening.

The international dimension

In most of the advanced countries the number of small firms is now increasing, as is their share of employment, reversing a downward trend in the sector prior to the late 1960s. SMEs are a vital part of all EU economies, accounting for 65 per cent of EU turnover. They dominate many service sectors, particularly hotels, catering, retailing and wholesaling, and are important in construction. In the USA it is estimated that small firms now generate 50 per cent of GDP. Small firms are a vital and growing part of business in all countries.

Small firms are important providers of employment. They generate 66 per cent of employment across the EU. In Italy the proportion is 79 per cent, in France it is 63 per cent and in Germany it is 60 per cent. In the UK they generate only 61.5 per cent of employment, but the figure is gradually increasing, and things are

Framfab is Europe's largest internet consultancy employing over 2570 people in 59 countries around the world and boasting a long blue-chip client list. *Forbes* magazine recently placed it as one of the top 300 companies in the world. And yet this Swedish company started life only in 1995, set up by **Jonas Birgersson,** when he was just 24 years old. Since then he has gone on to receive many awards and *Resumé* magazine even named him 'web guru'.

Jonas has a somewhat unusual background. He studied Military History at the University of Lund, specialising in military intelligence theory and military organisation theory. Prior to setting up Framfab he was director of the government subsidised Swedish Roleplaying and Conflict Gaming Federation (SVEROK), a network of gameplayers – from role playing and military strategy games. From there he went on to set up his own company and secured work with the Swedish telecoms company, Telia, on a project called Passagen – the world's first web-based conscious portal project. The success of this project launched the company on its growth path. Its strategy has included mergers and acquisitions as well as product/ service diversification, through its subsidiaries Framfab Innovations and Framfab Ventures, both designed to help entrepreneurs find funding for technology start-ups.

Log onto Framfab's website – www.framfab.com – and find out more about one of Europe's leading 'new economy' companies.

changing. Now the UK has one of the highest start-up rates in Europe. Over half a million new start-ups were recorded in 1999 and it is significant that the high start-up rate continued throughout the recession of the early 1990s. Indeed, in most other respects the UK now tends to have a fairly average profile for its small firm sector, compared to the rest of Europe.

Average firm size tends to be higher in the larger countries of Europe (ENSR, 1993). Within the small countries, firm size is largest in the central countries like Luxembourg and smallest in the peripheral countries. The proportion of small firms also seems to be inversely related to the economic development of the country, with higher proportions of small firms in countries like Spain, Portugal and Greece. One widely held misconception is that Britain has a smaller proportion of middle-sized, or '*mittelstand*', companies than in Germany. The high level of start-ups since the 1980s has made this seem to be the case but Storey (1998) concludes that 'the size structure of the UK and (pre-unification) Germany is in fact closer than between any other two large countries in the European Community'. However, Storey also concludes that employment in the USA, and to a lesser extent the UK, is still more concentrated in very large companies than in other EC countries or Japan.

Factors influencing the growth of small firms

A number of factors have contributed to the growth of small firms. A major influence has been the shift in most economies away from manufacturing towards the service sectors, where small firms often flourish because of their ability to deliver personalised, flexible, tailor-made service at a local level. The 'deconstruction' of larger firms into smaller, more responsive units concentrating on their core activities, often sub-contracting many of their other activities to smaller firms, has also contributed to the trend. Large firms and even the public sector became leaner and fitter in the 1980s in a bid to reduce fixed costs and reduce risks. Small firms have benefited, although they may be seen as dependent on large ones.

Technology has influenced the trend in three ways. Firstly, the new technologies that swept the late twentieth century have been pioneered by new, rapidly growing firms. Small firms have pioneered innovation in computers and the internet, although only time will tell whether these markets will start to consolidate and amalgamate into larger units as they mature. Secondly, these technologies have actually facilitated the growth of self-employment and small business by easing communication, encouraging working from home and allowing smaller and smaller market segments to be serviced. Indeed, information has become a product in its own right and one that can be generated anywhere around the world and transported at the touch of a button. Finally, many new technologies, for example printing, have reduced fixed costs so that production can be profitable in smaller, more flexible units.

Social and market trends have also accelerated the growth of small firms. Firstly, customers increasingly expect firms to address their particular needs. Market niches are becoming slimmer and markets more competitive – better served by smaller firms. Secondly, people are wanting to control their own destiny more. After periods of high unemployment, they now see self-employment as more attractive and more secure than employment. Redundancy pushed many people into self-employment at the same time as the new 'enterprise culture' gave it political and social respectability. The growth of 'new age' culture and 'alternative' lifestyles has also encouraged the growth of a whole new range of self-employment opportunities.

Some theoretical considerations

The question arises as to whether there are any underlying theories to explain the growth in number and importance of small firms. Marxist theory predicts that capitalism will degenerate into economies dominated by a small number of large firms and society will polarise between those that own them and those that work in them. To a Marxist, the rise of small firms is just another, subtler way for this trend to manifest itself. The small firms are dependant upon larger firms for their custom and well being. They absorb risk and push down pay and conditions for workers as they are rarely unionised. However, the successful growth of so many small firms over the period, the increasing fragmentation of industries and markets and the increasing popularity of self-employment by choice would seem to belie this theory.

People like Fritz Schumacher (1974) would have us believe that the growth of small firms is part of a social trend towards a more democratic and responsive society – 'small is beautiful'. To him the quality of life is more important than materialism. He is very much in favour of 'intermediate technology' – simpler, cheaper and easier to use – with production on a smaller scale and more locally based. However, the technologies that have fuelled the growth of small firms at the end of the twentieth century have been far from simple and for many quality of life has improved alongside materialism. Which leads us onto free-market economics. At one extreme the growth of small firms can be seen as the triumph of the free market and the success of the 'enterprise culture' promulgated by politicians like Ronald Reagan and Margaret Thatcher. Increasing numbers of small firms are the natural result of increased competition and a drive to prevent private and public monopoly. But what exactly does economic theory have to say about small firm creation?

Traditional industrial economists would explain the growth of new firms in terms of industry profitability, growth, barriers to entry and concentration. However, they are more concerned with 'entry' to an industry, rather than whether this is by a new or an existing firm. They assume an endless supply of potential new entrants. They would say that entry to an industry is high when expected profits and growth are high. Entry is deterred by high barriers to entry and high concentration, when collusion between existing firms can take place. However, much of this work does not specifically consider the role of new or smaller firms. Indeed, Acs and Audretsch (1989) show that entry by small, primarily new, firms is not the same as entry by large firms and that small firm birth is lower in highly concentrated industries and ones where innovation plays an important part.

By way of contrast, labour market economists have been more interested in what influences individuals to become potential entrants to an industry by becoming self-employed. Psychologists have also contributed greatly to this work which has focused on the character or personality of the individual, the antecedent influences on them such as age, sex, education, employment status, experience and ethnicity as well as other societal influences. This work has proved far more successful and informative and we examine it in detail in the next chapter.

Summary

In the late twentieth century the focus of business interest shifted from large to small firms. Their contribution to the economy became recognised as did the shortcomings of large companies. Start-ups like **Microsoft** demonstrated they could become world-class outstanding successes very quickly. Alongside this, the importance of entrepreneurs like **Richard Branson**, founder of **Virgin**, and **Anita** and **Gordon Roddick**, founders of **Body Shop**, became realised as they and their businesses became 'the stuff of dreams' – at least in the financial press.

Entrepreneurs use innovation to exploit or create change and opportunity for the purpose of making profit. They do this by shifting economic resources from an area of lower productivity into an area of higher productivity and greater yield, accepting a high degree of risk and uncertainty in doing so.

Owner-managers own the business they manage. Sole traders are owner managers. Managers of companies owning over 50 per cent of the share capital, and thereby controlling the business, are owner-managers. However, the term is also used loosely when a small group of managers own and control the business. Not all owner-managers are entrepreneurs, indeed most are not entrepreneurial. Entrepreneurs are defined primarily by their actions although, as we shall see in the next chapter, they can have certain identifiable characteristics. They are the particular type of owner-manager that the financial press love so much. They make 'the stuff of dreams' come true.

A small or medium sized enterprise (SME) is one with under 500 employees. A micro business has up to 9 employees, a small business up to 99 employees and a medium-sized business up to 499 employees. A defining characteristic of the small firm is the influence of the manager. It is managed in an informal, personalised way and the character and preoccupations of the manager is a significant influence on decision-making.

There are a number of other significant characteristics, which include shortage of cash and difficulty in raising finance, limitations in product or service range and markets they operate in, reliance on a small number of customers and the effects of their small scale on financial evaluation and decision-making. But perhaps the other defining characteristics are uncertainty, innovation and firm evolution.

Small firms and entrepreneurship are broadly overlapping sets. However, the two concepts are not necessarily synonymous. We broadly characterised small firms as either lifestyle – set up to allow the owner-manager to pursue an activity they enjoy – or growth – one set up to make money and grow. However, as in the case of **Fat Face**, one can change into the other.

Notwithstanding the success of firms like **JCB**, until the 1960s the UK saw a decrease in the importance of small firms. Since the 1970s this has been reversed. Now, with over half a million a year, the UK has one of the highest business start-up rates in Europe. The 3.7 million UK SMEs generate 61.5 per cent and micro and small businesses generate 49.5 per cent of employment, and the trend is upwards. SMEs now generate over a quarter of UK GDP; however, they still account for a smaller proportion of the economy than in other EU member states. They also provide a smaller share of employment; the EU average is 66 per cent, in Italy the proportion is 79 per cent, in France 63 per cent and Germany 60 per cent.

Most small firms in the UK do not grow to any size – almost two-thirds of businesses comprise of only one or two people, and often the second person is the spouse; some 95 per cent of firms employ fewer than 10 employees and 99 per cent fewer than 50 employees. The Swedish firm **Framfab** shows, however, that firms in all countries can grow rapidly to become international businesses. SMEs tend to have lower productivity than large firms, even in the same industry. They also vary widely in the resources they allocate to innovation. However, one-third of manufacturing SMEs spend nothing at all. Statistics indicate that the period of highest risk for a newly established business is in the first three years of its life, when almost 50 per cent cease trading.

The increasing number of small firms is a result of many trends – the move from manufacturing to the service sectors, the 'deconstruction' of many large firms and the trend towards sub-contracting, the influence of new technologies, and social and market changes.

Whilst Marxist theory would seem to be able to accommodate the growth of small firms, many politicians would claim that it is a manifestation of the success of free-market capitalism. But whilst industrial economists would have little to say to explain the phenomenon, labour economists and psychologists have been more successful.

⬤ Essays and discussion topics

1 Are small firms worthy of special treatment? If so, by whom and what form should it take?
2 List the pros and cons of running your own business.
3 Do you think you might have what it takes to be an entrepreneur? Return to this question after you have read the next chapter.
4 Do you think the definition of an entrepreneur is adequate?
5 How does the management of a small firm differ from the management of a large one?
6 What are the characteristics of small firms that distinguish them from large firms and what are their implications? Do these mean that small firms really are sufficiently different to warrant special study?
7 Are small firms sufficiently homogeneous to justify special study? What further segmentation might you suggest and what are the special and different characteristics of these segments?
8 Does the UK have a culture that encourages entrepreneurship and business start-ups?
9 What more can be done to develop a culture that encourages entrepreneurship and new business start-ups?
10 Is it good that so many businesses close in their first three years?
11 Why have the number of small firms been increasing since the late 1960s?
12 Does Marxism say anything to explain the increasing number of small firms?
13 Is small really beautiful?
14 What are the real defining characteristics of a small firm?

⬤ Exercises and assignments

1 Research the history and profile of an entrepreneur who set up their own business and grew it successfully.
2 Contact the DTI and obtain their most recent small business statistics. This should be available on their website on www.dti.gov.uk. What does this tell you about recent developments?
3 Visit the US Small Business Administration website on www.sbaonline.sba.gov and obtain US small business statistics. How do they compare to the UK?
4 Answer the following small business quiz. Circle the correct answer to the question: A, B or C.

---

1. The European Commission defines a 'micro business' as:
   A up to 1 employee
   B up to 4 employees
   C up to 9 employees

2 The European Commission defines a 'small business' as:
   A 2–49 employees
   B 5–99 employees
   C 10–99 employees

3 The European Commission defines a 'small and medium-sized enterprises (SMEs)' as:
   A under 100 employees
   B under 250 employees
   C under 500 employees

---

4   In 1998 the number of SMEs in the UK was:
    A   2.4 million
    B   3.7 million
    C   4.5 million

5   The % increase since 1979 was:
    A   34%
    B   44%
    C   54%

6   The % of total firms represented by SMEs was:
    A   99.9%
    B   96.9%
    C   93.9%

7   The % of employment generated by SMEs was:
    A   42%
    B   52%
    C   62%

8   The % of GDP generated by SMEs was:
    A   20%
    B   25%
    C   35%

9   The % of SMEs with less than 50 employees was:
    A   99%
    B   89%
    C   79%

10 The % of employment generated by these firms was:
    A   25%
    B   35%
    C   45%

11 The % of SMEs with less than 10 employees was:
    A   95%
    B   85%
    C   75%

12 The % of SMEs with no employees was:
    A   64%
    B   54%
    C   44%

13 The % of businesses ceasing to trade in their first three years of existence is:
    A   30%
    B   40%
    C   50%

14 The % of turnover generated by SMEs in the European Union is:
    A   45%
    B   65%
    C   85%

15 The % of employment generated by SMEs in the European Union is:
   A 56%
   B 61%
   C 66%

16 The % of GDP generated by small firms in the USA is:
   A 30%
   B 40%
   C 50%

17 The % of exports generated by firms with less than 20 employees in the USA is:
   A 20%
   B 35%
   C 50%

18 The % of households in the USA with at least one person involved in an emerging business is:
   A 27%
   B 37%
   C 47%

Check your answers. The correct answers are at the bottom of the page. What conclusions do you draw from the correct answers?

● Websites to visit

1 *Sunday Times* runs an Enterprise Network, sponsored by the DTI. It also has an excellent website on www.enterprisenetwork.co.uk. The main section of the website contains:

● Information – reports, newsletters, daily news features.
● Ask the experts – submit your own questions or view previous questions.
● Case studies – from *Sunday Times*, DTI and Design Council.
● Topical issues – for example, e-commerce, the Euro and so on.
● Ongoing issues – for example, raising finance, best practice, cost reduction and so on.

It also has events, special offers and chat line.

2 *Wall Street Journal* has a Start-Up website on startup.wsj.com. It contains articles about entrepreneurship, start-ups, franchising and day-to-day business problems. It has US franchise opportunities, businesses for sale, business angels with capital as well as an extensive database of venture capital firms. It also has a helpline as well as an on-line business plan outline.

Answers
1: C, 2: C, 3: C, 4: B, 5: C, 6: A, 7: C, 8: B, 9: A, 10: C, 11: A, 12: A, 13: C, 14: B, 15: C, 16: C, 17: C, 18: B.

● References

Acs, Z.J. and Audretsch, D.B. (1989) 'Births and Firm Size', *Southern Economic Journal*, vol. 55.

Anderson, J. (1995) *Local Heroes*, Glasgow: Scottish Enterprise.

Atkinson, J. and Meager, N. (1994) 'Running to Stand Still: The Small Business in the Labour Market', in J. Atkinson and D.J. Storey (eds), *Employment, The Small Firm and the Labour Market*, London: Routledge.

Birch, D.L. (1979) 'The Job Creation Process', unpublished report, *MIT Program on Neighbourhood and Regional Change*, prepared for the Economic Development Administration, US Department of Commerce, Washington, DC.

Bolton, J.E. (1971) *Report of the Committee of Inquiry on Small Firms*, Cmnd. 4811, London: HMSO.

Cannon, T. (1991) *Enterprise: Creation, Development and Growth*, Oxford: Butterworth-Heinemann.

Casson, M. (1982) *The Entrepreneur: An Economic Theory*, Oxford: Martin Robertson.

Crainer, S., Dearlove, D. (1998) *Gravy Training: Inside the Shadowy World of Business Schools*, Oxford: Capstone.

de Geus, A. (1997) *The Living Company*, Boston: Harvard Business Press.

Dewhurst, J. and Burns, P. (1983) *Small Business Finance and Control*, London: Macmillan – now Palgrave.

Economic News, The Small Business Advocate, February 1997, Washington, DC, Office of Advocacy, SEA.

ENSR (1993) *The European Observatory for SMEs*, Zoetermeer, Netherlands: EIM.

Penrose, E.T. (1959) *The Theory of the Growth of Firms*, Oxford: Basil Blackwell.

Schumacher, E.F. (1974) *Small is Beautiful*, London: Abacus.

Storey, D.J. (1998) *Understanding the Small Business Sector*, London: International Thomson Business Press.

Storey, D. and Sykes, N. (1996) 'Uncertainty, Innovation and Management', in P. Burns and J. Dewhurst (eds), *Small Business and Entrepreneurship*, London: Macmillan – now Palgrave.

Wynarczyk, P., Watson, R., Storey, D.J., Short, H. and Keasey, K. (1993) *The Managerial Labour Market in Small and Medium Sized Enterprises*, London: Routledge.

chapter two

Heroes and super-heroes

Contents

- Born and made
- Character traits
- Character traits of owner-managers
- Character traits of entrepreneurs
- Antecedent influences
- Entrepreneurial culture
- Summary

Learning outcomes

By the end of this chapter you should:

- Understand what are the influences that help develop owner-managers and entrepreneurs;
- Understand what are the character traits of owner-managers;
- Understand what are the character traits of entrepreneurs;
- Understand the methodological problems associated with trying to measure character traits and the linkages with growth businesses;
- Understand what antecedent influences are likely to influence owner-managers and entrepreneurs;
- Understand the concept and appreciate the importance of culture;
- Appreciate what constitutes an entrepreneurial culture and how it might be measured.

Born and made

Launching and running your own business, even a lifestyle business, is not easy. It requires, amongst other things, hard work, tenacity and a willingness to live with uncertainty in varying degrees. But if owner-managers are the heroes of this book, then entrepreneurs must be the super heroes. The personal character traits required to launch a business successfully are not sufficient to see it grow to any size. But what are these characteristics? Not withstanding this, we also know that the role of the entrepreneur needs to change as the business develops and all too often they are not able to make the transition.

Were it not for those who have a vested interest in identifying our super-heroes at an early stage in their business development, it is unlikely that economists, sociologists and psychologists would have paid this area so much attention. Because of this it remains an area of heated academic debate and constant development, not least over the question as to whether entrepreneurs are born rather than made.

Figure 2.1 shows the influences on individuals to start up and grow their businesses. The model proposes that entrepreneurs, and indeed owner-

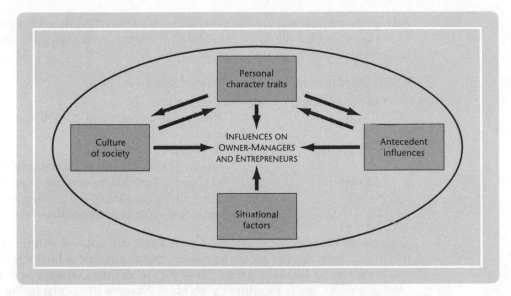

Figure 2.1 Influences on owner-managers and entrepreneurs

managers, are in fact both born and made. Whilst they do have certain personal character traits that they may be born with, they are also shaped by their history and experience of life. This comprises their antecedent influences – the social environment that they find themselves in for example, their family, ethnic group, work, education and so on – and the culture of the society they are brought up in. Some cultures encourage entrepreneurial activity, others discourage it. What is more, the situations entrepreneurs find themselves in can influence the decision. For example, if they are thrown out of work they may have little option but to try to start up their own business.

All these factors influence the decision whether to start up a business and whether to grow it. If all the factors are favourable the volume of start-ups should increase as, too, should the number of businesses that grow. Indeed both antecedent influences and the dominant culture of the society will almost certainly influence the personal character traits of individuals as they develop over time and visa versa – over time entrepreneurial characters will start to shape society and influence those they come in contact with. These three factors are interrelated.

However, of most interest to many people are the character traits and antecedents of our super-heroes – entrepreneurs. And that has a lot to do with trying to 'pick winners'. Entrepreneurs share certain character traits with owner-managers but they also have certain additional, almost magical, qualities that the average owner-manager does not possess.

Character traits

The issue of linking the character traits of an individual to the success of a business – picking winners – needs to be approached with caution. Even if it is possible to identify personal characteristics of owner-managers and entrepreneurs, it is not always possible to link them directly with a particular sort of business. So far we have considered three types of managers and implicitly linked them to three types of small firm:

Type of manager		Type of business
1　Owner-manager	⇨	Lifestyle firm. Often trade or craft based. Will not grow to any size.
2　Entrepreneur	⇨	Growth firm. Pursuit of growth and personal wealth important.
3　Manager	⇨	Manages a business belonging to someone else. Will build an organisation putting in appropriate controls similar to a large firm.

These were broad generalisations. The linkages are not that simple or direct all of the time. For example, an entrepreneur might manage a business belonging to someone else, at least for a time. Similarly, an owner-manager may find himself with a growth business, quite by accident. Success or failure in business, as we shall see later, comes from a mix of many different things. The character traits of the manager is just one factor in the equation. What is more, it takes time for the entrepreneur to prove that the business they manage is in fact a growth business, so do you measure aspirations or reality?

A further difficulty is that much of the research fails to distinguish between owner-managers and entrepreneurs, assuming anyone who starts their own business is an entrepreneur. However, research into the character traits of owner-managers of growth businesses, who should mainly be entrepreneurs, does allow us to come to some broad conclusions and to paint a picture of the different characters of owner-managers compared to entrepreneurs.

There are also a number of methodological problems associated with attempting to measure personality characteristics (Deakins, 1996):

- They are not stable and change over time.
- They require subjective judgements.
- Measures tend to ignore cultural and environmental influences.
- The role of education, learning, and training is often overlooked.
- Issues such as age, sex, race, social class and education can be ignored.

Clearly the area is an academic minefield. Notwithstanding this, many researchers do believe that, collectively, owner-managers have certain typical character traits, although the mix and emphasis of these characteristics will inevitably be different for each individual. Whether a clearly definable set of entrepreneurial characteristics exists is more controversial. Furthermore, many of the character traits that have been found are similar to those found in other successful people such as politicians or athletes (Chell, Haworth and Brearley, 1991). Perhaps, the argument goes, it just happens that the individual has chosen an entrepreneurial activity as a means of self-satisfaction. Certainly, even if you believe the character traits can be identified, they do not explain why the individual chose to apply them in an entrepreneurial context. Table 2.2 summarises the character traits associated with owner-managers and entrepreneurs.

Table 2.1 Character traits of owner-managers and entrepreneurs

Owner-managers

- Need for independence
- Need for achievement
- Internal locus of control
- Ability to live with uncertainty and take measured risks

Entrepreneurs

- Opportunistic
- Innovative
- Self-confident
- Proactive and decisive with high energy
- Self-motivated
- Vision and flair
- Willingness to take greater risks and live with greater uncertainty

Sources: Baty, 1990; Blanchflower and Meyer, 1991; Brockhaus and Horwitz, 1986; Caird, 1990; Chell, Haworth and Brearly, 1991; Kanter, 1983; McClelland, 1961; Schumpeter, 1996; Storey and Sykes, 1996.

Character traits of owner-managers

Owner-managers have a certain set of common character traits that they share with entrepreneurs.

Need for independence

Owner-managers have a high need for independence. This is most often seen as 'the need to be your own boss' and is the trait that is most often cited, and supported, by researchers and advisors alike. However, independence means different things to different people, such as controlling your own destiny, doing things differently or being in a situation where you can fulfil your potential. It has often been said that, once you run your own firm, you cannot work for anybody else.

Need for achievement

Owner-managers typically have a high need for achievement, a driving force that is even stronger for entrepreneurs. Achievement for the individual owner means different things depending what type of person they are. For example, the satisfaction of producing a beautiful work of art, employing their hundredth person, or making the magic one million pounds. Often money is just a badge of achievement to the successful entrepreneur. It is not an end in itself.

> 'We don't feel like millionaires at all. Money doesn't come into it. It's not really why you do it, it really isn't.'
>
> **Brent Hoberman**
> co-founder of **Lastminute.com**
> *Sunday Times* 19.09.99

Public recognition of achievement can be important to some owner-managers and entrepreneurs. And this can lead to certain negative behaviours or unwise decisions. For example, overspending on the trappings of corporate life – the office, the company car and so on (often called the corporate flagpole syndrome) – or the 'big project' that is very risky but the entrepreneur 'knows' they can do it. These can lead to cash flow problems that put at risk the very existence of the business.

> 'Most of the pleasure is not the cash. It is the sense of achievement at having taken something from nothing to where it is now.'
>
> **Charles Muirhead**
> founder of **Orchestream**
> *Sunday Times* 19.09.99

Internal locus of control

If you believe that you can exercise control over your environment and ultimately your destiny, you have an internal locus of control. If, however, you believe in fate, you have an external locus of control and you are less likely to take the risk of starting a business. Owner-managers typically have a strong internal locus of control, which is the same for many senior managers in large firms.

In extreme cases this trait also can lead to certain negative behaviours. In particular, it can show itself as a desire to maintain personal control over every aspect of the business. That can lead to a preoccupation with detail, over work and stress. It also leads to an inability or unwillingness to delegate as the business grows. Again, in extreme cases it might show itself as a mistrust of subordinates. Kets de Vries (1985) thinks these behaviours lead to subordinates becoming 'infantilised'. They are expected to behave as incompetent idiots, and that is the way they behave. They tend to do very little, make no decisions and circulate very little information. The better ones do not stay long.

This need for control also shows itself in the unwillingness of many owner-managers to part with shares in their company. They just do not want to lose control, at any price.

Ability to live with uncertainty and take measured risks

Human beings, typically, do not like uncertainty and one of the biggest uncertainties of all is not having a regular pay cheque coming in. That is not to say owner-managers like it. Uncertainty about income can be a major cause of stress. The possibility of missing out on some piece of business that might affect their income is one reason why they are so loath to take holidays.

> 'When I was made redundant self-employment was my only option and the work with the Business Link made it possible. The money was good, but I don't like the uncertainty – where the money for next month is coming from.'
>
> **Jean Young**
> Self-employed 1998–99

There are also other commercial aspects of uncertainty that the owner-manager has to cope with. Often they cannot influence many aspects of the market in which they operate, for example, price. They must therefore react to changes in the market that others might bring about. If a local supermarket has a special price promotion on certain goods it may well affect sales of similar goods in a local corner shop. A business with a high level of borrowing must find a way of paying interest charges but has no direct influence over changes in interest rates. Many small firms also have a limited customer or product base and this can bring further uncertainty. If, for whatever reason, one large customer ceases buying it can have an enormous impact on a small firm.

Hand in hand with their ability to live with uncertainty is their willingness to take measured risks. Most people are risk averse. They try to avoid risks and insure against them. Setting up your own business is risky and owner-managers are willing to take more risks with their own resources than most people. They might also risk their reputation and personal standing if they fail. However, they do not like it and try always to minimise their exposure. Hence, their preference to risk other peoples' money and borrow, sometimes too heavily, from the bank. Another example of this is the way they often 'compartmentalise' various aspects of their business. For example, an owner-manager might open a second restaurant but set it up as a separate limited company just in case it fails and should endanger the other. In this way they sometimes develop a portfolio of individually small businesses and their growth and success is measured not just in the performance of a single one but rather by the growth of the portfolio.

One important characteristic of owner-managers in their approach to dealing with uncertainty and risk is the short-term approach they take to all business decisions. It really is a case of not being certain that the business will survive until tomorrow. Therefore decision making is short-term and incremental. Strategies often evolve on a step-by-step basis. If one step

> 'The ideal business has no fixed overheads, commission only sales, large volume and low overheads.'
>
> **David Speakman**
> Founder of **Travel Counsellors**
> *Sunday Times 6.12.98*

works then the second is taken. At the same time the owner-manager will keep as many options open as possible, because they realise the outcome of their actions is very uncertain. Prudent entrepreneurs also seek to keep their fixed costs as low as possible, trying to minimise the risk they face. They also see assets as a liability rather than an asset, limiting the flexibility that they need, which is just as well since finding the resources for the business is usually a problem.

Character traits of entrepreneurs

Entrepreneurs share these characteristics with owner-managers. However, they have certain additional traits. Nevertheless, owner-managers can be entrepreneurial in some of their actions and the boundaries between the two are not always clear. Consequently, many of these traits are present in owner-managers, but to a far lesser extent.

Opportunistic

By definition, entrepreneurs exploit change for profit. In other words they seek out opportunities to make money. Often entrepreneurs see opportunities where others see problems. Whereas ordinary mortals dislike the uncertainty brought about by change, entrepreneurs love it because they see opportunity and they do not mind the uncertainty.

For many entrepreneurs the problem is getting them to focus on just one opportunity, or at least one opportunity at a time. They see opportunity everywhere and have problems following through on any one before becoming distracted by another. This is one reason why some entrepreneurs are not able to grow their business beyond a certain size. They get bored by the routines and controls, they see other market opportunities and yearn for the excitement of another start-up. They probably would be well advised to sell up and do just that. However, others realise this element of their character and become serial entrepreneurs, moving to set up and sell on one business after another. You see this very often in the restaurant business where an entrepreneurial restaurateur launches a new restaurant and makes it successful, then sells it on so as to move onto another new venture. They make money by creating a business with capital value, not necessarily income for themselves.

Anatomy of a serial-entrepreneur
Sir Terence Conran

1930: Born Esher, Surrey, England. Left Central School of Arts and Crafts half-way through textiles course to take up architectural job. Started designing and manufacturing furniture in his spare time from an old workshop in east London.

1952: Gave up architecture and moved to larger studio in Notting Hill to manufacture furniture full-time.

1956: Employed one assistant and four part-time designers but business still struggling. To generate more cash, started 'up-market soup kitchens' serving simple meals with bread and wine and kitted out with his furniture. Concept worked. Two sites opened in London and one in Cambridge. Expanded furniture business, producing catalogues and employing sales staff.

1959: Started design consultancy, specialising in shop interiors and exhibitions, employing 100 staff within two years.

1960: Sold restaurants.

1962: Sold £100 000 stake in business to Morgan Grenfell and used the money to start Habitat, opening the first shop on the Fulham Road.

1967: Habitat merged with Ryman but soon bought back the company and expanded overseas.

1981: Habitat went public and later merged with Mothercare.

1986: Merged with British Home Stores to form Storehouse.

1990: Retired from Storehouse.

1990s: Starts 19 restaurants and bars in London including Mezzo, Bibendum and Quaglino's, one in Paris and others soon in Stockholm and New York. Reopens the Great Eastern Hotel.

Innovative

Their ability to spot opportunities and to innovate are the two most important distinguishing features of entrepreneurs. Innovation is the prime tool entrepreneurs use to create or exploit opportunity. These characteristics sets entrepreneurs apart from owner-managers. Entrepreneurs link innovation to the market place so as to exploit an opportunity and make their business grow. Although innovation is difficult to define and can take many forms, entrepreneurs are always, in some way, innovative. We shall explore this in more detail in the next chapter.

Self-confident

Facing uncertainty, you have to be confident in your own judgement and ability to start up your own business. Many start up training programmes recognise this by trying to build confidence by developing a business plan that addresses the issue of future uncertainty. As well as a useful management tool, the plan can become a symbol of certainty for the owner-manager in an otherwise uncertain world and some even keep it with them at all

> 'My mother gave me a massive self-belief. I will always try things – there is nothing to lose.'
> **Richard Thompson**
> founder and chairman of **EMS**
> Rupert Steiner, *My First Break: How Entrepreneurs Get Started*, Sunday Times Books, 1999

times, using it almost like a bible, to reassure them of what the future will hold when the business is successful.

Entrepreneurs, therefore, need self-confidence a-plenty to grow their business given the extreme uncertainty they face. If they do not believe in the future of the business, how can they expect others to do so? However, the self-confidence can be overdone and turn to an exaggerated opinion of their own competence, and even arrogance.

Some researchers believe entrepreneurs are actually 'delusional'. In an interesting piece of research, two American academics tested the decision-making process of 124 entrepreneurs (defined as people who started their own firm) and 95 managers of big companies in two ways (Busenitz and Barney, 1997). Firstly, they asked five factual questions each of which had two possible answers. They asked respondents to rate their confidence in their answer (50 per cent, a guess; 100 per cent, perfect confidence). Entrepreneurs turned out to be much more confident about their answers than managers, especially those who gave wrong answers. Secondly, they were given a business decision. They were told they must replace a broken foreign-made machine and they had two alternatives. The first was an American-made machine, which a friend had recently bought and had not yet broken down, and the second a foreign-built machine, which was statistically less likely to break down than the other; 50 per cent of the entrepreneurs opted for the American machine but 90 per cent of the managers opted for the foreign one. The researchers concluded that the entrepreneurs were more prone to both delusion and opportunism than normal managers. So the question is raised, is entrepreneurial self-confidence so strong as to make them delusional, blinding them to the reality of a situation?

Proactive and decisive with high energy

Entrepreneurs tend to be proactive rather than reactive and more decisive than other people. They are proactive in the sense that they seek out opportunities, they do not just rely on luck. They act quickly and decisively to make the most of the opportunity before somebody else does.

Entrepreneurs are often seen as restless and easily bored. They can easily be diverted by the most recent market opportunity and often seem to do things at twice the pace of others, unwilling or unable to wait for others to complete tasks. Patience is certainly not a virtue many possess. Many entrepreneurs seem to work 24 hours a day and their work becomes their life with little separating the two. It is little wonder that it places family relationships under strain.

One important result of this characteristic is that entrepreneurs tend to learn by doing. They act first and then learn from the outcomes of the action. It is part of their incremental approach to decision-making, each small action and its outcomes contribute to the learning process.

> 'Neither my grandfather nor my father would be surprised if they could see me now. My success didn't just happen As a young boy, I was always working. My parents and my brothers and sisters all had high energy.'
>
> **Tom Farmer**
> founder of **Kwik-Fit**
> *Daily Mail* 11.05.99

Self-motivated

Entrepreneurs are highly self-motivated, amounting almost to a driving urge to succeed in their economic goals. This is driven by their exceptionally strong inner need for achievement, far stronger than with the average owner-manager. Running your own business is a lonely affair, without anyone to motivate and encourage you. You work long hours, sometimes for little reward. You therefore need to be self-motivated, committed and determined to succeed.

This strong inner drive – what psychologists call type 'A' behaviour – is quite unique and can be seen as almost compulsive behaviour. This is not to say that entrepreneurs are not motivated by other things as well, such as money. But often money is just a badge of their success that allows them to measure their achievement. What drives them is their exceptionally high need to achieve. 'A' types tend to be goal-focused, wanting to get the job done quickly. However, they also tend to be highly reactive, focusing on the future and often not in control of the present.

> 'I have never had anything to do in my life that provides so many challenges – and there are so many things I still want to do.'
>
> **Martha Lane Fox**
> co-founder of **Lastminute.com**
> *Sunday Times* 19.09.99

> 'I am motivated by my success not money. But success is partly measured by money.'
>
> **Wing Yip**
> founder of **W. Wing Yip & Brothers**
> *Sunday Times* 2.01.00

Vision and flair

To succeed, entrepreneurs need to have a clear vision of what they want to achieve. That is part of the fabric of their motivation. It also helps them bring others with them, both employees and customers. The flair comes with the ability to be in the right place at the right time. Timing is everything. Innovation that is before its time can lead to business failure. Innovation that is late results in copy-cat products or services that are unlikely to be outstanding successes. A question constantly asked about successful entrepreneurs is whether their success was due to good luck or good judgement? The honest answer in most cases is probably a bit of both.

Willingness to take greater risks and live with even greater uncertainty

It is worth stressing that, whilst all owner-managers are willing to take risks and live with uncertainty, true entrepreneurs are willing to take far greater risks and live with far greater uncertainty. Often they are willing to put their own home on the line and risk all, so strong is their belief in their business idea.

What is more, growth businesses face rapid change. Even with careful management they are extremely risky. Growth businesses require large amounts of capital and entrepreneurs are, if necessary, willing to risk all they own for the prospect of success. Faced with such extreme uncertainty a high degree of self-confidence is essential.

> 'When I gave up my job [with Boston Consulting Group] I was without income for four months. I had to borrow money for the business and I thought I would have to sell my flat. I was prepared to move into a bedsit.'
>
> **Ernesto Schmitt**
> founder of **People-sound.com**
> *Times 7.08.99*

> 'You have to have nerves of steel and be prepared to take risks. You have to be able to put it all on the line knowing you could lose everything.'
>
> **Anne Notley**
> co-founder of **The Iron Bed Company**
> *Sunday Times 28.01.01*

Antecedent influences

We are all born with certain character traits. However, we are also influenced by the social environment that we find ourselves in, for example, our family, ethnic group, education and so on. They influence our values, attitudes and even our behaviours. These are called antecedent influences and it has been held that owner-managers and entrepreneurs often share common antecedent influences which, again, distinguish them from other people (Carter and Cachon, 1988).

In many ways the academic research in this area is even more confusing, and sometimes contradictory, than with personal character traits. There are a myriad of claimed influences that are difficult to prove, or indeed, disprove. There are simply too many variables to control. A further confusion is between owner-managers and entrepreneurs. Most of the research is about influences on start-ups. But start-ups comprise both owner-managers and entrepreneurs.

However, there is a body of research on antecedent influences on managers of growth businesses which can apply, in the main, to entrepreneurs. The problem here is that some of the influences that seem to influence growth are not those that can be proved to influence start-ups. The only really safe conclusion is that, except for a handful of influences, the research is inconclusive.

Education

One influence that comes through on many studies for both start up and growth is educational attainment. Clearly there are problems measuring educational attainment consistently over studies, however, particularly in the USA, research consistently shows a positive association between the probability of starting-up in business and increases in educational attainment (Evans and Leighton, 1990). Similar research in other countries tends to support this result, albeit less strongly and not consistently. However, what is altogether stronger is the relationship between educational attainment and business growth. Storey (1994) reviewed 17 multivariate antecedent studies which gauged the influence of educational attainment (amongst other influences) and found that there was a positive influence in eight. This led him to conclude that there was 'fairly consistent support for the view that educated entrepreneurs are more likely to establish faster-growing firms'.

This is not a widely acknowledged result and perhaps one that is more true of the USA than Britain. It is the stuff of folk lore that the entrepreneur comes from a poor, deprived background and has little formal education. In fact some writers go further and claim that 'anecdotal evidence' suggests that too much education can discourage entrepreneurship (Bolton and Thompson, 2000). But times are changing and if you ask venture capitalists why they think certain firms will grow rather than others, they will tell you that they are looking for background and track record in the firm's management, and education counts. It is also particularly true of the new generation of entrepreneurs pursuing e-commerce opportunities.

The rationale for the relationship might be two-fold. Firstly, educational attainment might provide the basis for better learning through life, enabling entrepreneurs to better deal with business problems and giving them a greater openness and more outward orientation. Secondly, it might give them higher earning expectations that can only be attained by growing the business. What is more it might also give them greater confidence in dealing with customers and other business professionals.

Employment and unemployment

Storey's (1994) review of antecedent literature also came to some important conclusions regarding the influence of employment and unemployment. Reviewing three multivariate studies he found two had statistically significant relationships between unemployment and the probability of starting-up in business. However, when he came to look at growth four out of eight studies showed a negative relationship and the other four showed no relationship at all. What is more, four out of seven studies found a positive relationship between positive motives for setting up the business (for example, market opportunity, making money) and subsequent growth. This led Storey to conclude that 'if the founder is unemployed prior to starting a business, that firm is unlikely to grow as rapidly as where the founder is employed'.

It would seem that unemployment gives people a strong push into self-employment. They possibly have limited options open to them. However, they may not have the skills needed to grow the business and may have lower aspirations than those who leave employment to start their own business. It would seem that what is needed to make the firm grow is positive motivation – a real desire, an ambition, almost a need to achieve certain internally generated goals or pursue some market opportunity. Growth does not happen (often) by chance. The entrepreneur must want it.

Research in France also casts doubt on the long term viability of start-up generated by unemployed people (Abdesselam, Bonnet and Le Pape, 1999). They found that firms with the shortest life-spans were set up by the young (under 30) and unemployed. They also found that there was a high probability that they would be female and the business would be in the retail or wholesale sector. These results cast worrying doubt on the wisdom of any government policy to encourage the unemployed to start up their own business.

Other influences on start-ups

There are other influences on start-ups that have been cited, many supported by univariate research, for example the influence of family. In a survey of 600 respondents, Stanworth *et al.* (1989) found that between 30 per cent and 47 per cent of individuals either considering, about to start, or in business had a parent who had been in business. Another factor often cited is that immigrants to a

Anita Lucia Roddick, née Perilla, was born in Littlehampton, England in 1942, one of four children of Italian immigrants. Her parents settled in Littlehampton to run the Clifton Cafe. Her father died when she was ten and the children then helped to run the cafe. From school she went to Bath College of Education where she took a Teacher Training course. She started teaching, but wanted to live abroad so she got a job with the United Nations in Geneva. She had never had a holiday as a child and so, with the tax-free money she earned in Geneva, she decided to spend a year travelling around the world. She visited Polynesia, New Caledonia, Australia and Africa where her interest in the use of natural ingredients for cosmetic purposes was aroused. In Tahiti she saw local women plastering themselves with cocoa butter. Half the bean was used for chocolate and the other half was used as a cosmetic. In Morocco she saw women washing their hair in mud.

Returning to England, she met Gordon Roddick, a graduate of the Royal Agricultural College at Cirencester. He had farmed overseas and in the UK before settling in Littlehampton. They married in 1970. Originally they planned to travel overland to Australia and buy a pineapple plantation, but the arrival of first one and then two children made them change their plans. Instead they bought and ran a restaurant and later a small hotel in Littlehampton. In 1976 they opened their first tiny **Body Shop** in Brighton. Today, **Body Shop** is an international business and they are millionaires.

. . . to be continued

Table 2.2　Factors that could not be proved to influence start-ups

● Marital status	● Experience	● Gender	● Personality
● Children	● Age	● Social class	● Manager
● Previous wage	● Ethnicity	● School type	(in previous job)

country often go into self-employment. Examples such as the high incidence of self-employment in the Indian, Pakistani and Bangladeshi immigrant communities in the UK are often quoted. However, Storey in his review of multivariate analyses concludes that there is little support for the impact of family, family circumstances, cultural or ethnic influences on self-employment decisions. In countering the issue of immigrant populations he quotes the example of West Indian and Guyanese immigrant communities where the levels of self-employment are low. Other factors that Storey could not prove were influences are shown in Table 2.2.

It has to be said that Storey's cold analytical approach to the immigrant issue does not stand the test of observation. As Harper (1985) observed:

> The Indians in East Africa, the Armenians in Egypt, the Lebanese in West Africa, the Kikuyu in Masailand, the Mahajans all over India except in their desert homeland of Rajasthan, the Tamils in Sri Lanka, the Palestinians in Arabia and the British almost everywhere except in Britain; all have shown that dislocation and hardship can lead to enterprise. The very experience of living in a difficult environment, and of planning, financing and executing a move and then surviving in a new and often hostile environment requires the qualities of self-restraint, abstinence, hard work and voluntary postponement of gratification which are normally far more severe than those demanded by the lifestyle of those who remain at home, or of the indigenous people of the place in which these refugees relocate.

Starting and running your own business is not easy and immigrants often have the motivation to work the long hours. With few options often open to them, they have little to lose from failure and much to gain from success.

One interesting perspective on entrepreneurship is provided by Kets de Vries (1997) who believes entrepreneurs often come from unhappy family backgrounds. This makes them unwilling to accept authority or to work closely with others. He paints the picture of a social deviant or misfit who is both hostile to others and tormented in themselves:

> A prominent pattern among entrepreneurs appears to be a sense of impulsivity, a persistent feeling of dissatisfaction, rejection and pointlessness, forces which contribute to an impairment and depreciation of his sense of self-esteem and effect cognitive processes. The entrepreneur is a man under great stress, continuously badgered by his past, a past which is experienced and re-experienced in fantasies, daydreams and dreams. These dreams and fantasies often have a threatening content due to the recurrence of feelings of anxiety and guilt which mainly revolve around hostile wishes against parental figures, or more generally, all individuals in a position of authority.

In reality there is little support for this extreme view.

Other influences on growth

Storey's review of the research concludes that there are three further factors that are positively correlated with growth companies:

1 Growth companies are more likely to be set up by groups rather than individuals. This proves the venture capitalist's view that they invest in a management team not in a business and explains why they are so willing to invest in management buy-outs and buy-ins. Managing growth needs a range of different skills with managers able to work as a team. Attracting a strong management team can be a problem for a start-up. How do you tempt successful managers to leave secure jobs and face the risks associated with a start-up? The answer is by offering them a share in the business. In that way they share in the success of the business as well as the risks that it faces.

> **Lastminute.com** offers last minute deals on theatre tickets, flights, holidays and even restaurants. It was set up in 1998 by **Brent Hoberman** (30) and **Martha Lane Fox** (26), after raising £600 000 in venture capital. In 1999 it had a turnover of £195 000 and did not make a profit. By early 2000 the company was operating in the UK, France, Germany and Sweden, had 162 employees and 800 000 registered subscribers. In the same year it was floated on the Stock Market at a valuation of more than £400 million.
>
> The Board included Peter Bouw, former chairman and chief executive of KLM, Bob Colliers, vice president of Intercontinental Hotels, and Linda Fayne Levinson, who ran Amex Travel. All have experience of the products the company sells. Technology was headed by Dominic Cameron from Aztec and BBC Television, the European Director was Tom Virden, former head of Netscape Netcentre European Portal Sites. How did they attract such a strong management team? Martha Lane Fox explains:
>
>> We decided not to be greedy about equity but to recruit a highly talented and experienced management team by selling them a dream – a stake in lastminute.com.
>
> *The Times* 24.03.00
>
> . . . to be continued

2 Middle-aged owners are more likely to be associated with growth companies. Middle age does have some advantages. It bring experience, credibility and financial resources. With the family possibly grown up, middle-aged entrepreneurs can devote more time and resources to the business.

However, as with all research these results must be treated with caution. Findings like these come from looking at what has happened in the past and if situations change, the past may not be a good indication of what might happen in the future. Computing and e-commerce may well be changing the nature of the game of start-up and growth businesses.

Forged in the white heat of two great forces: the spirit of free enterprise introduced during their youth by Margaret Thatcher and a technological revolution. Never before have so many millions been made by people so young.

wrote the *Sunday Times* (17.09.99). Every day newspapers carry stories of these young self-made millionaires, usually following up e-commerce opportunities, mainly well educated, often raising many millions in venture capital by giving away some of their equity, with their businesses still in their infancy and not yet breaking even. Among the *Sunday Times* 'Top 100 Internet Tycoons' (3.11.99), the average fortune amassed was £40.3 million and 20 per cent were aged 30 or less. The youngest was Benjamin Cohen aged 17 who had amassed a modest £5 million from his website aimed at the Jewish community, Jewish.com, started with just £150.

UK millionaires in their twenties

All of the following are millionaires many times over and all made it in their twenties. There are many more.

- **Charles Nasser**, born 1969, an electronic engineering graduate, launched **Claranet**, an internet service provider, in 1996.
- **Jason Drummond**, born 1969, owner of **Virtual Internet**.
- **Jason Pickthall**, born 1970, launched **People Phones**, a company selling mobile phones, in 1989, aged nineteen.
- **Robert Bonnier**, born 1970, chief executive of **Scoot.com**, a telephone and internet information company.
- **Tahir Mohsan**, born 1971, launched **Granville Technology**, a computer mail order company, with his brother in 1987.
- **Joe de Sarem**, born 1972, launched **Rhodium**, a computer software company, in 1995.
- **Alexander Straub**, born 1972, head of **Modus.com**.
- **Ajaz Ahmed**, born 1973, a university drop-out, launched **AKQA New Media** in 1993.
- **Martha Lane Fox**, born 1973, joint founder with **Brent Hoberman** (born 1969) of **Lastminute.com**.
- **Charles Muirhead**, born 1975, dropped out from a university computer course to launch **Orchestream**, an internet company.

---

3   Owners with previous managerial experience are more likely to be associated with growth companies. This is likely to be the case because they bring with them both managerial and, probably, market experience. They also know their previous worth which may create salary expectations that can only be satisfied by a growth business.

The factors that Storey could not prove influenced growth are shown in Table 2.3. However, he also concludes that the picture is 'fuzzy' and that what the entrepreneur has done prior to establishing the business 'only has a modest

Table 2.3 Factors that could not be proved to influence growth

● Gender	● Training	● Family history
● Prior firm size experience	● Social marginality	● Prior self-employment
● Prior sector experience	● Ethnicity	

influence on the success of the business'. One factor frequently debated is that of the experience of prior business failure. Whether or not this is a positive experience is still to be adequately researched. Until then no conclusion can be drawn.

One curious conclusion is that the influence of training cannot be proved. If you believe that entrepreneurs are both born and made, then you must accept that they can be influenced. Just like an athlete or a musician, if they have the basic ingredients, then training should improve their performance. There are at least two major problems related to this variable. Firstly, there is the question of what constitutes training. Smaller firms are notoriously poor at undertaking formal training but that does not necessarily mean they do not undertake informal training. Secondly, those small firms that do seek out formal training are also likely to seek out other sources of help and so the influence of the formal training becomes more difficult to measure.

These studies of growth businesses allow us to draw an, albeit tentative, identikit picture of the antecedent influences on an entrepreneur which are most likely to result in them successfully growing their business. These are shown in Table 2.4. Remember, however, that they are generalisations. Whilst broadly supportable because of the samples on which they are based, they do not apply to every individual, as we can see from the anatomy of Sir Terence Conran. Just

> **Anatomy of a serial-entrepreneur Sir Terence Conran**
>
> ● Left university without completing degree.
> ● Very positively motivated.
> ● Only managerial job in his own business.
> ● Started own business aged 20 years.
> ● A one-man entrepreneur.

like small firms, entrepreneurs are not homogeneous. They are also based on ex-post research, that is analysis based on the past. Circumstances do change and sometimes the past is not always a good predictor of the future. What is more, if picking winners were really that easy there would be an awful lot of rich people around.

Table 2.4 Antecedent influences on the entrepreneur

● Well-educated
● Starts business because of positive motivations
● Leaves managerial job to start business
● Middle aged (or very young?)
● Willing to share ownership of business

Entrepreneurial culture

The final element in the jigsaw puzzle is culture. In his seminal work on the subject, Hofstede (1980) defined culture as the 'collective programming of the mind which distinguishes one group of people from another'. It is a pattern of taken for granted assumptions. An entrepreneurial culture is one that fosters positive social attitudes towards entrepreneurship. Cultures can change over time, albeit slowly. So, most people would argue that Britain has developed a more entrepreneurial culture from the 1970s through to today. What is more there may be subcultures within any dominant culture. So, for example, different ethnic groups in a country may be more or less entrepreneurial.

It has be argued that there is no such thing as one identifiable entrepreneurial culture; what is needed is a favourable environment which combines social, political and educational attributes (Timmons, 1994). However, many would consider the culture in the USA to be the most entrepreneurial in the world. It is an achievement orientated society that values individualism and material wealth. According to Welsch (1998):

> Entrepreneurship is ingrained in the fabric of North American culture. It is discussed at the family dinner table among intergenerational members, practised by pre-school children with their lemonade stands, and promoted every day through personal success human interest stories in the media. Furthermore, entrepreneurship is taught in school from kindergarten through to the twelfth grade, it has been integrated into college and university curricula, and is taught and promoted through various outreach and training programmes including government Small Business Development Centres in every state of the nation. Consequently, through one's life as an American citizen, entrepreneurship as a career option is espoused early and reinforced regularly.

Americans are said to have a 'frontier culture', always seeking something new. They are restless, constantly on the move. They have a strong preference for freedom of choice for the individual. The individual is always free to compete against established institutions. Rebellious, non-conformist youth is the accepted norm. If there is an 'American dream' it is that the humblest of individuals can become the greatest of people, usually measured in monetary terms. Achievement is prized and lauded throughout society. Individuals believe they control their destiny. Americans think big. Nothing is impossible. They prefer the new, or at least the improved. They worship innovation. Time is their most precious commodity. They are tolerant of those who make mistakes as long as they learn from them. Things need to get done quickly rather than always get done perfectly.

Measuring the dimensions of culture in a scientific way is extremely difficult. The most widely used dimensions are those developed by Hofstede (1981) who undertook an extensive cross-cultural study, using questionnaire data from some 80 000 IBM employees in 66 countries across seven occupations. From his research he established four dimensions (Figure 2.2):

High (upper quartile countries)		Low (lower quartile countries)
USA Australia New Zealand UK Canada France Germany	INDIVIDUALISM	South America Pakistan
Malaysia Philippines France South America	POWER DISTANCE	UK USA Scandinavia Germany
Greece Portugal Uruguay Guatemala France	UNCERTAINTY AVOIDANCE	Hong Kong Singapore UK USA
Japan Austria Italy UK USA Germany	MASCULINITY	North Europe

Figure 2.2 Hofstede's dimensions of culture

1 **Individualism vs collectivism** This is the degree to which people prefer to act as individuals rather than groups. Individualistic societies are loosely knit social frameworks in which people primarily operate as individuals or in immediate families. Collectivist societies are composed of tight networks in which people operate as members of ingroups and outgroups, expecting to look after, and be looked after by, other members of their ingroup. In the individualist culture the task prevails over personal relationships. In the collectivist culture the opposite is true. 'Anglo' countries (USA, Britain, Australia, Canada and New Zealand) are the highest scoring individualist cultures, together with the Netherlands. France and Germany just made it into the upper quartile of individualist cultures. South American countries were the most collectivist cultures, together with Pakistan.

2 **Power distance** This is the degree of inequality among people that the community is willing to accept. Low power distance countries endorse egalitarianism, relations are open and informal, information flows are functional and unrestricted and organisations tend to have flat structures. High power distance cultures endorse hierarchies, relations are more formal, information flows are formalised and restricted and organisations tend to be rigid and hierarchical. Low power distance countries tend to be Austria, Ireland, Israel, New Zealand and the four Scandinavian countries. The USA, Britain and Germany also make it into the lower quartile. High power distance countries are Malaysia, the Philippines and four South American countries, with France also making it into the upper quartile.

3 **Uncertainty avoidance** This is the degree to which people prefer to avoid ambiguity, resolve uncertainty and prefer structured rather than unstructured situations. Low uncertainty avoidance cultures tolerate greater ambiguity, prefer flexibility, stress personal choice and decision-making, reward initiative, risk-taking and team-play and stress the development of analytical skills. High uncertainty avoidance cultures prefer rules and procedures, stress compliance, punish error and reward compliance, loyalty and attention to detail. The lowest uncertainty avoidance countries are Hong Kong, Ireland, Jamaica, Singapore and two Scandinavian countries. The USA and Britain are in the lowest quartile group. The highest uncertainty avoidance countries are Greece, Portugal, Guatemala and Uruguay, with France also in the highest quartile group. Germany is about halfway.

4 **Masculinity vs femininity** This defines quality of life issues. Masculine virtues are those of assertiveness, competition and success. Masculine cultures reward financial and material achievement with social prestige and status. Feminine virtues are those such as modesty, compromise and cooperation. In feminine cultures issues such as quality of life, warmth in personal relationships, service and so on are important, and in some societies having a high standard of living is thought to be a matter of birth, luck or destiny (external locus of control). The most masculine countries are Japan, Austria, Venezuela, Italy and Switzerland. The USA, Britain and Germany all fall into the highest quartile. Four North European countries are the highest scoring feminine countries. France is about halfway.

Using Hofstede's dimensions, therefore, the USA, our role model for entrepreneurial culture, emerges as a highly individualistic, masculine culture, with low power distance and uncertainty avoidance. It is a highly individualistic culture, one that is fiercely competitive and the home of the 'free-market economy'. Assertiveness and competition are central to the 'American dream'. If there is a key virtue in the USA it is achievement, and achievement receives its monetary reward. It is an informal culture. All men are created equal, however, they also have the freedom to accumulate sufficient wealth to become very unequal. The USA is the original 'frontier culture'. It actually seems to like change and uncertainty and certainly rewards initiative and risk-taking.

Using Hofstede's dimensions, this, then, is the anatomy of an enterprise culture. One that encourages enterprise and entrepreneurship, one where the probability of an entrepreneur being made, rather than just born, is highest. This is the sort of culture that many other countries have been trying to encourage and develop because it seems to encourage the characteristics that are needed for successful management. This culture, combined with the other antecedent influences, is said to be likely to develop the largest number of that most valuable resource – entrepreneurs.

However, notice one thing from Figure 2.2; alongside the USA, at the extreme ends of these dimensions, is the UK and that can hardly have been held up to be the epitome of an enterprise culture at the time these studies were conducted. Perhaps the dimensions measured by Hofstede are just not relevant to entrepreneurship. Perhaps there are other equally relevant, important but uncharted dimensions. After all, his work was based upon IBM employees and they can hardly be described as the most entrepreneurial in the world, particularly just at the time when Microsoft was setting out in business. Whilst other countries try to emulate the enterprise culture of the USA, the jury is out on how precisely the dimensions of their enterprise culture are to be measured.

Notwithstanding this serious reservation about measurement, we know that deep cultures take time to change, if indeed they can be changed. There is little evidence, as yet, of different cultures around the world converging. What is more, we do not understand how best to go about changing cultures, even if you believe it desirable. Rather than trying to change a nation's culture perhaps the best thing to do may be to ensure that, at the very least, it does not inhibit entrepreneurship.

Summary

Owner-managers and entrepreneurs are both born and made. They have certain personal character traits that they are born with and are influenced by antecedent factors as well as the culture into which they are born. The issue of linking the character traits of an individual to the success of a business – picking winners – needs to be approached with caution because it is not always possible to link individuals. Success or failure in business comes from a mix of many different things. The character traits of the manager is just one factor in the equation. What is more there are a number of methodological problems associated with trying to measure personality traits:

● They are not stable and change over time.
● They require subjective judgements.
● Measures tend to ignore cultural and environmental influences.
● The role of education, learning and training is often overlooked.
● Issues such as age, sex, race, social class and education can be ignored.

Owner-managers have the following character traits:

● Need for independence.
● Need for achievement, strongest in entrepreneurs like **Brent Hoberman** and **Charles Muirhead**.
● Internal locus of control, that is a belief that they can control their own destiny.
● Ability to live with uncertainty and take measured risks, unlike **Jean Young**.

In addition, entrepreneurs have the following character traits, however, some more entrepreneurial owner-managers might exhibit them, albeit to a lesser degree:

● Opportunistic, creating or exploiting change for profit, like the serial-entrepreneur **Sir Terence Conran.**
● Innovative, using innovation as their prime tool to create or exploit opportunity.
● Self-confident, like **Richard Thompson**.
● Proactive and decisive with high energy, like **Tom Farmer**.
● Self-motivated, like **Martha Lane Fox**.
● Vision and flair.
● Willingness to take greater risks and live with greater uncertainty, like **Ernesto Schmitt** and **Ann Notley**.

Education is an important antecedent influence on start-ups but more particularly entrepreneurial growth businesses. Whilst unemployment is a strong push into self-employment, entrepreneurial growth businesses are more likely to set up for more positive motives. It is possible that having a parent who was previously self-employed is more likely to lead a person to set up their own firm. Observation tells us that another influence is immigration to a foreign country. **Anita Roddick**, founder and Chairman of **Body Shop**, fits this profile fairly well.

Growth companies are more likely to be set up by groups rather than individuals often, like **Lastminute.com**, sharing ownership to attract experienced managers. They are more likely to be set up by middle-aged owners with previous managerial experience who leave their job for the start-up. However, observation tells us that this might be changing with computers and e-commerce creating a whole generation of very young millionaire entrepreneurs who have set up companies such as **Claranet**, **Virtual Internet**, **People Phones**, **Scoot.com**, **Granville Technology**, **Rhodium**, **Modus.com**, **AKQA**, **New Media**, **Lastminute.com** and **Orchestream.** Probably the youngest is Benjamin Cohen aged seventeen who had amassed £5 million from his website aimed at the Jewish community, **Jewish.com**, started with just £150.

Culture – 'the software of the mind' – also influences the decision whether to set up your own firm and whether to grow it. Culture can be measured in four dimensions: individualism vs collectivism; power distance; uncertainty avoidance; and masculinity vs femininity. The USA is probably the role model for an entrepreneurial culture. It emerges as a highly individualistic, masculine culture, with low power distance and uncertainty avoidance. Whether or not you accept these dimensions of culture as saying anything about entrepreneurship, what is true is that entrepreneurship is ingrained into the fabric of culture in the USA, part of the 'American dream'.

⬤ Essays and discussion topics

1 Are entrepreneurs born or made?
2 Do you think you have what it takes to be an owner-manager or entrepreneur?
3 Which character traits of owner-managers and entrepreneurs might have negative effects on a business?
4 What factors do you think effect the success or otherwise of a business venture?
5 Can you 'pick winners'?
6 How do entrepreneurs cope with risk and uncertainty?
7 What are the defining characteristics of an entrepreneur?
8 Are immigrants more entrepreneurial?
9 Can training help develop entrepreneurship?
10 Has your education, so far, encouraged you to be entrepreneurial? If so, how? If not, how could it be changed?
11 Does this course encourage entrepreneurship?
12 Is entrepreneurship really just for the middle-aged?
13 Are there advantages to setting up your own business when you are young?
14 Why might so many e-commerce entrepreneurs be young and well-educated?
15 Is it really better to set up in business with other individuals?
16 Does previous business failure mean that you are more likely to succeed in the future?
17 Have attitudes to entrepreneurs changed in this country over the last twenty years?

18 Does this country have an enterprise culture?
19 How can enterprise culture be encouraged?
20 Why is the USA considered the most entrepreneurial culture in the world?
21 Which other countries would you consider to have an entrepreneurial culture?
22 Are their any other dimensions along which an enterprise culture could be measured?

Exercises and assignments

1 List the questions you would ask an owner-manager or entrepreneur in trying to assess their character traits.
2 Use the list of questions developed in exercise 1 to conduct an interview with an owner-manager of a local small firm. Summarise the most important observation and insights you have gained from the interview. Write an essay or report describing their character. Make sure to justify your conclusions about their character with evidence from the interview.
3 Find out all you can about a well-known entrepreneur and write an essay or report describing their character. Give examples of their actions that lead you to make the conclusions you do about their character.
4 Evaluate your own character against the results of the previous exercises.

Entrepreneurship exercise

Go to the Entrepreneurship Exercise at the back of the book to see whether you really have what it takes to become an entrepreneur.

References

Abdesselam, R., Bonnet, J. and Le Pape, N. (1999) 'An Explanation of the Life Span of New Firms: An Empirical Analysis of French Data', *Entrepreneurship: Building for the Future*, Euro PME 2nd International Conference, Rennes.

Baty, G. (1990) *Entrepreneurship in the Nineties*, New Jersey: Prentice Hall.

Blanchflower, D.G. and Meyer, B.D. (1991) 'Longitudinal Analysis of Young Entrepreneurs in Australia and the United States', *National Bureau of Economic Research*, Working Paper no. 3746, Cambridge, Mass.

Bolton, B. and Thompson. J. (2000) *Entrepreneurs: Talent, Temperament, Technique*, Oxford: Butterworth-Heinemann.

Brockhaus, R. and Horwitz, P. (1986) 'The Psychology of the Entrepreneur', in D. Sexton and R. Smilor (eds), *The Art and Science of Entrepreneurship*, Cambridge , Mass: Ballinger Publishing Co.

Busenitz, L. and Barney, J. (1997) 'Differences between Entrepreneurs and Managers in Large Organisations: Niases and Heuristics in Strategic Decision Making', *Journal of Business Venturing*, vol. 12.

Caird, S. (1990) 'What Does it Mean to be Enterprising?', *British Journal of Management*, vol.1, no. 3.

Carter, S. and Cachon, J. (1988) *The Sociology of Entrepreneurship*, , Stirling: University of Stirling Press.

Chell, E., Haworth, J. and Brearley, S. (1991) *The Entrepreneurial Personality*, London: Routledge.

Deakins, D. (1996) *Entrepreneurs and Small Firms*, London: McGraw-Hill.

Evans, D.S. and Leighton, L.S. (1990) 'Small Business Formation by Unemployed and Employed Workers', *Small Business Economics*, vol. 2, no. 4.

Harper, M. (1985) 'Hardship, Discipline and Entrepreneurship', *Cranfield School of Management*, Working Paper no. 85.1.

Hofstede, G. (1980) *Culture's Consequences: International Differences in Work-related Values*, Beverly Hills: Sage.

Hofstede, G. (1981) *Cultures and Organisations: Software of the Mind*, London: HarperCollins.

Kanter, R.M. (1983) *The Change Masters*, New York: Simon & Schuster.

Kets de Vries, M.F.R. (1985) 'The Dark Side of Entrepreneurship', *Harvard Business Review*, November–December.

Kets de Vries, M.F.R. (1997) 'The Entrepreneurial Personality: A Person at the Crossroads', *Journal of Management Studies*, February.

McClelland, D. C. (1961) *The Achieving Society*, Princeton, New Jersey: Van Nostrand.

Schumpeter, J.A. (1996) *The Theory of Economic Development*, edn copyright 1983, New Jersey: Transaction Publishers.

Stanworth, J., Blythe, S., Granger, B. and Stanworth, C. (1989) 'Who Becomes an Entrepreneur?', *International Small Business Journal*, vol. 8, no. 1.

Storey, D.J. (1994) *Understanding the Small Business Sector*, London: International Thomson Business Press.

Storey, D. and Sykes, N. (1996) 'Uncertainty, Innovation and Management', in P. Burns and J. Dewhurst (eds), *Small Business and Entrepreneurship*, London: Macmillan – now Palgrave.

Timmons, J. (1994) *New Venture Creation*, Boston: Irwin.

Welsch, H. (1998) 'America: North', in A. Morrison (ed.), *Entrepreneurship: An International Perspective*, Oxford: Butterworth Heinemann.

chapter three

Opportunity and innovation

Contents

- Tools of entrepreneurship
- Invention and innovation
- The father of innovation
- Sources of opportunity
- Innovation in small firms
- Innovation in large firms
- Deconstructing large firms
- Growth of small firms and self-employment
- Global markets, fragmented segments and e-commerce
- Summary

Learning outcomes

By the end of this chapter you should:

- Understand the nature of innovation and why it is so difficult to define;
- Understand the critical role of the entrepreneur and intrapreneur in the process of innovation;
- Understand the importance of innovation for world economic growth;
- Understand how innovation can be stimulated in businesses of all sizes;
- Understand how large firms go about encouraging innovation by establishing structures that imitate many aspects of small firms;
- Understand how that is leading to the distinctions between large and small firms becoming increasingly blurred;
- Appreciate the opportunities, particularly offered by e-commerce, to develop global markets and narrower market niches.

Tools of entrepreneurship

In Chapter 1 entrepreneurs were defined by their use of innovation to exploit or create change and opportunity for the purpose of making profit. Change creates opportunity and entrepreneurs create value by exploiting or creating change, for example in technology, materials, prices or demographics. They create new demand or find ways of exploiting existing markets. Entrepreneurs are the key to identifying commercial opportunities and then exploiting them and this is why they are so valued in today's society. As Michael Porter (1990) put it: 'Invention and entrepreneurship are at the heart of national advantage.'

Are you an innovative thinker?

Innovation is the prime tool entrepreneurs use to create or exploit opportunity and is one of the two most important distinguishing features of their character. The Innovative Potential Indicator (IPI) was developed by Dr Fiona Patterson based upon research on employees in established companies. It is published by Oxford Psychologists Press. It claims to be the only psychometric test able to identify those people who have the potential to become innovative thinkers. Dr Patterson identifies ten types of people:

1 The *Change Agent* who thrives on change and is independent, who conjures up the strangest ways to solve problems and who does not stick to what they were told. This is the innovative thinker who embodies one of the most essential characteristics that differentiates entrepreneurs from owner-managers.
2 The *Consolidator*, whose rigidity and independence militates against innovative thinking but is a safety net because of their preference for the status quo.
3 The *Harmoniser*, who likes the challenge but does not disclose good ideas for fear of upsetting other people.
4 The *Firefighter*, who flits from one idea to another in an imaginative but unpredictable way.
5 The *Cooperator*, who likes change but 'goes with the flow'.
6 The *Catalyst*, who is good at thinking up ideas but soon loses interest.
7 The *Inhibited Innovator*, whose brainwaves could be valuable but lacks the confidence to push it forward.
8 The *Incremental Innovator*, who dreams up radical ideas but likes to implement them in a step-by-step way which can appear inflexible.
9 The *Spice-of-Life*, whose dominant characteristic is the need to be doing something, anything, new.
10 The *Middle-of-the-Road*, who is good at blending ideas but is ambivalent about them.

The IPI questionnaire asks for agreement/disagreement to 36 statements about how you approach change, how adaptable you are and how you stand up to others. Based upon your answers, it scores you on four main areas of behaviour which Patterson's research shows can be used to establish whether a person has innovative potential. Scores can be between 20 and 80 on each dimension. The dimensions are:

● Motivation to change (MTC).
● Willingness to behave in a challenging way (CB).
● Willingness to adapt and use tried and tested approaches (AD).
● Consistency of working style which indicates efficiency and orderliness (CWS).

Change Agents have high MTC and CB scores, and low AD and CWS scores. So for example, Trevor Baylis, the inventor of the clockwork radio, had a MTC score of 70, a CB score of 60, an AD score of 25 and a CWS score of 35 (*The Times*, 14.03.00)

The ability to spot opportunities and to innovate are the two most important distinguishing features of entrepreneurs. Innovation is the prime tool entrepreneurs use to create or exploit opportunity, and firms that grow do so because they innovate in some way. However, entrepreneurs are not the only people who try to practice innovation. For all firms, of any size, innovation has become something of a holy grail to be sought after and encouraged.

So how is innovation to be encouraged? Can it be pursued in a systematic way? Can entrepreneurs learn anything from this? Indeed, can large firms learn anything about the process of innovation by observing how entrepreneurs go about it? Do small firms innovate? What changes in the future will create opportunities for entrepreneurs to pursue? Before we address any of these issues we must try to define innovation.

Invention and innovation

Innovation is an illusive thing. It is usually associated with the development of a new or better product or process; an extreme example would be a new invention. However, examples abound of inventions that are not commercially successful. Thomas Edison, probably the most successful inventor of all time, was so incompetent as an innovator that his backers had to remove him from every new business he founded.

Innovation, therefore, is more than just invention and it is not, necessarily, the product of research. It can be many things, for example the substitution of a cheaper material in an existing product, or a better way of marketing an existing product or service, or even a better way of distributing or supporting an existing product or service. Small firms in particular are often innovative in their approach to marketing. Innovation then is about doing things differently.

Mintzberg (1983) defines innovation as 'the means to break away from established patterns', in other words doing things really differently. Therefore, simply introducing a new product or service that has customers willing to buy it, is not necessarily innovation. Innovations have to break the mould of how things are done. New cars are rarely truly innovative, despite what the marketing hype might say. However, the Mini was innovative because it changed the way cars were designed and changed the way people perceived vehicle size. To really innovate Minzberg says that 'one engages in divergent thinking aimed at innovation; the other is convergent thinking aimed at perfection'.

Like it or loath it, **McDonald's**, the ubiquitous hamburger chain, brought true innovation to the food industry. It developed a standardised, high quality hamburger sandwich, produced using entirely new cooking procedures, delivered with the speed of just-in-time preparation by meticulously trained people, in clean surroundings and at a bargain price. This was something entirely new for customers and it spawned a completely new market called 'the fast-food industry'.

But innovation is even more than this. What is needed to make the innovation potentially successful is for it to be linked to customer demand – existing or in the future. Even process innovation, which may involve no change to the product itself, to be successful, must be linked to customer demand through cost/price, quality lead times, and so on.

Video recorders were invented by an American firm called Ampex in 1954. They were reel-to-reel devices, about the size of a juke box, and were used by television networks to record and then transmit programmes in different time zones. However, the real innovators were the Japanese companies Sony (with their Betamax system) and, to a greater extent, JVC (with their VHS system) who realised that the big market for video recorders would be in the home. They succeeded in producing a small video recorder at an affordable price. Like all the best innovations it did not replace an existing product but created its own market. In the 1980s Japanese video-cassette recorders accounted for half of Japan's consumer electronics industry's annual sales of $30 billion and three-quarters of its combined profits.

To innovate effectively, therefore, requires insight – into customers and markets, into what is possible and what is not, and into how to make things happen. It is also helped by good luck. What is more, innovation may be a necessary condition for establishing a growth business, but it is not a sufficient condition. To exploit an innovation successfully requires a strength of personal character, managerial ability and often money, which bring us back to the central role of the entrepreneur.

Bolton and Thompson (2000) associate invention closely with creativity but link it with entrepreneurship if the invention is to become a commercial opportunity to be exploited. 'Creativity is the starting point whether it is associated with invention or opportunity spotting. This creativity is turned to practical reality (a product, for example) through innovation. Entrepreneurship then sets that innovation in the context of an enterprise (the actual business), which is something of recognised value.' To them creativity and innovation need the entrepreneurial context to become a business reality – supported by a certain mix of talents and temperaments and based on appropriate knowledge and skills.

In 1991 **Trevor Baylis** was watching a TV programme about the Aids epidemic in Africa. It got him thinking about how information about Aids prevention might be broadcast to people in a country where there was no electricity and batteries were prohibitively expensive. He quickly came up with a design for a clockwork radio. Despite being featured on radio and TV he could not convince people that it was a commercially viable product.

It was only when he teamed up with an entrepreneur, **Christopher Staines**, and a company called **Liberty Life** that the radio was produced and marketed. The entrepreneur was able to exploit the innovation in a way the inventor was not able to do. Production began in 1994 and 120 000 radios are now made each month. Without the entrepreneur the invention would not have reached the marketplace.

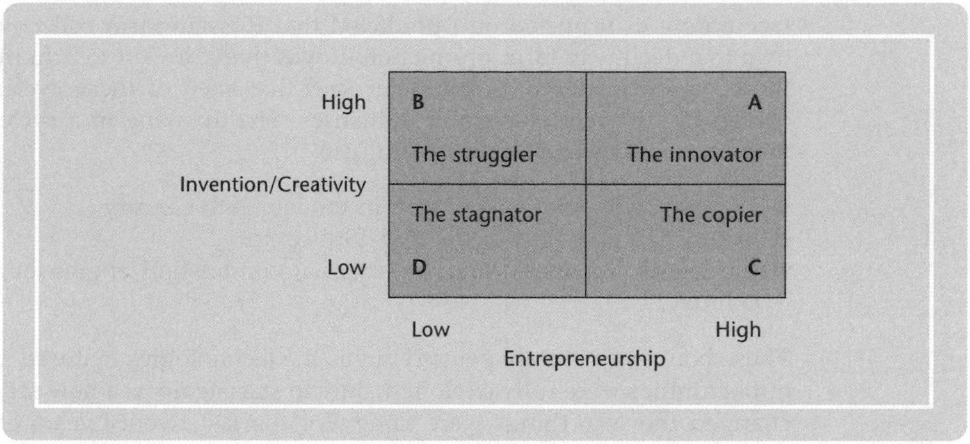

	Low	High
High (Invention/Creativity)	B The struggler	A The innovator
Low	The stagnator D	The copier C

Invention/Creativity — High / Low
Entrepreneurship — Low / High

Figure 3.1 Invention and entrepreneurship

The matrix in Figure 3.1 shows the relationship between invention and the entrepreneur. Only in quadrant A is there a winning combination of invention and entrepreneurship. In quadrant B there is a firm struggling with too many wasted ideas. It lacks an entrepreneur with the ability both to see the commercial application of the idea and to exploit it. In quadrant C there is a firm that lacks invention and creativity but can at least copy and perhaps improve on inventions coming from other firms if they have a commercial application. Firms in quadrant D lack both invention and entrepreneurship, are certain never to grow and indeed their very survival may be questioned.

Lifestyle businesses are rarely innovative. They do not invent new ways of doing things and they are not run by entrepreneurs. The owner-manager of a corner shop may be making an adequate income to support himself, he may have risked all his savings to set up the shop, but he is not doing anything different. Most small firms therefore do not innovate. If an owner-manager wants to establish a growth business, however, they will probably have to innovate in some way and in doing that they are being entrepreneurial.

The father of innovation

It is the work of Joseph Schumpeter (1996), an Austrian economist, that most strongly links entrepreneurship to innovation. He was the first economist to challenge classical economics and the way it sought to optimise existing resources within a stable environment and treating disruptions as a 'God sent' external force. For Schumpeter a normal healthy economy was one that was continually being 'disrupted' by technological innovation producing the 50 year cycles of economic activity noticed earlier by the Russian economist, Nikolai Kondratieff.

Using data on prices, wages and interest rates in France, Britain and the USA, Kondratieff first noticed these 'long waves' of economic activity in 1925. Unfortunately he was executed by Stalin some ten years later because he (accurately as it turned out) predicted that Russian farm collectivisation would lead to a decline in farm production. It was therefore left to Schumpeter to study these waves in depth. Schumpeter said that each of these cycles was unique, driven by different clusters of industries. The upswing in a cycle started when new innovations came into general use:

- Water power, textiles and iron in the late 18th century.
- Steam, rail and steel in the mid-19th century.
- Electricity, chemicals and the internal combustion engine in the early 20th century.

These booms eventually petered out as the technologies matured and the market opportunities were fully exploited, only to start again as a new set of innovations changed the way things were done. For the last twenty years of the cycle the growth industries of the last technological wave might be doing exceptionally well. However they are, in fact, just repaying capital that is no longer needed for investment. This situation never lasts longer than twenty years and returns to investors then start to decline with the dwindling number of opportunities. Often this is precipitated by some form of crisis. After the twenty years of stagnation new technologies will emerge and the cycle will start again.

However, the other factor at work is that innovation – particularly technological innovation – also seems to generate growth that cannot be accounted for by changes in labour and capital. Although the return on investment may decline as more capital is introduced to an economy, any deceleration in growth is more than offset by the leverage effects of innovation. Because of this the rich Western countries have seen their return on investment increasing, whilst the poorer countries have not caught up.

But innovation does not happen as a random event. Central to the process is the entrepreneur. It is they who introduce and then exploit the new innovations. For Schumpeter, 'the entrepreneur initiates change and generates new opportunities. Until imitators force prices and costs into conformity, the innovator is able to reap profits and disturb equilibrium' (O'Farrell, 1986). By way of contrast, early classical economists such as Adam Smith saw the entrepreneurs as having a rather minor role in overall economic activity. He thought that they provided real capital, but did not play a leading or direct part in how the pattern of supply and demand was determined.

Schumpeter described five types of innovation:

1   The introduction of a new or improved good.
2   The introduction of a new process.
3   The opening up of a new market.
4   The identification of new sources of supply of raw materials.
5   The creation of new types of industrial organisation.

In fact, there are considerable problems interpreting these criteria for innovation. For example, what constitutes a new product? When a sofa manufacturer produces a 'new' sofa, is that a new product? Economists would probably argue that it was not (the cross elasticity of demand is unlikely to be zero), but the entrepreneur might disagree. What if the sofa manufacturer starts manufacturing chairs? At what point does the firm start producing genuinely new products?

Sources of opportunity

If Schumpeter was the father of innovation, Peter Drucker (1985) probably helped to deliver the baby. He believes that

> innovation is the specific tool of entrepreneurs, the means by which they exploit change as an opportunity for a different business or a different service. It is capable of being presented as a discipline, capable of being learned and capable of being practised. Entrepreneurs need to search purposefully for the sources of innovation, the changes and their symptoms that indicate opportunities for successful innovation. And they need to know and to apply the principles of successful innovation.

Drucker, therefore, believes innovation can be practised systematically. Firms that practice innovation systematically search for change then carefully evaluate its potential for an economic or social return. Change provides the opportunity for innovation to make an economic return.

He lists seven sources of opportunity for firms in search of innovation. Four can be found within the firm itself or from the industry of which it is part and are therefore reasonably easy to spot. They are 'basic symptoms – highly reliable indicators of changes that have already happened or can be made to happen with little effort'. They are:

- The *unexpected* – be it the unexpected success or failure or the unexpected event.
- The *incongruity* – between what actually happens and what was supposed to happen.
- The *inadequacy in underlying processes* – that are taken for granted but can be improved or changed.
- The *changes in industry or market structure* – that take everyone by surprise.

These sources of opportunity need to be dissected and the underlying causes of change understood. The causes give clues about how innovation can be used to increase the economic return.

The other three factors come from the outside world:

- *Demographic changes* – population changes caused by changes in birth rates, wars, medical improvements and so on.
- *Changes in perception, mood and meaning* – that can be brought about by the ups and downs of the economy, culture, fashion and so on.
- *New knowledge* – both scientific and non-scientific.

Drucker lists the seven factors in what he sees as an increasing order of difficulty, uncertainty and unreliability, which means that he believes that new knowledge, including scientific knowledge, for all its visibility and glamour, is in fact the most difficult, least reliable and least predictable source of innovation. Paradoxically, this is the area that government, academics and even entrepreneurs pay most attention to. Drucker argues that innovations arising from the systematic analysis of mundane and unglamorous unexpected successes or failures are far more likely to yield results. They have the shortest lead times

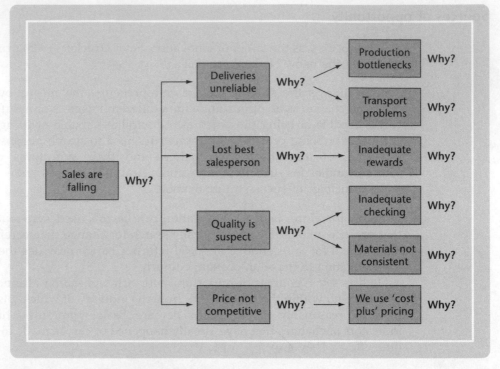

Figure 3.2 Why? Why? diagram

between start and yielding measurable results and carry fairly low risk and uncertainty.

One technique for getting to the root cause of these 'unexpected events', 'incongruities' or 'inadequacies' is the 'Why? Why?' diagram. This is used to explore options related to the event. Figure 3.2 shows a diagram exploring the reason for a fall in sales (Vyakarnham and Leppard, 1999). From it you can see there are several possible reasons, although the trails have not been taken to completion. The root cause will lie at the end of the 'why?' trail.

Drucker advocates a five stage approach to purposeful, systematic innovation:

1   Start with the analysis of opportunities, inside the firm and its industry and in the external environment. Do not innovate for the future, innovate for now. Timing is everything. The right idea at the wrong time is worth nothing.
2   Innovation is both conceptual and perceptual. Therefore look at the financial implications but also talk to people, particularly customers, and analyse how to meet the opportunity.
3   To be effective, an innovation must be simple and has to be 'focused'. Don't try to be too clever. Don't try to do too many things at once.
4   To be effective, start small. Don't be grandiose. Take an incremental approach.
5   Aim at leadership and dominate the competition in the particular area of innovation as soon as possible.

Oxford Asymmetry International is a British example of a world-class firm that specialises in the systematic development of invention and high technology. When British Petroleum withdrew its financial support for a research project analysing the small-scale manufacturing of certain chemicals, Stephen Davies, an Oxford University professor, secured £500 000 backing from two business angels to continue his work and, in 1992, set up the company with only 4 employees.

The company provides a one-stop shop in chemical discovery and promotes itself as a partner to drug manufacturers who are looking to innovate and are willing to out-source this activity. Successful innovation is the result of an effective partnership, each partner bringing different qualities to the relationship.

Over lunch in 1995 at Oxford University's Innovation Centre, Stephen happened to meet a senior manager from Pfizer and this led to the formation of a joint venture company called Oxford Diversity Pfizer, the company that developed Viagra.

Oxford Asymmetry International now works with companies like Astra, Bayer, Eastman Chemicals, Leukosite, Pfizer, Vanguard Medica and Vertex. It was floated in 1998 with a staff of 200 (40% with PhDs) and a market capitalisation of £120 million, a figure that doubled within a year.

Firms with a good track record for innovation, therefore, practice it systematically. It does not happen by chance. They look for small changes that can be made to the way they do things. Indeed so systematic can the search for innovation be that some firms have been set up specifically to undertake it. However, these and other firms seeking innovation must also foster an entrepreneurial approach in the individuals seeking it. This requires them to be internally driven, motivated by a need for personal achievement, money, power, fame or simple curiosity. Entrepreneurs clearly matter, but nobody knows how much.

Whilst innovation may be encouraged through a systematic approach, entrepreneurs realise that it is not always arrived at in an orderly and linear fashion. Scientific discoveries do indeed sometimes lead to commercial opportunities which entrepreneurs can exploit. However, the linkages are not always as you would expect. William Shockley had to invent a theory of electrons and 'holes' in semiconductors to explain why the transistors that he and his colleagues at Bell Laboratories in the USA had invented in 1948 actually worked. What is more, he and his colleagues took the transistor idea to Palo Alto in California and started a company that eventually became Intel. Similarly, whilst it was British universities that 'invented' the internet to facilitate communication between a European group of university observatories, it was an American academic and American companies that exploited it.

How innovations, particularly technical innovations, see the light of commercial day is complex. It involves a labyrinthine series of interrelationships and feedback networks, often with an entrepreneur at the centre, almost like a spider weaving a web. The lesson from this is that simply pouring money into R&D does not necessarily guarantee innovation that will yield a commercial return.

Innovation in small firms

Few small firms introduce really new products into their product range. Even fewer introduce really new products into the economy as a whole. This role is more likely to be undertaken by larger firms because of the resources they command. However, small firms can, and often do, introduce products or services that are clearly differentiated from those of the 'competition', to the point where one might question whether there is any direct competition. Indeed, this ability to differentiate clearly is a major element in their success. Is this innovation? Perhaps it is, but one would have to stretch Schumpeter's first or even his third criteria (opening up of a new market) to accommodate it.

This is not to decry the importance of small firms in the process of product innovation. Studies suggest that, although they are much less likely to conduct R&D than large firms, they conduct them more efficiently and introduce new products to the marketplace faster than big companies. Studies measuring only R&D expenditure must be treated with caution because of the inability of small firms often to separate out this expenditure. However, a US study (Acs and Aaudretsch, 1990) found that small firms produce 2.4 times as many innovations per employee as large firms. Another UK study (Pavitt, Robinson and Townsend, 1987) concluded that small firms are more likely to introduce fundamentally new innovations than large firms.

What seems clear is that innovative behaviour is not entirely related to firm size. It also relates to business activity, the industry, the nature of the innovation, and the type of company. Large firms outperform small firms where resources are important – because of capital intensity, because of scale of spending on R&D, advertising and so on, or simply because of barriers to entry. Rothwell (1989) shows that, where no such prerequisite exists, the share of small firm in innovation is substantial. He concludes that

> innovative advantage is unequivocally associated with neither large nor small firms. The innovatory advantages of large firms are in the main associated with their relatively greater financial and technological resources, that is, their material advantages; small firm advantages are those of entrepreneurial dynamism, internal flexibility and responsiveness to changing circumstances, that is, their behavioural advantages.

Small firms are most likely to provide something marginally different to the competition, in terms of the product or service, and thus find a market niche. They are also far more likely to innovate in terms of marketing and customer service (often low cost options). They often find new routes to market first, for example 'direct' selling, via the phone with the growth of call centres located in low cost areas or via the internet offering similar advantages through the 'virtual' organisation. Small firms are often innovative in their approach to key account management and customer relationships. They find ways of networking with customers and suppliers so as to cut costs and lead times. Which of Schumpeter's categories do these fall into?

If Schumpeter's description of innovation is inadequate, it is because of the myriad forms it can take. What is more, the central role of the entrepreneur needs to be explicitly acknowledged in any definition. Therefore, this illusive thing called innovation might be defined as:

A 'mould-breaking' development in new products or services or how they are produced – the materials used, the process employed or how the firm is organised to deliver them – or how or to whom they are marketed, that can be linked to a commercial opportunity and successfully exploited.

Innovation is important if a small firm wants to grow and be successful. In a study of fast-growing small firms matched against slow-growing firms, Storey *et al.* (1989) concluded that the owner-managers of the fast-growing firms were much more likely to emphasise competitive advantage as being in areas such as innovation and product or service quality. By way of contrast, the owner-managers of the slow-growing firms emphasised price. Innovation, therefore, is not only the vehicle for their faster growth but also a means of fending off competition and being able to charge a higher price.

In fact, Schumpeter said nothing about whether innovation could be best carried out by small or large firms. To him this was irrelevant. An entrepreneur could just as easily work in a large as in a small firm. However, small firms do have the inherent flexibility needed to spot market opportunities and capitalise on them quickly if, that is, they are run by an entrepreneur. Small firms typically lack the bureaucratic, hierarchical structures of large firms. As Cannon (1985) points out:

> The ability of the entrepreneurial mould-maker to break free from bureaucratic rigidities, fan the flames of innovation and create new situations has been the basis of the growth of many of today's great corporations. Ford, Dupont, Kellogg, Singer, Krupp, Eastman, Courtauld, Daimler, Biro, Siemens and Daussault all built giant enterprises which are virtually synonymous with their industries.

However, large firms can also have advantages; capital, high degree of market power with existing products, comprehensive distribution and service facilities, access to technical expertise, access to professional management, greater ability to protect the innovation. As has been pointed out (Vossen, 1998), the advantages of large firms are generally the disadvantages of small firms and visa versa, and therefore collaboration between the two sizes can create powerful synergistic relationships.

By the time Schumpeter died in 1950 the next cycle of boom was starting based upon oil, electronics, aviation and mass production. Another started in the 1980s based upon digital networks, software and new media. This is currently enjoying added growth through the development of e-commerce. Each cycle seems to be shorter and the current one may only last until 2010. One reason for the shortening cycle may be the more systematic approach entrepreneurs now have towards exploiting innovation.

Innovation in large firms

Many truly successful innovations, particularly product innovations but certainly the ones involving large amounts of capital, originate from large not small companies. There are few Dysons in this world who successfully struggle to bring a genuinely new product to the market themselves, against all the odds.

(James Dyson invented a completely new 'cyclone' vacuum cleaner and then successfully claimed against Hoover for infringing his patents with their 'vortex' cleaner.) There are just too many problems to sort out – not least of which is finding the finance. Moreover it is easier for a middle-sized or large company to sort out these problems because it has more resources, more experience – more of everything to throw at a problem. But how does the process of intrapreneurship – entrepreneurship within a big company – actually work? How do successful big companies encourage innovation?

Incremental improvements to products and services are one thing. They can be addressed systematically. But these changes, important as they are, do not conquer new markets. Often what is needed is the mould-breaking innovation and big companies can put bureaucratic barriers in the way to this. When the personal computer was first introduced it was considered simply a toy and the market leader in computers, IBM, ignored it for many years. However, the personal computer turned the whole computer industry on its head and nearly caused the demise of IBM. Not only did IBM not lead in this major innovation, it also tried to ignore it – and paid the price.

Successful big firms do find ways of creating a culture that encourages innovation and intrapreneurship. More than a century ago National Cash Register (NCR) devised a scheme for paying employees for new ideas. Many of today's companies find different ways of doing it. There certainly is no one model.

> **3M** generates a quarter of its annual revenues from products less than five years old. It tries to make innovation part of the corporate culture by encouraging staff to spend 15% of their time working on pet ideas that they hope one day will become new products for the company. They also get money to buy equipment and hire extra help.
>
> To get an idea accepted, it must first get the personal backing of a member of the main board. Then an interdisciplinary team of engineers, marketing specialists and accountants are set up to take the idea further.
>
> Failure is not punished, but success is well-rewarded.

However, central to any model is a product champion – in a large company we call them an intrapreneur. Art Fry invented the now ubiquitous 'Post-It' notes for 3M. He was looking for a way to mark places in a hymn book – a paper marker that would stick, but not permanently. At the same time the company had developed a new glue which, unfortunately as it seemed at the time, would not dry. Art spotted a use for the product but what was different was the way he went about persuading his bosses to back the project. He produced the product, complete with its distinctive yellow colour, and distributed it to secretaries who started using it throughout 3M. Art then cut their supplies, insisting that there would be no more unless the company officially backed the product. The rest is history.

Drucker maintains that intrapreneurial management does not happen by chance in big companies. It has to be made to happen. Firstly, it requires a culture

When **Bayer** came up with an innovative new technology capable of providing high quality, short-run colour printing quickly and at low cost, the company was not planning to expand into that area. However, it realised that there was a gap in the market between office printers or photocopiers and conventional printing.

It therefore spun-off a new company, **Xeikon**, which it set up in Belgium in 1988, providing it with full support including seed capital, advice and facilities. By 1998 the company had a turnover of over £45 million and employed 160 people.

that is receptive to innovation and willing to see change as an opportunity rather than a threat. The company must do the hard work for the intrapreneur. Secondly, systematic measurement of intrapreneurial and innovatory performance is necessary. The company must also build in learning from its successes and failures so as to improve its performance. Thirdly, intrapreneurial management needs to be structured, staffed and remunerated appropriately. Big firms can learn valuable lessons in this from the more successful small firms.

Many companies believe that the initial stages of innovation require such a different culture that completely separate premises from the corporate offices need to be found. This leads them to set up separate 'research' establishments. But research is not the same as development and even then the innovation has to be exploited commercially. Having separate locations for many of these activities allows them to maintain different cultures as well as the different structures, staffing and remuneration that Drucker refers to.

Taking this idea further, big companies often 'spin-off' new ventures, creating completely new, small companies that are lean and flexible and focused on getting their product to market. However, often the big company has to put in place mechanisms to make this happen, mini organisations within the big company with the task of spotting innovative opportunities and facilitating their

Xerox may have problems with its core copier business but it has managed to push through many innovations. Many were pioneered by its Palo Alto Research Centre (PARC). But initially few were taken up by Xerox, who left them to be exploited, often very successfully, by others. The one (major) exception was, of course, the laser printer. It was only when it set up a separate company, **Xerox Technology Ventures**, located almost as far away in the USA as you can get from both Xerox head office and PARC, that things began to change. This company was to exploit technologies that did not 'fit' into Xerox's product portfolio.

If a product was turned down by head office it could be offered to the new venture group. Once a working model was perfected, the founders, who would be rewarded with a 20% stake in the new business, were moved out of the plush PARC laboratories and into low cost commercial premises and professional management put in to bring the product to market.

After ten years the company now has more than a dozen young firms established.

development. Ideally these are run by an intrapreneur, wheeling and dealing to make the most of the opportunities the market presents and the innovations the big company cannot use in its mainstream activities.

In the UK, Dixons, the high street electrical goods retailer, spun-off Freeserve, the internet access provider, because this innovative opportunity was completely different from its mainstream activity. However, it used its retail base to give away disks so that Freeserve could gain market share and 'first-mover' advantage in the UK. What is also interesting in this example is that the distinctions between what is a large and what is a small firm are becoming very blurred. Even after its £1.5 billion stockmarket float in 1999, Dixons kept some 82 per cent of the shares. Freeserve then had a turnover of some £2.5 million. The floatation made Freeserve Europe's 'largest' publicly traded net company. But how do you measure size? At the time of the stock market float Freeserve was only about a year old and had only 16 employees. What is more, it had never made a profit. How can a firm with only 16 employees that has never made a profit be worth £1.5 billion? The answer is that the market was valuing potential, which is why so many of today's entrepreneurs – in big as well as small companies – are interested in e-commerce.

Large firms are innovative and they can develop their own intrapreneurs. The distinctions between large and small firms are, in many ways, beginning to blur. So where is all this leading?

Deconstructing large firms

Big companies are not only seeking to replicate the flexibility of the small firm but also encourage more managers to be entrepreneurial and innovative by changing their structure, in fact 'deconstructing', that is, breaking themselves down into smaller units. Peter Chemin, CEO of the Fox TV empire believes that 'in the management of creativity, size is your enemy' (*Economist*, December 1999). He has tried to break down the studio into small units, even at the risk of incurring higher costs.

Amar Bhidé (2000) believes that, rather than trying to reinvent themselves, large firms should concentrate on projects with high costs and low uncertainty, leaving those with low costs and high uncertainty to small entrepreneurial firms. As ideas mature and risks and rewards become more quantifiable, large firms can adopt them. Even in capital intensive businesses such as pharmaceuticals, entrepreneurs can conduct early stage research, selling out to large firms when they reach expensive, clinical trial stage. About a third of drug firms' revenue now comes from licensed-in technology. Many large companies, like General Electric and Cisco, have adopted the policy of buying up small firms who have developed new technology.

Asea Brown Boveri (ABB) is the largest power engineering company in the world. But in fact it is made up of some 1200 separate companies each employing, on average, only 200 people. Even their Zurich headquarters has less than 200 employees.

John Naisbitt (1994) also feels the future lies very much with small firms, whether owner-managed or 'deconstructed' from large firms. His book is based upon the apparent paradox that 'the bigger the world economy, the more powerful its smallest players'. He sees much of the growing importance of smaller firms, and with them entrepreneurs, coming from larger firms which will have to restyle themselves into 'networks of entrepreneurs' if they are to survive. In his view

> downsizing, re-engineering, the creative networking organisation, or the latest virtual corporation, whatever it is called, it comes down to the same thing. Corporations have to dismantle bureaucracies to survive. Economies of scale are giving way to economies of scope, finding the right size for synergy, market flexibility, and above all, speed.

He observes that

> to survive, big companies today – ABB, AT&T, GE, Grand Metropolitan, Coca-Cola, Benetton, Johnson & Johnson, British Petroleum, Honda, Alcoa, Xerox – are all deconstructing themselves and creating new structures, many as networks of autonomous units. Deconstruction is now a fashion, because it is the best way to search for survival.

If imitation is the sincerest form of flattery then the small firm has at last been acknowledged as an outstanding success. And the facts back this up. Already over 50 per cent of US exports are created by micro firms with less than 20 employees. The same is true in Germany. Under 7 per cent of US exports now come from firms with over 500 employees.

The other side to this trend towards downsizing and deconstructing large firms is that they will increasingly concentrate on their core activities, where they have competitive advantage, and the subcontracting of non-core activities will increase. This enables them to reduce their fixed cost base and thus the risk they face, flatten their organisation structure thereby ensuring a quicker response time to changes in the marketplace. Indeed the very nature of the company of the future is likely to change. The successful company of the future will be a 'knowledge' company whose core activity will focus on the capture and retention of its most valuable asset; knowledge, in all its different forms. This will also accelerate the trend to change business structures, radically reshaping the relationship between employer and employee.

The trend towards flattening organisational structures started in the USA in the 1980s and then came to Europe. In 1994, BT cut 5000 middle and senior managers in one year, reducing its layers of management from 12 to six. W. H. Smith cut 600 store managers in the same year reducing its layers of management from four to two. In the following year Shell got rid of 1200 managers from its head office. In the late 1980s and early 1990s the entire banking industry has seen over one-third of its managers leave the industry. This is not just about deconstructing, it is about changing the attitudes of the remaining managers about the security of their jobs as well as putting many middle-aged managers in the position of having few alternatives other than self-employment (although the early retirement payment helped soften the blow, as well as set up their own businesses). No wonder self-employment blossomed over the same period.

Growth of small firms and self-employment

The trend to out-source all but core activities should encourage the growth of more small, specialist niche subcontractors, particularly in the manufacturing sector. 'Partnership sourcing' is likely to increase, whereby a close relationship is built between the bigger company and the smaller subcontractor, with one helping the other to grow. The development of e-commerce for supply chain management will just accelerate this trend. This is despite the recent experience in Japan and with Marks & Spencer in the UK, when small subcontractors faced severe problems as their big partners dropped them to ensure their own survival. Alongside 'partnership sourcing' goes the danger of over-dependence on a small number of customers.

Charles Handy (1994) predicts that there will be a growth of 'shamrock organisations' amongst larger firms, the three leaves being core staff, temporary staff to ease them over peaks and troughs in work and small organisations supplying specialist services, deeply embedded in and dependant upon the larger firm. These sort of opportunities for small firms in the marketplace – 'pull' factors – will make setting up a business attractive. What is more, social changes such as unemployment and early retirement – 'push' factors – are likely to accelerate the trend.

An increasing number of people are likely to have more than one job, often dipping into self-employment as a part-time activity or between periods of employment. Almost 1 million people in the UK already have more than one job. People already realise that there is no-longer any such thing as a 'job for life', therefore keeping all the options open by having a part-time, self-employed occupation to fall back on is likely to appear increasingly attractive.

Home-working, both in employment and as part of self-employment, is also likely to increase. Already it is estimated that 4 per cent of workers in the UK and 10 per cent in the USA work this way. And if that occupation develops into a

---

In 1998 **Roger Penfound** was faced with a difficult situation. Approaching 50 years old and having worked for the BBC all his working life as a director of TV and video programmes, mainly at the Open University, he faced redundancy as the organisation slimmed down and cut out 'peripheral' activities. He had few alternatives as the entire industry was moving towards a subcontract basis.

Using his redundancy package, he set up **Performance Media**, a company producing training and promotional videos. He used his contacts in, and knowledge of, the industry to provide the video crews and editing facilities. His contacts from the BBC and OU were his initial client base. He did a good job, and now he could do it for a fraction of the price. Initially he worked from home, with a professional telephone message-taking service. Within six months he had taken a small office, using part-time administrative support. One year hence and he was earning what he had earned at the BBC and expanding his client base beyond his old contacts.

lucrative market opportunity, self-employment may offer more independent security than employment. As Charles Handy put it:

> It is the end of the age of the mass organisation, the age when we could all confidently expect to be employed for most of our lives if we so wanted, and over 90% so wanted . . .What we do, what we belong to, why we do it, where we do it – these may all be different and could be better . . . Change comes from small initiatives which work, initiatives which, imitated, become fashion. We cannot wait for great visions from great people, for they are in short supply at the end of history. It is up to us to light our own small fires in the darkness.

This means that individuals will have to take more responsibility for themselves and their future, investing in their education, training and development. They must become the knowledge workers that the companies of tomorrow will need. They will have to invest in themselves as distinct brands and seek to secure their future in what ever way is best. For many that will mean self-employment rather than employment. For some it will mean both. Knowledge workers, working from home or within larger organisations, are likely to become the self-employed craftsmen of the twenty-first century.

All in all, the twenty-first century should see a enormous growth in self-employment and the number of small firms. Many of these new small firms will come from the large firms of today. Some will be the result of deconstruction. Many will be set up by ex-managers from large firms, perhaps because they see market opportunities, perhaps because they are made redundant or face job insecurity. They will face a different and uncertain future.

Global markets, fragmented segments and e-commerce

The pace of change in the commercial world continues to accelerate. Product life cycles have shortened dramatically because of fashion and technology. The cycles of economic activity are shortening as new waves of innovation present opportunities for entrepreneurs. Working methods and patterns have also altered dramatically, some might say not always for the better. The service sector has now become the major driver of economic activity.

Tom Peters (1987) refers to it as 'a world turned upside down' and 'in chaos'. Charles Handy (1989) describes it as 'the age of unreason', where there is no 'logic' or 'order' underlying seemingly random occurrences in the business world. Others (Cannon, 1991) think they 'bear all the hallmarks of a major industrial revolution'. So can the entrepreneur cope? What are likely to be the new waves of innovation? How will markets be organised?

Global markets have already arrived for many companies such as McDonald's, Coca-Cola and Microsoft. This reflects common product values and globalisation of life-styles. At the same time markets have become more dispersed as barriers to entry of national or local markets have been dismantled, particularly across Europe. Alongside this there is an accelerating trend towards fragmented market segments, with niches becoming smaller in terms of product or service specification, but growing in terms of the ability to service this market segment globally.

QXL is an online auction house that is Britain's equivalent of America's eBay, a company on which the idea is based. Founded by **Tim Jackson**, a freelance journalist who has written books on Richard Branson and Intel, in the space of two short years he founded the company, raised two lots of venture capital, initially £500 000 and then £7 million and then floated the company at a market capitalisation of some £750 million.

QXL has auction sites in Britain, France, Germany and Italy and has seen sales increasing exponentially at 20% a month. It organises auctions between individuals wanting to buy and sell second-hand goods as well as involving companies wanting to sell products to the highest bidder.

E-commerce is accelerating these trends. It is the single most important innovation affecting business in the early twenty-first century and is creating enormous opportunities for small firms. It will be as significant as the railways in the nineteenth century. E-commerce entrepreneurs will exploit the immediate market opportunities to create the e-commerce structures. Like the railways before them, these businesses are highly valued, indeed probably overvalued. But this just reflects their fundamental importance. Their lasting legacy, however, will be the new routes to market that small firms can now take. Almost any market on the planet is now accessible by the smallest of firms, given the will. Indeed e-commerce creates the opportunity to be physically small but still have a global presence. With market barriers coming down, competition is therefore likely to intensify.

Some firms will compete on price but others will use e-commerce to differentiate themselves more effectively and target niche markets for their products or services on a global basis. The number of market niches therefore seems to be growing incrementally. The trend towards narrower market niches creates obvious opportunities for small firms that recognise these trends and are able to match identified market needs. What is more, they can create a global brand for their product or service in their narrow market niche. But they will only do so if they have an entrepreneur at the helm.

As smaller companies specialise to an ever greater degree than before they will also form closer relationships with the customers they serve. E-commerce will allow them better to understand their customer needs. If they service large companies they will increasingly be linked to them and their supply chain through the internet. Indeed the immediate benefit of e-commerce is for business-to-business trading. Many people feel that retail e-business will really only take-off when digital television is more commonplace.

Another of the effects of e-commerce is to give business access to customers directly, without going through the middleman. This is called 'disintermediation'. It can already be seen in many markets, for example in finance, where you can find firms looking for venture capital and individuals offering it.

The web is an anarchic system that is likely to destabilise many traditional markets and entrepreneurs will make the most of the opportunities this generates. What is more, the new routes to market created by the web will mean that in the future small firms will be better able to compete against large firms.

Sandiford Computer Services Ltd is a small software company set up in 1988. It employs some 15 people. As a byproduct of its main activity of developing bespoke process control software, it developed a unique software product that enables engineers to develop plant schematics on personal computers and then transfer the display files specifically to a Honeywell TDC3000 distributed control system.

The Honeywell system is very expensive and is used to control process plant, such as those used by power stations, that need to be kept running night and day. By removing the need for plant schematic development to take place while a plant is running, Sandiford's system offers considerable savings to the user as well as increased plant utility and safety.

Despite its size, the company now sells this software product to dozens of countries, including the USA and Japan. It sells this unique product exclusively to users of the Honeywell system, a clearly defined and easily identifiable market segment, that Honeywell actually help them market to by identifying users. Sandiford have succeeded in finding a niche in a global market.

Networks, cooperations, partnerships, alliances and joint ventures of all sorts will all increase as firms of all sizes seek out ways of achieving these closer relationships with their customers and suppliers on a global basis. For example, smaller UK accountants are increasingly forming alliances with other firms not only in the UK but also on mainland Europe. These alliances offer clients specialisations that the original firm might not have as well as geographical coverage. They are an attempt to offer a better service and gain competitive advantage in an industry that is finding it increasingly difficult to differentiate between one firm and another.

With large multinationals concentrating on their core activities to deliver high quality goods or services to ever narrower product markets, and the growth of specialist niche players and the increase in self-employed knowledge workers, medium-sized companies are likely to be squeezed. They will increasingly be either swallowed up by very large global companies, or disintegrate into smaller units. They face the danger of being saddled with the bureaucracy and lack of responsiveness of large companies, but without the size to benefit from economies of scale. Indeed, even the large companies will increasingly have to be aware of competition from the niche companies who are likely to keep nibbling away at their markets. The very large companies, however, will have the pick of the successful niche players as they grow. Those who become successful are likely to be bought out even before they make it to medium-sized status.

Summary

Innovation is difficult to define. It is about introducing new products, services or processes, opening up new markets, identifying new sources of supply of raw materials or creating new types of industrial organisation. But it is more than that. It is about breaking the mould – doing things differently. That might involve invention or developing an innovative processes, as with **McDonald's**. But it must be linked to customer demand. An inventor, like **Trevor Baylis**, cannot necessarily create innovation, and such persons need the help of an entrepreneur.

Innovation has been a prime source of economic growth across the world. It is therefore encouraged by government and is something firms of all sizes seek to facilitate. Small firms produce more than their fair share of innovations and seem to do it more efficiently than large firms. However, they tend to do this in sectors where resources, in particular capital, are less important. Using new knowledge, including scientific knowledge, is the most difficult form of innovation. Innovation stemming from the systematic analysis of unexpected successes or failures, or the incongruities between what actually happens and what was supposed to happen are far more likely to yield commercially viable innovations.

Innovation is the prime tool of entrepreneurs. Entrepreneurs link innovation to the market place. Without the entrepreneur the innovation may not make it to the market place. However, how it gets there is not straightforward. It involves a labyrinthine series of interrelationships and feedback networks with the entrepreneur at the centre. Transistors were not exploited by the company that invented them, **Bell Labs**. However, as we saw with **Oxford Asymmetry International**, these networks can be set up and exploited systematically.

Small firms need to innovate to grow. They can be particularly innovative in the area of marketing. Many small firms manage to differentiate themselves very effectively from competitors and this can also be seen as a form of innovation. However, most small firms are not at the forefront of true innovation, particularly technical innovation, that results in new products being introduced. Most true innovations that have an effect on the whole economy come from large firms. Whilst they can create cultures and structures that encourage innovation they still need the essential ingredient – an entrepreneur or intrapreneur – to make it happen, like Art Fry at **3M**.

Large companies often spin-off new companies to allow them to focus on getting a new product to the market place, as **Bayer** did with its print technology company, **Xeikon**. However, they often need internal structures to make this happen. Thus, **Xerox** has **Xerox Technology Ventures** to see that innovations are indeed exploited.

All this means that the distinctions between large and small firms are beginning to blur. This is not only with respect to definition, as we saw with **Freeserve**, but also with regard to actual structure. **ABB** is the largest engineering firm in the world but it is made up of 1200 small firms. More and more large firms are starting to downsize and deconstruct as a commercial response to markets that are seeing acceleration in the pace of change. The other side to this, as we saw with **Performance Media**, is managers being made redundant by their companies and then setting up their own small firms.

This trend is also offering opportunities to small firms. Increasingly they are able to sell to a global market, as we saw with **Sandiford Computer Services**. Thus small firms can focus on increasingly narrow market niches, satisfying very precise customer needs but selling to more customers than they ever dreamt of. Central to this is the growth of e-commerce, which presents the major opportunity of the century. Similar in importance to the railways of a century ago, we are already seeing new, small firms such as **QXL** going to the stockmarket and yielding enormous returns to entrepreneurial founders. However, the real importance of the web is the unhindered access to markets it offers small firms. Competition will intensify and small firms are likely to be the beneficiaries.

As change accelerates, the role of the entrepreneur, and the intrapreneur, will become even more important. They are the person linking change with opportunity and with innovation. Without them our society will not progress and prosper. Indeed it may not be able to cope with the ever increasing pace of change. At the start of the twenty-first century we are likely to see more small firms, not less, as large firms deconstruct themselves and the opportunities of a global market place become real for firms of all size because of technology and, in particular, e-commerce.

● Essays and discussion topics

1 What do you think constitutes innovation? Give examples.
2 What is the relationship between innovation and change?
3 What are the major political, economic, social and technological changes that you expect to see over the next 10 years? What are their likely consequences and how might they be exploited commercially?
4 Over the next 10 years, what are the main commercial opportunities that small, as opposed to large, firms might be best advised to exploit?
5 List the advantages and disadvantages small firms have over large firms in introducing innovation.
6 How do you think large firms will develop over the next 10 years?
7 How do you think small firms will develop over the next 10 years?
8 How do you think self-employment might develop over the next 10 years?
9 What are the main barriers to innovation and entrepreneurship in large firms?
10 What are the main barriers to innovation in small firms?
11 Are there any differences between an intrapreneur and an entrepreneur?
12 Are all entrepreneurs innovators? Are all innovators entrepreneurs?
13 Why do many people believe the creative process is best handled in a small, entrepreneurial firm?
14 Why will entrepreneurship become more important in the future?
15 Is the development of e-commerce really as important as the development of the railways in the last century?
16 How will e-commerce affect the small firm?
17 What opportunities does the rise of e-commerce create?
18 What are the problems of working from home?
19 What are the implications of knowledge becoming the most valuable commodity that the firm possesses?
20 Can a small firm really have a global brand?

● Exercises and assignments

1 Write up a case study of successful innovation in a large firm (for example, 3M's Post-It labels).
2 Write up a case study of successful innovation in a small firm (for example, James Dyson and his 'cyclone' cleaners).
3 Contact the DTI and obtain their most recent reports on innovation.
4 Find out how Britain performs compared to other countries in terms of its ability to innovate.

5　Review the financial press to discover why are telecom firms like BT and AT&T splitting themselves up?

6　Review the financial press for other recent examples of large companies deconstructing themselves. Find out why they are doing this.

7　Review the financial press to see which are the most successful growing, small firms. What opportunities are they pursuing? Is there a pattern?

8　Answer the Innovation Potential Indicator questionnaire and assess your innovative potential. You can get more details of how to obtain it from the website of Oxford Psychologists Press on www.opp.co.uk.

9　Research the reasons for the success of VHS rather than Betamax video format. What are the lessons from this?

10　Research the commercial reasons for the success of the Mini. How important is good marketing to the success of an innovation?

Websites to visit

1　The Business and Innovation Centre site on www.bbic.co.uk.
2　The Business Technology Best Practice Programme site on www.etsu.com/etbpp.
3　The Information Society Initiative (ISI) Programme for Business site on www.isi.gov.uk. This is an industry–government partnership aimed at encouraging British business to exploit information technology.
4　Information on Insight Training and their approach to creativity and innovation training can be found on www.innovate.gb.com.

References

Acs, Z.J. and Audretsch, D.B. (1990) *Innovation and Small Firms*, Cambridge, Mass: MIT Press.

Bhidé, A. (2000) *The Origin and Evolution of New Businesses*, Oxford: Oxford University Press.

Bolton, B. and Thompson, J. (2000) *Entrepreneurs: Talent, Temperament, Technique*, Oxford: Butterworth-Heinemann.

Cannon, T. (1985) 'Innovation, Creativity and Small Firm Organisation', *International Small Business Journal*, vol. 4, no. 1, 33–41.

Cannon, T. (1991) *Enterprise: Creation, Development and Growth*, Oxford: Butterworth-Heineman.

Drucker, P. (1985) *Innovation and Entrepreneurship*, London: Heinemann.

Handy, C. (1989) *The Age of Unreason*, London: Hutchinson.

Handy, C. (1994) *The Empty Raincoat*, London: Hutchinson.

Mintzberg, H. (1983) *Structures in Fives: Designing Effective Organisations*, London: Prentice-Hall.

Naisbitt, J. (1994) *Global Paradox*, Book Clubs Association.

O'Farrell, P.N. (1986) *Entrepreneurs and Industry Change*, Irish Management Institute.

Pavitt, K., Robinson, M. and Townsend, J. (1987) 'The Size Distribution of Innovating Firms in the UK: 1945–1983', *Journal of Industrial Economics*, vol. 45.

Peters, T. (1987) *Thriving on Chaos*, London: Pan.

Porter, M.E. (1990) *The Competitive Advantage of Nations*, New York: Free Press.

Rothwell, R. (1989) 'Small Firms, Innovation and Industrial Change', *Small Business Economics*, vol. 1, 51–64.

Schumpeter, J.A. (1996) *The Theory of Economic Development*, edn copyright 1983, New Jersey: Transaction Publishers.

Storey, D.J., Watson R. and Wynarcyzk P. (1989) 'Fast Growth Small Business: Case Studies of 40 Small Firms in North-east England', Department of Employment, Research Paper No. 67, London: HMSO.

Vossen, R.W. (1998) 'Relative Strengths and Weaknesses of Small Firms in Innovation', *International Small Business Journal*, vol. 16, no. 3, 88–94.

Vyakarnham, S. and Leppard, J. (1999) *A Marketing Action Plan for the Growing Business*, 2nd edn, London: Kogan Page.

chapter four

Start-up

Contents

- The start-up decision
- The idea
- Personal attributes
- Customers
- Competitors
- Generic marketing strategies
- Resources
- Planning
- Summary

Learning outcomes

By the end of this chapter you should:

- Understand what motivates people to start-up their own business, what prevents them from doing so and what influences this process;
- Understand what is needed to successfully launch your own firm;
- Understand how business ideas might be generated;
- Appreciate the personal attributes needed to run your own business;
- Understand the importance of linking the idea for a business to customer need;
- Appreciate the importance of understanding who your competitors are and how you might be different to them;
- Be able to evaluate the competitive rivalry in a sector or industry;
- Understand the generic marketing strategies;
- Understand the basis for economies of scale and economies of small scale;
- Appreciate the basis for differentiation and market focus;
- Appreciate the wide range of resources needed to start up a business and that they do not always have to be owned to be used;
- Appreciate the importance of using informal and formal networks to marshal resources and gain credibility;
- Appreciate the importance of planning;
- Be able to generate and critically evaluate ideas for a business start-up.

The start-up decision

Why does anybody want to take the risk of starting up their own business? It is hard work without guaranteed results. But millions do so every year around the world. The start-up is the bedrock of modern-day commercial wealth, the foundation of free market economics upon which competition is based. So can economists shed light on the process?

An economist would tell us that new entrants into an industry can be expected when there is a rise in expected post-entry profitability for those entrants. In

> **Steve Hulme** retired from teaching on health grounds, aged 50, in 1997. Over two and a half years he got by on his pension and the salary earned by his wife. However, he became restless and decided to write a textbook for teenagers about problem solving and lateral thinking. Based on this he decided to become self-employed and run courses for the young unemployed to introduce them to the kind of 'joined up' thinking skills he believed industry was looking for.
>
> He set up his training business, aged 52, with the help of the Prince's Initiative for Mature Enterprise (Prime). It is a scheme, set up in 1999, to provide advice, support and loans for those over-45s who are jobless.

other words, new entrants expect to make extra profits. They tell us that the rate of entry is related to the growth of that industry. They also tell us that entry is deterred by barriers such as high capital requirements, the existence of economies of scale, product differentiation, restricted access to necessary inputs and so on. What is more, the rate of entry is lower in industries with high degrees of concentration where it may be assumed that firms combine to deter entry. However, research also tells us that, whereas the rate of small firm start-up in these concentrated industries is lower, the rate of start-up for large firms is higher (Acs and Audretsch, 1989).

These seem useful, but perhaps obvious, statements about start-ups. But do they really explain what happens and why? Somehow economists fail to explain convincingly the rationale for, and the process of, start-up. They seem to assume that there is a continuous flow of entrants into an industry just waiting for the possibility of extra profits. But people are just not like that. They need to earn money to live, they have families who depend on them. Leaving a secure job to start up a business, for example, needs more of a rationale than just 'extra profits'. Certainly the personal characteristics of owner-managers and entrepreneurs and their antecedents are factors that economists are both unfamiliar and uncomfortable with. Economists are not really interested in the individual – who is likely to set up their own firm – and their motivations for doing so. Economists are just interested to explain how many might be interested to do so and into which sectors they might be expected to go. What is more, economists are not altogether happy with the idea that the number of start-ups can be influenced by non-economic factors like antecedence and culture, but most people believe they are.

> **Jessica Hatfield** thought she was 'God's gift' to advertising, so when the advertising agency she worked for rejected her idea for point of sale promotional material she decided to prove them wrong and set-up her own company. **The Media Vehicle** was set up in 1995 with a £12 000 overdraft. It puts advertisements on supermarket trolleys and along the aisles of shops and co-ordinates national campaigns for clients. Profits in the first year were only £11 000 on sales of just over £400 000. However, five years later this has risen to £1 million on sales of almost £5 million.

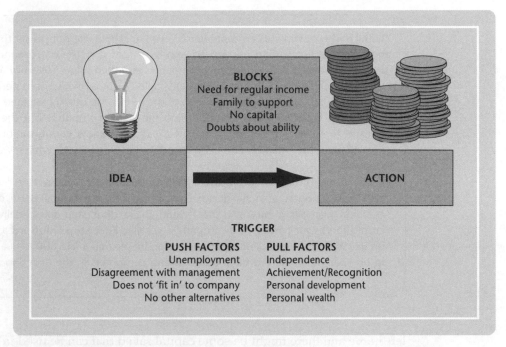

Figure 4.1 Reasons for setting up in business

Figure 4.1 seeks to explain how start-ups happen and why, sometimes, they do not. Most people, at some time in their life, have an idea that could form the basis for establishing their own business. But few people chose to do so. What is needed is a trigger to spur them into action, to turn the idea into reality. These triggers can take the form of 'push' or 'pull' factors. Push factors are those that push you into self-employment – unemployment or forced redundancy, disagreement with your boss, being a 'misfit' and not feeling comfortable in an organisation for some reason, or simply having no alternative because, for example, you have a physical disability or illness. These are very strong motivations for self-employment, but not necessarily to grow your business. Worse still, unemployment as a strong push factor may indicate a higher probability that the business will have a short life span. A growth business is far more likely to be established because of the positive motivation or pull factors – the need for independence, achievement and recognition, personal development and wealth. Sometimes the factors combine and an entrepreneur emerges with a positive motivation, for example, to make a success of an innovative idea, having felt a 'misfit' in their old organisation.

All too often these triggers are blocked by other factors – the need for regular income, a family to support, no capital or a doubt about your own ability. These all boil down to two things – insufficient self-confidence and an inability to cope with high risk and uncertainty. Without these key ingredients the business will not get past the ideas stage.

It is no coincidence that many people try to start up their own businesses either at an early age or in their late thirties and forties. The blocks are fewer. This is particularly the case later in life when children will probably have grown up and

Richard Thompson was entrepreneurial even at school. He got his mother to make more packed lunch than he needed and then sold it in the playground. He even bought stationery from liquidating companies and then sold it to family and friends.

He left school at 16 to join a company called Copycat which sold peripherals in the rapidly growing computer market of the 1980s. He quickly decided that there were more lucrative opportunities selling the actual computers but the company refused to move into an area that it felt it did not know enough about. Richard investigated the market and developed industry contacts whilst working for Copycat.

Because of his frustration at the unwillingness of the company to move into the personal computer area he decided to set up his own business. He drew up a business plan for a business that would make door step sales, delivering the computers by mail order. The company was called **First Stop Solutions** and was set up in 1986. On the back of his business plan he secured a £15 000 loan and, at first in his spare time, started buying and selling computers in the Croydon area.

. . . to be continued

left home and there might be some capital saved that can be used in the start-up. At the same time the prospective entrepreneur will have gained experience and confidence and, very possibly, be seeking new challenges for self development.

Motivations can be difficult to disentangle and, although growth businesses are more likely to be set up as a result of pull factors, often people face a combination of push and pull factors. What is more, size of business may not feature in their vision at start-up. Indeed motivations change over time. Many owner-managers may start out with no wish to grow their company to be a future Microsoft or Virgin. However, if a business shows potential for being successful, few owners will hinder growth until their personal resources are really stretched. At this point the owner reaches a watershed.

A start-up perspective on the entrepreneurial character has been developed by Cooper (1981). He provides probably the most comprehensive framework for explaining the various factors that contribute to the decision to start-up your own business, and these factors are set out in Table 4.1. Cooper classified them into three groups:

1   The antecedent influences on the entrepreneur: their background, family, age, education, job experience and so on.
2   The incubator organisation in which they have previously been working: its location, market sector, skills required and so forth.
3   The environmental factors external to the individual that contribute to the decision: the economy, role models, availability of finance, advice, staff and other support, and so on.

But more is needed than just an idea and a trigger to establish a successful business. As we saw from the failure statistics, too many start-ups fail within the first three years. For the idea to be translated into a reality with a chance of success you need to have the personal skills and personal qualities needed to run the business. You need to find customers and understand the market. You need

Table 4.1 Influences on the start-up decision

Antecedent influences	Incubator organisation	Environmental influences
Genetic factors	Geographic location	Economic conditions
Family influences	Nature of skills and knowledge	Accessibility of finance
Education	Contact with other start-ups	Entrepreneurial role models
Previous career experience	Motivation to stay or leave organisation	Opportunities for interim consulting
	Experience in a small business setting	Availability of staff and supporting services
		Accessibility of customers

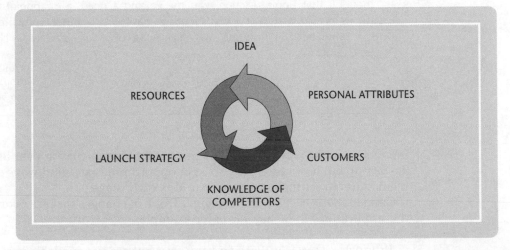

Figure 4.2 What you need to start your own business

to know who your competitors are and how you might be certain you will attract the customers rather than them. You need to think through how you are going to market the product or service. Finally, you need to ensure that you have sufficient resources. And that usually means raising finance. All of these factors are summarised in Figure 4.2.

The idea

Most people usually base their business upon skills, experience or qualifications that they have already gained from a previous job, or through a hobby. Often they think that their employer is not making the most of some opportunity. Sometimes they have an idea but cannot persuade their employer to take it up, so they decide to try it themselves. Often they have contacts in the industry they believe they can exploit to their own advantage.

Other people spot gaps in the market: opportunities that are not being taken by existing businesses. The entrepreneur has been distinguished from the owner-manager as being a person who is likely to spot these opportunities and be

In 1976 **Anita Roddick** set up the first **Body Shop** in Brighton:

I know everyone wants to think that it is like an act of God – that you sit down and have a brilliant idea. Well, when you start your own business it does not work like that. I remember walking through Littlehampton with the kids, one in a pushchair and one walking beside me. We went into the sweet shop, then into the greengrocer and then to Boots. In both the sweet shop and the greengrocers I had choice. I could buy as much, or as little, as I wanted. I could buy half a pound of gob-stoppers or a kilo of apples, the quantities were up to me. In Boots I suddenly thought 'What a shame that I can't buy as little as I like here too. Why am I stuck with only big sizes to choose from? If I'm trying something out and don't like it, I am too intimidated to return it, so I'm stuck with it.' That one thought, that single reaction, was me voicing a need, a disappointment with things as they were. But if that's a need I have, lots of other women must have the same need, I thought. Why can't we buy smaller sizes – like in the greengrocers?

Anita Roddick
Personal interview
. . . to be continued

innovative in the way they take them up. Motivations may appear little different at start-up but how entrepreneurs spot opportunities and find ways of exploiting them starts to set them apart even at this early stage.

Gaps in markets come from change. Think of changes that are taking place and the implications they may have; for example:

- Products or services that you have seen but are not available in your area can mean there are opportunities. Experience of overseas countries and markets is always valuable.
- Changes in customer demands or fashions can mean needs are not being met.
- Changes in markets can lead to opportunities; for example, the opening up of new retail outlets or shopping areas.
- Changes in legislation can create opportunities; for example, changes in Health and Safety at Work regulations and Food Hygiene regulations have created opportunities in the past.

Michelle Clark, a New Yorker, opened her first 'nail bar' in London in 1999. Her company is called **The New Nail Company** and the idea comes from the USA.

Look what happened to the market for American-style coffee shops and juice bars. Every woman has her nails done in America. Why not here? The goal is to create the market for manicure bars and become the market leader.

Sunday Times 14.11.99.

> **David Vanrenen** thinks he has an angle on e-commerce with his company, **EarthPort.com**. Currently his company has only 150 000 subscribers, but is quoted on the Ofex stock market in London.
>
> The company acts as a kind of global internet 'wallet'. You obtain an account with the company by logging your personal and credit card details with them. You can then use your account to buy goods and services from other internet suppliers without having to repeatedly fill out forms and give out your credit card details. This 'locks' subscribers into the site and there is the added advantage of having a ready made customer base and valuable personal information.

Of course you can create your own change and your own opportunity through innovation; for example, innovation could mean:

- Invention. Although, as we saw in the previous chapter, this is not necessarily the same thing as innovation. Often inventors are best advised to sell-on their idea rather than to try to exploit it themselves.
- Ways of doing things better or cheaper. Better is good; cheaper, as we shall see, can lead to problems.
- New developments in technology; for example computers and e-commerce.
- New ways of getting goods or services to markets; for example, direct selling via telephone or internet.

> **James Dyson** is the inventor of the revolutionary cyclone vacuum cleaner who challenged established large companies in the market to gain a market share in excess of 50 per cent. Inventor of the 'Ballbarrow', a light plastic wheelbarrow with a ball rather than a wheel, the idea came to him in 1979 because he was finding that traditional cleaners could not clear all the dust he was creating as he converted an old house. Particles clogged the pores of the dust bags and reduced the suction. He had developed a small version of large industrial cyclone machines, which separate particles from air by using centrifugal force, in order to collect paint particles from his plastic-spraying operation for Ballbarrow. He believed the technology could be adapted for the home vacuum cleaner, generating greater suction and eliminating the need for bags.
>
> Working from home, investing all his own money and borrowing on the security of his home and drawing just £10 000 a year to support himself, his wife and three children, he produced 5000 different prototypes. However, established manufacturers rejected his ideas and venture capitalists declined to invest in the idea. It was not until 1991, 12 years after the idea came to him, that he was able to obtain finance from Lloyds Bank to manufacture the machine. Early sales were through mail order, then followed a deal with John Lewis and later Comet and Currys.
>
> Today James Dyson's personal wealth is estimated to be over £500 million. Dyson's major competitor, Hoover, paid him the ultimate complement of copying his design with their Vortex range. In 2000 he won his case against them for infringing his patents.

Bolton and Thompson (2000) suggest that there are three basic approaches to innovation in this context, which are not mutually exclusive:

1   Have a problem and seek a solution. They cite as an example Edwin Land's invention of the Polaroid camera because his young daughter could not understand why she had to wait to have pictures of herself printed.
2   Have a solution and seek a problem. They cite 3M's Post-It notes as an example of a product with loosely sticking qualities that was applied to the need to mark pages in a manuscript.
3   Identify a need and develop a solution. The example they cite is James Dyson's dual cyclone cleaner that he developed because of his frustration with the inadequate suction provided by his existing vacuum cleaner when he was converting an old property.

There are many sources of potential business ideas. They could come from:

- Existing businesses;
- Existing franchises;
- Innovations;
- Patents;
- Licences;
- Research institutes;
- Industry and trade contacts;
- Industry and trade shows;
- Newspapers and trade journals;
- Business networks and contacts;
- Television and radio.

Inventors of board games are usually best advised to sell their idea on to companies with an existing range of games. However, there are exceptions. **Abalone** is a game invented by two Frenchmen, **Michel Lalet** and **Laurant Levy.** With a hexagonal board and 15 black and 15 white marbles, the idea is to position your marbles in a way that pushes the opponent off the side of the board.

Lalet and Levy could not raise the finance to produce and market the game from either banks or publishers and after eight months were about to give up when they happened to discuss the idea with a neighbour. He wanted a business plan – no more than 20 pages long – and then agreed to put in FFr500 000. Unfortunately, this was only one-third of what they originally thought they needed. Whilst it was enough to pay for an initial production run, it left precious little for marketing. Their reaction was novel. They took the game around bars and clubs giving demonstration games and creating their own PR and hype over the game. They sold the game to shops themselves. The approach worked, in the first three months they sold 9000 copies and the pair have now become quite famous in France.

The game became a craze spawning a jazz record label and other merchandising. Over two years they sold 130 000 copies. Lalet and Levy then sold their share of the business to their neighbour in exchange for a royalty on sales. Abalone is now sold in 30 countries and turnover is some FFr15 million.

One significant factor, of course, will be the sectors and markets in which small firms are currently growing most quickly, for example, e-commerce. It is here where opportunities currently exist. But will you be able to capitalise on these developments as quickly as existing firms?

We are now starting to understand how the creative process works. The brain has two sides that operate in quite different ways. The left side performs rational, logical functions. It tends to be verbal and analytic, operating in a linked, linear sequence. The right side operates intuitive and non-rational modes of thought. It is non-verbal linking images together to get a holistic perspective. A person uses both sides, shifting naturally from one to the other. However, the right side is generally thought to be the creative side. The implication of this is that to encourage creative thinking you need to encourage the right side. Mintzberg (1976) makes the interesting suggestion that the very logical activity of planning is essentially a left-brain activity whilst the implementation of the plan, that is the act of management, is a right-brain activity. He bases this claim on the observation that managers split their attention between a number of different tasks, preferring to talk briefly to people rather than to write, reading non-verbal as well as verbal aspects of the interaction, take a holistic view of the situation and rely on intuition. He argues that truly effective managers are those that can harness both sides of the brain. The point being that you need to develop right-brain activity and try to be creative.

To overcome the habit of logic it is necessary to deliberately set aside this ingrained way of thinking. Creative or lateral thinking is different in a number of dimensions to logical or vertical thinking. Edward de Bono (1971) set out the various dimensions of difference, and Figure 4.3 is based on his work.

One technique for encouraging creative thinking is called brainstorming, which is practised in a group. In the session you do not question or criticise ideas; the aim is to encourage their free flow. Participants encourage and copy ideas down as they come by facilitating all the dimensions of creative thinking in Figure 4.3. This allows the right side of the brain full rein, and the left brain is only engaged later on to analyse the ideas that have come up.

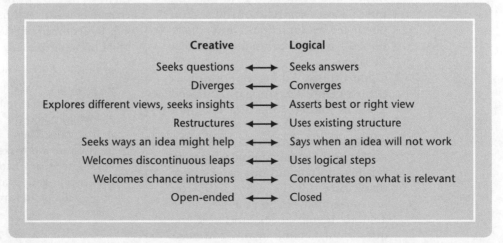

Creative		Logical
Seeks questions	←→	Seeks answers
Diverges	←→	Converges
Explores different views, seeks insights	←→	Asserts best or right view
Restructures	←→	Uses existing structure
Seeks ways an idea might help	←→	Says when an idea will not work
Welcomes discontinuous leaps	←→	Uses logical steps
Welcomes chance intrusions	←→	Concentrates on what is relevant
Open-ended	←→	Closed

Figure 4.3 Dimensions of creative (lateral) vs logical (vertical) thinking

The important thing with ideas is to write them down; all too often good ideas are forgotten. But a good idea is not necessarily a good commercial opportunity; it must be linked to market demand. And often the first attempt at putting that product or service together in a marketable way fails, so what may be necessary is a series of trial-and-error iterations. Howard Head, the inventor of the steel ski, made some 40 different metal skis before he finally made one that would work consistently.

Personal attributes

It goes without saying that, if certain operating skills are needed to run a business, somebody in the firm must have them. Normally that person will be the founder. You cannot be a carpenter without having the skills of a carpenter. However, if you have six carpenters working for you, the primary skills you might need could be those of a salesperson. In fact a self-employed carpenter probably needs to be a salesperson too, as well as an administrator and bookkeeper. The smaller the business the more the owner-manager needs to be a jack-of-all-trades, an all-rounder. Only as the business grows can they afford the luxury of buying in specialist help.

However, it is not just relevant operational skills that you need. You are likely to have the characteristics of owner-managers and entrepreneurs that we have already discussed. But you also need certain personal qualities:

- Stamina: You work long hours with few holidays in your own firm, so you need the stamina for hard work. Robert Wright, who set up a small airline company called Connectair in the 1980s after leaving Cranfield University, called it '90% perspiration, 10% inspiration'.

- Commitment and dedication: In order to be motivated to put in that hard work you need to be committed and dedicated. And that can put a strain on relationships. You need to be tenacious and disciplined, willing to make personal sacrifices.

- Opportunism: taking opportunities almost before they appear. You need to be in the right place at the right time.

- Ability to bounce back: It is often said that the most common word in business is 'no' and this can be very dispiriting. All the more so if you are self-employed. So you need to be able to bounce back and ask the question again and again. You need to be persistent.

> **Gary Frank** started up the **Delicious Doughnut Company** in 1989 with £15 000 borrowed from family and friends. By 1999, helped by a change of image and better branding, the company makes £400 000 profit on turnover of £7 million.
>
> In those days I employed a girl to help me make the doughnuts. We started making them at midnight and this lasted four or five hours. Then I would load up the van and make the deliveries. After that I had to do the paperwork and snatch a few hours sleep before starting again.
>
> *Sunday Times 5.9.99*

Born in 1955 in Seattle, **Bill Gates**, founder of **Microsoft**, is probably the most successful entrepreneur of his generation and he started young. With his friend Paul Allen, he 'begged, borrowed and bootlegged' time on his school's computer to undertake software commissions.

The two went to Harvard University together, using the University's computer to start their own business. Bill's big break came when he approached Altair, a computer company in Albuquerque, New Mexico, trying to sell it a customised version of the Basic programming language for the PC it produced. The only problem was that, at the time, he and his partner, Paul Allen, had not finished writing it. He had a vision of what it would look like and how it would operate, but no software. That was not finished until some weeks later. This package was later licensed to Apple, Commodore and IBM. IBM later commissioned Microsoft to develop its own operating system and that was how Microsoft Disk Operating System (MS DOS) was born.

- Motivation to excel: You need be results orientated, with high but realistic goals and a drive to achieve them. One thing is for certain; it can be very lonely running your own firm, so you need to be self-motivated.
- Tolerance of risk, ambiguity and uncertainty: If you crave certainty, regular routine and clear job definitions, do not go into business on your own.

Running your own business is not an easy option. It needs people with outstanding qualities and they deserve our admiration.

Customers

Ralf Waldo Emerson once said: 'If a man can make a better mousetrap than his neighbour, though he builds his house in the wood, the world will make a beaten path to his door'. He was wrong. Two further things are essential:

1   The world must need the mousetrap. There must be a market demand for a business idea for it to be capable of being transformed into a viable business. Customers will buy a product or service because it solves a problem for them, meets a need they have or adds value to them.
2   The world must know about the mousetrap and be persuaded to buy it. Customers must know about a new product or service and be persuaded that it will perform as promised before they will buy it. That can also mean understanding their motives for buying and tailoring the product or service better to meet those needs.

Inventors are particularly prone to mousetrap myopia; they tend to focus on the product and not on the market. But market demand is the key to commercial viability, and you need to start with basics:

- Who is going to buy the product or service? Name names and describe the customers.
- Why will they buy it?

- What needs do they want the product or service to meet?
- Is the customer reachable? If so, how?
- What are the channels of distribution?
- Is the market for the product or service new or mature?
- Is the market growing or declining?
- How big is the market?
- Does it have boundaries (for example, geographic location)?
- Are there competitors? If so, why should customers buy your product or service rather than that of the competitor?
- Is the product or service unique in any way?
- Is the market highly concentrated or fragmented?

Many of these things are difficult to assess at start-up, but some market research really is vital. One of the things you are trying to estimate is the sales potential of your product or service. This will, amongst other things, determine the scale and nature of the resources you need. Estimating the size of a completely new market for a completely new product or service can be a daunting task. For example, the market for PCs was completely underestimated when they were first introduced. However, where there are existing markets for similar products or services the task will be easier. Nevertheless, sometimes the quickest and cheapest way of finding out these things is by starting the business, limiting the costs and risks, and closely monitoring the outcomes. This approach is attractive to owner-managers because they are action orientated and learn by doing. However, all too often it is just an excuse for not undertaking any market research at all.

Competitors

It is particularly important that a start-up understands the nature of the competition it faces. This involves undertaking market research to develop a detailed knowledge of competitors and how your product or service compares to theirs. Research indicates that low growth firms have the least understanding of their competitors (Storey, Keasey, Watson and Wynarczyk, 1987). Ultimately you will have to find some form of competitive advantage over them if you are to be successful. A major survey of over 2500 small firms concluded that there was an inverse relationship between the number of competitors and growth performance (Cosh and Hughes, 1998). In other words, as you might expect, the fewer competitors the better.

However, few competitors can also be a bad thing, in some circumstances. If you are entering a market where there is high concentration, then it may be that these competitors will combine to deter entry. High concentration can also mean bigger, more powerful companies as competitors. You need to think carefully before entering a market dominated by big companies because they will have well established market positions and the resources to fight off new entrants.

Location can be an important factor dictating competition. In the UK, as in other countries, there can be marked variations in the sectoral, size and age structure of firms in difference regions of the country and at different points in time. Whilst in the past surveys have found that small firms in the UK have tended to grow more quickly in rural rather than urban areas (ESRC, 1992), the

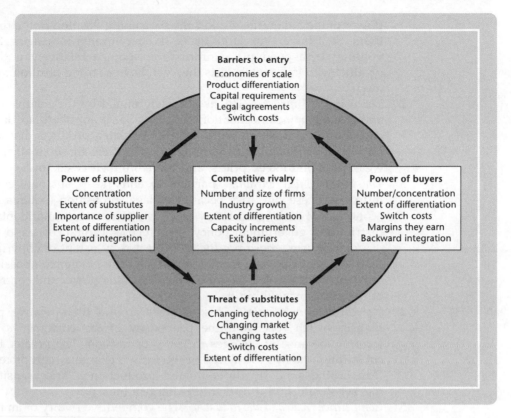

Figure 4.4 Porter's Five Forces

survey noted earlier, which is more recent, found the opposite. Of course, some of this may be due to factors other than competition. So for example, whilst firms in the south east of England face fiercer competition than firms in other parts of Britain, the survey also noted that they tended to enjoy higher growth rates. One reason for this might be because the market for their goods or services was growing faster and therefore greater competition could be sustained.

The structure of the market – the customers, suppliers, competitors – and the potential substitutes and barriers to entry determine the degree of competition and therefore the profitability you are likely to achieve. Michael Porter (1985) developed a useful structural analysis of industries which he claims goes some way towards explaining the profitability of firms within it. The aim of any competitive strategy, he says, 'is to cope with and, if possible change, the rules in favour of the company'. Unfortunately, a small firm is unlikely to be able to change those rules, so it pays to understand them. Porter claims that five forces determine competitiveness in any industry. These are shown in Figure 4.4.

1   *The power of buyers* This is determined by the relative size of buyers and their concentration. It is also influenced by the volumes they purchase, the information they have about competitors or substitutes, switch costs and their ability to backward integrate. Switch costs are the costs of switching to another product. The extent to which the product they are buying is differentiated in some way also affects relative buying power. The greater the

power of the buyer, the weaker the bargaining position of the firm selling to them. So if buyers are large firms, in concentrated industries, buying large volumes with good price information about a relatively undifferentiated product with low switch costs they will be in a strong position to keep prices low.

2 *The power of suppliers* This is also determined by the relative size of firms and the other factors mentioned above. So, if suppliers are large firms in concentrated industries, with well differentiated products that are relatively important to the small firms buying them, then those small firms are in a weak position to keep prices, and therefore their costs, low.

3 *The threat of new entrants* Barriers to entry keep out new entrants to an industry. These can arise because of legal protection (patents and so on.), economies of scale, proprietary product differences, brand identity, access to distribution, government policy, switch costs, capital costs and so forth. For example, a firm whose product is protected by patent or copyright may feel that it is relatively safe from competition. The greater the possible threat of new entry to a market, the lower the bargaining power and control over price of the small firm within it.

4 *The threat of substitutes* This revolves around their relative price performance, switch costs and the propensity of the customer to switch, for example because of changes in tastes or fashion. The greater the threat of substitutes, the less the ability of the firm to charge a high price. So, a small firm selling a poorly differentiated product in a price sensitive, fashion market should find it difficult to charge a high price.

5 *Competitive rivalry in the industry* The competitive rivalry of an industry will depend on the number and size of firms within it and their concentration, its newness and growth and therefore its attractiveness in terms of profit and value added together with intermittent over-capacity. Crucially important is the extent of product differentiation, brand identity and switch costs. The greater the competitive rivalry, the less the ability of the firm to charge a high price.

These five forces determine industry profitability and, in turn, are a function of industry structure – the underlying economic and technical characteristics of the industry. These can change over time but the analysis does emphasise the need to select industries carefully in the first place. It also provides a framework for predicting, *a priori*, the success or otherwise of the small firm. For example, a small firm competing with many other small firms to sell a relatively undifferentiated product to a few large customers in an industry with few barriers to entry is unlikely to do well without some radical shifts in its marketing strategies. How many small firms face just such a situation?

Generic marketing strategies

There have only ever been three ways of selling products or services and at the launch of your business you need to decide which one applies to you. You see two of them being used every day in any street market. At one end of the market there is a street trader offering the cheapest goods in the market – fruit, vegetables or whatever; at the other end there is another offering something

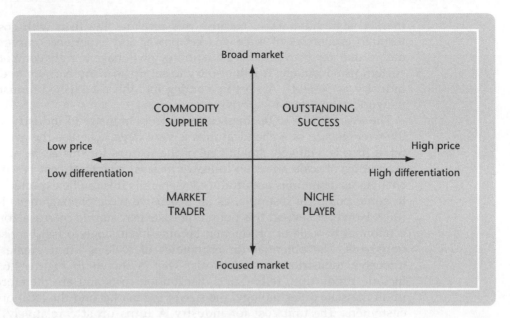

Figure 4.5 Generic marketing strategies

different – freshest or organically-grown fruit, vegetables or whatever. The more different you are, the higher the price you can charge. But there is also a third way to charge a higher price – not to go to the market, but rather to take the product to the customer. This is focusing on the customer and their needs.

Many centuries later, Michael Porter (1985) gave this piece of common-sense the catchy title of 'generic marketing strategies' and argued that there are only three fundamental ways of achieving sustainable competitive advantage:

- Low price;
- High differentiation;
- Customer focus.

These lead to the four market positions, or 'generic marketing strategies', shown in Figure 4.5.

Commodity supplier

This is where the firm sets out to be the lowest price producer in the industry appealing to a very broad market with a relatively undifferentiated product. To have the lowest price means you must have the lowest costs. This assumes that costs can be reduced, for example through economies of scale, and that this is important to the customer. The risks this firm faces are that cost leadership cannot be sustained, competitors might imitate and technology changes or any basis for that all important cost leadership might be eroded.

This strategy is an inherently unattractive alternative for most smaller firms as they can rarely achieve the economies of scale of large firms and seldom have the capital to invest constantly in new technology. What is more, it is likely that sustainable cost leadership can only be achieved by means of 'substantial relative market share advantage' because this provides the firm with cost advantage through economies of scale, market power and experience curve effects. This means that any firm pursuing this strategy will have to fight competitors hard to sustain its advantage. It will also try to set up as many barriers to entry into the industry as possible. A start-up coming into this established industry will have its work cut out just to survive.

The average size of businesses varies from industry to industry. For example, the average size of a chemical firm is very large, whereas the average size of a retail firm is relatively small. One of the reasons for this is the extent to which economies of scale affect an industry; that is, how total cost per unit produces changes as more units are produced. Generally this can be expected to decline up to some point, for example, as an expensive piece of machinery is used more fully. However beyond this point unit costs may start to increase, for example, as economies of scale of production become increasingly offset by rising distribution costs. The potential for economies of scale is often greatest in capital-intensive industries like chemicals. This is shown in Figure 4.6. Total costs include production, selling and distribution costs and are therefore dependent upon the state of technology, the size of the market and the location of potential customers. The unit cost for industry A turns up at a relatively low level of output, implying the optimal size of firm is relatively small, in contrast to industry B where there are considerable economies of scale. Porter calls these 'fragmented' industries where economies of scale just do not exist and large firms cannot, therefore, dominate the industry. These are clearly easier industries for a small business start-up. Where economies of scale are considerable, and they are valued by the customer, this is an industry that a small business start-up should avoid.

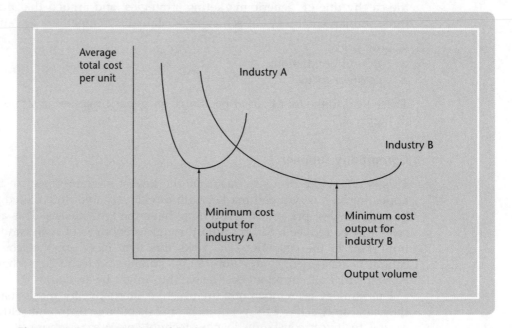

Figure 4.6 Economies of scale

Market traders

And yet, we do see very small businesses surviving in highly price-competitive markets where economies of scale exist. Just visit your local Saturday market to see some examples. How do they do it? The answer lies in businesses that are classified as market traders.

When an economist draws a production cost curve it looks like Figure 4.7. It is almost assumed that there will be economies of scale and that minimum cost output will be at some point A yielding a unit cost of A1. But what happens to the left of the curve? In many industries it is possible to start up with an absolute minimum of overheads enabling you to compete with bigger companies who achieve the economies of scale. For example, consider the consultant working from home or the 'metal-basher' operating from a low-cost workshop under the railway arches. The average cost of production might then actually be lower than that of the big firm, for example B1. The problem is that that will only hold true of production levels up to a certain level, say B. To grow the business beyond this size means that the firm must increase its overheads and then it starts to move down the cost curve. In order to cross the 'no-man's-land' between B and A the firm will need high investment and it will need to move quickly. The chances of making this dash successfully are therefore relatively low. Businesses in this category are therefore unlikely to see growth.

Small firms, therefore, can compete on price as market traders. They may also compete in industries where economies of scale exist but are either unimportant to the customer or cannot be achieved because of limitations in the size of the market, either in total or geographically, and therefore economies of scale cannot be achieved. This happens particularly in highly specialist industries.

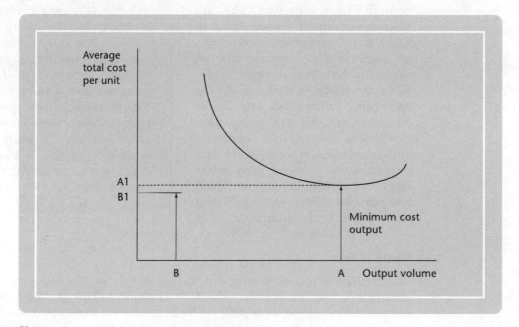

Figure 4.7 Economies of small scale

If a firm sets up in an industry where economies of scale are achievable and are important to customers, it must grow quickly just to survive. A firm can find itself in this situation when the market or product may be new and economies of scale have yet to be developed. Firms may not yet have grown to their optimal size to achieve these economies and the battle is on to see who can get there first. However, achieving market dominance in this sort of industry is risky and the road to high growth has many casualties along the way.

An example of the effects of economies of scale is the microcomputor industry. Born in the late 1970s with unknown demand for its products and no established producers, it has grown rapidly. However, the industry offers substantial economies of scale, particularly in R&D for hardware and software. Conse-quently the market has consolidated, with many small firms going out of business. The survivors have been one of two types of firm. First, there are firms like Microsoft for software and Apple Corporation for hardware, which recognised that the industry would eventually be dominated by a few large firms offering low cost or premium quality products. Microsoft's big break came when IBM chose its operating system for its first PC in 1981 and the company was then able to ride to market dominance on the back of IBM's entry into the PC market. Secondly there were firms like Sun Microsystems which specialised in CAD/CAM equipment and aimed at even smaller specific market segments. Sun Microsystems established an effective market niche for itself and headed off any direct competition with big companies. Customers valued their expertise and economies of scale were less important. As often happens, it has been the middle-sized firm which has pursued neither strategy which has suffered in this industry.

> The **Apple Corporation** realised that economies of scale were achievable and would become increasingly important to customers as the basic microcomputer became more and more a commodity. Based upon an excellent product range, Apple grew rapidly, grabbing market share worldwide, so that it was in a good position to compete with big company entrants to the hardware industry such as IBM.
>
> However, even Apple made mistakes, and the worst was keeping control of its operating systems so that the PC, using the ubiquitous Microsoft operating system, came to dominate the market. With market dominance came greater economies of scale. Companies like Dell have become expert at keeping their cost base as low as possible by using the internet to help manage their supply chain and direct marketing. Now Apple is trying hard to compete on things such as capability and design rather than price.

Niche player

Differentiation means setting out to be unique in the industry along some dimensions that are widely valued by customers. This is called developing a unique selling proposition (USP). The firm sets out to establish itself as unique and different from its competitors in some ways. It can then charge a premium price.

Where the firm combines this with a focus on a narrow target market segment is said to be following a strategy of 'focused differentiation', better known as a niche strategy. Economists call this occupying the 'interstices' of the economy. Clear differentiation often goes with well-aimed segmentation as it is easier to differentiate yourself in a small, clearly identified market. The key to segmentation is the ability to identify the unique benefits that a product or service offers to potential customers. Thus, for example, there may be two electrical engineers producing similar products but, whereas one is a jobbing engineer producing a range of products for many customers with no particular competitive advantage, the other might differentiate itself on the basis of its market – that it sells to a few large companies with whom it has long-term relationships, being integrated into their supply chains.

Being a niche player involves four things:

1   Finding out what elements in the marketing mix are 'unique' to the business. That means understanding what the customers really want when they buy the product or service and why they buy it from you rather than a competitor. Uniquenesses can be product- or market-based.
2   Specialising in customers and/or products rather than methods of production, which is important when competing on price. You must understand your customer thoroughly and ensure that your product or service precisely meets their needs. Ongoing, thorough market research is essential.
3   Stressing the inherent strengths of the firm and the USPs of the product or service, such as innovation, flexibility or personalised service, over its competitors.
4   Emphasising in your marketing the non-price elements of the marketing mix (see page 100) that differentiate you from the competition. Niche players should be able to charge a premium price and sustain a high margin, clearly a very attractive option for smaller firms.

It is vital that any firm understands the basis of its competitive advantage. For a firm pursuing a differentiation strategy this means understanding the basis for its differential advantage. This can be based in law (a licence, copyright, patent and so on), upon elements of the product (quality, design and so on), the service offered or intangible things like image. For a shop it may be based on location (the only shop on the estate). The more elements that the firm can claim set it apart from the competition the better. However, these elements must be a real benefit and add value to the customer. If the firm has elements of differentiation then it should aggressively promote them, usually through a strong brand identity.

> One Huntingdon-based family company that has been very successful in differentiating its products and selling to a small but lucrative market segment is **Quad Electroacoustics**. Its silvery grey, bizarrely sculptured audio equipment looks like no others. When Japanese 'competitors' bring out new models every year, Quads stay the same and last forever. Its original electrostatic loudspeaker was in production for 28 years. Current models sell for some £3000 and still 70 per cent of Quad's sales are exported, especially to Europe and Japan.

Establishing a market niche is most effective when aimed at a narrowly defined market segment. Sometimes this can involve concentrating on gaps in the market-place left by larger companies. One problem of a niche market is its very narrowness, which limits it, but, what might be limited for larger companies offers smaller firms a range of opportunities. Entrepreneurs often run businesses in different niches, finding growth through diversification. However the environment can change; markets grow or shrink, technology changes and customers move around. As the picture changes, so do opportunities, and what might offer a good niche in one decade may turn into a free-for-all in another.

The general thrust of research strongly suggests that market positioning is a key contributor to growth and that developing a market niche by differentiating a business from its competitors is a strategy that offers smaller firms the best chance of success and possibly sustainable growth. For example, in a survey of some 1500 smaller companies across Europe, it was found that those companies that had seen their sales and/or profit grow in the 1990s were those who had 'better or different products or services', and this led to weak-to-normal levels of competition (Burns and Whitehouse, 1994). Those that had seen sales, but particularly profits, decline competed on price and encountered fierce competition. Another survey into 3500 of Britain's 'Superleague Companies' concluded that most of these high-growth companies served niche markets (3i, 1993). Storey *et al.* (1989) concluded that the owner-managers of the fast-growing firms were much more likely to emphasise competitive advantage as being in areas such as innovation and product or service quality. By way of contrast, the owner-managers of the slow growing firms emphasised price.

One company, that arguably could make even higher margins by charging a higher price for its products, is the **Morgan Motor Company**. Founded in 1909, it is the world's oldest privately owned car manufacturer.

Every Morgan is hand-built and looks like it came from the 1930s. Each car is different, with a choice of 35 000 body colours and leather upholstery to match. It takes seven weeks to build a car and customers are invited to the factory to see the process. Morgan sells only about 500 cars a year, half overseas, and demand exceeds supply, cushioning the company from the vagaries of demand.

Back in the 1970s **Alan Pound** was making sound-mixing equipment in his garage and selling it through trade magazines. But in 1988 he moved into the computer-telephony market and started making hardware and software that is used in voice mail systems. **Aculab** became more and more specialist and sales topped £10 million.

In 1999 Aculab was the most profitable company in the *Sunday Times* Fast Track 100 companies. He was quoted as saying: 'the company's success stems from picking a profitable niche in an area where there is little competition, high margins and huge barriers to entry'.

There are, of course, risks with any marketing strategy. The risks associated with a policy of differentiation are that the basis for differentiation cannot be sustained as competitors imitate or that the USP becomes less important to customers. If the premium charged for the product or service is too high, customers may decide not to purchase. The risks associated with a policy of focus are that the segment becomes unattractive for some reason, or that smaller segments start to appear chipping away at what is already a small customer base, or that the basis for segmentation disappears as the differences between segments disappear. Despite these risks, the niche player stands the best chance of launching and then growing a successful start-up.

Outstanding success

Sometimes firms that differentiate themselves effectively turn out to have a very broad market appeal, and what may have started out as a niche business turns out to be an outstanding success and experiences rapid and considerable growth. However, it is unlikely that many businesses will start life here, except perhaps in areas of real innovation. Commodity suppliers try desperately to differentiate themselves, with varying degrees of success. Those companies that succeed in differentiating themselves do so through the effective use of branding.

Eventually even the big company can feel threatened by a large number of extremely effective niche companies. The computer industry as a whole has now fragmented into many different segments and no company other than IBM now tries to compete in every segment, including Japan's Fujitsu, Hitachi and NEC. Every other firm concentrates on the area where it can be best. Apple, Sun Microsystems, Intel, Compaq and Microsoft have all thrived in recent years despite brutal price wars. Companies with broader product lines based on large machines, such as DEC, Bull, Siemens-Nixdorf and Japan's computer makers have seen their profits collapse. This process is nowhere more evident than in IBM. Its profits evaporated and it had to completely reorganise to face the competition from effective niche marketers.

Based upon these generic marketing strategies, a specific launch strategy for the business needs to be developed and that needs resources and careful planning.

Anita Roddick opened the first **Body Shop** in a back street in Brighton in 1976. It sold only about a dozen inexpensive 'natural' cosmetics, all herbal creams and shampoos, all in simple packaging. She thought it would only appeal to a small number of customers that shared her values. Her husband, Gordon, even went off to ride a horse across the Americas about a month after it opened. However, Anita was wrong.

Today Body Shop is a multinational company with stores on every high street. What started out as a niche business rapidly became an outstanding success as Anita found that the Body Shop concept had a very broad market appeal.

. . . to be continued

Resources

The next consideration is resources. The resources needed will depend ultimately upon the size of the business and this is difficult to predict at start-up. Most start-ups need money, but sometimes this can be minimised by borrowing resources or obtaining assets on lease or hire purchase. Certainly in the early days it does not pay to be burdened by high interest payments and flexibility is crucial. A golden rule in start-ups is to keep your fixed costs as low as possible, thus keeping that all important break-even point low.

However, there are other less obvious resource needs. The business needs customers, suppliers,

> **Katy** and **Maurice Ostro** set up **Glasay International** in 1992. It sells the Mon Glace range of frozen yogurt. It is a lean and mean business, employing only seven staff, three of them family members. Overheads are low. It outsources everything, from production to warehousing and distribution, allowing the firm to concentrate on sales and marketing. The company has now broken into the airline industry which liked Glasay's Dryce box, a dry ice box that keeps the yogurt frozen for 12 hours. By 2000 sales were £2.5 million.

perhaps employees and a landlord. Even if it is to borrow the money, it will need a banker. The process of assembling these resources is a difficult one and is crucially dependent on one factor – credibility. The whole process has been likened to the credibility merry-go-round, shown in Figure 4.8, that can be mounted at any point (Birley and Norburn, 1984).

If you go to a banker with an ill-thought-through proposal, not knowing how much money you need, your credibility in terms of whether you are likely to

> **Richard Thompson** quickly decided to leave Copycat and concentrate on his business full time. **First Stop Solutions** first rented an office in a shared workspace. But Richard wanted to sell premier brand computers such as IBM or Compaq to blue-chip customers.
>
> His first problems came with trying to persuade IBM to give him a dealership. Part of the process was a visit to his offices by IBM. Convinced that he would have a credibility problem with IBM if they realised how small his business was and that he shared office space, he persuaded the owner of the workspace to let him take down their sign and put up one saying First Stop Solutions. He also persuaded the other businesses sharing the space to pretend to be part of the business for the day. He introduced a company specialising in importing car parts as his administration department and another selling office supplies as his accounts department.
>
> The trick worked. He got the dealership and within two years the company was voted 'IBM Quality Dealer of the Year'. It soon dominated the local area but then went national, supplying computers to companies like McDonald's. By 1994 it was making profits of £400 000 on sales of £4 million.
>
> *. . . to be continued*

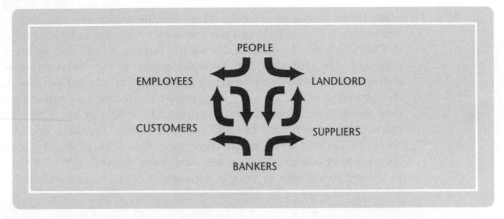

Figure 4.8 The credibility merry-go-round

manage the start-up effectively will be very low. The banker is looking to have you persuade them that your start-up will succeed. They might suggest you go out and get your first customer. But if you go to a customer and ask them to place an order for your product or service they might ask about reliability or after-sales service. They might also reasonably expect to see the product. They might even ask for evidence of previous satisfied customers. The same problem happens when you approach suppliers or a landlord. They will ask for a bank reference, or look to a trading track record – none of which you have. So how do you get off the merry-go-round?

Credibility can be established in a number of ways. Education and track record are important. If you can demonstrate achievements, particularly in the industry that you want to start-up in, it counts for a lot. Personal contact is the key to any relationship and networks of friends and commercial contacts can be important. A strong personal relationship can bring with it credibility. Your network of contacts might provide you with your first customer, or provide you with low cost or free office space. They might even provide you with the cash that the banker is so reluctant to provide. Networks can also provide you with professional advice and opinion, often without charge. Formal networks such as Chambers of Commerce, Business Links in the UK, Small Business Development Centres in the USA and Trade Associations can be invaluable for this.

Deciding what resources are needed, when and how to acquire them are important strategic decisions for a start-up. Entrepreneurs typically seek to use the minimum

> **Richard Branson** may have been lucky to find someone willing to let him have the premises for his first Oxford Street record shop rent free, but when he launched **Virgin Atlantic** he showed that he understood that high capital costs lead to high risks. He minimised these risks by leasing everything and then being able to offer a good quality service at attractive prices.
>
> Richard Branson's main skills are said to be networking, finding opportunities and securing the resources necessary for their exploitation.
>
> *. . . to be continued*

amount of resources at each stage of the business. The important thing to remember is that you do not have to own a resource to be able to use and control it. Owning a resource normally means buying it and that ties up capital which increases the risk that the business faces. It has even been suggested that entrepreneurs who do not own a resource are in a better position to commit and de-commit quickly, giving them greater flexibility and reducing the risks they face (Stevenson, Roberts and Grousebeck, 1985). In the USA, minimising the resources that you own but still use and control is called 'bootstrapping', more formally defined as a 'multistage commitment of resources with a minimum commitment at each stage or decision point' (Bhidé, 1992). Clearly, to bootstrap you need to tap into as wide a network of contacts as possible.

Planning

Assembling the resources needed to start up a new business needs careful planning. Writing down what you intend to do and what you need helps ensure that you do things systematically, in a coordinated fashion. It means others can comment upon and help improve your plans. For many people it also adds a touch of certainty to an otherwise highly uncertain activity. For them, the plan represents the vision of what they want the business to become and how they will go about achieving it. It can become a symbol of what they are striving for. Self-employment creates uncertainty about income generation and small firms face greater market uncertainty than large firms. As we saw in a preceding chapter, the ability to deal with uncertainty is a central feature of entrepreneurship. Planning helps address this issue.

> In 1994 **Richard Thompson** set up a second business called **EMS**, which placed trained staff into computer stores to represent manufacturers. By 1996 this had grown so large that Richard decided to sell the old business to his employees for a few hundred thousand pounds. By 1998 EMS had grown to employ 500 staff on sales of £4.9 million and profit of £700 000. He then sold it to the Mosaic Group for some £5 million, continuing as Chairman.

What is needed is a business plan, and what goes into that we address in later chapters. However, it means that we need to address three issues:

1　**Viability** – customers, competition and marketing strategy, but also the profitability of the business. These are the bare bones of the business plan.
2　**Resources** – people and other resources, but most important of all the money needed to finance the start-up, over what period and how it will be repaid. This requires a cash flow forecast.
3　**Credibility** – track record and experience. This is important if you are to use the plan to assemble the resources you need.

Of course, a plan will not make uncertainty go away or even diminish it. It is simply that planning is the best way man knows of preparing for uncertainty, both practically and psychologically. It is also the best way we have of convincing others that we are prepared and addressing the issue of credibility. It is not that there is any simplistic formula for successfully starting a business. It is just that by planning you give yourself a better chance of avoiding at least some of the pitfalls.

In many ways it is the planning process that is more valuable than the plan itself, unless, perhaps, you are seeking finance. So the plan itself needs to be fit for purpose. A plan which seeks to convince others to lend to or invest in a business will be something of a selling document. The more money being sought, the longer that plan. A plan which is for your own purposes can be a brief working document. Whatever its purpose, it needs to be flexible because the only thing that is certain in life is that the future is not. So it is quite likely that plans will have to adapt or even change completely.

Advice to start-ups:

1 Network – find out who your mentors are.
2 Find out what you want to do and look at the competition and decide on how you can improve on the competition.
3 What is your USP? What is it about your business that makes you different from anyone else. And once you have found those little uniquenesses state them time and time again because those little uniquenesses are the thing the competition will find it difficult to duplicate.

Anita Roddick,
founder of **Body Shop**
Personal interview

. . . *to be continued*

Networks of friends and colleagues can be an invaluable source of advice and opinion about your business plan. What is more, advice is available from a myriad of more formal sources. Many banks produce free booklets detailing what is needed to set up your own business and how to go about developing a business plan. There are government agencies in many countries that give start-up advice, usually without charge. In England local Business Links and the Small Business Service perform this service. In the USA it is Small Business Development Centres and the Small Business Administration (SBA). Further details about UK sources of help and advice are in the next chapter. The more rapid the growth your business will face, the more likely you are to need advice. Indeed, evidence shows that fast growth firms are more likely to seek out and use advice than average growth businesses (Cosh and Hughes, 1998). However, it cannot be proved directly that the advice they received led to their growth.

Summary

Many people have business ideas but few start up their own business. The blocks to doing so include the need for regular income to support a family, the lack of capital and self-doubt. What is needed is a trigger. This can be a push factor such as unemployment or a pull factor such as a desire to make money. As we saw with **Steve Hulme**, it can be a combination of these factors. **Jessica Hatfield** set up **The Media Vehicle** to prove that an idea her employers had turned down would work. Generally businesses set up for positive motives or pull factors are most likely to grow.

Influences upon this decision can be antecedence such as family, the incubator organisation in which they have worked or other environmental factors, such as general economic conditions. Often seeds of entrepreneurship can be seen at an early age, as in the case of Richard Thompson who went on to set up **First Stop Solutions**. To start a business, not only do you need an idea, you also need certain personal attributes, customers, an ability to deal with competitors, a launch strategy and finally resources. Business ideas can come from many sources. They can come from an individual's skills and experiences, from spotting gaps in the market – like **Anita Roddick** and **Body Shop** – or from innovation – as with **James Dyson**. **Abalone** invented and successfully marketed a new board game; **EarthPort.com** found a new angle on e-commerce. You need to brainstorm ideas in an uncritical way, remembering to write them down, before exploring them in more detail.

To run your own firm you must be willing to work hard for long hours like **Gary Frank** and his **Delicious Doughnut Company** You must be committed and dedicated. Like **Bill Gates** you must be opportunistic, able to bounce back in adversity, motivated to excel and tolerant of risk.

An idea is of no use unless it is linked to market demand. There must be a need for the product or service in the market place that is capable of being exploited. You need to know who your customers will be and why they will buy from you rather than competitors. Careful research needs to be undertaken into the sector or industry that you are launching the business. You are most likely to succeed where there is little direct competition. However, even if there are few competitors, if they are large firms you might still face an up hill struggle. Porter's Five Forces is a useful way of making judgements about the degree of competition in a market. It looks at the power of buyers and suppliers, the threat of new entrants and substitutes and the competitive rivalry within the industry.

You need a launch strategy for your business, but you first need to understand that there are only three fundamental ways of achieving sustainable competitive advantage:

- Low price;
- High differentiation;
- Customer focus.

These combine to provide four generic marketing strategies:

- *Commodity supplier*: where you are selling a commodity on price alone. You therefore need to be the lowest cost producer, making the most of any economies of scale that are available.
- *Market trader*: where you are still selling on price but using economies of small scale, in particular low overheads, to keep costs low. However, in these circumstance you must be aware of the limitations to the size of your market and the risks you face in trying to grow the business.
- *Niche player*: selling a differentiated product or service to a targeted, narrow market segment, like **Quad Electroaccoustics**. This strategy offers the best chance of success for a small firm, as **Alan Pound** and **Aculab** have proved.
- *Outstanding success*: sometimes niche firms become outstanding successes as the market they originally sold to expands beyond their expectations, as was the case with **Body Shop**.

Apple Corporation realised that they had to grow fast in their early years to achieve economies of scale that would become important to the customers. More recently, however, they have started to differentiate themselves in terms of machine capabilities and design.

Most business start-ups require a broad range of resources and acquiring them can be a problem because of the lack of credibility of the entrepreneur. What is more, it is important for most businesses that overheads and the break-even point are kept as low as possible. As in the case of **Glasay International**, this can also help the firm focus on what is important to make the business a success. However, like **Richard Branson**, you do not always have to own resources to use them and if you need to own them you do not always need to purchase them outright. You can beg and, as in the case of **First Stop Solutions**, borrow them. Using informal and formal networks of contacts can be vital in helping you do this.

Finally, the start-up needs to be thought through and the business plan is a vital tool in allowing you to do this. It can be no more than a brief, working document that allows you to marshal your ideas in a systematic way, however, if you need it to raise finance it will have to be more comprehensive and much more of a 'selling document'.

● Essays and discussion topics

1 What are the blocks you personally face in starting up your own business? Against each block consider the changes that would be needed for it to be removed.
2 Can people be trained to be creative and generate business ideas?
3 How can government persuade more people to set-up their own business? Should they attempt to do so?
4 Do you think you have the personal attributes needed to run your own business?
5 Why do you need to undertake market research before setting up in business? What sort of market research do you need to undertake?
6 Can a lifestyle business still cater for customer needs?
7 If a business idea is good, is it not the case that there is bound to be competition?
8 Is it better to have big company or small company competitors?
9 Why might many small firms perceive themselves as having no competition?
10 Are there really only three ways to sell a product or service?
11 How might you go about driving down costs, if you were a commodity supplier?
12 What are the risks that a market trader faces in growing a business? How might they be overcome?
13 Do you know of any small firms that compete successfully on price? How do they do it? Can they grow?
14 Do you know of any niche players? How do they differentiate themselves? What market segment(s) do they sell to?
15 Can a niche player grow? If so, how and what are the dangers they face in doing so?
16 How important is a brand in communicating differential advantage?
17 Can differential advantage be sustained indefinitely?
18 Why are networks important?
19 How do you generate a network of contacts in a systematic way?
20 How important is 'good luck' in setting up your own business?
21 If the future is uncertain, what is the point of planning?
22 What is meant by 'flexibility' with regard to the business plan? Why is this important?

⬤ Exercises and assignments

1 Write a mini case study on the motivations of and other influences on an entrepreneur you know who set up their own business.
2 Select a market or industry and, using library data, evaluate the competitive forces within it using Porter's Five Forces.
3 List 10 ways a product or service can be differentiated from competitors. Against each, list how that differential advantage might be sustained.
4 Consider the market for a commodity, for example petrol. List the different market segments this sells to, whether the segments offer the opportunity to develop a differential advantage and if so what these are. Note whether there are pricing difference between the segments.
5 Select a product or service that is clearly differentiated. List the ways it is differentiated, the value to the customer and how these differential advantages are communicated to the customer.
6 Write a mini case study about how an entrepreneur you know who set up their own business managed to assemble all the resources they needed.
7 List the friends, relatives and contacts that might be useful to you were you to set up your own business. Against each name jot down why they might be useful.

⬤ Start-up exercise

Undertake steps 1 to 3 of the start-up exercise at the back of the book.

⬤ Websites to visit

1 The *Sunday Times* runs an enterprise network website on www.enterprisenetwork.-co.uk. Review some of the 'My First Break' case studies to see where entrepreneurs got ideas and the problems they faced in setting up their businesses.
2 Visit the *Wall Street Journal* start-up website on www.startup.wsj.com. Review some of the start-up case studies to see where entrepreneurs got ideas and the problems they faced in setting up their businesses.

⬤ References

Acs, Z. and Audretsch, D.B. (1989) 'Births and Firm Size', *Southern Economic Journal*, vol. 55.
Bhidé, A. (1992) 'Bootstrap Finance: The Art of Start-Ups', *Harvard Business Review*, November–December.
Birley, S. and Norburn, D. (1984) 'Small versus Large Companies: The Entrepreneurial Conundrum', *Journal of Business Strategy*, vol. 6, no. 1, Summer.
Bolton, B., and Thompson, J. (2000) *Entrepreneurs: Talent, Temperament, Technique*, Oxford: Butterworth-Heinemann.
Burns, P. and Whitehouse O. (1994) *Winners and Losers in the 1990s*, 3i European Enterprise Centre, Report no. 12.
Cooper, A.C. (1981) 'Strategic Management: New Ventures and Small Business', *Long Range Planning*, vol. 14, no. 5.
Cosh, A. and Hughes, A. (eds) (1998) *Enterprise Britain: Growth Innovation and Public Policy in the Small and Medium Sized Enterprise Sector 1994-97*, Cambridge: ESRC Centre for Business Research.
de Bono, E. (1971) *Lateral Thinking for Management*, Harmondsworth: Penguin.
ESRC Centre for Business Research (1992) *The State of British Enterprise: Growth, Innovation and Competitive Advantage in Small and Medium-Sized Firms*, Cambridge: ESRC.
Mintzberg, H. (1976) 'Planning on the Left Side and Managing on the Right', *Harvard Business Review*, 54: July–August.

Porter, M.E. (1985) *Competitive Advantage, Creating and Sustaining Superior Performance*, New York: The Free Press.

Stevenson, H.H., Roberts, M.J. and Grousebeck, H.I. (1985) *New Business Ventures and the Entrepreneur*, Homewood, Ill: Irwin.

Storey, D.J., Keasey, K., Watson, R. and Wynarczyk, P. (1987) *The Performance of Small Firms: Profits, Jobs and Failures*, London: Croom Helm.

Storey, D.J., Watson R. and Wynarcyzk P. (1989) *Fast Growth Small Business: Case Studies of 40 Small Firms in North East England*, Department of Employment, Research Paper No. 67, London: HMSO.

3i European Enterprise Centre (1993) *Britain's Superleague Companies*, Report no. 9.

chapter five

Start-up: making it happen

Contents

- Marketing strategies
- Price
- Differentiation
- Customer focus
- Entrepreneurial marketing
- Market research
- Selling skills
- Legal forms of business
- Sources of help and advice in the UK
- Summary
- Appendix: UK checklist of regulations to be met in setting up a business

Learning outcomes

By the end of this chapter you should:

- Understand why customers buy products or services;
- Understand the difference between features and benefits;
- Understand what is meant by the term marketing mix and how it can be used to describe elements of the marketing strategy;
- Appreciate the influences on pricing decisions and understand how price is determined;
- Understand basic cost terminology and be able to calculate break-even;
- Appreciate what is needed to differentiate a product or service;
- Understand how markets can be segmented and what is meant by market focus;
- Be able to construct an appropriate marketing mix for different market segments;
- Understand the different forms of market research and how to go about collecting information;
- Be able to develop a market research questionnaire and a market research plan;
- Understand what is needed to sell effectively and have developed selling skills;
- Be able to decide on the appropriate legal business form for a start-up;
- Know where to go for help and advice.

Marketing strategies

How do you decide which of the generic marketing strategies to adopt? This depends upon a thorough understanding of customers (what they want), competitors (how their product or service compares) and the degree of competition in the market (Porter's Five Forces). The fiercer the competition in the industry, the better the product or service competitors have to offer, then the more a start-up will have to compete on price.

However, the first thing is to understand why customers buy a product or service. Take as an example why people might buy a mundane item like a drill bit. They do not buy it for its aesthetic qualities, they buy it because they want to drill a hole, perhaps to fix something to a wall. The drill solves the problem of creating a hole or fixing something to a wall. If there happens to be a more efficient or easier way of making holes or fixing things to walls, the drill manufacturer is in trouble. A founder of a successful cosmetics firm once said that in the factory he made perfume but in the shops he sold dreams.

In marketing terms, this is called understanding the *benefits* the customer is looking for. They do not buy the *features* that describe the product or service, they buy the benefits it brings to them. You do not buy oil for your car because of its colour or viscosity as such, you buy it because it makes the engine run smoothly, extends its life and reduces repair bills. The features might convince you of the benefits, but it is the benefits you really want. So, different people buying a pen might be looking for different benefits. Of course it must write, but if that were the only benefit they were looking for, why would anybody buy anything but the cheapest pen available? An expensive pen is rarely bought just as a writing implement (for the *consumer*), but more usually as a gift that reflects warmly on the giver (the *customer*). If the customer is different to the consumer then a product or service must offer benefits to both. The customer is buying intangible benefits such as status or esteem for the recipient. The consumer will derive benefit from a writing implement that is aesthetically pleasing and the fact that the donor held them in such esteem that they went to the trouble and expense of buying the gift. There is a market for both cheap and expensive pens, but to different customers.

Understanding the difference between features and benefits is the cornerstone of marketing. It is important in tailoring the marketing offered to customers, deciding on your competitive advantage and building a growth strategy to sustain it. It is real tangible benefits to the customer that differentiate a product or service and allow a premium price to be charged. Unfortunately, many owner-managers like to define their products in physical terms and therefore think they are selling one thing, only to find customers are buying something else.

Features can be turned into benefits, for example:

Feature		Benefit
Our shop takes credit cards	⇨	You can budget for your purchases to suit your pocket
Our shop stays open later than others	⇨	You get more choice when to shop
Our shop is an approved dealer	⇨	You can be guaranteed that we know and understand all technical aspects of the product
Our shop is a family business	⇨	You get individual, personal attention from somebody who cares

So, listing the features of a product or service can be the start of the process of understanding the benefits that the customer is seeking from them. However, it is

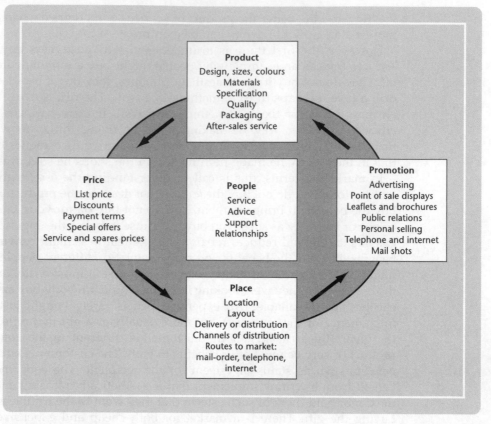

Figure 5.1　Marketing mix: The five Ps

more convincing to start with the benefits that customers are looking for and then construct features that provide those benefits. Which actually comes first is a little like the chicken and the egg.

One technique that is widely used to describe the features of a product or service is called the marketing mix or The Five Ps, a convenient short-hand for a range of sub-elements consisting of product (or service), price, promotion, place and people. This is shown in Figure 5.1.

The customer buys the marketing mix as a package, and the mix must be consistent to reinforce the benefits that the customer is looking for. The marketing mix is only as strong as its weakest link. As we saw in the last chapter, there is a trade-off between price and the other elements of the mix. The stronger or more distinctive and different these elements, the higher the price you are normally able to command. Too many small firms compete primarily on price because they believe the other elements of their marketing mix are insufficiently different from their competitors. However, price is more usually a barrier to sale rather than a positive inducement.

Central to the whole marketing mix is the entrepreneur and their personal approach. Their personal approach will probably, of necessity, involve a very much hands-on, face-to-face way of marketing. They will develop relationships with customers in this way and this in itself can be a distinct form of competitive advantage over large firms.

Adrian Wood set up **GTI**, a publishing company, whilst at university. Adrian and two friends, Mark Blythe and Wayne Collins, were thinking about their futures and realised they did not know much about the job they were thinking about going into. The idea was to explain to students what was involved in various occupations. Adrian first thought of the idea in his second year studying economics at Reading University. He decided that he needed to 'sell' the idea to students – and more importantly to advertisers – by attracting some well-known business names to contribute articles to the magazine. So he wrote to dozens of well-known people and some, including Sir John Harvey-Jones, agreed to do it.

Initially, Adrian and his two friends each put £200 into the business and used the university careers adviser as a consultant. Their first publication tackled quantity surveying and property. They took a week off studying and interviewed lecturers in different departments. They even got the backing of the head of education of the Royal Institute of Chartered Surveyors. About half the publication was devoted to advertising and they personally delivered copies of it around the country. It made £6000 profit.

And so the company was born. The following year five magazines were published and sales came to £120 000. In 1990 they bought an office in Wallingford, Oxfordshire. Today GTI employs some 40 people, publishes over 30 titles and generates sales of over £3 million.

The appropriate marketing mix depends on the benefits the customer, and consumer, are looking for. Take for example a pen, bought simply as a writing implement. It is sold in many high street shops, with only point of sale display materials (probably self-service), with no promotion and minimum service at a very low price. The benefit is that it writes and can be easily obtained. Other elements of the marketing mix are relatively unimportant, so there is strong price competition. On the other hand, a pen bought as a gift has an expensive looking exterior, is also sold in the high street but probably from behind locked glass display stands that can be accessed only with the help of an assistant. They come with a guarantee and are promoted at Christmas time with the realisation that most are bought as gifts not by the consumer. The customer probably wants to spend, say, £25 on a gift and even a so called 'rational man' would not consider buying a box of 250 cheap, disposable pens as a substitute gift, even though they are likely to last longer than the expensive pen. The way to go about marketing these two, apparently, similar products is therefore totally different. The point is that you need to know what the customer and consumer is buying – which may not be the same as you think you are selling.

Customers do not usually sit and wait for a new business to open its doors. They need to be informed of what it has to offer and convinced to try it and word of mouth recommendations can take time. Advertising is only one, very expensive, form of promotion. Many small firms cannot afford it and indeed prefer more personal forms of communication with customers. More recently, large firms have started calling this relationship marketing. Once established, small firms have an advantage in this because the relationship is usually sincere and built on the trust that the owner-manager will deliver the product or service they promise. If they do not, they face the risk of going out of business.

Many firms do not advertise because of its expense and because all too often it is not targeted at specific customers. Body Shop does not advertise, preferring instead to use the considerable PR skills of its founder, Anita Roddick, and window displays on the high street. J. Barbour & Sons, the manufacturer of upper-class but utilitarian waterproof jackets, spend very little on advertising, preferring to sponsor outdoor events such as horse trials.

Stokes (1998) makes the point that owner-managers typically prefer 'interactive marketing' – interacting on a one-to-one basis with customers – because they have strong preferences for personal contact with customers rather than impersonal marketing through mass promotions. He points out that this extends to their preference in terms of market research. They prefer to talk to and observe customers, rather than undertake desk or other more formal research. Promotion is often by word of mouth and recommendation – something that can be crucial to purchasing decisions in some consumer and business-to-business markets (Bayus, 1985). One reason for this preference is, of course, cost but the other is that this is something that large firms are not as good at. This preference for interactive marketing also underlines the importance of networking. In small firm marketing the most important P is probably the personality of the entrepreneur.

The term 'place' in the marketing mix encompasses channels of distribution. Not all businesses sell direct to the end users. Many sell through intermediaries – agents, wholesalers, mail order companies, retailers, specialist outlets or other routes. Often these are established routes to particular markets offering the advantage of loyal customers and local knowledge as well as possible savings in terms of distribution costs or reduced stock holding. For a start-up it might be difficult and risky to ignore these established distribution channels. Although, that is precisely what many e-commerce start-ups are doing. For example, a designer and producer of novel greeting cards had little practical alternative but to sell his cards through high street shops. However, he decided to sell directly to selected shops rather than to go through wholesalers, selling to small shops rather than chains. Doing things differently can be risky, but the rewards of success can be high. The decision about channels revolves around matching the product or service to the customer and their needs in a way that provides an adequate return. However, the evidence points towards small firms rarely being adventurous in their choice of distribution channels.

The elements of the marketing mix, related to the customers they are targeted at, together make up the marketing strategy of the firm. The strategy is just a series of related tasks that, taken together, have a coherence and give direction to the firm. The strategy adopted at the launch of a new business may change as it becomes more established. For example, special price offers may be appropriate at launch, in order to get customers to try the product or service and then repeat buy. On the other hand, if the product or service is sufficiently unique and different, then it may be possible to premium price at launch, particularly if the product or service is unlikely to be repeat purchased quickly. Similarly, some advertising or a mail-shot might be appropriate at launch to inform customers of the new business, whereas, because of expense, word of mouth recommendation might be relied on more later on.

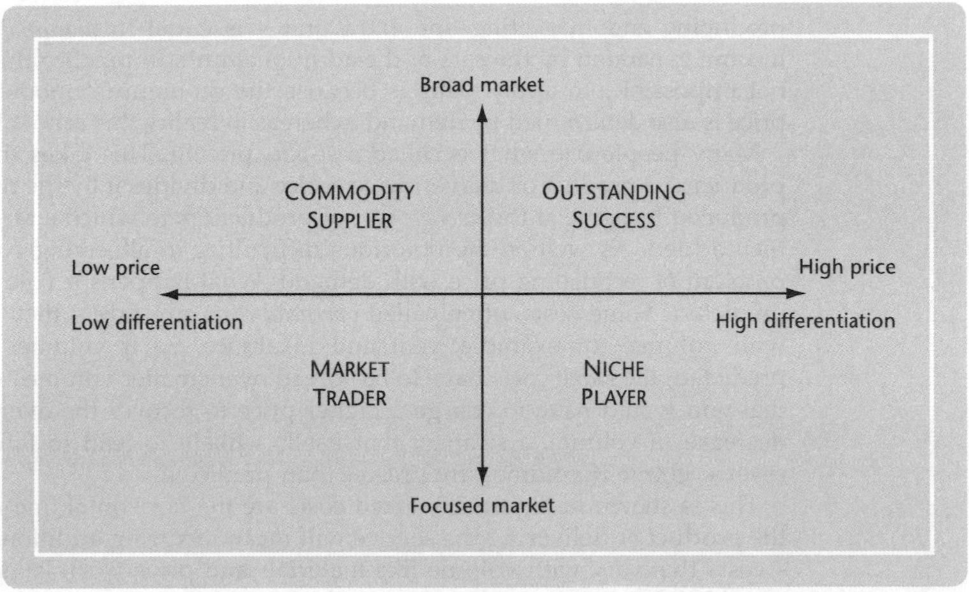

Figure 5.2 Generic marketing strategies

Let us return to the three fundamental ways of achieving sustainable competitive advantage shown below in Figure 5.2 – low price, high differentiation and customer focus – and explore what this means for a start-up. In Chapter 7 the effects of e-commerce on this model will be explored.

Price

Many start-ups are uncertain about how to set prices. They often feel that they must be cheap to attract customers and feel insecure about charging a premium price compared to the competition. To sustain a low-price strategy you must be a low-cost provider and do whatever is needed to drive costs down. However, there are other approaches to pricing.

The price charged for a product or service ought to reflect the value of the package of benefits to the customer. The value can be different to different customers and in different circumstances. Take, for example, the price charged for emergency, compared to routine, plumbing work. A premium price reflects the benefit to the customer of preventing their house being flooded. However, the features of that emergency service, as reflected in the marketing mix, must reflect the benefits the customer is looking for; for example, ease of telephone call-out, 24-hour fast, efficient service, clear-up, facilitation of insurance claims and so on. Similarly, a railway company is able to charge a range of different prices for what is essentially the same service, transportation from one place to another. Given these things, there is often a 'going rate' for a similar product or service.

One factor in the pricing decision is the costs you face in doing business. There are many cost concepts and this book does not intend to go into them in detail. The conventional profit maximising model developed by economists tends to indicate that price should be set at a point where *marginal cost* – the cost of producing and marketing one extra unit – is equal to *marginal revenue* – the income generated by the sale of the additional unit. In practice this is difficult, if not impossible, to apply. This is because the economists' model assumes that price is also determined by demand, whereas in reality this is not always the case.

Many people use what is called *cost-plus* pricing. This takes the total cost of producing a product or delivering a service and divides it by the number of units produced to arrive at the *average cost* of production, to which a target mark-up is then added. As well as the notorious difficulties in allocating cost there is the problem of reconciling price with demand. What happens if volumes are not as predicted? Some costs, often called *overhead costs*, are *fixed* – they do not change with volume, for example, rent and insurance. So if volumes are less than predicted, the same costs have to be spread over smaller volumes – which means that you would have to charge a higher price to recover the overheads and the decrease in volume, a strategy that itself is likely to lead to falling sales. The reverse is true if volumes are greater than predicted.

This is shown in Figure 5.3. Fixed costs are the horizontal line AB. Producing the product or delivering the service will mean incurring additional *variable costs* – costs that vary with volume like materials and piece-work labour. Every time an additional unit is produced and sold, an additional cost is incurred. Line AC therefore represents the total cost of producing the product or delivering the service – the fixed cost plus the variable cost. Over large volumes, this line may curve downwards as the effects of economies of scale are felt. Line LM represents the revenue generated by sales – sales volume multiplied by unit price. At volume X all costs are covered by revenue. This is called the *break-even point*. At volume Y a certain target profit is reached. Obviously the problem with this sort of approach to pricing is that it tends to assume that at a given price, a given number of products will be sold, whereas in reality the quantity sold will be

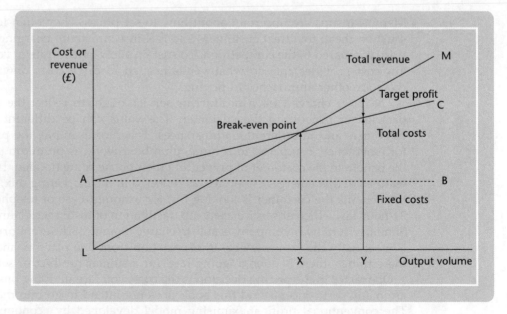

Figure 5.3   Costs, volume and revenue

linked in some way to the price charged. The break-even point can be easily calculated. To do so requires two further terms to be defined. *Contribution* is the difference between sales price and variable cost. *Total contribution* is the difference between total sales (or turnover) and total variable costs for a specified period. *Contribution margin* expresses this as a percentage of sales price or total sales. For example (assuming sales of 100 units per week):

Sales price	£10	Total sales	£1000
Variable cost	£ 6	Total variable costs	£ 600
Contribution	£ 4	Total contribution	£ 400
Contribution margin	0.40 or 40%	Contribution margin	0.40 or 40%

Break-even (expressed in £ turnover) is defined as:

$$\frac{\text{Total fixed costs}}{\text{Contribution margin}}$$

If total fixed costs are £200 per week, the break-even point is:

$$\frac{£200}{0.40} = £500 = 50 \text{ units}$$

Verifying:

Break-even sales 50 units @ £10	£500
Variable costs 50 units @ £6	£300
Total contribution	£200
Total fixed costs	£200
Profit	–

Once above the break-even point, each £1 of sales contributes £0.40 or 40 per cent to profits. So, if the target profit is £400 per week then sales would have to be:

$$\frac{£400}{0.40} = £1000 \ \textit{above the break-even point} = £1500$$

Verifying:

Sales	£1500
Total contribution @ 40%	£ 600
Total fixed costs	£ 200
Profit	400

As we shall see in the next chapter, break-even is an important concept for many reasons, and a break-even worksheet is provided at the end of this chapter.

However, whilst competitors may know about costs, customers rarely do and, just sometimes, as in the case of prestige pens bought as gifts, they may want to pay a high price. How demand holds up to changes in price is determined by the elasticity of demand. The more differentiated the product or service, the more price inelastic is demand – it does not vary greatly with changes in price. The more the product or service is a commodity, the more price will be elastic – it will be affected by price changes. Price elasticity may sound a highly theoretical concept, but the practical applications of it are important.

When **Jean Young** set up as a sole trader offering training to the healthcare sector she estimated her sales in the first year to be a modest £17 200. Deciding on a *per diem* charge was easy, the market would pay in the range of £300 to £1200 per day. Whilst she was experienced, Jean was a start-up so she reckoned that a safe rate would be £400. At this rate she already had some days booked and she estimated that she could sell 43 days in her first year.

With no variable costs she had a contribution margin of 100%. Her fixed costs were reasonable as well since she worked from home. The main element was depreciation on her car and computer equipment. Her fixed costs for the year were estimated at:

Depreciation	£2667
Secretarial wages	330
Transport	430
Telephone	450
Stationery	570
Repairs	350
Other	285
Insurance	100
Total	£5182

She therefore worked out her break-even point as £5182 of turnover, and that included the depreciation on her car that she would keep with or without the business. Since she already had firm commitments for training work totalling over £6000, she felt certain the business was viable.

Table 5.1 shows the increase in sales volume required to maintain the same level of profitability as a result of a price reduction. This depends on the contribution margin before the price cut. If the contribution margin is only 20 per cent and you were tempted to cut prices by 15 per cent, you would have to increase sales volume by a massive 300 per cent, or quadruple sales, just to make the same amount of profit as before. The higher the margin, the less the effect. But even at 40 per cent margin, you would still have to increase sales by 27 per cent. In the face of static or declining sales many owner-managers would be tempted to cut prices. The table makes you think twice about that strategy. Of course there may be other important factors influencing the decision such as reducing stocks

Table 5.1 Percentage increase in sales volume required to achieve the same level of profit after a price cut

Price reduction	Contribution margin		
	20%	30%	40%
−5%	+33%	+20%	+14%
−10%	+100%	+50%	+33%
−15%	+300%	+100%	+60%

Table 5.2 Percentage decrease in sales volume required to achieve the same level of profit after a price increase

Price increase	Contribution margin		
	20%	30%	40%
+5%	−20%	−14%	−11%
+10%	−33%	−25%	−20%
+15%	−43%	−33%	−27%

or bringing in some much needed cash. However, seeking to increase profits by increasing sales at low prices is fraught with dangers.

The arithmetic of pricing is even more persuasive when it comes to price increases. Table 5.2 shows the decrease in sales volume that could sustain the same level of profitability in the face of a price increase. The same 20 per cent margin could see a reduction in sales volume of 43 per cent in the face of a 15 per cent price increase and would still achieve the same level of profitability. Of course the effect is less the higher the margin. Nevertheless such deep reductions in volume may see profits actually increase as overheads are cut (why maintain the same level of staff with less work?). Alternatively you might decide to improve the level of service offered so as to justify the higher price. What is more, the lower volumes mean that stock holdings and other capital costs are likely to come down, not an unimportant consideration if capital is scarce.

The actual effect of price on volumes sold depends on the price elasticity of demand and a small firm can decrease it by attempting to differentiate itself from the competition as much as possible and, in so doing, charging as high a price for its goods or services as the market will bear. This price must, however, be consistent with the other elements of the marketing mix. Tables 5.1 and 5.2 give you some indication of the price–volume–profit effects – so long as you know the contribution margin.

In 1988 **Neil Summers** was discharged from the Royal Marines because of an agonising and potentially crippling back disorder. Never one to give in, he came up with an idea for relieving pressure on the back which involved stretching backwards over a wooden stool. This became the, now famous, **Back Stretcher** – a curved wooden block in which are placed rolling slats. He started selling it at dinner parties and within months was producing dozens. In 1995 he won Britain's Inventor of the Year award. Now he produces hundreds of thousands each year and his company has a rapidly increasing turnover of over £3 million.

However, all did not go smoothly. It was a painful discovery that it would cost over £120 to produce the device in Britain when he knew that he could only sell it for about £80. The answer was to set up the factory in Posnan in Poland with a partner, which is where the device is now manufactured. What continues to be even more painful are his attempts at selling the device in Britain. Whilst the Back Stretcher is now as well-known in Japan as a Dyson vacuum cleaner is in Britain, the paucity of specialist outlets makes the British market a difficult nut to crack.

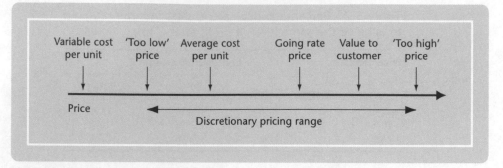

Figure 5.4 The pricing range

Pricing, therefore, is a question of judgement. It is certainly not a science. The range of prices that a business can charge is shown in Figure 5.4. At the bottom of the range is variable cost – the cost of producing one additional unit. If the price charged falls below this then any additional sale costs more than the revenue it generates. The top end of the range depends totally on the differential advantage the firm enjoys – and how well the firm can capitalise upon it. However, no business can afford to ignore competition. Even products or services that are unique face price resistance and ultimately there will be a price that is 'too high' for the customer. At the other extreme there will be a price that is so low that customers will not believe the product or service can deliver the claims that it makes. Indeed for some products, like the exclusive pen bought as a gift, price is very much part of what the customer is buying.

Whilst you may have a longer-term pricing policy, in relation to this there are two further pricing options to be considered at start-up stage as part of a well-thought-through launch strategy, consistent with other elements of the marketing mix:

1 *Skimming* – charging a high initial price at launch. This tends to work best when demand is relatively price inelastic, or there are likely to be a number of different groups of customers and you can appeal to those who will pay a higher price first and move on to the rest later, or little is known about the costs of producing and marketing the product or service. So, for example, when camcorders were first offered for sale the initial price was high and it was sold very much as an innovative, exclusive product. Prices today are much lower and it is much more of an everyday product. Skimming generates high profits and, as the volume sold is usually low, the capital needed for the business is reduced.

2 *Penetration* – charging a lower price at launch. This tends to work best when demand is relatively price elastic or competitors are likely to enter the market quickly, or there are no distinct price-customer groupings or there is the possibility of achieving economies of scale if volume sales can be achieved. It builds sales quickly where no regular customers exist. So, for example, when a new washing powder is launched there may be special 'two for the price of one' offers to get customers to try it. Special offers of this sort are particularly useful as they benchmark the price at a higher level and creates the expectation that the price will rise at some future date. Without that there might be resistance to any subsequent price rise.

Differentiation

Differentiation is about being different and distinctive. It can come from being innovative in some way. Remember the definition of innovation in Chapter 3:

A 'mould-breaking' development in new products or services or how they are produced – the materials used, the processes employed or how the firm is organised to deliver them – or how or to whom they are marketed, that can be linked to a commercial opportunity and successfully exploited.

However, many firms might not be described as innovative but are still clearly differentiated from the competition. For both a product or a service differentiation can come about through function, design, quality, performance, technology or other tangible characteristics. So, for example, Mercedes Benz and Bang & Olufsen aim to differentiate themselves through quality in their respective sectors. McDonald's does it, in part, through quality of service (speed, cleanliness and so on). Differentiation might come from the other elements of the marketing mix, for example, the channels of distribution. When Direct Line started selling motor insurance over the telephone it was so radically different that it was seen as an innovation in financial service delivery that had applications in other sectors. And yet the innovation was simply the use of another, much cheaper, channel of distribution.

Differentiation can, however, prove costly if the basis that is chosen subsequently proves inappropriate. So, for example, Sony devised the Betamax format for its video recorders but ultimately had to adopt JVC's VHS system. Companies try to protect the basis for differentiation in any way possible. It might be that a product can be patented, the design registered or, for written material, copyrighted.

Differentiation is helped by clear branding. A brand should be the embodiment of the product or service offering to customers. So, for example, the Mercedes Benz, Jaguar and BMW brands all convey quality. Virgin is the embodiment of Richard Branson; brash, entrepreneurial, different, anti-establishment. Body Shop is environmentally friendly. The Co-op bank is ethical whereas Coutts Bank is for the wealthy. Many so-called brands, however, fall far short of this instant recognition of values and virtues, being

In the ubiquitous mobile phone market you might think it hard to differentiate yourself. When **Charles Dunstone** set up **Carphone Warehouse** in 1986 with his savings of £6000 he was only 24 years old. His original vision was to sell mobile phones from shops so that people could browse before they bought. Nobody else was selling mobile phones in this way at the time.

Whilst making the most of a high growth market, the real opportunity to differentiate the firm came when Vodafone and Cellnet started offering packages with different combinations of rental and call charges. Customers had to decide which tariff was best for them and many were confused about the packages on offer. Carphone Warehouse set itself up to offer independent, reliable advice, something few other retailers offered. In a highly competitive marketplace the firm was able to claim some element of differentiation, a claim that it used extensively in its advertising.

little more than expensive logos. What do the Barclays, Shell or BT brands convey, other than a knowledge of what the firm sells?

In a world where products and services are often all too homogeneous, a good brand is a powerful marketing tool that must be the cornerstone of any strategy of differentiation. Not only can it help turn prospects into customers, if everything else is right it can turn them into regular customers. What is more, as shown in Figure 5.5, it can help turn them into supporters – regular customers who think positively about the brand – or even advocates – who are willing to recommend the product and bring in new customers. This is an approach far more in tune with interactive marketing, one that is easier to achieve with the personal touch.

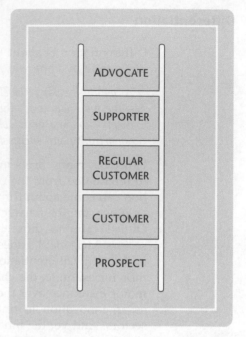

Figure 5.5
The customer loyalty ladder

Body Shop is now a global brand, but what does it stand for and what are customers buying? Even Anita Roddick admits they are not just buying cosmetics – 'oil and water will not make their hearts sing'.

The marketing mix comprises cosmetics made from high quality, natural ingredients which do not involve cruelty to animals. They can be bought in a range of refillable containers, including trial sizes, that are plain and simple with clear factual statements about their ingredients. Tester bottles are freely available in shops and staff are trained not to sell products 'hard' and to respond to questions honestly, if necessary going to the Product Information Manual. The company does not advertise, relying instead on PR, particularly through Anita Roddick, and their prime-site shop windows that often promote environmental issues rather than products. The green shop decor with its ambience of a sweet shop reinforces the environmental, no-frills image. Staff receive regular training, not only on business but also on environmental issues. They are encouraged to work in the community, on company time.

Unlike other cosmetics companies, Body Shop is selling a feel-good factor of a different sort, with a strong ethical dimension. It campaigns on behalf of many environmental issues such as the destruction of the Brazilian rain forests, 'trade, not aid', recycling and, famously, animal testing of cosmetics. Anita is outspoken on many issues such as the role of business in the community and female issues. The Body Shop brand is deeply emotional, based upon a marketing mix that reinforces the 'save the planet' image and really does 'make the heart sing'.

. . . *to be continued*

Branding and things like patents and copyrights are about securing differential advantage for as long as possible and creating barriers to entry into the market. The bigger the market, the more difficult and expensive this is to achieve. That is why differentiation is most successful when combined with a strategy of customer focus.

Customer focus

Focus involves breaking down markets into different groups of customers; these are called *segments* – groups of customers who have similar characteristics or needs. The key for most start-ups is to focus their attention and resources on just three or four clearly defined market segments, tailoring the marketing mix to the needs of customers in those segments and communicating the benefits to them in an appropriate way and through an appropriate medium. This is the starting point of niche marketing referred to in the last chapter. Studies show that there is a relationship between profitability and gaining a high market share of a particular segment.

There are many ways of segmenting markets. You are looking for groups of customers with similar needs that can be identified and described in some meaningful and useful way. For consumer markets these include personal characteristics (demographics) such as age, gender, socio-economic group, occupation, location of home, stage in family life-cycle, and so on. If the group can be identified in this way information on their buying habits is relatively easy to obtain and it is also possible to find out the best media through which to reach them. For example, ACORN (A Classification of Regional Neighbourhoods) breaks down the whole of the UK into about 40 different neighbourhoods, each identified by postcode. So, for example, large inner-city Victorian houses near universities may, reasonably, be assumed to house a lot of university students, which could be important if that is your target market.

For business markets, segments might include type of business, size, location, nature of technology, credit-worthiness and so on. The most commonly used classification is the official standard industrial classification (SIC), which breaks down all businesses into broad groups and sub-groups according to activity.

Market segments can be any one – or a combination of – descriptive factors associated with the product or service, the customer, channels of distribution, sales territories and so forth. As shown in Figure 5.6, it is also possible to vary the degree of aggregation of segments.

Radio Spirits Inc. is certainly a niche business. Based in Illinois, USA, it sells old-time radio shows such as 'The Lone Ranger', 'Dragnet', 'The Jack Benny Show' and 'The Burns and Allen Show'. Collecting these shows started as a hobby for its founder, Carl Amari. It now has a catalogue of over 4000 shows that it mails to 350000 potential customers across the USA. It also has a pay-per-listen website. Despite being a niche business the company still managed sales of over $8 million in 1999.

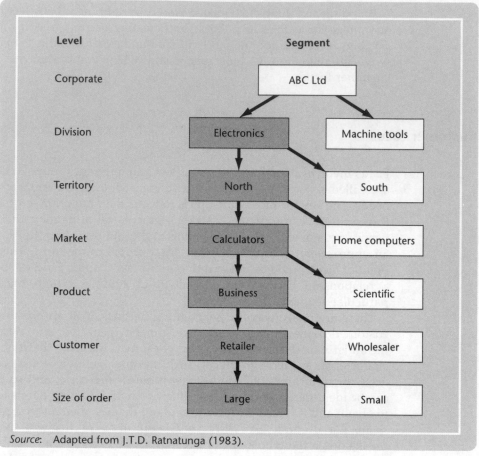

Level	Segment	
Corporate	ABC Ltd	
Division	Electronics	Machine tools
Territory	North	South
Market	Calculators	Home computers
Product	Business	Scientific
Customer	Retailer	Wholesaler
Size of order	Large	Small

Source: Adapted from J.T.D. Ratnatunga (1983).

Figure 5.6 Segmentation levels

Unfortunately there are no prescriptive approaches to segmentation. It requires creative insight into customers' buying habits as well as an understanding of the unique benefits offered by the product or service to these groups. This means understanding the market and competitors, but most of all the customers.

The slimmer the market segment that the product or service is tailored to suit, the higher customer satisfaction is likely to be. We all like personal service and the ultimate market segment comprises just one customer. However, this might not be an viable segment economically. The trend is towards slimmer and slimmer market segments. The danger facing firms selling to slim market segments is their over reliance on a small customer base. If tastes change the segment might disappear. It is vital therefore that niche businesses keep in close touch with the changing needs of their customers.

One small firm producing motor components found itself competing unsuccessfully against a large multinational that undercut it on price. It decided to rethink its whole marketing strategy and found there were many opportunities for products manufactured to a high technical specification, in which quality and supplier reputation were more important than the price charged. By focusing its

Chris Hutt set up **Unicorn Inns** in 1986 and sold it to Moorland ten years later for over £13 million. But it was not until 1991 that he analysed the successful Newt & Cucumber formula that was worth so much.

Newt & Cucumber is a prime-sited town or city-centre free house close to offices, shopping centres and focal points of entertainment, feeding off continuous pedestrian flow. It has a 'traditional but trendy' atmosphere and serves regional real ales alongside national lagers and premium bottled beers. It is open all day and offers food. It is designed to appeal to a wide and varying target market according to the time of day and time of week. It has an informal, basic and unpretentious decor, combining hard-floored, stand-up drinking areas and soft-carpeted, sit-down eating sections. It has a large open vista but there are also intimate corners. It is meant to display 'traditional' pub values – the primacy of beer over any elaborate and frivolous decoration. In this way it is meant to appeal to a wide range of drinkers. It feeds off heavy pedestrian flows. It offers:

- A wide range of premium liquor brands;
- Tasty, filling, value-for-money lunch-time meals, served fast;
- Competitive pricing;
- A warm, traditional and lively atmosphere;
- Efficient, friendly service by motivated staff;
- A safe, secure environment with no games of pool or juke boxes.

An extract from the firm's 1991 business plan, showing their target markets and marketing mix is shown in Table 5.3.

. . . to be continued

marketing strategy on these segments, the company was able to establish itself as a niche player in what was otherwise a highly competitive industry.

Once you understand what your customers or market segments are looking for, you can start to tailor the product or service that you offer. Once you understand your competition, you will start to understand the strength or otherwise of your competitive advantage. With this in mind you can decide which of Porter's generic marketing strategies is most appropriate to each product/market offering. From that you start to understand the imperatives you face and what tasks need to be addressed in your marketing plan. The advantages of developing a market niche can be considerable. If done properly it is profitable and avoids confrontation and competition.

Research indicates that small firms often go about the process of niche positioning in a 'bottom-up' sort of way (Dalgic and Leeuw, 1994). Often they start by pursuing an opportunity by matching innovative ideas to their resources, testing it by trial and error in the market place. The entrepreneur does not always use formal research at this stage, relying perhaps more on intuition. If the idea attracts customers (whether or not they conform to an expected profile), the entrepreneur gets to know them through regular contact. Expansion then comes by looking for more customers with the same profile. Often this is, again, a gradual process of self-selection with some encouragement from the entrepreneur rather than a process involving formal research and deliberate choice.

Table 5.3 Newt & Cucumber's business plan

SEGMENTS:	Shoppers	Office/ professionals	Pensioners/ low paid
Time	12–5	12–2	12–2
Male/female split	10/90	40/60	90/10
Marketing Mix:			
Product:	Coffee/tea, soft drinks	Choice of good food	Cheap beer
Service:	Friendly	Fast	Low priority consideration
Price:	Competitive	Food up to £3.50	Worthington Bitter £1.04
Place:			
– environment	Safe, sit down, clean toilets	Clean, comfortable	Warm
– convenience in choice of pub	90%	80%	50%
Critical Sucess Factors	Safe, clean environment	Rapid delivery of tasty, filling, good value meals	Cheap beer

Entrepreneurial marketing

One dimension in which entrepreneurial marketing is different to conventional marketing is its heavy reliance on relationships. More recently this has been recognised and christened 'relationship marketing', which can be contrasted to the more traditional transaction marketing. Supporters of this 'new' approach – in fact, long used by small firms – believe that it can deliver sustainable customer loyalty (Webster, 1992). The two approaches are contrasted in Table 5.4. This approach may not be viable with all products or services, but it does add yet a further dimension to Porter's generic marketing strategies. Relationship marketing can be mixed with any of the four strategies to create a relationship hybrid that implies a different set of strategic imperatives from those implied by a transaction marketing approach.

However, a reliance on relationships may not in itself be sufficient to mark out the entrepreneurial firm. Chaston (2000) says that truly entrepreneurial firms have a distinctively different approach to marketing which he defines as 'the philosophy of challenging established market conventions during the process of developing new solutions'. The entrepreneurial marketing process is essentially simple, involving understanding conventional competitors and then challenging the approach they adopt. The process of 'rational entrepreneurship' is shown in Figure 5.7. In essence, what he is suggesting is that marketing is judged to be entrepreneurial by its degree of innovation. Since this is the essence of entrepreneurship, this is difficult to dispute.

Unemployed	Office/ professionals	Students	Regulars	Pre-clubbers
2–5	5–7	anytime	7–11	7–11, Fri/Sat
90/10	60/40	50/50	60/40	60/40
Cheap beer	Wide range of quality drinks	Wide range of quality drinks	Wide range of quality drinks	Fashionable brand leaders
Low priority consideration	Friendly	Low priority consideration	Friendly	Fast
Worthington Bitter £1.04	20% discount	Competitive	Competitive	Low priority consideration
Music/TVs	Upbeat atmosphere	Relaxed, safe	Home from home	Lively, 'in place'
50%	80%	70%	50%	80%
Cheap beer	Cheap drinks and upbeat atmosphere after work	Relaxed atmosphere and used by other students	Good service and atmosphere	'In place' reputation

As Chaston points out, even relationship marketing can be copied, although larger firms may find it more difficult to sustain than smaller firms. Here again he encourages the entrepreneur to do things differently. For example, many internet businesses foster relationships with their customers by generating a sense of community on their website. Chaston's approach is deceptively simple as he points out that there are many conventions that can be challenged. He suggests three categories:

1 Sectoral conventions are the strategic rules that guide the marketing operations of the majority of firms in a sector such as efficiency of plants, economies of scale, methods of distribution and so on. So, for example, insurance used to be delivered through insurance brokers until Direct Line came along, challenged the conventional wisdom, and began to sell direct, over the telephone.
2 Performance conventions set by other firms in the sector such as profit, cost of production, quality and so forth. In the 1960s Japanese firms ignored Western performance conventions en-masse and managed to enter and succeed in these markets.
3 Customer conventions which make certain assumptions about what customers are looking for from their purchases, for example price, size, design and so on. Anita Roddick redefined the cosmetic industry's 'feel-good factor' to include environmental factors.

Table 5.4　Relationship vs transactional marketing

Relationship marketing	Transactional marketing
● Encourages close, frequent customer contact.	● Limited contact.
● Encourages repeat sales.	● Orientated towards single purchase.
● Focus on customer service.	● Limited customer service.
● Focus on value to the customer.	● Focus on product/service benefits.
● Focus on quality of total offering.	● Focus on quality of product.
● Focus on long-term performance.	● Focus on short-term performance.

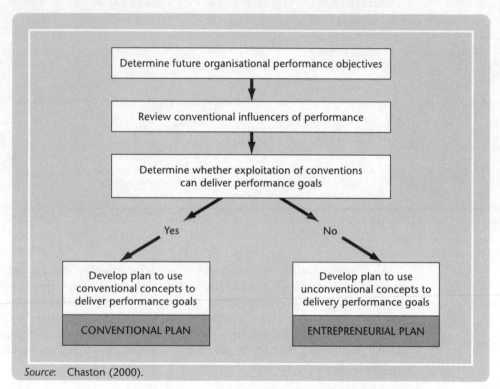

Source:　Chaston (2000).

Figure 5.7　Entrepreneurial vs non-entrepreneurial planning pathway

In most sectors there are factors that managers believe are critical to the success of their business. Chaston encourages entrepreneurs to ask 'why?' These conventions are all worth questioning and doing things differently is what entrepreneurship is about, but doing things differently is risky and Chaston is the first to say it takes careful research and analysis, matching opportunities to the firm's capabilities. He proposes a somewhat different approach to marketing planning which he calls 'mapping the future'. This eight-stage process is shown in Figure 5.8. Although shown as linear and sequential, the process is interrupted as new market information is discovered and earlier decisions are revisited. The process also includes small scale market entry and trial to gain further information.

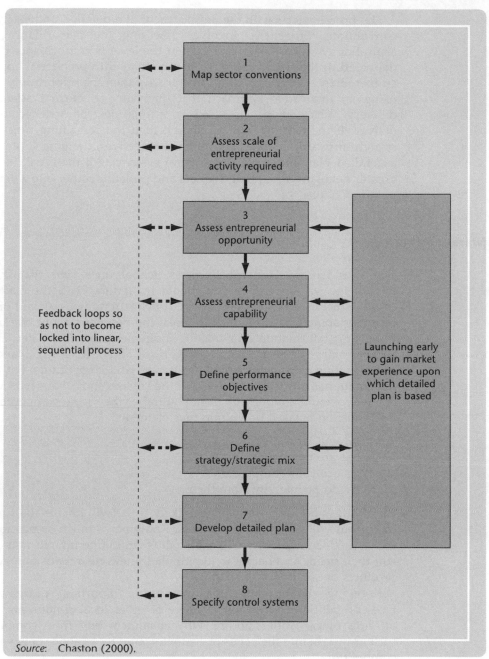

Source: Chaston (2000).

Figure 5.8 The entrepreneurial marketing planning process

The process starts with the development of a detailed understanding of sector conventions. Stage two involves assessing the performance gap between aspirations of future performance and the level of performance currently being delivered. If the size is sufficient to attract an entrepreneurial approach (that is, an incremental approach is not warranted), then the opportunity is investigated using an innovative approach that questions all current assumptions about delivery. Whatever that approach is, it must next be matched to the ability to deliver. If the firm has the capability, then the remaining processes are more straight forward; defining performance objectives, defining strategy, developing a detailed plan and specifying control systems. All these will be considered in greater detail in subsequent chapters and pulled together into a detailed business plan in Chapter 8.

Market research

The President of Harvard Business School once said that if you thought knowledge was expensive, you should try ignorance. Some market research is essential before a business is started. It helps minimise risk and uncertainty and provides some basis on which to make the decisions about marketing strategy. Collecting information and making judgements on it are key entrepreneurial competencies (Carson, Cromie, McGowan and Hill, 1995). Market research is about getting information about customers and competitors. For a start-up any information is probably of value, but the key question that needs to be answered is – why should anyone buy from you rather than from competitors? To answer this question break it down into four elements:

1   Who will buy?
2   What are they buying?
3   Who are your competitors?
4   Why do people buy from them?

Clarifying who the customers are likely to be will enable the firm to focus on those that will give it most business. Knowing as much as possible about them and why they might buy will enable the firm to fine tune its marketing better to suit their needs and help it to identify both new customers and, eventually, new products or services.

Knowing who the competitors are is just as important. A pizza restaurant may face competition from a whole range of other local restaurants, not just those offering pizza. Understanding why customers buy from competitors gives a further insight into the needs of customers and ideas about how you may combat competition.

Market research, therefore, might involve estimating the size and nature of the market including profiling of consumer or industrial customers. A consumer profile might include age, sex, income, occupation, social status, geographic location and so on. An industrial profile might include sector, size, geographic location and so forth. It might involve understanding why, where and when customers buy, the nature of distribution channels and the nature of economic and other environmental trends that might affect the business. It might involve analysing competitors in terms of their product/service offering, size,

Mark Dorman was an advertising executive who had worked for 20 years in the business. In 1995 he was sitting in a hotel bar in the USA feeling jet-lagged. The barman offered him a vodka or a coffee, black or white, to help him come round. Something registered in his mind – what a brilliant idea if you could really have black vodka. It would be completely unique and instantly branded as it was poured into the glass.

When he got back to the UK he decided to investigate the idea. He asked for help from a friend, Christopher Hayman, who worked for Beefeater Gin. After some experimentation they found that it could be done by colouring the vodka with black catechu, a Burmese herb. There was also the added advantage that if you put a mixer in first, as the Americans do, the vodka floats to the top, giving a distinctive cocktail. He also found out that there was a lucrative market out there with more than 350 million cases of vodka sold annually.

By 1997 Mark had invested some £750 000 of his own money in the idea, a third of which was simply the legal costs of registering the product in different countries. He had a company, imaginatively called the **Black Vodka Company**. However, he had run out of money and was still unable to produce the vodka in volume.

The story has a happy ending. Mark was able to find a private backer who shared his faith in the product and bought a share of the company. In 1998 black vodka went on sale in Britain and the USA. It was a success. In 1999 Francarep, the capital development arm of the Rothschild family, bought a 27 per cent stake in the company on projected sales of 100 000 cases. Not bad for an idea from a barman!

profitability, operating methods. If a new product or service is involved, it might involve some testing so as to get customers' reaction. The important thing is to start by specifying what market information is needed.

There are two ways to research a market (Table 5.5):

1   Field research;
2   Desk research.

Field research can involve conducting face to face individual or group interviews, telephone surveys or administering postal questionnaires. Simple observation and discussion will go a long way without costing much other than time. Asking questions of potential customers face-to-face, by mail shot or by telephone will provide a lot of valuable information. Visiting competitors at their place of business, perhaps buying their product or service and talking to other customers will give an insight into how they operate.

Research based on interviewing has to ensure that a representative sample of respondents is seen and that, where a structured interview is used, the subject areas are covered comprehensively. When questionnaires are used, the questions must be clear and unambiguous. They should not be 'lead' respondents by implying an answer to the question. Their design should facilitate interpretation and possible data processing.

For retailers, location is obviously very important. Once prospective premises have been identified, local trade needs to be checked out. Find out how many and what type of customers pass by the location. Are shops in the immediate vicinity an advantage or disadvantage? Location can be important for other businesses,

Table 5.5 Advantages and disadvantages of field vs desk research

	Field research	Desk research
Advantages	● Reflects your needs. ● You control quality. ● Up to date.	● Cheap. ● Quick. ● Good for background information.
Disadvantages	● Expensive. ● Takes time. ● Can tell competitors what you are up to.	● Not specific to your business. ● Can be incomplete or inaccurate. ● Can be out of date.

Table 5.6 Advantages and disadvantages of different types of field research

	Personal interview	Telephone interview	Postal questionnaire
Quality of data	Very good	Good	Good
Quantity of data	Very good	Fair	Poor
Speed	Good	Very good	Poor
Response rate	Good	Good	Poor
Cost	High (your time)	Fair	Fair

for example proximity to customers or a workforce. Many start-ups locate where the owner-manager happens to live. It is not a positive decision. Some lifestyle businesses also locate where the owner-managers want to live. The advantages of different types of field research are shown in Table 5.6.

Desk research can provide information quickly and cheaply. Information on markets, sectors and industries is published in newspapers, trade magazines, industry surveys and reports, trade journals or directories, many of which will be available at the local business library. There may be websites that provide information. Desk research can provide information on product developments, customer needs or characteristics, competitors and market trends. However, for many start-ups local information is of far more importance than regional or national information and that might come from local Chambers of Commerce and other local sources of help and advice.

For many start-ups the easiest and cheapest way to undertake market research is to test-market and launch the business in a low-cost way, constantly reviewing what is happening and how customers react and refining the product or service offered to them. However, this can be a very expensive way of doing market research if things go wrong and some basic market research is essential for just about any start-up. The bigger the start-up, the more important is proper market research.

Whilst any and all information is probably worth having, we need to know what we are looking for. The vital need is to understand why customers buy and how they might be influenced. We need to understand how to go about matching what the firm is capable of producing with what the customer needs – and that is called marketing. Marketing is first and foremost an attitude of mind about always putting the customer first. Understanding customer needs and motivations is central to marketing.

Euravia Engineering is a Lancashire-based company that repairs and overhauls aircraft engines. It was started in 1988 by **Dennis Mendoros**, a Greek who originally came to Britain to study aeronautical engineering but returned to Greece to work in the aero-industry.

When he decided to set up the business he also had to decide where to locate it. He decided on Britain rather than the USA or other European locations because of lifestyle reasons but also because of the UK's established markets, engineering standards that were almost universally recognised and the international reputation of its aero-industry. He decided on Lancashire because of its concentration of aeronautical companies.

Initially he located near to Manchester airport, but that proved to be a mistake because it was expensive and he could not get suitably qualified staff. He quickly moved 40 miles to Barnoldswick where Rolls-Royce Aero-engines had recently closed a factory leaving a pool of highly skilled and experienced engineers. His staffing problems were solved. He also set the business up in an old textile mill so as to keep down costs.

In 1994, with 15 employees, the company moved to a new factory in Kelbrook, a few miles south, where it now remains. Euravia Engineering is thriving and now has a workforce of over 50.

Selling skills

Whatever the 'theory' of marketing might be, the practical reality is that most owner-managers will have to do at least some of their own selling at start-up. The first thing to do is to identify the customer. It sounds obvious but, particularly for business-to-business products or services, the consumer or user of the product or service is not always the buyer. Indeed to get a sale you might have to persuade a range of people – called the 'decision-making unit' (DMU) – each with different interests. The DMU tends to increase with the size of firm you are selling to. The DMU might involve, say, two engineers, a buyer and somebody from the finance department, each looking for different things. Each one has to be satisfied.

It is important to plan a sales interview so as not to waste time or create a bad impression. This starts with knowing as much as you can about the prospective customer and being clear about what you want from the interview. It is important to be able to evaluate the business potential from each customer so as to make the most of your time. The other variable here is their attitude towards you, but whilst you can affect attitude, you are unlikely to be able to affect business potential. Figure 5.9 shows a selling potential matrix that a salesman can use to improve their use of time. Most time should be spent with friendly customers with high potential. Salesmen tend to spend time with any and all friendly customers, in fact they must husband their time between these and the high business potential customers, so as to move these from less friendly to more friendly over time.

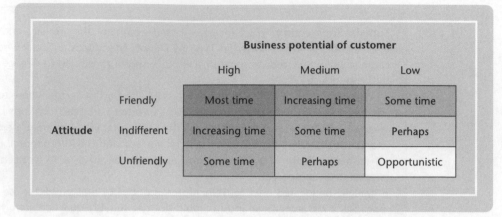

Figure 5.9 The selling potential matrix

It is important to gain the customer's attention, arouse their interest and build confidence. All the time you are trying to find out three important things:

1 What they want.
2 How to match this to the product or service you have to sell.
3 How to build up agreement that it does indeed meet their requirements.
4 How then to close the sale.

The sales interview is the ideal opportunity to bridge the gap between a customer's needs and the benefits offered by a product or service. If you can do that, and convince the customer that the product or service does indeed meet their requirements, you have a sale. Sales interviews can be started in a number of ways:

- *Question*: You might ask a question that ascertains that the customer buys these sort of products or services.
- *Statement*: You might state the benefits of the product or service directly, for example 'our service will save the average household 20% on their phone bills'.
- *Reference*: You might give a personal reference like 'Mr Smith in your other factory was impressed with our service and said you might be interested . . .' You can equally use impersonal references like an article in the trade or national press.
- *Sales aids*: You might launch straight into looking at photographs, brochures and so on.
- *Demonstration*: If you have the product with you, a demonstration may be the best way to get going.
- *Link to earlier contact*: You may have phoned or made contact earlier and agreed to the meeting.

Once you have opened, your aim should be to state the features and benefits of the product and start matching them to the needs of the customer. There are various techniques to help get your message across. Visual stimuli like support materials, demonstrations or presentation all help. Building the relationship is vital. Small things can be important to help achieve this in the short space of time

Goldsmith's Fine Foods was set up by Mark Goldsmith in Manchester immediately after leaving university. It is a wholesaler that sells savoury snacks and cakes to a range of customers, but mainly small restaurants and snack bars. Early on Mark realised that he was not just selling snacks and cakes. To the owners of these outlets he was selling the opportunity to make additional income from their customers by tempting them with something they might not otherwise buy – this was the benefit. An additional feature to enhance this benefit is the advice Mark gives on the positioning of various products, including his own, so as to maximise the spend from each of their customers. This service has allowed Mark to differentiate himself, for this target market segment, from other wholesalers and develop close relationships.

available. For example, dressing appropriately, being punctual, keeping eye contact, being confident and enthusiastic about the product or service, listening to the customer and trying to see things from their point of view, being courteous and polite, and avoiding negative body language like looking bored. The most important advice of all, particularly if the interview goes wrong, is to let the customer talk and to really listen to what they are saying. All the time they are giving you information which should enable you to match the benefits of your product or service to their needs. This entails understanding how to turn features into benefits, as discussed earlier. Relationships are built on over time and networks of contacts can be developed through good customer relationships, so pressurising a customer is unlikely to pay off in the long run.

Selling benefits means understanding both the product or service and the needs of the customer, being able to match the two and then convince the customer that they should buy. That often means avoiding jargon and talking the customer's language.

As the sales interview progresses the customer may show a lack of interest. If this is the case, then the opening was probably not sufficiently interesting and you need to discover what other areas of need – if any – the product or service might meet. In other words you need to ask questions. If the customer raises an objection – which is more than likely at some point in the interview – then at least they are showing an interest and in raising the objection they are providing additional information. If the customer has a fundamental objection, for example, you are trying to sell double glazing and it turns out to be a new house, then it may be time to move on. But just sometimes this is not the case and it may be worth asking why they do not see the need for the product or service. It may just be worth trying to convince them of the benefits it offers over what they already use, even if the time to change is some way in the future. There are six other types of objection, some of which can be dealt with. They are:

- *Feature objection*: Where some of the features do not meet the customer's approval. This can be dealt with by emphasising the positive reasons for these features.
- *Information seeking objections*: Where the customer is not fully convinced by some aspect of the presentation. This provides the opportunity to give them relevant information and tailor it to their requirements.

- *Price objections*: This may be fundamental but often can be made in the hope of negotiating a lower price. Benefits should be restated compared to the price difference in competing products. Value for money needs to be stressed and a discount only offered as a last resort, perhaps using it to secure a larger order.
- *Delay objection*: The customer wants to put off making a decision. This is difficult if the delay is genuine. Arranging a return visit when the time is right may be all you can achieve.
- *Loyalty objection*: There may be an established relationship with a competitor. Stress the benefits of the product or service and never 'knock' the competitor. Try to find reasons why they should change supplier, for example, are they being taken for granted in terms of the service they receive? Always keep contact as it may just take time to convince them to try you.
- *Hidden objection*: The buyer prevaricates for no obvious reason. This is another difficult situation. It is important to get to the unstated objection and deal with it, so ask questions.

Some people actually have problems recognising buying signals and can continue relentlessly through their presentation long after the customer actually wanted to buy the product or service. Buying signals can be many and various; the customer becoming interested and animated, positive body language such as leaning forward or wanting pick up or try the product. If interest is confirmed by asking a few questions, the whole process can be short-circuited and you can go to the most important stage of all – closing the sale.

There are six well-known techniques used for closing the sale:

- *The trial close*: You can try this one immediately you see a buying signal. This close uses the opportunity of an expression of interest to ask a further question which implicitly assumes a sale. For example, 'You will want to take our extended credit, won't you?' or 'It is the quality of the product that has convinced you, hasn't it?' Notice the trial close ends with a question and if the answer is positive then you can proceed straight to close the sale.
- *The alternative close*: This forces the customer to a decision between options. For example, 'Do you want 1000 or 5000?' or 'Can we deliver next month or would you prefer next week?'
- *The summary close*: This is useful if the buyer is uncertain about the next step. It summarises what has been said and sets out the next steps. For example, 'So those are the advantages our service offers over the one you are using at the moment and I think you would agree we are better in every respect. Do you agree?'
- *The concession close*: Concessions are usually on price. They may secure orders but should not be given away too soon, only at the end of the interview when you judge it necessary to tip the balance in your favour. For example, 'And if you place an order in December, there is a special 5% discount.'
- *The quotation close*: Often you have to provide a formal quote at the end of the sales interview. If this is the case, then it should be followed up with another visit to the customer to clarify the main points, answer any queries and secure the sale.
- *The direct close*: Just sometimes it is actually necessary to ask for the order directly – and then remain silent and listen to the answer. If the answer is 'no' at least it should provide some objections that you might be able to overcome.

Successful selling means knowing your product or service inside out and understanding the needs of your customers. It is not just about winning orders, it is about building relationships – vital for a small firm that does not have the advertising and promotion budget that a large firm might have. Relationships are built on trust and respect and, if you cannot get these from the customer, then you are simply an order-taker and the business could easily disappear at any time.

Legal forms of business

Nothing, in the overregulated world of today, is ever simple. Before a new business is launched thought should give some to the legal problems that need to be dealt with. Appendix 1 to this chapter provides a check-list of the regulations facing business. The first issue is the legal form for the business. The three most popular are: the sole trader (almost 60 per cent of businesses), partnership and limited liability company.

Sole traders

This is the business owned by one individual. The individual is the business, and the business is the individual. The two are inseparable. A sole trader is the simplest form of business to start – all that is needed is the first customer. It faces fewer regulations than a limited company and there are no major requirements about accounts and audits, although the individual will pay personal taxes which will be calculated based upon the profits made by the business.

There are two important limitations, however. The first is that a sole trader will find it more difficult to borrow large amounts of money than a limited company because lending institutions prefer the assets of the business to be placed within the legal framework of a company, because of the restrictions then placed upon the business. It is, however, quite common for a business to start life as a sole trader and incorporate later in life as more capital is needed.

The second disadvantage is that the sole trader is personally liable for all the debts of the business, no matter how large. That means creditors may look both to the business assets and the proprietor's assets to satisfy their debts. However, this disadvantage should not be over emphasised because of the widely adopted practice of placing some family assets in the name of the spouse or another relative and because, even as a limited company, a bank is likely to ask for a personal guarantee from the proprietor before giving a loan.

Partnerships

Some professions, such as doctors and accountants, are required by law to conduct business as partnerships. Partnerships are just groups of sole traders who come together, formally or informally, to do business. As such it allows them to pool their resources, some to contribute capital, others their skills. Partnerships, therefore, face all the advantages of sole traders plus some additional disadvantages.

The first of these disadvantages is that each partner has unlimited liability for the debts of the partnership, whether they incurred them personally or not.

Clearly partnerships require a lot of trust. The second disadvantage is that the partnership is held to cease every time one partner leaves or a new one joins, which means dividing up the assets and liabilities in some way, even if other partners end up buying them and the business never actually ceases trading.

Generally, if you are considering a partnership you would be well-advised to draw up a formal partnership agreement. It is very easy to get into an informal partnership with a friend, but if you cannot work together, or times get hard, you may regret it. If there is no formal agreement, then the terms of the Partnership Act 1890 are held to apply. Partnership agreements cover such issues as capital contributions, division of profit and interest on capital, power to draw money or take remuneration from the business, preparation of accounts and procedures when the partnership is held to 'cease'. Solicitors can provide a model agreement which can be adapted to suit particular circumstances.

Limited companies

A company registered in accordance with the provisions of the Companies Acts is a separate legal entity distinct from its owners or shareholders, and its directors or managers. It can enter into contracts and sue or be sued in its own right. It is taxed separately through Corporation Tax. There is a divorce between management and ownership, with a board of directors elected by the shareholders to control the day-to-day running of the business. There need be only two shareholders and one director, and shareholders can also be directors.

The advantage of this form of business is that the liability of the shareholders is limited by the amount of capital they put into the business. What is more, a company has unlimited life and can be sold on to other shareholders. Indeed there is no limit to the number of shareholders. Therefore a limited company can attract additional risk capital from backers who may not wish to be involved in the day-to-day running of the business. Also, because of the regulation they face,

Table 5.7 Advantages and disadvantages of different forms of business

	Sole trader	Partnership	Limited company
Advantages	● Easy to form ● Minimum of regulation	● Easy to form ● Minimum of regulation	● Limited liability ● Easier to borrow money ● Can raise risk capital through additional shareholders ● Can be sold-on ● Pays Corporation Tax
Disadvantages	● Unlimited personal liability ● More difficult to borrow money ● Pay personal tax	● Unlimited personal liability for debts of whole partnership ● More difficult to borrow money ● 'Cease trading' whenever partners change ● Pay personal tax	● Must comply with Companies Acts ● Greater regulation ● Greater disclosure of information

bankers prefer to lend to companies rather than sole traders, although they may still require personal guarantees. Clearly this is the best form for a growth business that will require capital and will face risks as it grows.

Nevertheless there are some disadvantages to this form of business. Under the Companies Acts, a company must keep certain books of account and appoint an auditor. It must file an annual return with Companies House which includes accounts and details of directors and shareholders. This takes time and money and means that competitors might have access to information that they would not otherwise. Advantages and disadvantages of different forms of business are summarised in Table 5.7.

The easiest way to set up a company is to buy one 'off the shelf' from a Company Registration Agent at a cost of some £150. This avoids all the tedious form-filling that is otherwise required. It also saves time. Agents will also show you how to go about changing the company's name if you want to.

Franchises

These are not so much a legal form of business as a way of doing business. They are increasingly popular, particularly with individuals who are less entrepreneurial but wish to run their own business. A franchise is a business in which the owner of the name or method of doing business (the franchisor) allows a local operator (the franchisee) to set up a business under that name. The local operator may be a sole trader or a limited company.

In exchange for an initial fee (anything from a few thousand to hundreds of thousands of pounds) and a royalty on sales, the franchisor lays down a blueprint of how the business is to be run; content and nature of product or service, price and performance standards, type, size and layout of shop or business, training and other support or controls. Since the franchise is usually a tried and tested idea, well-known by potential customers, the franchisee should have a ready

> **Body Shop** is an international franchise chain of shops. Body Shop International Ltd. is the franchisor. Franchisees pay an initial fee plus an annual operating charge for a fixed term, renewable franchise. Franchisees buy a 'turn-key' system with a tightly controlled retail format providing shop fitting and layout, staff training, financial and stock control systems and even help with site identification. Body Shop can also help arrange finance to purchase the franchise. Body Shop also, of course, makes a margin on the products it sells to the franchisees.
>
> Franchisees receive regular visits from company representatives who provide assistance with display, sales promotion and training. Information packs, newsletters, videos and free promotional material are made available and franchisees have to return a monthly report on their sales. This enables the company to monitor both trading results and the local sales performance of individual products. The company closely monitors the use of The Body Shop trade mark in all franchisees' literature, advertising and other uses.
>
> *. . . to be continued*

Table 5.8 Advantages and disadvantages of being a franchisee or franchisor

	Franchisee	Franchisor
Advantages	● Business format proved. Less risk of failure. ● Easier to obtain finance than own star-up. ● Established format. Start-up should be quicker. ● Training and support available from franchisor. ● National branding should help sales. ● Economies of scale may apply.	● Way of expanding business quickly. ● Financing costs shared with franchisees ● Franchisees usually highly motivated since their livelihood depends on success.
Disadvantages	● Not really your own idea and creation. ● Lack of real independence. Franchisor makes the rules. ● Buying into franchise can be expensive. ● Royalties can be high. ● Goodwill you build up dependent upon continuing franchise agreement. This may cause problems if you wish to sell. ● Franchisor can damage brand	● British Franchise Association rules take time and money to comply with. ● Loss of some control to franchisees. ● Franchisees can influence the business. ● Failure of franchisee can reflect on franchise. ● May be obligations to franchisee in the franchise agreement.

market and a better chance of a successful start-up. Indeed only about 10 per cent of franchises fail.

There are hundreds of franchises in the UK as well as tens of thousands of franchisees. Most established franchisors are members of the British Franchise Association, which has a code of conduct and accreditation rules, based on codes developed by the European Franchise Association. One key principle is that the franchisor shall have operated the business concept with success for a reasonable time, and in at least one pilot unit before starting the franchise network. Table 5.8 summarises the advantages and disadvantages of being a franchisee and a franchisor. The DTI produces free booklets on buying a franchise (DTI, 1998a) and on franchising your business (DTI, 1998b).

Sources of help and advice in the UK

There are many sources of help and advice in the UK. Owner-managers might decide to join business associations such as the local Chamber of Commerce or Trade Association, membership of which gives them access to certain support and services, often financed by membership fees. These are largely self-selecting, self-regulating groups although the British Chambers of Commerce have developed their own rather onerous accreditation and quality assurance system. The services provided by these associations varies enormously. However, studies have shown that their services are predominantly low-cost, low-frequency and low-duration (Bennett, 1996 and Bennett, 1998) – in other words they can provide you with information and advice cheaply and quickly. Chambers generally attract a higher proportion of SMEs as members and are locally-based, thereby providing good opportunities for local networking.

Regionally-based Learning and Skills Councils (formerly Training and Enterprise Councils) and their Scottish counterparts, Local Enterprise Councils (LECs), are government-funded bodies with largely private sector boards of management. They provide advice, information, training (particularly in Investors in People), diagnostic consultancy and support to firms. They can also provide information and advice on grants and subsidies. The Scottish LECs are integrated into the networks of Scottish Enterprise and Highlands and Islands Enterprise. This provides more substantial consultancy, larger grant aids infrastructure and export support than English equivalents (Bennett, Wicks and McCoshan, 1994).

Local advice and consultancy to SMEs is offered in England through the Business Link network, in Scotland a similar network called Business Shop and in Wales through Business Connect. These organisations are designed as first-stop shops offering general advice on business and grant and subsidy availability through to specialist advice on topics such as marketing, exports, innovation and product design (Priest, 1999). The English Business Links tend to offer a greater range of services than Business Shops and Business Connects. All are financed mainly by government and are closely related to Learning and Skills Councils and LECs.

There are also some 200 locally-based, not-for-profit Enterprise Agencies around the UK. Their financial backing is variable – most are sponsored by local governments or TEC/LEC contracts, with large companies giving significant in-kind and financial support in many cases (Bennett, 1995). They offer advice and consultancy particularly to start-ups and micro businesses across a wide range of fields, but particularly business strategy and planning, and finance. They are also an invaluable source of information on local grants. They offer a personal service that is often free of charge; however, they have been criticised in terms of their quality control procedures and the impact they have on their clients (Bennett and Robson, 1999).

Across the UK, the Small Business Service provides information and advice via telephone and internet, working closely with Business Links and their equivalents. The Department of Trade and Industry (DTI, 1999) can also be helpful and provides a free comprehensive guide to help for small firms. Many of the banks also provide free information and advice. For example, Barclays provides free Business Information Fact-sheets which give information on size of market, types of customers, competition, advertising, start-up costs, qualifications and legal matters relevant to particular fields of business. They also provide more general start-up information in the form of free booklets (Barclays Bank, 1998). However, do not forget your network of friends and colleagues who might be willing to help and advise.

Summary

Customers buy products or services to obtain benefits. Sometimes there are separate customers and consumers for the product or service, both looking for benefits. It is important to understand what benefits they are looking for. All too often owner-managers focus just on the features of the product or service.

One way of describing the features is the marketing mix, or 5 Ps:

- *Product*: the tangible characteristics of the product or service;
- *Price*: the price, including discounts or special offers;
- *Promotion*: advertising, point of sale displays, PR, selling and so on;
- *Place*: location, layout, channels of distribution and so on;
- *People*: the service, advice, support and relationships, particularly important to owner-managed businesses.

The marketing mix must be consistent, reinforcing the benefits the customer is looking for. It is only as strong as its weakest link. The stronger, more distinctive and different the other elements of the marketing mix, the higher the price that can be charged. Like **GTI**, it is essential to understand what your customers are looking for in order to build a strong marketing mix. The elements of the marketing mix, related to the customers they are targeted at, together make up the marketing strategy of the firm.

Owner-managers prefer 'interactive marketing' – doing things themselves and using one-to-one contact with customers for anything from market research to promotion. For them the fifth P in the marketing mix is their personality.

Too many small firms sell on price because they fear competition. The price charged ought to reflect the benefits customers obtain from a product or service. Therefore similar products or services might be able to command different prices with different target markets. There is a pricing range available to most firms with a number of other benchmarks: variable cost, average total cost and, important for **Jean Young**, the going rate. Also important is the break-even point. Many firm 'cost-plus' price based upon break-even and a target level of profitability.

Whether it is possible to charge a higher price depends on the elasticity of demand which in turn depends, in part, on the uniqueness of the product or service. There are considerable benefits to being able to charge a higher price and, for many firms, small increases can more than compensate for relatively large reductions in the volume of sales. In setting price, information on the variable and average cost of production is relevant, but there will be a going rate that is influenced by the value to the customer and the price charged by competitors. Ultimately however, for any product or service, there will be a price that is too low for credibility and one that is too high. **Back Stretcher** had to engineer its costs so as to be able to pitch the product at a price customers were willing to pay, no matter how unique it was. Variations in pricing strategy at start-up might include skimming or penetration, depending on product-market characteristics.

Differentiation is about being different or distinctive in some way. As with **Carphone Warehouse**, it does not necessarily involve innovation but can be made up from a myriad of small distinguishing features. Differentiation is helped by clear, effective branding – like **Body Shop**. Differentiation can be safeguarded by patents, design registrations and copyrights. A brand should be the embodiment of the product or service offering to the customer. A good brand can help turn prospects into customers and move customers up the loyalty ladder. It helps a business secure differential advantage.

Customer focus involves breaking markets down into segments that have similar characteristics or needs. For a start-up this allows resources to be focused on segments where there is the highest possibility of making a sale. It can also lead to niche positioning, which can be very profitable. The slimmer the market segment, the easier it is to defend against competition, but slim segments carry the danger that customers' tastes might change and the market disappears. **Unicorn Inns** demonstrates how a slightly different marketing mix can be applied to each market segment.

As we saw with **Radio Spirits Inc**., there are many different markets segments and there is no prescriptive way of segmenting a market. It requires creative insight into customers' buying habits as well as an understanding of the unique benefits offered by the product or service. If you want to be entrepreneurial in your approach to marketing you need to understand what the conventions in your marketplace are and try to do things differently, if you have the capabilities. Market research is important for a start-up. It minimises risk and uncertainty and provides information on which to build a marketing strategy. The key question to be answered is why someone should buy from you rather than from competitors. As we saw with the **Black Vodka Company**, the range of information needed can vary enormously. There are two approaches to getting information; field research and desk research. Field research involves discussions and interviews. It might use postal questionnaires or telephone surveys. It might involve simple observation. Desk research involves getting published information from a variety of sources. It is quick and cheap and can provide invaluable background information. It helped **Euravia Engineering** decide on the location for the business.

Many start-ups do not undertake formal market research. They treat the launch as market research, constantly reviewing customer reaction. However, if things go wrong this can be an expensive form of research.

The ability to sell is important at start-up. Selling is about matching the benefits of the product or service to the needs of a customer and then convincing them to buy. As with **Goldsmiths Fine Foods**, the benefits customers are looking for are not always obvious, but the sales role is important in finding out what they are. Over time the salesperson can build a relationship of trust and respect that can lead to new customer networks being developed. Selling skills can be developed with practice. There are ways to start a sales interview; there are sales aids that can be used in the interview itself. There are techniques to handle objections and to help close a sale.

There are sole traders, partnerships and limited liability companies. Sole traders are easy and quick to set-up but, if the business is to grow, it is probably best to form it into a limited company sooner rather than later. Franchise is a popular, low-risk way of setting up in business using the ideas, expertise and systems of an established organisation like **Body Shop**.

Advice from a network of contacts is invaluable. In the UK help and advice is available from Learning and Skills Councils, LECs, Business Links, Business Shops, Business Connects, Chambers of Commerce, Trade Associations, Enterprise Agencies and the Small Business Service.

● Essays and discussion topics

1 Are customers logical?
2 Why are people willing to pay quite high prices for bottled water?
3 Why do owner-managers prefer interactive or personal marketing?
4 Why is it said that the three most important elements of the marketing mix for a retail business are location, location and location?

5   Advertising is the most expensive way of one person talking to another. Discuss.
6   What is marketing?
7   What is the difference between marketing and selling?
8   Why is marketing important?
9   Costs determine prices. Discuss.
10 Is there really a limit to the price you can charge for a product or service?
11 Can you really sell less and make more profit?
12 How can you charge different prices for the same product or service?
13 How different does a product or service have to be to mean that you are following a strategy of differentiation?
14 Every product or service is different. Discuss.
15 Why is branding so important?
16 Is creating a brand easier or more difficult for a small firm?
17 What makes a good brand?
18 Is Carphone Warehouse really different to other shops selling mobile phones? If so, how? If not, why not? Does it matter?
19 We spent most of the twentieth century creating mass markets and will spend most of the twenty-first breaking them down. Discuss.
20 Is market segmentation an art or a science?
21 Is market research worthwhile?
22 Do most small firms set about market positioning in a haphazard sort of way with the result that success or failure is really just luck?
23 Business is 90% perspiration and 10% inspiration. Discuss.
24 If you think knowledge is expensive, try ignorance. Discuss.
25 How do you go about undertaking market research prior to starting a business?
26 How do you find out who your customers might actually be?
27 Describe some sorts of customers that might not be interested in the service that Goldsmith's Fine Foods provides. What elements of the marketing mix might they be more interested in?
28 Selling is not an honourable profession. Discuss.
29 Why are franchises an attractive business opportunity?
30 What is the best legal form of business?
31 Is the organisation of small business support services across the UK a confusing muddle?
32 Where would you go for help and advice in setting up your own business? Why?

● Exercises and assignments

1   Select five products or services. List their features and translate these into benefits for the customer. Alongside this list any proof that might be needed to convince the customer that the benefit is real.
2   Place the five products or services in each of the four boxes of Porter's Generic Marketing Strategies. Explain why you place them where you do.
3   Select one product or service and write up its history – how it got to be where it is, what strategies the firm followed and how competitors reacted.
4   If a company has fixed costs of £160 000 and sells only one product at £25, with a variable cost of £17, calculate its break-even point. If the same company introduces a second product to increase sales above the break-even point and achieves total sales in this year of £960 000 against total variable costs of £720 000, calculate the new break-even point. Fixed costs remain unchanged. Calculate the profits it makes at this level of sales. Why has the break-even point changed? Is the change good or bad?
5   List as many generic ways as you can think of to differentiate a product or service. Alongside them jot down what you need to do to sustain these differences.

6 Develop a market research questionnaire to find out what benefits existing customers of a health club are looking for from their membership.

7 Develop a market research plan to evaluate the commercial potential of opening a shop selling sports wear in a small market town.

8 Select a product or service from Exercise 1. Team up with two other students, one as a customer, another as an observer. Conduct a role playing sales interview lasting 15 minutes with the customer. Make certain each of you understands the role you are playing. Plan your interview using the outline contained in this chapter. When it is finished, get the observer to give you feed-back on how you performed.

● Start-up exercise

Undertake steps 4 to 9 of the Start-up exercise at the back of the book.

● Websites to visit

1 Barclays Bank website contains a Business Opportunities Profiles Service which gives information such as potential customers, competition and start-up costs for selected business sectors. Visit the site and see if there is any information relevant to your business idea. The site is on: www.smallbusiness.barclays.co.uk.

2 The following websites provide help, support and advice for business start-ups. Visit each one to see what it has to offer.
- LivewireYoung Entrepreneurs: www.shell-livewire.org.
- Small Business Service: www.businessadviceonline.gov.uk.
- Business Links: www.businesslink.co.uk.
- National Federation of Enterprise Agencies: www.smallbusinessadvice.org.uk.
- Master Planner: www.masterplanner.co.uk.
- Barclays Bank: www.smallbusiness.barclays.co.uk.
- NatWest Bank: www.natwest.co.uk.
- British Franchise Association: www.british-franchise.org.
- Business incubators: www.ukbi.co.uk.
- 3i: www.3i.com.

● Appendix   UK check list of regulations to be met in setting up a business

	Area	Requirement	Help & Advice
Business Structure	Sole Trader	If trading with a name other than your own, must display name and address of owner at premises and on stationery	Business Link: 0845 6009006
	Partnership	As above. Set up a formal deed of partnership (otherwise terms of the Partnership Act, 1890, apply)	
	Limited company	Register name and office with Registrar of Companies (Companies House). If trading with a name other than full corporate name, must display name and address of owning company. Must file annual return	Companies House: 0870 333636
	Co-operatives	*Either:* register (as above) with Companies House. Name must be acceptable *or:* register under Industrial and Provident Societies Act Register of Friendly Societies. Must be *bona fide* co-operative and name acceptable	Industrial Common Ownership Movement: 0113 246 1737
	Franchises	Need contract with franchisor. Legal advice essential	British Franchise Assn: 01491 578050

Appendix continued overleaf

Area	Requirement	Help & Advice	
Tax	VAT	Check whether registration necessary because of turnover level	CWL1 booklet available from local VAT or Inland Revenue office gives information and CWF1 to notify all departments
	Tax	Notify local Inland Revenue office on form CWF1 and submit P45	
	National insurance	If self-employed, register for Class 2 contributions on form CWF1 at back of CWL1 booklet	
Health and Safety	Health and safety	Most factories and workshops need to register with the Health and Safety Executive and offices, shops and other premises with the local authority. Processes causing pollution must register. If food is being prepared or stored, contact the local authority Environmental Health Department	HSE INFOLINE: 0870 545500

DTI Advice: 0207 215 5000 Leaflets available |
| | Fire certificate | Fire certificate may be necessary (for example, guest houses, hotels, residential nurseries). Check with local Fire Authority | |
| | Environment | If business uses refrigeration, air conditioning, fire fighting equipment or cleaning solvents legislation may apply
If business produces, disposes of, imports or exports waste legislation may apply | |
Employees	Rights	Employment protection legislation applies. If an existing business is taken over, existing terms must be maintained	DTI Advice: 0207 215 5000 Leaflets available
Premises	New	If new building or change of use is involved, consult local authority Planning Department	
	Existing	If business involves plant or machinery installed within an industrial site but outside a building or the premises will require structural alteration, consult local authority Planning or Building Regulations Departments	Local authorities have booklets available
Licences		Cinemas, theatres, child minders, taxis, indoor sports venues, public entertainment venues, street traders, pet shops or kennels, scrap metal dealing, sex shops, residential care, nursing homes or agencies need to apply to the local authority Licensing Department	
		Scrap metal processing, waste management, abstraction of water or discharge of effluent need to apply to the Environmental Agency	Tel: 08457 333111
		Hotels, restaurants, abattoirs, hairdressers, mobile shops (food sales), massage, skin piercing (including tattooing), work with asbestos need to apply to local authority Environmental Health Department	
		Heavy goods or public service operators need to apply to the area office of the Vehicle Inspectorate Executive Agency	Tel: 01265 41461
		Possession or sale of weapons need apply to local police	
		Sale of alcohol in shops, public houses, clubs, nightclubs, restaurants, hotels and so on need to apply to the local magistrate	
		Money lending, credit arrangement, debt collection, credit cards, credit reference agencies, hiring, leasing or renting goods all require a Credit Licence from the Office of Fair Trading	Tel: 0207 211 8608
		If you keep information on people on computer you must be registered with the Data Protection Agency	Tel: 01625 545740

Source: Adapted from *Setting up in Business: A Guide to Regulatory Requirements*, DTI (1998).

● References

Barclays Bank (1998) *Setting up and Running your Business,* London: Barclays Bank, October.

Bayus, B.L. (1985) 'Word-of-Mouth: The Indirect Effects of Marketing Efforts', *The Journal of Advertising Research,* vol. 25, no. 3, June/July.

Bennett, R.A., Wicks, P. and McCoshan. A. (1994) *Local Empowerment and Business Services: Britain's Experiment with TECs,* London: UCL Press.

Bennett, R.J. (1995) 'The Re-focusing of Small Business Services in Enterprise Agencies; the Influence of TECs and LECs', *International Small Business Journal* , no. 13.

Bennett, R.J. (1996) 'Can Transaction Cost Economics Explain Voluntary Chambers of Commerce?', *Journal of Institutional and Theoretical Economics,* no. 152.

Bennett, R.J. (1998) 'Business Associations and their Potential Contribution to the Competitiveness of SMEs', *Entrepreneurship and Regional Development,* no. 10.

Bennett, R.J. and Robson, P.J.A. (1999) 'Intensity of Interaction in Supply of Business Advice and Client Impact', *British Journal of Management,* vol. 10, issue 4.

Carson, D., Cromie, S., McGowan, P. and Hill, J. (1995) *Marketing and Entrepreneurship in SMEs,* London: Prentice Hall.

Chaston, I. (2000) *Entrepreneurial Marketing: Competing by Challenging Convention,* Basingstoke: Macmillan – now Palgrave.

Dalgic, T. and Leeuw, M. (1994) 'Niche Marketing Revisited: Concept, Applications and Some European Cases', *European Journal of Marketing,* vol. 20, no. 1

DTI (1998a) *Buying a Franchise,* London: HMSO.

DTI (1998b) *Franchising your Business,* London: HMSO.

DTI (1999) *A Guide to Help for Small Business,* London: HMSO, April.

Priest, S.P. (1999) 'Business Link SME Services: Targeting Innovation and Change', *Environment and Planning C; Government and Policy,* no. 17.

Ratnatunga, J.T.D. (1983) *Financial Controls in Marketing: The Accounting–Marketing Interface,* Canberra College of Advanced Education, Canberra.

Stokes, D. (1998) *Small Business Management: A Case Study Approach,* London: Letts Educational.

Stokes, D., Blackburn, R. and Fitchew, S. (1997) *Marketing for Small Firms: Towards a Conceptual Framework,* Report to Royal Mail Consulting, Small Business Research Centre, Kingston University, July.

Webster, J.E. (1992) 'The Changing Role of Marketing in the Corporation', *Journal of Marketing,* vol. 56, October.

● Answers to exercises and assignments

4. Contribution margin 1 $= \dfrac{\pounds(25-17)}{\pounds 25}$ $= 0.32$

Break-even 1 $= \dfrac{\pounds 160\,000}{0.32}$ $= \pounds 500\,000$

Contribution margin 2 $= \dfrac{\pounds(960\,000 - \pounds 720\,000)}{\pounds 960\,000}$ $= 0.25$

Break-even 2 $= \dfrac{\pounds 160\,000}{0.25}$ $= \pounds 640\,000$

Profit 2 $= \pounds(960\,000 - 640\,000) \times 0.25 = \pounds 80\,000$

Break-even point has moved up, which makes the firm more risky. On the other hand it is now making a profit of £80 000 which it was not before. If it could have made sales of £960 000 from the original product alone, it would have been better off.

chapter six

Start-up: control and decision-making

Contents

- Cash flow and Death Valley
- The profit statement
- The balance sheet
- Financial drivers
- Break-even
- Decision-making
- Summary
- Appendix: information for control

Learning outcomes

By the end of this chapter you should:

- Understand the importance of cash flow, particularly for a start-up;
- Be able to draw up a cash flow forecast;
- Understand how money flows around the business;
- Appreciate the difference between profit and cash flow;
- Understand the information conveyed in a profit statement and balance sheet;
- Understand what financial information is needed to control a small firm and be able to record and collect it;
- Understand the key financial drivers of a business and appreciate the importance of monitoring them on a regular and timely basis;
- Understand how financial information can be used to help decision making, in particular how to use profit-cost-volume information;
- Appreciate the need for a start-up to minimise its fixed overhead costs and maximise its contribution margin.

Cash flow and Death Valley

Cash flow is the lifeblood of a business; it pays the bills and the wages, but most small firms are short of it. A start-up spends cash on premises, equipment, stock and so on even before the first customer walks through the door. Even that first sale might be on credit and it can take time before debts are collected. During this time the business will have a negative cash flow. It is called the Death Valley Curve and is shown in Figure 6.1. Many firms do not survive to come through the other end.

Death Valley may not be a problem if you have sufficient capital – your own or borrowed – so that you can trade all that time when no cash is coming in. But you need to map out Death Valley to see what you face. Work out its depth – how

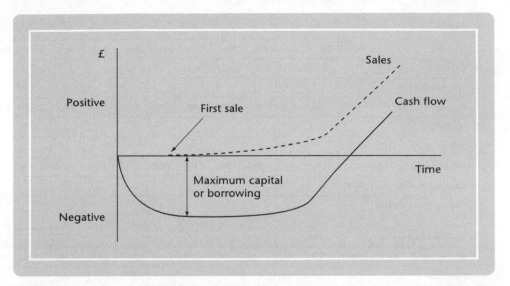

Figure 6.1 The Death Valley curve

much cash is needed – and its length – how long you will need the cash. Death Valley might be deeper and longer than you expect. Indeed if you get some unexpected orders and sales really take off, Death Valley could get longer or deeper, or both.

The way to chart a path through Death Valley is by preparing a cash flow forecast which lists the estimated cash receipts and payments of the business. This can be done on a daily, a weekly or, more normally, a monthly basis. The total cash receipts minus the cash payments in any period is called cash flow. In Death Valley cash flow is negative. Cash flow is added to (or subtracted from) the balance in the bank at the end of the previous period to show the bank balance at the end of the period.

An example of a cash flow forecast is shown in Figure 6.2 using a pro forma Cash-flow Worksheet. Jean Young is a start-up sole trader offering consultancy and training to the health sector. She is working from home, so her overheads are low. She also has a working husband so they have agreed that she does not have to withdraw cash from the business until March. Below are her best estimates of what the business will face during its first year of trading.

1   Sales estimates are the key to any business plan. In most cases sales at start-up are overestimated. It takes longer for a start-up to gain customers than the owner-manager usually appreciates. In this case, however, Jean Young plans a modest build-up of her training days, selling only one day at £400 in November. This she will invoice (+ VAT) immediately and she assumes the invoice will be paid one month later, which are her normal terms of trade.
2   £2000 is the capital introduced to pay for the capital purchases (see below).
3   The VAT reclaim of £299 relates to the capital expenditure on computer equipment (£1701 plus VAT 17.5%).
4   Expenditures are estimated cash payments in appropriate months. Capital purchases are a printer, software and other expenditure (including £299 VAT).

Month:	Nov	Dec	Jan	Feb	Mar	April	May	June	July	Aug	Sept	Oct	Total
SALES													
Volume: days	1	1	2	2	3	4	5	5	5	5	5	5	43
Value:	400	400	800	800	1200	1600	2000	2000	2000	2000	2000	2000	17200
RECEIPTS													
Sales – cash													
Sales -debtors +VAT		470	470	940	940	1410	1880	2350	2350	2350	2350	2350	17860
Capital introduced	2000												2000
Grants, loans and so on.													
VAT on cap.ex		299											299
TOTAL *(A)*	2000	769	470	940	940	1410	1880	2350	2350	2350	2350	2350	20159
PAYMENTS													
Materials													
Wages/salaries Sec	10	120	20	20	20	20	20	20	20	20	20	20	330
Rent													
Heat/light/power													
Advertising													
Insurance		100											100
Travel – Petrol	10	10	20	20	30	40	50	50	50	50	50	50	430
Telephone	120			100			100			100			420
Stationery/postage	130	40	40	40	40	40	40	40	40	40	40	40	570
Repairs/renewals		200						150					350
Local taxes													
Other Prof. fees	50											125	175
Other …………		10	10	10	10	10	10	10	10	10	10	10	110
Capital purchases	2000												2000
Loan repayments													
Drawings/dividends					820	850	970	860	730	770	875	785	6660
VAT on purchases													
VAT paid to C&E		70			350			840			1050		2310
TOTAL *(B)*	2320	550	90	190	1270	960	1190	1970	850	990	2045	1030	13455
CASH BALANCES													
Cash flow *(A) – (B)*	(320)	219	380	750	(330)	450	690	380	1500	1360	305	1320	
Opening balance	–	(320)	(101)	279	1029	699	1149	1839	2219	3719	5079	5384	
Closing balance	(320)	(101)	279	1029	699	1149	1839	2219	3719	5079	5384	6704	6704

Figure 6.2 Cash flow forecast for Jean Young

5   VAT is payable on invoiced sales only. It is paid to the Customs and Excise authorities on a quarterly basis in the month indicated. VAT reclaimable has not been estimated (except for capital purchases) as it is unlikely to be large and would be complicated to calculate.

Because of the low level of overheads, Jean Young only has a negative cash flow in November and then in March as a result of her starting to take drawings out of the business. If she were to take an economic wage from the business from start-up, Death Valley would be much longer. A comprehensive and more complex example of a cash flow and profit forecast for an existing business is included in the appendix to Chapter 11. In fact, Jean Young's turnover is sufficiently low to mean that she does not have to register for VAT.

The profit statement

It is important to realise that profit is not the same as cash. Profit is the difference between sales and costs or unit selling price and unit cost. It tells you how all the assets of a business have grown (or shrunk) through trading. You can make a profit but have no cash, for example because the person who has bought the good or service has not yet paid for it. It is true that eventually the profit should turn into cash, but meanwhile bills and wages need to be paid, and if you do not have the cash to pay them you may go out of business. Figure 6.3 shows how profit is made and, at the same time, money flows around the business. Start at the top, at 1, and work through the diagram in the sequence detailed below.

1   A business starting up needs to find cash. This could be in the form of a sole trader's own money or, for a company, shareholders contributing share capital, both perhaps supplemented by bank borrowings.
2   This is now invested in assets to be used in the business. The assets will comprise long-term or fixed assets such as plant and machinery, office equipment, computers, vehicle and so on, and assets for use on a day-to-day basis. These will also include stocks of goods for resale, stocks of consumables to be used in the office, and, of course, cash to pay the bills. These are usually called current assets. The cash has now turned into other assets, but all these funds are still retained in the business.
3   The assets are then used to generate sales. Goods are resold, services are rendered. This is the first stage on the way to making profits.
4   Of course, making sales is not enough to guarantee profits. Sales might be high, but if day-to-day business costs are higher, then a loss rather than a profit will emerge. So there is a need for management to control day-to-day costs and produce an operating profit. Other non-operating costs, such as loan interest, might also have to be deducted.
5   The result is net profit. This is still not, necessarily, cash since customers might still owe you money or you might not have paid all your bills. However, it does represent an increase in the total assets – or funds – of the business. If the business is established as a sole trader, money may now be withdrawn. If the business is a limited company, corporation tax is deducted, and then dividends may be paid to shareholders. Sole traders pay income tax on the profits of the business and shareholders pay income tax on their dividends.

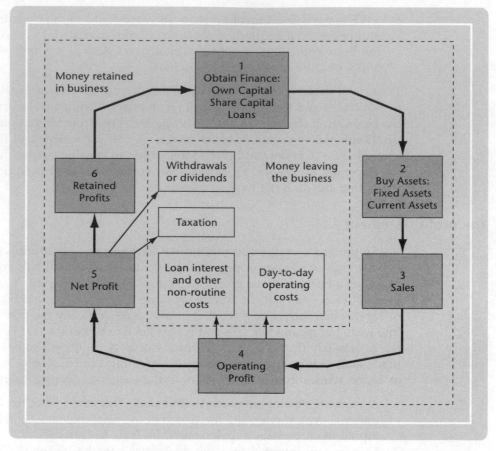

Figure 6.3 The flow of money

6 The balance of retained profits represents another injection of capital into the business. However, this capital is not, necessarily, cash. This is important as any business will need a constant flow of capital to replace existing assets which are used up and/or to expand or grow. As we know, many small firms prefer to finance their expansion using their own money rather than borrowing or giving equity away.

Successful businesses sell their goods or services for more than they cost to produce, so this flow of finance will continually increase. However, the hidden ingredient in this is time. By speeding up the flow of funds you can decrease the amount of capital you need – or simply take more out of the business.

The key to this is debtors and creditors. Debtors are those customers that owe you money because they have not paid immediately and creditors are those suppliers that you owe money to. By getting debtors to pay quickly you speed up the flow of funds. You can speed up the collection of debts by:

● Choosing customers carefully to start with and invoicing them immediately upon sale. In choosing credit customers always ask for, and check up on, trade references, ask for a bank reference, make credit checks with other suppliers, check any published information (such as accounts) about the customer and, if possible, visit their premises.

- Setting appropriate credit limits and making payment terms clear. Once the customer's references are checked they can be set a credit ceiling that must be kept. This minimises exposure to any bad debts. Bad debts are expensive. If you are making a 20 per cent margin, you need to increase sales by £4 to recover each £1 of bad debt.
- Taking the right measures to speed up payments. These include sending statements, following up outstanding debts by telephone – it could be there is a problem with the delivery or the cheque has gone astray, offering discounts for prompt payment or charging interest on overdue accounts, withholding supplies, threatening to reclaim your goods, taking legal action or using debt collectors when all else fails.

By getting creditors to wait for payment you also speed up the flow because you have the use of their money. But you must always handle creditors carefully because, if you get a reputation for late payment, you may find it difficult to get credit at all. If you make an arrangement, then stick to it. Always try to agree good terms at the beginning, try for part payment of large orders or buy in small quantities, do not pay early and, if in trouble, keep talking to your creditors – silence is often taken as a sure sign of bad news.

It is one thing to realise that profit is not the same as cash flow, but it is altogether more difficult to reconcile the two figures. Let us go back to the example of Jean Young. At the end of October she projected a healthy £6804 would be in her bank account. Her projected profit statement, reproduced from the previous chapter, looked like this:

Sales		£17 200
Overheads:		
Depreciation	£2667	
Secretarial wage	330	
Transport	430	
Telephone	450	
Stationery	570	
Repairs	350	
Other	285	
Insurance	100	£ 5182
Net Profit		£12 018
Drawings		£ 6660
Profit retained in business		£ 5358

The question therefore is, what this profit retained in the business represents and how it reconciles to the increase in cash of £6704. The reconciliation is shown overleaf.

Profit statement		Cash flow		Reconciling items		Note
INCOME:		RECEIPTS:				
Sales	£17 200	Paid	£15 200	Debtor outstanding	£2 000	15
		+ VAT	£2 660	+ VAT outstanding	£350	
		Total	£17 860	Total	£2 350	2
		Capital	£2 000	Capital	£2 000	5
		VAT reclaim	£299	VAT reclaim	£299	
		Total	£20 159			
EXPENSES:		PAYMENTS:				
Sec. wage	£330	Sec. wage	£330			
Transport	£430	Transport	£430			
Telephone	£450	Telephone	£420	Tel. bill outstanding	£30	4
Stationery	£570	Stationery	£570			
Repairs	£350	Repairs	£350			
Other	£285	Other	£285			
Insurance	£100	Insurance	£100			
Depreciation	£2 667			Depreciation	£2 667	3
		Capital purch.	£2 000	Capital purchase	£2 000	3
		VAT paid	£2 310	VAT paid	£2 310	5
Drawings	£6 660	Drawings	£6 660			
Total	£11 842	Total	£13 455			
Retained	£5 358	Cash	£6 704			

Notes:

1 Jean has not received payment for all the work she has done. The outstanding debtor – a current asset of the business – is the sale invoiced in October but not expected to be paid until November. The invoice is for £2000 + £350 VAT.

2 Jean introduced capital in the form of cash of £2000. This is not part of the trading profit of the business.

3 The fixed assets of a business wear out over time and lose their value. Depreciation is a way of showing this in the profit statement. The simplest way of doing this is called 'straight-line depreciation' which writes off the asset in equal amounts over its life. For example, if there was an asset that cost £5000 and would have a working life of 5 years, at which time it could be sold off for £1000, the annual depreciation would be:

$$\frac{\text{Initial cost} - \text{final or residual value}}{\text{Working life}}$$

$$= \frac{£(5000 - 1000)}{5}$$

$$= £800$$

The value of the asset would go down each year by £800. At the end of year one it would have a value of £4200, year two £3400 and so on, until year five when it would be £1000. Depreciation does not represent any cash expenditure. That takes place when the asset is purchased. In Jean's case the depreciation is on her car and computer equipment and the actual calculation is not shown. However, the computer equipment was purchased with the £2000 she put into the business (£1701 + £299 VAT).

4 The telephone charges outstanding are an estimate of the call charges for September and October that have not yet been invoiced or paid, but are nevertheless a liability of the business. These are called accrued liabilities.

5 VAT can be complicated. A business collects it on behalf of the Customs and Excise Authority and it is therefore not part of the trading income of the business. However, it may deduct from the amount collected any VAT that it pays to suppliers, paying over only the net amount. VAT does therefore affect cash flows. Jean Young can reclaim £299 of VAT on the capital purchases. VAT is charged to customers on her sales of £17 200 is £3010 (£17 200 × 17.5%). It is, if you like, her problem that she has so far only collected £2660 leaving £350 owing still from customers. Since she has only paid £2310 to the Customs and Excise Authorities, she still owes them £700 (£3010 - £2310).

The profit statement, therefore, can tell you how the assets of the business are growing through trading. As we have seen it does not tell you about cash. It is not an exact figure since it involves elements of judgement, for example in the calculation of depreciation or an accrued liability. However, there are some other things it does not do. It does not tell you about the profitability of individual product lines. Nor does it tell you, on its own, how well you are doing. If you make a profit of £50 000 from a capital investment of £2.5 million you are making a return of only 2 per cent (£50 000 ÷ £2 500 000) and would be better off putting your money in the Building Society. It does not tell you about capital investment – for that you have to go to the balance sheet.

The balance sheet

The balance sheet is a snap shot at a point in time that shows two things:

● Where the money in a business is invested;
● Where this money came from.

Money initially comes from the capital the owner puts in (called share capital, if it is a limited company) and loans. It is increased by the profits that are retained in the business. This money is invested in the assets of the business – fixed assets; things the business means to keep such as vehicles, machinery and so on, and working capital; things the business means to sell or turn over. Working capital comprises current assets such as stock, debtors or cash less current liabilities such as creditors and accrued expenses. In other words, the balance sheet gives details of all the money retained in the business as shown in Figure 6.3.

There are two sides to a balance sheet and they always balance. If £1000 were put into a business as cash the balance sheet would balance:

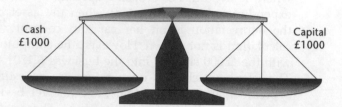

Cash
£1000

Capital
£1000

This would be shown as:

| Where money is invested: | Cash | £1000 |
| Where it came from: | Capital introduced | £1000 |

If £500 of this is spent on machinery and £500 on stock the balance sheet would not change much:

Machinery	£ 500
Stock	£ 500
	£1000
Capital introduced	£1000

Only when the business starts trading do additional funds start to be generated in the form of profit as you can see from Figure 6.3; if the stock were to be sold for cash of £1000, a profit of £500 would be made and the balance sheet would still balance:

Machinery	£500
Cash	£1000
	£1500
Capital introduced	£1000
Retained profit	£ 500
	£1500

If the balance sheet does not balance then either assets are missing or there is an arithmetical mistake.

To see how a balance sheet is constructed let us turn back to the case of Jean Young. If we were told that her car was valued at £12 130 (excluding VAT) and the computer equipment £1504 at the start of the year (both of which she introduced to the business), and that together with the other equipment she purchased for £1701 these were expected to last five years at which point only the car would have a residual value of £2000, then her depreciation charge would be:

$$\frac{(£12\,130 + £1504 + £1701) - £2000}{5} = £2667$$

And these fixed assets at the end of the year would have a value of:

$$(£12\,130 + £1504 + £1701) - £2667 = £12\,668$$

From this and the information in the previous section we could draw up her balance sheet as a sole trader at the end of October:

Fixed assets			
Car			£12 130
Computer and other equipment			3 205
			£15 335
less: Depreciation			2667
			£12 668
Current assets			
Debtors		£2 350	
Cash		6 704	
		9054	
less: **Current liabilities**			
VAT		£700	
Telephone		30	
		£730	
Net current assets			£ 8 324
Total assets			**£20 992**
Represented by:			
Capital introduced			
Cash			£ 2 000
Other assets			£13 634
			£15 634
Net profit for year			£12 018
less: Drawings			£ 6 660
Total capital			**£20 992**

As with profit statements, you can have projected balance sheets or historic balance sheets – ones that explain what actually happened. A start-up will prepare projected cash flows and profit statements, possibly balance sheets. Once the business starts running it needs to monitor how it is doing against these projections to make certain thing are going as planned. Historic profit statements and balance sheets are derived from the books of account that are used to control a business. The appendix to this chapter explains what information a business needs to keep and shows how it can be recorded.

Financial drivers

Accounting systems can provide enormous amounts of information, including full profit statements, balance sheets and details of outstanding debtors, creditors and stock-holding levels. Sometimes they produce so much information that owner-managers cannot cope and prefer to ignore it. In fact, most small firms can be controlled by monitoring, on a timely basis, just six pieces of information that tell the owner-manager different, but vital information on the performance of the business. These are called the financial drivers of small firms. They are like the instruments on a car dashboard. They tell you different things about the engine and different pieces of information are important at different times and in different circumstances. On a road with a speed restriction you watch your speedometer. When changing gear at speed you watch your rev-meter. When low on petrol your eye never strays from the petrol gauge. The financial drivers tell you all you need to know about driving the business. The six financial drivers are:

1. Cash

As we have already seen, it is vital to monitor cash. Without cash the bills cannot be paid. For a start-up or when it is in short supply cash may have to be monitored on a daily basis, but most small firms need to keep an eye on it at least on a weekly basis. Actual balances need to be compared to forecasts.

2. Sales

This tells the firm about the volume of activity it is experiencing. This should also be compared to forecasts. If sales are running ahead of forecasts, does the firm have the resources to meet these demands? Current sales may be a good indicator of future sales, but if not, then order books may also have to be monitored. It is sales that always drive cash flow and profitability. It should be monitored on a daily or weekly basis for most start-ups and at least monthly even for an established business.

3. Profit margins

In the process of setting prices in line with projected costs, the owner-manager will also be setting profit targets. These can only be achieved if the sales volume targets are met, at the appropriate prices, and costs are controlled. Profit margins give the owner manager this information. They should be compared to original forecasts and kept as high as possible. Margins probably need only be monitored on a monthly basis. It might be that it is sufficient simply to monitor contribution margin. This would be the case if fixed overheads are unlikely to change dramatically or quickly. In the example of Jean Young, there are no variable costs and in this case it is therefore more appropriate to monitor net profit margins. The net profit margin is net profit expressed as a percentage of total sales. In the previous example of Jean Young this is:

$$\frac{\text{Net profit} \times 100}{\text{Sales}}: \quad \frac{12\,018 \times 100}{17\,200} = 70\%$$

Jill and **Peter Donnely** started **Eisenegger**, a clothing retailer, from the living room of their London house. By 1998 sales were £8.7 million but it is still run from their home, now in Lancashire.

The company has 24 shops selling fashionable outdoor leisure/sports wear. The products are made in the Far East and shipped direct to the shops, cutting storage costs. The average cost of an item is £10–£15.

4. Margin of safety or break-even

Break-even is an important reference point and we shall be looking at this important concept in more detail in the next section. However, as a business grows the break-even point is likely to increase. That is a fact of business. In order to grow most businesses must, at some point, take on more fixed overheads. This increases the break-even point. What is important is not so much the absolute level, but rather how much above it the firm is operating. The margin of safety is a measure of how far sales are above break-even, expressed as a percentage of total sales. In the example of Jean Young, because she has no variable costs, this happens to be the same as the net profit margin and is:

$$\frac{(\text{Total sales} - \text{Break-even sales}) \times 100}{\text{Total sales}} : \quad \frac{(17\,200 - 5182) \times 100}{17\,200} = 70\%$$

The higher the margin of safety the better, because the safer the firm is in terms of maintaining its profitability should sales suddenly decline. Margin of safety is therefore a measure of operating risk. However, it reflects a number of factors; level of sales, ability to maintain contribution margins and ability to control fixed overheads. It is therefore a powerful piece of information and needs to be checked monthly.

The margin of safety is of great interest to bank managers. If you started up in business manufacturing, say, umbrellas and anticipate sales reaching 2000 per month shortly after the factory opens, at this level of sales your margin of safety will be 10 per cent. A bank would be worried about granting a loan with such a small margin of safety. They know from bitter experience that sales forecasts, particularly for new ventures, are notoriously unreliable. On a risky lending proposition most bank managers would be looking for a margin of safety of at least 50 per cent. However, be aware that if sales were actually to start falling and the company approached its break-even point, a prudent businessman would try to cut their fixed costs – particularly discretionary ones that they control – and thus reduce the break-even point and perhaps restore the margin of safety. In other words the break-even point, and therefore the margin of safety, are not set in concrete, they can be engineered to minimise the risks.

5. Productivity

For most firms the single largest and most important expense they face is their wage costs. It therefore needs to be controlled carefully. However, as with break-even, as a firm grows its wage costs are likely to increase. Wages are therefore best measured in relation to the productivity that they generate. For many firms this is most easily measured by the simple percentage of wages to sales. Often there are industry norms that can be used to measure productivity. For example, in the licence trade the benchmark for this is 20 per cent. Wages of bar staff should be about 20 per cent of sales. If higher, the pub is over-staffed, if lower, it is under-staffed – a crude but simple and effective measure that needs to be checked weekly or monthly.

6. Debtor or stock turnover

Similarly most firms will have one important current asset on their balance sheet that represents over 50 per cent of their total assets. For a service business this will be debtors. For a retail business it will be stocks. For a manufacturing business it could be both. This asset needs to be monitored on a monthly basis. However, as with previous figures, as the firm grows it is likely to increase, so what is important is not its absolute size but rather its relationship to the level of activity or sales of a business. Two statistics are widely used:

1. Debtor turnover: $\dfrac{\text{Sales}}{\text{Debtors}}$

If sales were £120 000 per year and debtors stood at £20 000, debtor turnover would be 6. This means debtors turnover six times a year. In other words, debtors pay after every 2 months. This can be compared to the plan, the terms of trade and the industry norm to judge whether debtors are being controlled effectively. If they are not, the firm will be having problems with its cash flow.

2. Stock turnover: $\dfrac{\text{Sales}}{\text{Stocks}}$

If sales were £120 000 and stocks stood at £30 000, stock turnover would be 4, meaning that stock turns over four times a year, equivalent to every 3 months.

Chris Hutt believed that rigorous, centrally applied financial controls were the key to profitable operation at **Unicorn Inns**. He appointed Geoff Jones, aged 30, as Finance Director in 1993 on a part-time basis to provide the Board with in-house financial management skills. As part of Chris's emphasis on control, the company ensures:

- Daily checks on cash takings and bankings, carried out by telephone and direct computer input to the company's bank account.
- Weekly sales and profit performance measured within 16 hours of each week ending. Results are reviewed immediately by management and priorities for action identified.
- Weekly stocktaking to ensure there were no stock losses and gross margin targets were attained.
- Labour costs, as a percentage of sales, monitored through monthly management accounts, mailed to all affected parties no later than 10 working days after each period.

All of these factors were linked to targets set for each pub manager and tied into their bonus scheme.

Chris believed that two of the key pieces of financial information any growing business needs to monitor are the break-even point and the margin of safety. He monitored this data monthly and above his desk he kept a graph showing sales against break-even point. (The difference between the two is the margin of safety.) It makes interesting reading, showing the gradual improvement in the margin of safety because of the high margins and low fixed costs as Unicorn Inns rolled-out the Newt & Cucumber concept.

. . . to be continued

This can be compared to the plan and the industry norm to judge whether stock is being controlled effectively. If not, the firm is likely to be having problems with its cash flow.

It is important for a growing firm to have appropriate and relevant financial information that can be produced promptly and on a timely basis, at an acceptable cost. The financial drivers give the owner-manager simple, understandable information. They can be reproduced on a single piece of paper. They provide the headline information on how the business is doing. If they disclose a problem then more information might be needed to decide on the appropriate course of action. For example, if debtors are not being controlled effectively only a detailed list of debtors and when the amounts owing were due for payment (called an *aged listing of debtors*) will provide the information needed so that action can be taken.

Break-even

Figure 6.4 reproduces the familiar Cost–profit–volume chart introduced in the last chapter. However, the simplified profit–volume chart in Figure 6.5 is far easier to interpret and use and emphasises the two most important financial principles of start-up:

1 **Keep fixed overheads as low as possible**. The lower the fixed cost AB, the lower the break-even point and therefore the lower the risk. If fixed costs AB can be lowered, line AC moves parallel and to the left in Figure 6.5 – and therefore the lower the risk. High fixed operating costs are called high *operating gearing* or *leverage*. One way of measuring this is as the proportion of total costs represented by fixed overhead costs. This percentage should be kept as low as possible, particularly at start-up. Remember, higher fixed assets also mean higher depreciation charges and therefore higher fixed overheads. Investment in fixed assets can therefore increase a business's break-even point.

High borrowings – perhaps to finance investment in fixed assets – mean high interest costs, which are

David Speakman is a serial entrepreneur. But when his second business, a restaurant, failed losing him £500 000 he decided to list the prime attributes of the ideal business. He wrote: 'no fixed labour costs, commission only sales, large volume and low overheads'.

He was already running a small travel agency with a turnover of £548 000, but the experience of failure decided him to re-jig it. The result was **Travel Counsellors**, a firm that four years later had grown to a turnover of £16 million in 1998. The firm has a small head office with some 20 people handling marketing, billing and supplies. But it relies mainly on some 50 travelling counsellors equipped with portable computers and mobile phones who visit customers homes mapping out itineraries and 30 online counsellors working from their own homes, fielding telephone and Teletext enquiries and arranging visits to customers.

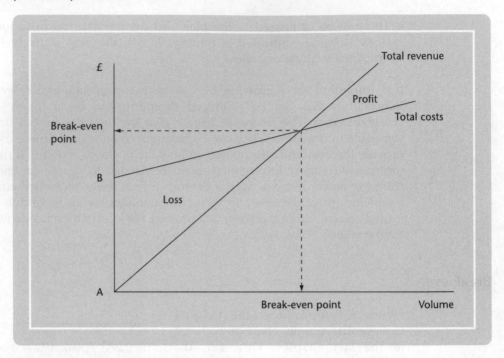

Figure 6.4 Cost–profit–volume chart

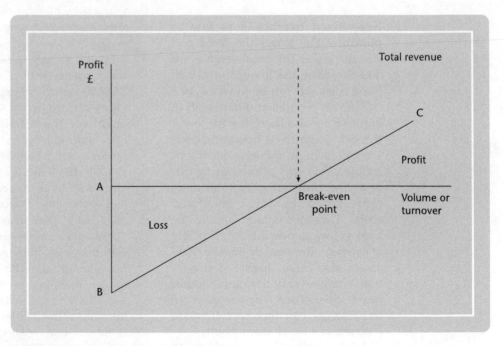

Figure 6.5 Profit–volume chart

fixed and over which there is little discretion. If turnover goes down, interest payments stay the same. Indeed, sometimes interest rates, and therefore interest payments, can go up when turnover and therefore profit goes down. This is the classic situation that happens when interest rates go up in order to decrease overall demand in the economy. The small firm faces a squeeze with higher costs and lower turnover. High financing costs are called high *financial gearing* or *leverage*.

Businesses with high operating or financial gearing (or both) need to make certain they achieve their sales targets. They have very little day-to-day influence over their fixed costs therefore their business imperative is to attract a sufficient volume of customers – and that is about marketing and sales. They can afford to offer special price deals if their margins are high, so as to attract different market segments at different prices. For example, running a train from London to Manchester incurs mainly fixed costs and the train operator must

Ed White was made redundant by Andersen Consulting in 1991, so he decided to set up his own consulting firm, **Ed White & Co**, specialising in IT consultancy for the banking and motor industries. Clients of the Buckinghamshire firm include Lloyds TSB, Mercedes-Benz and VW.

In 1998 sales were £4.3 million, of which 50 per cent was to mainland Europe. The interesting point about the company, however, is that it employs only 12 full-time staff, preferring to remain 'lean and flexible' by employing 90 freelance consultants.

Flitwick Manor Hotel is a country house hotel in Bedfordshire. With a turnover of £922 000 per annum, it has high fixed costs of £426 000, of which 34 per cent represents permanent staff and 20 per cent loan interest; 82 per cent of its variable costs represents consumables such as food and wine. It lets out rooms and sells food and drink and therefore the average contribution margin can be used to calculate its break-even point:

Turnover (ex VAT)	£922 000	
Total variable cost	£326 000	
Contribution	£596 000	64%
Fixed costs	£426 000	
Profit	£170 000	

$$\text{Break-even} \quad \frac{£426\,000}{0.64} = £666\,000$$

Margin of safety = 27.8%

With the high fixed costs and high contribution margin it is important that Flitwick keeps its beds and restaurant full. It therefore spends heavily on promotion. It also has a luncheon club, offering cheap lunches to regular customers, who also receive regular promotions from the hotel.

fill the train as full as possible. They do this by offering a range of fares with all sorts of different terms and conditions or facilities to a range of different customers. In that way a business man might pay eight times as much as the off-peak student traveller on the same train and yet not feel that they are getting a bad deal.

As we saw in the previous chapter, the lowest price at which a product or service can be offered is its variable cost. Above this every £1 is extra contribution to fixed costs or, if the business is operating above its break-even point, extra profit. If, in addition to high fixed costs, a firm faces low variable costs, then it is able to offer its product or service at a very low price in order to attract marginal business – extra business it would not otherwise have. So, for example, our railway company may offer a £1 special offer fare, possibly linked to other conditions or purchases, and would still make £1 extra profit. The only problem with this is that, unless you are able to make this product or service sufficiently different from the normal product or service you offer, all your regular customers might be attracted to it and sales might never be high enough to meet fixed costs.

Marginal business can be very attractive, particularly to businesses with high fixed costs, such as railways, airlines and hotels. The railway has to run its trains to a predetermined timetable and so the marginal cost of an extra passenger is very, very low – hence all the special schemes and discounts to encourage people to travel on the off-peak services. Standby tickets for air flights are a similar case, as are weekend bargain breaks in hotels. The danger, of course, is that all the customers end up wanting cut-price fares and you end up not making a profit at all.

2 **Keep contribution margins as high as possible**. Do not sell just on price, find a differential advantage. Higher margins increase the angle of line AC, pivoting it in an anticlockwise direction about A, and lowering the break-even point. Once past the break-even point every £1 of sales revenue yields even higher profits. However, high contribution margins generally mean high differential advantage.

As its name implies, **Penforth Sofa Beds** makes sofa beds. Selling to large retail outlets, its margins are squeezed and, despite low fixed costs of £102 000, it makes a contribution margin of only 17 per cent on a typical sofa bed.

Selling price (ex VAT)	£200	
Variable cost	£166	
Contribution	£ 34	17%

Break-even $\dfrac{£102\,000}{0.17} = £600\,000$

78 per cent of the variable costs represent materials and 12 per cent represent piecework labour. With this cost structure and because Penforth cannot influence the price it charges, it is vital that all variable costs are tightly controlled. Materials must be sourced from the lowest cost provider and labour costs kept down to a minimum.

. . . to be continued

Businesses with low contribution margins cannot afford to cut their prices. What is more, their business imperative must be to control these high variable costs. For them, a 1 per cent reduction in the contribution margin can have disastrous effects on their profitability, so cost control and cost minimisation is a vital day-to-day activity for the owner-manager.

Decision-making

Break-even analysis is a powerful tool. As we have seen, it gives you the tools you need to make decisions about pricing and how the finances of a business should be structured. These are basic, important principles. However, it also gives you the tools to answer four other sorts of important business questions:

1 'How well is the business doing?' questions;
2 'What if?' questions;
3 'Which product or service is more profitable?' questions;
4 'Where should I focus limited resources? questions.

> When **Anita Roddick** opened the first **Body Shop** in 1976 her husband – Gordon, an accountant – left to ride a horse from Buenos Aires to New York. He left her with one piece of advice: 'You've got to take over £300 a week to cover your overheads and be able to invest in more stock. If you don't, give it all up and come over with the kids and join me in Lima.' Essentially, this was the first Body Shop's break-even point – which was easily exceeded. Gordon came back from South America early and the rest is history.
>
> *. . . to be continued*

How well is the business doing?

The break-even point is a benchmark, above which the business starts to make profit. But if you know the break-even point and the contribution margin, it is very easy to *estimate* the level of profitability – given the level of sales – without needing to resort to an accounting system. The formula to use is:

$$\text{Profit} = \frac{(\text{Sales} - \text{Break-even sales})}{\text{Contribution margin}}$$

So, we saw in the last chapter that, when Jean Young had sales of £17 200, her profit was £12 018. This can be calculated simply and quickly using the formula above:

$$\frac{(£17\,200 - £5182)}{1} = £12\,018$$

Similarly, if break-even were £500 a week and contribution margin were 40 per cent, at sales of £1500 the profit would be:

$$\frac{(£1500 - £500)}{0.40} = £400$$

What if?

The most asked question in business, particularly for a start-up, is 'what-if?' What if I invest in a van? What if I place that expensive advertisement in the newspaper? Contribution analysis can help answer the question by giving information about the additional sales needed to make sufficient profit to recoup the cost. This may not make the decision about what to do, but it does provide invaluable information on which to base it. So, for example, if the advertisement costs £1000 and the contribution margin is 40 per cent, the extra sales needed would be £2500. This can be calculated using a simple formula:

$$\text{Extra sales needed}$$

$$= \frac{\text{Increase in fixed costs}}{\text{Contribution margin}}$$

$$= \frac{£1000}{0.40}$$

$$= £2500$$

Penforth Sofa Beds sold between 4000 and 5000 sofas a year, giving it a turnover of £800 000–£1 million and a profit of £34 000–£68 000. **John Douglas**, the owner-manager, was also the company salesman. He often thought about hiring another salesman. If he paid a basic salary of £15 000 with a 5% commission, to justify hiring he would have to increase sales by:

$$\frac{£15\,000}{(0.17 - 0.05)} = £125\,000$$

$$= 625 \text{ sofas}$$

Since he was far from certain he could get a good salesman for this salary package, and because in a good year the company was pretty near to full capacity, so far he had decided against trying to recruit anybody.

Contribution analysis can also be used to answer 'what if' questions about price. Suppose that a competitor to a business selling skateboards at £20 each starts price-cutting, selling equivalent boards at just £16. The problem is to decide whether to match the price reduction, or to seek a more profitable alternative strategy. Look at the calculation below. Column 2 shows the effect on profits if prices are maintained with the result that there is a one-third fall in sales. Column 3 shows the effect on profits if prices are reduced in order to maintain the level of sales.

	1 Current position	2 Competitor lowers price & we hold price	3 Competitor lowers price & we lower price
Price	£20	£20	£16
Variable cost	£12	£12	£12
Contribution	£8	£8	£4
Sales volume	£ 3 000	£ 2 000	£3000
Total contribution	£24 000	£16 000	£12 000
Fixed costs	£16 000	£16 000	£16 000
Profit	£ 8 000	£ –	£(4000)

As we see from column 3, the business will actually lose money (£4000 per month) if it follows the price lead of the competitor. If it maintains its prices, the position is rather better, although it will still not make a profit (column 2). However, there may also be the opportunity in this situation to reduce overheads to reflect the lower sales, or even to spend more on advertising to persuade customers that the board is better and worth £20. Despite the evidence that an analysis of this kind often reveals, many companies automatically cut prices as a 'knee-jerk' reaction to competitive pressures, without appreciating the real costs or evaluating the alternatives.

Which product or service is more profitable?

For any business producing more than one product or service the question as to which is the more profitable, and therefore the one which is to have its sales 'pushed' hardest, is an interesting one, the answer to which is not as straightforward as you might think. However, it is a fundamental question in deciding upon the mix of sales.

Suppose the skateboard company can produce three versions; 'Standard', 'All-terrain' and 'Freestyle', and the costs and margins are as follows:

	Standard	All-terrain	Freestyle
Price	£25	£32	£50
Variable cost	£10	£16	£30
Contribution	£15	£16	£20
Contribution margin	60%	50%	40%

This shows that Freestyle gives the highest £ contribution per board, but that Standard has the best contribution margin. So which is the one that the firm should encourage the sales of most? The answer depends on the market that the different products are selling to.

Let us say that the total market for skateboards is limited and selling more of one reduces demand for the others. In this case, as can be seen below, for every £500 spent the company can make a bigger profit from selling the Standard board, with its higher contribution margin.

	Standard	All-terrain	Freestyle
Price	£25	£32	£50
Variable cost	£10	£16	£30
Contribution	£15	£16	£20
Contribution margin	60%	50%	40%
Contribution from £500 sales	£300	£250	£200

However, where the products or markets are independent, that is if the Freestyle board sold to one customer, the Standard to another and the All-terrain to a third, then selling one does not reduce the budget available for the others. In which case, sell as much as you can of the Freestyle board first, moving onto the All-terrain board and finally the Standard board.

The general rule therefore is, where you are selling products or services which compete with each other in the same market, push the sales of those products which have the highest contribution margin. Where you are selling independent products which do not compete against each other, first sell the items that give the highest £ per unit contribution.

In the case of the customer with a limited budget, the firm has to take account of a limiting factor, the amount of money available to buy their products. This is a special case of the situation considered next.

Where should I focus limited resources?

All businesses face some form of limiting factor. For example, think about possible constraints which might limit the launch of a new product or service. Apart from the obvious constraint of demand, there can be several other factors that limit an organisation's ability to expand, such as a lack of skilled labour, limited machine capacity, shortage of raw materials, lack of management expertise, or shortage of money. Retailers often regard available shelf space as being their main limiting factor, while for a fast growing manufacturing business the limiting factor may well be the availability of cash to finance their working capital needs.

Where a limiting factor exists, then a business will maximise its profits by making the best use of the limiting resource. For example, retailers need to make the best use of their available shelf space.

Assume that the skateboard company has a shortage of machinery which reflects itself in availability of machine hours. It needs to decide how to use the machine hours available to maximise its profits. This is done by looking at the contribution per machine hour:

	Standard	All-terrain	Freestyle
Price	£25	£32	£50
Variable cost	£10	£16	£30
Contribution	£15	£16	£20
Machine hours needed per 100 boards	1	0.5	2
Contribution per machine hour	£1500	£3200	£1000

As we see, the contribution per machine hour is greatest from the All-terrain boards. Every 1 hour of machine work produces 200 boards and yields £3200 contribution. Therefore, if machine hours really is the key limiting resource, they should produce All-terrain boards first, until demand is satisfied, followed by Standard boards, until demand is satisfied, and make up any unfilled capacity finally with the Freestyle board.

The general rule, where a limiting factor exists, is that the business should give priority to those products or services (or to those customers and markets) which generate the highest contribution per unit of limiting factor.

As always, the real world doesn't behave quite like a mathematical formula. If a supermarket filled its shelves entirely with small, high margin items it might find it had a lot of dissatisfied customers unable to find the bread, sugar and washing powder. Similarly, a manufacturer may prefer to sell to reliable large customers rather than to take greater risks selling to small traders, even though the contribution per sale may be higher in the latter case.

Another practical problem when a company has a range of products, each with different contribution margins is interpreting just what the break-even point means. The calculation is easy. It does not change. But what does this mean in terms of the sales mix? The answer is that the mix of sales at break-even is identical to the mix of sales that yields the average contribution margin. The problem is that if the sales mix changes, so too does the break-even point.

If the fixed costs for our skateboard company were £190 000 and the sales were as detailed below, producing an average contribution margin of 50 per cent, we could go on to calculate the break-even point using the usual formula:

	Standard	**All-terrain**	**Freestyle**		**Total**
Volume	8000	2000	4000		
Price	£25	£32	£50	Turnover	£464 000
Variable cost	£10	£16	£30	Variable cost	£232 000
Contribution	£15	£16	£20		
Contribution	£120 000	£32 000	£80 000		£232 000
Margin	60%	50%	40%		(50%)
				Fixed costs	£190 000
				Profit	£42 000

$$\text{Break-even} = \frac{£190\,000}{0.50} = £380\,000$$

The problem is that this break-even point only holds if the mix of sales always remains the same, that is for every eight Standard boards sold we always sell two All-terrain boards and four Freestyle boards. Should the mix change, then the break-even point will change.

Notwithstanding this, an understanding of which products, customers or markets generate the best contributions, and of the optimal way to utilise limited resources, can make a significant difference to the overall profitability of the business. You will be in a much better position to optimise the sales mix if you know which products are most profitable. It is also essential to know the break-even point, together with its limitations and manage it in the appropriate way.

Summary

Cash flow is the lifeblood of a business. You can be making a profit and still run out of cash which means that bills go unpaid. Start-ups face the danger of Death Valley; they need to chart its length and depth by producing a cash flow forecast like **Jean Young** and using it to plan to meet their financing needs.

Money flows around the business and it is important to make sure it keeps flowing as quickly as possible. That means making sure debtors pay as quickly as possible – choosing credit customers carefully, invoicing promptly, setting credit limits and following up promptly on late payment. Stocks should be kept to a minimum, buying only the minimum needed, and all available supplier credit is taken.

Profit represents the growth in the assets of a business that comes about through trading. Profit can be represented in any asset, not just cash. The balance sheet is a snap shot at a point in time that tells you where the money in a business comes from and where it is invested. Fixed assets, such as equipment and vehicles, are things the business means to keep. Working capital, which comprises current assets such as stocks and debtors and current liabilities such as creditors, is the thing the business means to sell or turn over.

Most businesses, like **Unicorn Inns**, can be controlled by monitoring six important financial drivers on a regular and timely basis. These drivers are:

1　Cash;
2　Sales;
3　Profit margins;
4　Margin of safety;
5　Productivity;
6　Debtor or stock turnover.

Companies such as **Eisenegger**, **Travel Counsellors** and **Ed White & Co.** understand that it is vital to keep fixed overhead costs as low as possible, particularly at start-up. It is also important to keep contribution margins as high as possible. Whilst **Flitwick Manor Hotel** had high operating and financial gearing, it also had high contribution margins. When operating gearing is high it is important that sales targets are met. A high contribution margin gives some discretion on pricing, allowing very low prices to be charged based upon the low marginal cost involved. However, this should only be tried when differential pricing – charging different prices to different customers – is practical. **Penforth Sofa Beds** had low fixed costs but also low contribution margins. Low contribution margins make it imperative that variable costs are closely monitored. They also make it impossible to drop prices any further.

Contribution and break-even analysis are powerful tools. They tell you about the risk the business faces and the imperatives for management. As Anita Roddick found out when she set up the first **Body Shop**, break-even is a benchmark above which a business starts to make profit. If you know how much above your break-even you are operating at, and your contribution margin, then it is easy to estimate your profitability.

Contribution analysis can also be used to answer 'what if?' type questions such as the question for **Penforth Sofa Beds** as to whether to recruit a new salesman or not. It tells you the value of extra sales needed to cover the increased fixed costs. Contribution analysis tells you which products or services are most profitable and, when some critical resource is limited, which to push the sales of. All in all, contribution analysis is a vital tool for the owner-manager.

■ Essays and discussion topics

1　Why is cash flow not the same as profit?
2　What would you do to ensure your start-up makes it through Death Valley?
3　There is no such thing as certainty, therefore there is no point in trying to forecast the future. Discuss.

4 The most important three pieces of advice for a start-up are:

- Think customer;
- Plan ahead;
- Don't run out of cash.

Discuss.

5 Profit is just something that an accountant constructs. The amount of profit depends on the assumptions the accountant decides to make. Therefore profit is not objective and means nothing. Discuss.

6 Why do you think owner-managers are not interested in accounting and control?

7 Do you think computer-based accounting systems make the task of controlling a small business easier?

8 What steps would you take in your start-up business to ensure debtors are kept to a minimum?

9 What steps would you take in your start-up business to ensure stocks are kept to a minimum?

10 Do you really think you can control a business by monitoring six financial drivers?

11 Entrepreneurs make decisions by instinct and not by using financial analysis. Discuss.

12 Cost-profit-volume analysis reflects the way owner-managers think. Discuss.

13 The margin of safety tells you about the long term viability of a business, the risks it faces and the earning quality of each £ of turnover. Discuss.

14 Behind every successful entrepreneur there is an accountant. Discuss.

● Exercises and assignments

1 Put a tick in the appropriate box (sometimes more than one) for the direct effects of each of these transactions:

	Increase cash	Increase profit	Decrease cash	Decrease profit
(1) Sales of stock on credit				
(2) Sale of old fixed assets				
(3) Purchase of fixed assets				
(4) Purchase of stock for cash				
(5) Payment of creditors				
(6) Payment of wages				
(7) Payment of dividends				
(8) Receipts from debtors				
(9) Issue of new shares				
(10) Receipt of loan				
(11) Repayment of loan				
(12) Payment of interest				

2 Work out the straight-line depreciation plus the recorded value of the assets each year for an asset originally costing £4000 using the following assumptions:

	Life expectancy	Residual value
A	5 years	£1000
B	8 years	£400
C	10 years	nil

3 Check your understanding of how balance sheets are drawn up. Put a tick in the appropriate box (sometimes more than one) for the direct effects of each of these transactions.

	Increase cash	Decrease cash	Increase other assets	Decrease other assets	Increase profit	Decrease profit	Increase liabilities	Decrease liabilities
(1) Purchase of fixed asset for cash	☐	☐	☐	☐	☐	☐	☐	☐
(2) Sale of fixed asset at balance sheet value for cash	☐	☐	☐	☐	☐	☐	☐	☐
(3) Sale of fixed assets for more than balance sheet value for cash	☐	☐	☐	☐	☐	☐	☐	☐
(4) Sale of fixed asset for less than balance sheet value for cash	☐	☐	☐	☐	☐	☐	☐	☐
(5) Depreciation of fixed asset	☐	☐	☐	☐	☐	☐	☐	☐
(6) Increase in value of freehold land	☐	☐	☐	☐	☐	☐	☐	☐
(7) Advance payment of rates	☐	☐	☐	☐	☐	☐	☐	☐
(8) Receipt of advance payment of subscription	☐	☐	☐	☐	☐	☐	☐	☐
(9) Write-off bad debt	☐	☐	☐	☐	☐	☐	☐	☐
(10) Estimate of telephone charges not yet received	☐	☐	☐	☐	☐	☐	☐	☐

4 To check your knowledge of accounting, complete the following short test. It is not comprehensive, but should give you an indication of your understanding. Tick the appropriate box to show that you agree or disagree with a statement; if you do not understand any of the technical terms, tick the 'Don't know' column.

	Agree	Don't know	Disagree
(1) The balance sheet tells you how much a business is worth.	☐	☐	☐
(2) All the fixed assets of a business are shown at their market value.	☐	☐	☐
(3) By depreciating the fixed assets of a business, you ensure that you have sufficient cash to replace them at the end of their life.	☐	☐	☐
(4) All capital is good; therefore you want as much working capital as possible.	☐	☐	☐
(5) It is always better to borrow money from the bank than to seek further equity, perhaps from other shareholders.	☐	☐	☐
(6) Loans are repaid out of accumulated profits.	☐	☐	☐
(7) Reserves represent the cash the business has accumulated over its life.	☐	☐	☐
(8) A company that is making profits can always pay its bills.	☐	☐	☐
(9) Any company making higher profits than another is doing better than that company.	☐	☐	☐
(10) To understand accounting you have to be able to do double-entry book-keeping	☐	☐	☐

5 An engineering company can produce an additional 1500 units of either valve A or valve B per year. The additional fixed costs to be invested to achieve this production would be £15 000 for A and £20 000 for B. A sells for £35 and variable costs per valve total £15 (contribution £20 per valve). Valve B sells for £36 and variable costs per valve total £11 (contribution £25 per valve). Which valve should it produce?

6 Given the data below, which products would you 'push' the sales of?

	A	B	C	D	E
Selling price per unit	£1.30	£1.00	£1.00	£1.00	£1.70
Variable costs per unit	£0.68	£0.49	£0.66	£0.68	£1.80
Contribution per unit	£0.62	£0.51	£0.34	£0.32	(0.10)
Contribution margin	48%	51%	34%	32%	NA

7 If you only had 2000 machine hours which product would you 'push' the sale of?

	A	B	C	D
Selling price per unit	£1.30	£1.00	£1.00	£1.00
Variable costs per unit	£0.68	£0.49	£0.66	£0.68
Contribution per unit	£0.62	£0.51	£0.34	£0.32
Contribution margin	48%	51%	34%	32%
Product time per 1000 units (hours)	2	1	4	2

8 If each line had limited sales potential how much of each would you actually produce?

	A	B	C	D
Contribution per unit	£0.62	£0.51	£0.34	£0.32
Contribution margin	48%	51%	34%	32%
Product time per 1000 units (hours)	2	1	4	2
Contribution per 1000 units per hr	£310	£510	£85	£160
Ranking	2	1	4	3
Sales potential (1000 units)	250	1000	750	500

9 How much profit would you make if fixed costs were £450 000?

10 Building on the previous exercises, what is the break-even point for the company, given the final outcome of your analysis?

£000s	A	B	D	Total
Sales	£325	£1000	£250	£1575
Variable costs	£170	£ 490	£170	£ 830
Contribution	£155	£ 510	£ 80	£ 745
Fixed costs				£ 450
Profit				£ 295

11 What does this mean in terms of the sales mix?

12 What happens if this mix changes?

13 A company has come to you for a £10 000 loan to finance its expansion. Currently its contribution margin is 60 per cent and this is expected to be maintained. Annual repayments of the loan, including interest, amount to £1200. How much extra sales turnover does the firm have to make to cover the annual loan repayments?

14 A company currently sells 200 000 units at a selling price of £25 and a variable cost of £15. Fixed costs are £1 400 000. It is currently considering three business strategies:

   (1) Halve the price and double the sales volume;
   (2) Drop price by £5 and increase sales by 20%;
   (3) Increase price by £5 and allow sales to fall by 20%.

   Which would you recommend?

15 ABC Co. produce plastic bottles. The company could fit another bottle-making machine in its factory without increasing existing overheads. However, it is not sure it can sell all of its production. The machine would cost £20 000 and last 5 years, and therefore depreciation would be £4000 per year. The machine operator would be paid £8500 per year. Materials and other variable costs would come to £0.15 per 100 bottles, and they could be sold at £0.65 per 100 bottles.

   (1) Calculate the breakdown point;
   (2) Calculate the profit on sales of:
        (a) 3 million bottles.
        (b) 4 million bottles.

16 Irene runs a hair salon and is considering opening late to offer 'half-price' hair cuts, perms and so on, to pensioners. The additional 28 hours opening time will be staffed using three girls working for £3.00 an hour. Each girl will handle 2 customers an hour and each customer will pay £10.00. Other additional variable costs come to £9.00 per hour. Is the idea worth doing?

17 A special Mediterranean Sea Cruise for a liner costs £250 000 to undertake in terms of staff, fuel, depreciation and so on. Each passenger has additional variable costs (food, linen and so on) of £200. The price for a ticket is £700 and one week before departure 500 tickets have been sold, 200 tickets remain unsold. What price can be charged for them?

18 Check your understanding of the appendix to this chapter. Using the Accounting Worksheet below, record the following transactions and draw up the balance sheet and profit statement.

- A £1000 cash from share capital received. £500 cash from bank loan received;
- B Fixed assets purchased on credit for £1100;
- C Stock purchased on credit for £550;
- D Some stock sold on credit for £500;
- E Pay creditors £1250;
- F Receive £1250 from debtors;
- G Pay cash expenses (no invoices) of £30;
- H Depreciation of fixed assets charged at £110;
- I Stock at the end of the period is £350;
- J Repair work to the value of £40 undertaken, still awaiting invoice.

19 Arrange for a presentation of the Sage accounting system. Visit the company's website on www.sage.com and investigate the range of packages available.

⬤ Accounting worksheet

| | Assets £ | | | | = | Capital £ | | Liabilities £ | |
	Cash	Debtors	Stocks	Fixed Assets		Shares	Profit	Bank Loan	Creditors
A					=				
A					=				
B					=				
C					=				
D					=				
E					=				
F					=				
G					=				
H					=				
I					=				
J					=				
					=				

⬤ Start-up exercise

Undertake steps 10 and 11 of the start-up exercise at the back of the book.

Appendix Information for control

The Companies Acts require that all companies keep certain accounting records to show and explain the companies' transactions. This involves keeping the following:

1 A record of day-to-day cash receipts and expenditures;
2 A record of assets and liabilities;
3 A statement of stock at the end of each financial year, and a statement of stocktaking from which it was prepared;
4 Except for ordinary retail trade, statements of all goods sold and purchased showing the goods and the buyers and sellers.

Whilst sole traders and partnerships are not required formally to keep all these records, they would be well advised to do so. After all, without adequate accounting information it is impossible to monitor the performance of the business.

It is reckless to run a business without any accounting records and yet many smaller firms do just that. The simplest accounting system can be very cheap and relatively easy to operate. It can provide regular and timely financial information. As the size of a business grows, so too does the complexity of the task of controlling it. However, computers have come to the rescue providing an increasingly cheap way of processing a lot of data. Nevertheless, any system, manual or computerised, is only as good as the information entered into it. If you put garbage in, then you will get garbage out.

Let's start with the simplest accounting system, where the only accounting record is a cash book showing receipts and payments. This is the barest essential for any business since they need cash to pay the bills and, without a record of it, they might have nothing in the bank account to pay them. Cash books take many forms. The simplest comprise four columns:

- One column to describe the transaction;
- One column to record amounts deposited;
- One column to record amounts spent;
- The final column recording the resulting balance in the account.

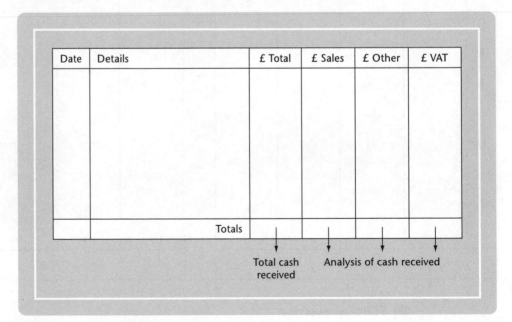

Figure 6.6 Cash receipts book

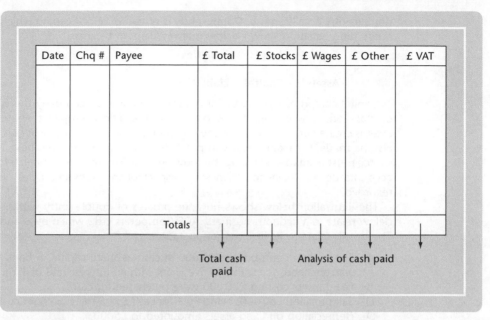

Figure 6.7 Cash payments book

Only slightly more complicated are the ones that separate out receipts and payments and provide some detailed analysis of where the cash came from and where it is going. An example of this given in Figure 6.6 and 6.7. Typically, the cash book records the cash held in the bank rather than actual cash on hand in the business. The balance in the bank is the difference between total receipts and total payments, plus or minus any amounts brought forward in the account. As you might expect, this does not always agree to the balance shown on your bank statement as being in your account. This is because transactions may be recorded in your accounting system at different times to the bank's. These are called 'timing differences'. However, other differences could arise because of recording errors, bank errors – or theft! Because of these differences, it is important that any cash book is reconciled with the bank statement regularly.

Most firms will also have some cash, however small an amount, actually on hand. This is normally called 'petty cash'. The easiest way to control and account for this if it is a small amount is through what is called an 'imprest system'. You start with a cash file with, say, £100 in it. Every time cash is needed to purchase something the cash is replaced with either an invoice or a properly authorised petty cash voucher describing what was purchased. At any time that total value of cash plus invoices plus vouchers will always be £100. At the end of every week or month, or simply when the cash runs out, the vouchers are replaced with cash from the bank account and the invoices and vouchers written up in the normal way. If the volume of cash transactions is too great for this system then a separate cash book for the cash on hand will have to be kept.

Cash books can form part of accounting systems and all accounting systems are based on the idea of double entry book-keeping. You will recall the earlier comment that the balance sheet should balance. This means that the idea of liabilities and assets balancing may be viewed as being an equation. If one part of such a balancing equation were to change, so another corresponding change should be recorded to ensure that the equation, and thus the balance sheet, remains in balance. For example, if the asset cash decreases because a bill is paid, so the liability of creditors should also be reduced. This leads to the idea of double entry book-keeping. Double entry is system of book-keeping which ensures that the accounting equation shown below is always kept in balance:

Capital = Assets − Liabilities

or

Assets = Capital + Liabilities

Capital comprises the capital introduced – in a limited company this is by way of share capital – and retained profit. The process of recording is simple: every time an additional asset is created or purchased for the organisation, recognition of where it came from must also be made. For example, if you put £1000 in cash into the business, recognition of its source must be made, let us say, by showing £1000 increase in capital. If for any reason the accounts do not 'balance', then some aspect of the transaction has not been properly recorded.

The illustration below shows how the process of double entry works. The transactions below relate to a fictitious business, ACE Computers Ltd., which buys and resells software. The details relate to its first year of operations.

A   The owners contributed £25 000 in cash as share capital. A bank loan for £10 000 was obtained, repayable in five years with an interest rate of 10% per annum.
B   Fixed assets costing £20 000 were purchased for cash.
C   Sales totalled £60 000, being 50% for cash and 50% to account customers on credit.
D   Depreciation on fixed assets amounted to £5000.
E   Sundry operating expenses totalled £10 000 of which £1000 remained unpaid at the year end.
F   Loan interest of £1000 was paid.
G   Stock costing £25 000 was purchased on account.
H   Trade creditors were paid £20 000 in cash.
I   Debtors paid £25 000 in cash.
J   Stocks at the end of the year had cost £10 000.

The details above are to be used to construct an accounting worksheet for ACE Computers, shown in Figure 6.8.

Explanation of ACE Computers worksheet

A   Cash of £25 000 is obtained as capital from the owners. Cash increases by £25 000 on the assets side; on the liabilities side capital increases by £25 000 and the accounting equation remains in balance. A bank loan of £10 000 is obtained. Cash increases by £10 000 on the assets side with the bank loan, a liability, increasing by the same amount.
B   Fixed assets are purchased for £20 000. Cash decreases on the assets side by £20 000. This is one asset being exchanged for another so fixed asset increases by £20 000
C   Here, the sales figures are recorded. On the assets side, cash goes up by £30 000 (50 per cent of the sales for the year) with debtors also increasing by £30 000 (the other 50 per cent). All of the £60 000 is recognised as a sale even though some of the cash from debtors may not have been received. This is an important accounting idea – sales can be recorded as sales and thus increase profits whether or not the cash inflow has taken place or not. In this case the increase of £60 000 on the assets side of the accounting equation is balanced by an addition to Profits of £60 000 on the Liabilities side.
D   Depreciation is calculated as being £5000 for the year. This results in, on the assets side, fixed assets being reduced by £5000, with profits on the liabilities side being decreased by the same amount.
E   Here, the sundry operating expenses are recorded. As with the accounting idea of cash not having to be received to be recognised as a sale, so we see an illustration of cash not having to be paid to be recognised as a charge against profits. Although only

	Assets £				=	Capital £		Liabilities £	
	Cash	Debtors	Stocks	Fixed Assets		Shares	Profit	Bank Loan	Creditors
A	+25 000				=	+25 000			
A	+10 000				=			+10 000	
B	−20 000			+20 000	=				
C	+30 000	+30 000			=		+60 000		
D				−5 000	=		−5 000		
E	−9 000				=		−10 000		+1 000
F	−1 000				=		−1 000		
G			+25 000		=				+25 000
H	−20 000				=				−20 000
I	+25 000	−25 000			=				
J		−15 000			=		−15 000		
	+40 000	+5 000	+10 000	+15 000	=	+25 000	+29 000	+10 000	+6 000

Figure 6.8 Accounting worksheet for ACE Computers Ltd

£9000 of the £10 000 sundry operating charges has been paid, accountants charge all of the £10 000 against profits, recognising the unpaid £1000 as an accrued charge – a liability. Thus on the assets side cash goes down by £9000; on the liabilities side profit decreases by all of the £10 000 with sundry accruals being increased by £1000. The entries recorded keep both sides of the accounting equation in balance – a decrease of £9000 on the assets side and a net increase of £9000 on the liabilities side. It's worth noting that the £1000 increase against sundry accruals could have been shown as an increase against Trade creditors as an acceptable alternative.

F The loan interest paid results in cash on the assets side going down by £1000 with profits going down by £1000 on the liabilities side.

G Stocks being purchased on credit for £25 000 is reflected in stocks on the assets side increasing by £25 000, with the same increase in creditors on the liabilities side.

H The payment of £20 000 to creditors results in both cash and creditors decreasing by that amount.

I Here the payment of some of the sums owed by debtors is recorded. Cash increases by £25 000 and debtors decreases by £25 000. Note that although this sum is associated with sales there is no impact upon profit. This is because we recorded the debtors' impact upon sales earlier (the £30 000 in line D)

J   This line relates to the fact that stocks costing £10 000 are left at the year end. We know (from line H) that stocks costing £25 000 were purchased. If stocks costing £10 000 are left then stocks costing £15 000 must have been sold (hopefully not stolen). Thus on the assets side stocks decreases by £15 000 with a corresponding decrease against profits on the liabilities side.

The final row shows the totals for each column. We see that, at the end of the year:

● There is £40 000 in the form of cash and in the bank;
● Debtors owe £5000;
● There are unsold stocks to hand which had cost £10 000;
● Fixed assets, having originally cost £20 000, are now valued at £15 000;
● £5000 is owed to trade creditors and £1000 to other creditors in respect of accrued sundry operating expenses, whilst £10 000 is still owed to the bank in respect of the bank loan;
● No further capital has been introduced BUT, as a result of operations, profits of £29 000 have been made. This amount is shown as capital as it is held on behalf of the owners by the organisation, owed back to them. Until such time as the owners take back some or all of the profits, the profits are retained and shown on the balance sheet as capital.

A simple accounting worksheet like this can be used to record the transactions of a very small business but proper books of account will soon be needed. Indeed, these days computer-based accounting systems such as Sage and Quickbooks are so cheap that more and more start-ups are using them from day one. Computers are excellent at dealing with large volumes of repetitive tasks quickly and accurately. However, they often do not reduce the time taken to keep the records, rather they improve the information generated by them. Most small firms still need a bookkeeper to run the computerised system. However, one option is to out-source the bookkeeping function and either have a professional come in to undertake the accounting work, say one day a week, or take details of the transactions to them on a regular basis.

The worksheet in Figure 6.8 contains all the information needed to construct the financial statements. The profit statement details are contained in the profits column. These are represented in the form of a profit statement below:

ACE Computers: profit statement for the year

		£000s	£000s
Sales	for cash	30	
	on account	30	60
less:			
cost of stock sold			15
Gross profit			45
less:			
operating expenses			10
depreciation		5	15
Operating profit			30
less:			
bank loan interest		1	1
Net profit			29

The profit statement is divided into sections. The first section determines the gross profit. This is the profit ACE Computers makes on buying and reselling stock. It is important as it is this gross profit figure from which other expenses are deducted. If the gross profit is low but other expenses are high a loss will result. In Jean Young's profit statement she did not have a gross profit line because she did not buy and sell goods.

For ACE the remaining expenses and charges are sundry operating expenses (£10 000), depreciation (£5000) and bank loan interest (£1000). Not all of these other items are charged in one section – the bank loan interest is kept apart from the operating expenses and the depreciation charge. By grouping these latter items together and deducting them from the gross profit we arrive at a profit figure which reflects the surplus – the operating profit – of £30 000 made on day-to-day activities. The bank loan interest is not an operations expense; rather it is a cost of financing. Although the loan interest (£1000) is deducted from the operating profit to give the net profit of £29 000, the day-to-day performance of management teams is normally related to the generation of operating profits.

Since ACE Computers is a limited company, the final net profit figure is the figure from which dividends can be paid. In their case there are no dividends so this is also the profit retained in the business. Compare this to Jean Young's profit statement. She also had net profit from which her drawings as a sole trader were deducted to arrive at the profit retained in the business. The balance sheet at the end of the first year for ACE Computers is shown below. It comes directly from the worksheet.

ACE Computers: balance sheet at end of first year

	£000s	£000s
Fixed assets		
at cost	20	
less: depreciation to date	5	15
Current assets		
cash/bank	40	
debtors	5	
stocks	10	55
less:		
Current liabilities		
creditors	(5)	
accruals	(1)	(6)
Net current assets		49
Total assets		64
less:		
creditors falling due after one year		
bank loan	(10)	(10)
Net assets		54
Represented by:		
Shareholders funds		
share capital	25	
retained profit	29	54

This balance sheet shows the company's assets and liabilities at the year end. However, the balance sheet also reveals whether shareholders' funds have increased or decreased over the year with a resulting change in the net worth of the organisation. In this case the shareholders' funds (and so the net assets) has increased from the original investment of £25 000 to £54 000 as a result of the profit made and retained of £29 000. Notice, however that cash increased only by £15 000 from £25 000 to £40 000. The difference is represented in the other assets shown in the balance sheet which increased by £14 000, net of liabilities.

● **Answers to exercises and assignments**

1

	Increase cash	Increase profit	Decrease cash	Decrease profit
(1) Sales of stock on credit		✓		
(2) Sale of old fixed assets	✓			
(3) Purchase of fixed assets			✓	
(4) Purchase of stock for cash			✓	
(5) Payment of creditors			✓	
(6) Payment of wages			✓	✓
(7) Payment of dividends			✓	✓
(8) Receipts from debtors	✓			
(9) Issue of new shares	✓			
(10) Receipt of loan	✓			
(11) Repayment of loan			✓	
(12) Payment of interest			✓	✓

Notes: Other balance sheet effects:

(1) Decrease stocks and increase debtors
(2) Decrease fixed assets
(3) Increase fixed assets
(4) Increase stocks
(5) Decrease creditors
(6) None
(7) Often called an 'appropriation' of profit
(8) Decrease debtors
(9) Increase share capital
(10) Increase loan capital
(11) Decrease loan capital
(12) None

2

	Straight line					
	A		B		C	
	Charge £	Asset value £	Charge £	Asset value £	Charge £	Asset value £
Original cost		4000		4000		4000
Year 1	600	3400	450	3550	400	3600
Year 2	600	2800	450	3100	400	3200
Year 3	600	2200	450	2650	400	2800
Year 4	600	1600	450	2200	400	2400
Year 5	600	1000	450	1750	400	2000
Year 6			450	1300	400	1600
Year 7			450	950	400	1200
Year 8			450	400	400	800
Year 9					400	400
Year 10					400	nil

3

	Increase cash	Decrease cash	Increase other assets	Decrease other assets	Increase profit	Decrease profit	Increase liabilities	Decrease liabilities
(1) Purchase of fixed asset for cash		✓	✓					
(2) Sale of fixed asset at balance sheet value for cash	✓			✓				
(3) Sale of fixed asset for more than balance sheet value for cash	✓			✓	✓			
(4) Sale of fixed asset for less than balance sheet value for cash	✓			✓		✓		
(5) Depreciation of fixed asset				✓		✓		
(6) Increase in value of freehold land			✓		✓			
(7) Advance payment of rates		✓	✓					
(8) Receipt of advance payment of subscription	✓						✓	
(9) Write-off bad debt				✓		✓		
(10) Estimate of telephone charges not yet received						✓	✓	

4 Answers to this question are given below. In fact, all the statements are false; your ticks should all be in the 'disagree' column.

(1) What a business is worth depends entirely on what a buyer will pay for that business. It may depend upon the use to which they are put. Anyway, the assets shown in the balance sheet are generally valued at their historic cost, not what they are worth today.

(2) Only land and buildings may be shown at market value. All other assets are shown at depreciated historic cost.

(3) Depreciation is an accounting transaction that reflects how the costs of an asset are allocated as charges against profit. A proportion of cost is charged against each

over the asset's life. Depreciation does not represent any cash flow. Equally, profit (even after depreciation) does not represent availability of cash to replace the asset.

(4) Capital is the funds invested in the business. The best companies get the highest returns from the smallest capital. These achieve high rates of return on their net assets (or capital). Working capital is particularly large for most companies and can be decreased by good control.

(5) If you borrow money you have to pay the interest, whether or not the business is making profit. Dividends paid to shareholders need only be paid when the company is making a profit. Loans will normally be repaid at some predetermined point in the future. Shareholders may liquidate their investment but normally only by selling their investment to another shareholder. Also the amount that you can borrow normally depends upon the amount of money shareholders have put in. In other words, there are many circumstances when further equity investment could be preferable to borrowing money.

(6) Loans are repaid out of cash, not profit.

(7) Reserves represent growth in all the assets of a business, not just cash. Indeed the other assets of a business could have grown to such an extent that cash might actually have decreased.

(8) Profit is not the same as cash. A profitable company can still have insufficient cash to pay its bills, because it has over-expanded its other assets.

(9) It is the profit obtained in relation to the net assets that is important, not just profit. For example, a business may make a profit of £200 on net assets of £1000, compared to another business making a profit of only £30 but on net assets of £100. The first business has a return of 20 per cent, the second 30 per cent. The second is making better use of the assets it controls. Given £1000 it might be able to make profits of £300.

5 The break-even point for A is 750 valves (£15 000/£20) and for B is 800 valves (£20 000/£25). If the company can sell its production of 1500 valves, valve A would generate a profit of £15 000 ((£35 − £15) × 1500 − £15 000)) and valve B a profit of £17 500 ((£36 − £11) × 1500 − £20 000)). The profit-volume charts for A and B are shown below.

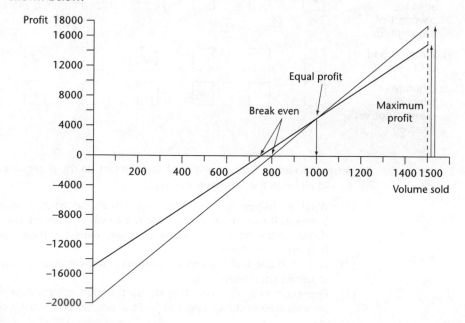

Since the business can invest in either valve A or valve B, but not both, the decision depends critically upon the estimate of sales. If sales are above 1000 per year, A yields a higher profit (or a lower loss). In other words valve B offers the change of a higher return, but this has to be set against the risk of a greater loss, and losses occurring when sales fall below only 800 valves.

6   Drop product E and push the sales of all other products, but particularly B since it has the highest contribution margin.

7   From the analysis below, you should push products B, A, D and C, in that order, since this is the ranking of the products with the highest contribution per machine hour. Machine hours are the limiting factor for this product.

	A	B	C	D
Contribution per unit	0.62	0.51	0.34	0.32
Contribution margin	48%	51%	34%	32%
Product time per 1000 units (hrs)	2	1	4	2
Contribution per 1000 units per hr	310	510	85	160
Ranking	2	1	4	3

8   Actual sales and profit:

	A	B	C	D	Total
Sales potential (1000 units)	250	1000	750	500	
Ranking	2	1	4	3	
Actual production (1000 units)	250	1000	Nil	250	
Productive hours taken	500	1000	Nil	500	2000
Contribution per 1000 units	620	510	NA	320	
Actual production (1000 units)	250	1000		250	
Contribution per 1000 unit	620	510		320	
Total contribution (£000)	155	510		80	745
Fixed costs (£000)					450
Profit (£000)					295

9   Profit calculation:

£000	A	B	D	Total
Sales	325	1000	250	1575
Variable costs	170	490	170	830
Contribution				745
Fixed costs				450
Profit				295

10   Break-even point:

Average contribution margin: $\dfrac{745}{1575} = 47.3\%$

Break-even point: $\dfrac{450\,000}{0.473} = £951\,350$

11   Sales mix:

	A	B	D
Actual production (1000) units	250	1000	250
Sales mix	1:	4:	1

The sales mix is assumed to stay the same at the break-even point. Therefore:

$\dfrac{\text{Break-even}}{\text{Actual sales}} = \dfrac{951\,350}{£1\,575\,000} = 60.4\%$

Break-even sales = Actual × 60.4%. Therefore:

	A	B	D
Actual production (1000) units	250	1000	250
Break-even production (1000) units	151	604	151

12 The break-even point will change and will have to be recalculated. This is a major shortcoming with the technique if the products sold have widely different margins.

13 Extra sales needed to cover loan repayments:

$$\frac{£1200}{0.60} = £2000$$

14 The answer is C.

At this price contribution rises to £15. A 20% drop in sales means 160 000 units and a contribution of £2.4 million (160 000 × £15). Definitely the best option.

For the others:

A: This does not make sense at all. Each unit currently makes a contribution of £10 (£25 − £15). At £12.50 each unit would actually make a loss of £2.50 (£12.50 − £15). The more you sell, the higher the loss. If you sold 400 000 units, the loss would be £1 million.

B: At this price contribution drops to £5. A 20% increase in sales means 240 000 units and a contribution of (240 000 × £5) £1.2 million. Unfortunately previously it was (200 000 × £10) £2 million. So this is not a good idea either.

15(1) Contribution = £0.65 − £0.15 = £0.50 per 100 bottles

Contribution margin = 77%

$$\text{Break-even point} = \frac{£4000 + £8500}{0.77} = £16\,250$$

(This is equivalent to 2.5 million bottles at £0.65 per 100)

15(2)

	3 million £	4 million £
Total sales	19 500	26 000
Break-even sales	16 250	16 250
Sales above break-even	3 250	9 750
Contribution margin	77%	77%
Profit	2500	7500

16 Irene's Hair Salon:

Incremental revenue per week:

£10.00 × 2 per hour × 3 staff × 28 hours   = £1680.00

Incremental costs:

(£5.00 per hour × 28 hours) + (£9.00 per hour × 28 hours)

= £420.00 + £252.00   = £ 672.00

Surplus   = £1008.00

Answer, therefore, is 'yes'

However, might some customers transfer to take up the half-price offer?

17 The liner:

$$\text{Break-even point} = \frac{£250\,000}{£(700 - 200)} = 500 \text{ passengers}$$

The liner is therefore covering its fixed costs at the moment and therefore any price above the variable cost per passenger (£200) makes an additional contribution to the profit of the cruise.

However, thought must be given to how other passengers feel about some passengers paying only, say, £201. If next time all the passengers waited until the last week and paid only £201 the cruise would make a loss:

Contribution = (£201 − £200) × 700 passengers =   £   700

Fixed costs   = £250 000

Loss   £249 300

For this reason, the cruise liner might decide not to drop its price at all.

18 The Accounting Worksheet is shown on the next page. The balance sheet at the end of the period will be:

Fixed assets		£ 990
Current assets:		
stock	£350	
debtors	£300	
cash	£420	£1070
Current liabilities:		
creditors		£ 440
Total assets		£1620
Liabilities due over 1 year:		
bank loan		£ 500
Net assets		£1120
Represented by:		
share capital		£1000
retained profit		£ 120
		£1120

The profit statement will be:

Sales	£500
Cost of sales	£200
Gross profit	£300
Overheads	£180
Net profit	£120

Accounting worksheet

	Assets £				=	Capital £		Liabilities £	
	Cash	Debtors	Stocks	Fixed Assets		Shares	Profit	Bank Loan	Creditors
A	+1000				=	+1000			
A	+500				=			+500	
B				+1100	=				+1100
C			+550		=				+550
D		+500			=		+500		
E	−1250				=				−1250
F	+200	−200			=				
G	−30				=		−30		
H				−110	=		−110		
I			−200		=		−200		
J					=		−40		+40
	+420	+300	+350	+990	=	+1000	+120	+500	+440

chapter seven

E-business

Contents

- The e-commerce opportunity
- Business-to-business trading
- Business-to-consumer retailing
- Information and special interest sites
- Setting up a website
- How e-business affects marketing strategies
- Help and advice
- Summary

Learning outcomes

By the end of this chapter you should:

- Appreciate the impact e-commerce will have, particularly on small business;
- Understand how internet service providers work and how they are likely to develop in the future;
- Understand how the internet is currently used for trading and how it might develop in the future;
- Understand the commercial considerations in setting up a business website;
- Understand how e-businesses make money and appreciate where the entrepreneurial opportunities lie in e-commerce;
- Understand the effect of e-commerce on marketing strategy;
- Know where to go for help and advice on e-commerce.

The e-commerce opportunity

Earlier in the book the advent of the internet was likened to that of the railways of the nineteenth century. It is the single most important innovation affecting business so far in the early twenty-first century and is creating enormous opportunities for entrepreneurs. It will be as significant as the railways and its effects just as lasting. In the same way as then, there are two ways for entrepreneurs to capitalise on it. The first is to establish the network and, like America Online (AOL) and Freeserve, become an internet service provider (ISP) or portal through which traders and their customers gain entry to the network or marketplace. The second is to be one of the traders in this marketplace and set out your stall to do business.

There may be fortunes to be made from being an ISP or portal at the moment but, just like the railways, this bubble will burst at some time in the near future as portals become established and trading patterns stabilise. However, for the time being, as nobody really knows what these trading patterns will look like, the potential and the opportunities are enormous. What is needed is a portal that offers something of particular value. Freeserve, AOL, Altavista and Yahoo! are consumer portals that generate some income from the charges for the call line, but most income comes either from the advertisers in the portal or the actual e-commerce going on through it. Some also operate as traders on it. Portals can also specialise in business-to-business trading. Thus Sage, being the dominant accounting software used by the small-business sector in the UK and many other countries, has launched its own portal aimed at the small-business market. However, it could take more than just market presence to succeed in this market, ISPs increasingly need to add real value for the user.

Advertising is a major source of revenue for portals and many other websites. However, although advertising revenues are increasing overall, the number of sites to advertise on is increasing even faster meaning many general, undifferentiated portals and sites are suffering. What is more, it seems that the number of 'click throughs' – the proportion of surfers who click onto an advertisement – is decreasing. They are estimated to have more than halved in the three years to 2000, increasing the pressure on falling advertising rates.

It is likely that, increasingly, some ISPs will start to segment the market and appeal to narrower and narrower market segments with their specialisms. This will happen in both the retail and business-to-business sectors. In this way advertisers will be more assured of reaching their target markets. Alongside this, the mass market retail portals will probably start to compete more and more on the content they offer, pulling in the consumers they need to generate income directly and from advertisers.

The merger in 2000 of AOL and Time Warner to form AOL Time Warner created the world's biggest on-line media company (valued about £220 billion) and indicated the way that the retail side of the internet might develop in the future. Time Warner owns the Time publishing empire, CNN, Warner Bros., Time Warner Cable, Sports Illustrated, People, HBO, Fortune and Entertainment Weekly. The merger gives Time Warner the opportunity to deliver all of its products over the internet, as the technology allowing it to do so develops, and signals the start of linkages between ISPs and the content providers to develop what is being called 'new media'. It probably also signals the start of the consolidation amongst the mass market, retail service providers, at least in the USA. In parallel

Internet companies can make a lot of money for their founders, fast. In July 1997 **Fast Search & Transfer** was a two-man business in Oslo, Norway. One year later it had more than 60 employees and was valued at $600 million. Soon it hopes to be the world's 'most comprehensive' search-engine, a challenge to the US firm Inktomi. All of this makes the company's chief executive, **Espen Brodin**, a millionaire, on paper at least.

Similarly, **Ben Way** spent the months leading to his 19th birthday negotiating a £25 million investment that allowed him to launch his e-commerce search engine, **Waysearch**, in 2000.

with this, 2000 also saw the merger of Vodafone Airtouch and Mannesmann to form Europe's largest company and a major world force in mobile communications. It is quite possible that the next step in the development of this sector will involve links with ISPs, as mobile phones are increasingly used for internet communications.

One essential ingredient on which portals compete is the search-engines they use. Indeed, many portals offer a choice of search engines (such as Alta Vista and Google). Search-engines trawl and catalogue internet content. They need to be fast, accurate and user-friendly to find precisely what the customer wants as quickly as possible without losing their interest. Anybody who has used the internet will know that some searches can generate thousands of possible results and any site on the list above about number 50 is unlikely to be visited. Most search-engines allow searches to be refined using more words, however, even this can still leave you with hundreds of possible results. Portals often charge more for a higher placement on a search, particularly for some of the more obvious words such as 'travel' or 'music' which may lead browsers to retail sites. Selecting the key words for a search is an essential element in good web design which can generate more 'hits' and therefore more business.

Another area of opportunity is domain names. These are the identities that companies have on the web. Early in the life of the internet, entrepreneurs started registering these names and then licensing them to companies that wanted to use them. Most established brand or company domain names are now registered and the opportunity is past.

Whilst the internet infrastructure is important, the e-business being conducted on it is probably of far greater significance. At present the biggest volume of trade by far is business-to-business (B2B), typically for suppliers of large companies. Several technology companies such as Dell, Cisco and Oracle have transferred almost all of their purchasing to the web and, indeed, much of their sales. There are four types of e-business being conducted on the web (see Figure 7.1). The other three types are:

- Business-to-consumer (B2C): this is normal web-based retail activity such as book-selling by Amazon.com.
- Consumer-to-business (C2B): this, as yet smaller, marketplace drives transactions the other way round with buyers bidding for products or services. So, for example, you might bid £50 for an airline ticket to New York on Priceline.com and let the airline decide whether to accept the offer.
- Consumer-to-consumer (C2C): this is the consumer auction – the car boot sale of the internet – where consumers offer things for sale to other consumers.

> **Virtual Internet** was set-up by **Jason Drummond** in 1996 to licence and protect domain names and host websites. It was the first web hosting company to launch on the Alternative Investment Market (AIM) and moved to a full listing in 2000. It is now the largest such company in the UK with sales of £6 million, serving 60 per cent of the FTSE 100 index companies and employing 126 staff with offices in Paris, Milan, New York and Sydney.

	Business	Consumer
Business	**B2B** GM/Ford/Daimler Benz EDI networks	**B2C** Amazon Dell
Consumer	**C2B** Priceline Accompany	**C2C** eBay QXL

Source: *The Economist*, 26 February 2000.

Figure 7.1 The e-commerce matrix

Many new firms such as Amazon, QXL, eBay and Autobytel are pioneering e-commerce and exploring innovative ways of doing business. The most original of these are the auction and bid sites (C2C and C2B) which organise auctions between buyers and sellers for a whole range of different products from cars to professional services. Most operate the same basic model. They make it easy for sellers and buyers – whether businesses or consumers – to find each other, they arrange for payment and they take a cut. Many auction sites for services also use a rating system to give buyers some indication of what they are getting. A variant on an auction site is the reverse auction site where a buyer for a car, for example, posts their requirement and then awaits bids from dealers.

Crucial to success in e-commerce is the 'business model' – how income will be generated. One of the most successful is that of the auctioneer **eBay**. Its success comes from being nothing more than an intermediary – software running on a web server. The customers, both buyers and sellers, do all the work. Sellers pay to set up their own auction, buyers use eBay's software to place their bids, shipping and payment are arranged between the seller and buyer and eBay takes between 7–18 per cent of the selling price as commission for letting them use their software. EBay holds no stocks and its involvement in the trade in minimal. It also sells advertising space. It is little wonder that in the quarter to December 2000 eBay's gross margin was over 80 per cent and operating margins were 20 per cent, yielding profits of $25 million.

At the core of eBay's business is software rather than people. The company has bought software companies to gain exclusive use of their technologies and make the auction process more efficient. It therefore faces enormous economies of scale in attracting as many auction transactions as possible and, with that in mind, has moved into new areas, such as used cars, and even plans to host storefronts for small merchants. It has also started to sell private-label versions of its service to companies, for a fee.

Where did we get the World Wide Web?

The first electronic mail transfer took place in July 1970 in the laboratories of consultants Bolt, Baranek and Newman. Building on the work of **Paul Baran** of the RAND Corporation, it was the result of a contract placed by the US Advanced Research Projects Agency (ARPA) to build a distributive network that enabled researchers at one site to log onto and run programmes at another. **Roy Tomlinson**, who wrote the programme, initiated the use of the symbol @ to separate the name of the sender from the mailbox ID. He chose it because it was the only symbol that was unlikely to form part of a name or an ID.

Computer networks were also being built elsewhere and ARPA brought researchers from Britain, France, Italy and Sweden to form an international Network Working Group to investigate how the various networks could be connected. In 1973 there was a breakthrough as researchers realised that instead of trying to create a common specification, all they had to do was use dedicated computers as gateways between each network, thus creating a 'network-of-networks'. In 1977 the concept was made a reality as a message was sent on a 94 000 mile round trip from San Francisco to University College, London and back to the University of Southern California. An international network – or 'internet' – was created. The system continued to be used but only by scientists and specialists for many years.

In 1990 an Englishman, **Tim Berners-Lee**, working at CERN, the European Particles Physics Laboratories in Geneva, proposed a solution to the problem they faced of capturing and co-ordinating the work of the scientists and then locating it in such a way that this accumulating knowledge was easily available. He devised a 'hypertext' system that would give access across the internet, allowing users to access the same information from different computer systems and add their own links to information. It also enabled links to be made to live data that kept changing. The system was called the World Wide Web. Shortly after this he devised a 'browser' that linked the resources on the internet in a uniform way. He also devised a protocol to specify the location of the information – the Unique Resource Locator (URL) – and one to specify how information exchanges between computers should be handled – the Hypertext Transport Protocol (HTP). Finally, he invented a uniform way to structure documents, proposing the use of Hypertext Mark-up Language (HTML). In 1992 the browser was made publicly available to anyone with an internet connection to download.

In 1993 a University of Illinois team working at the National Centre for Supercomputer Applications (NCSA), developed the CERN system, which used high-powered workstations and the Unix operating system, to operate on PCs and Macintosh. In the same year one of the team, **Marc Andreesen**, posted a message on some specialist Usenet conferences. It read: 'By the power vested in me by nobody in particular, alpha/beta version 0.5 of NCSA's Motif-based networked information systems and World Wide Web browser, X Mosaic, is hereby released. Cheers, Marc.' The World Wide Web, as we know it, had been born.

With the help of Jim Clark, the wealthy founder of Silicon Graphics, Marc Andreesen and others in the team went on to set up **Netscape**. When the company went public it was valued at $3 billion, a valuation that in those days was huge.

There are also bulk buying sites, such as letsbuyit.com, that pull together a consortium of online buyers for a range of consumer products. As the number of buyers goes up, the price comes down because the site is using the power of bulk buying to extract a discount from the supplier, part of which is passed on to the online buyers.

Alongside these developments, a market for infomediaries (Hagel and Singer, 1999) has developed. These do two things – help consumers and businesses navigate their way around the internet or help them conduct business in a more efficient or less risky way. So, for example, if you take part in a consumer auction you run the risk of one party in the bargain not paying or not delivering the goods. To counter this, escrow agents, such as I Trust You.com, have set up. For a fee, they hold the money or anything of value until all the conditions of the contract have been met, or the parties involved agree to the release of the money or property held in escrow.

The lasting legacy that the internet will give us is the new routes to markets that change the balance of power in the small versus large firm equation of competition. Almost any market on the planet is now accessible by the smallest of firms. With barriers down, competition is likely to intensify. Some firms will compete on price, others will try to differentiate themselves, but the great ability the internet offers is that of being able to focus or target precise market segments – in other words, niche marketing. The number of market niches is set to increase exponentially and this is the area in which small firms excel. At the same time niches will become slimmer and slimmer, defined in terms of customer need, but the market for that focused product-market offering will be global, generating the potential for enormous returns and redefining the nature of small business.

What will be essential to succeed in this new global marketplace for B2B and B2C markets will be good search-engines, but also good brands. Brands help identify products or services in customers' minds and short circuit the search and buying process. They are the ultimate key words.

Business-to-business trading

There are now more than 750 B2B markets across the world. There are more than 20 industry exchanges publicly traded at a market value of more than $100 billion. B2B markets are big business and if a start-up intends selling to other businesses it probably needs to establish a web presence immediately.

Buying supplies, checking specifications, getting copies of user manuals can all be done very quickly on the internet. However, the market can be extremely competitive. Many large firms buy solely on price, given the product specification. A particular area of growth has been the development of 'integrated supply chains' for large assemblers. These allow orders to be placed with suppliers on a just-in-time basis and eliminates the need to keep large stock. Supply chains can also be linked to customers' orders so as to minimise stock holding even further. With this degree of close collaboration comes a number of risks for small suppliers, for example, an over dependence on one customer and having to hold stocks for them which ties up scarce capital. The advantages for the large assemblers are obvious, but small suppliers might see a different picture.

Dell Computers is a pioneer of e-business, not least because it sells $15 million worth of computers from its website each day. Based in its factory on the outskirts of Limerick, on the west coast of Ireland, it take orders from all over Europe.

But what makes **Dell** special is its 'fully integrated value chain'. Suppliers, including many small firms, have real time access to information about customer orders and deliveries via the company's extranet. They organise supplies of hard drives, motherboards, modems and so on, on a 'just-in-time' basis so as to keep the production line moving smoothly. From the parts being delivered to the orders being shipped out takes just a few hours.

Dell have created a three-way 'information partnership' between itself and its customers and suppliers by treating them as collaborators who together find ways of improving efficiency.

. . . to be continued

Many industry giants are now joining together in consortia to set up these B2B markets. In 2000, America's Sears Roebuck and France's Carrefour set up a retail consortium called GlobalNetExchange that brings together $80 billion of annual purchases. In the same year Cargill, DuPont and Cenex Harvest, a US cooperative, set up Rooster.com to supply farmers and sell their crops. However, perhaps the most significant of all is the consortium of Ford, General Motors and DaimlerBenz setting up their joint, fully integrated supply chain, which other car makers may join. This purchases some $240 billion worth of parts from tens of thousands of suppliers. But what makes these joint venture networks so different and so important is that they are independent networks that also allow inter-company trading between the suppliers. The consortium members own the network and take a small cut of the huge number of transactions and thus generate an additional income stream. Everybody is able to trade using nothing more than standard software and an internet browser, finding precisely what they need at competitive prices and reducing their inventories because the exchange smoothes out demand. Supply chains can be disaggregated, allowing trading and greater competition at every point. Everybody in the system gains. Clearly the potential for global B2B trading using the internet is enormous and is growing rapidly.

Whilst important now, these B2B markets are new and there is the question of how they might evolve and develop. Kaplin and Sawhney (2000) argue that this depends on the structure of the industry. Because of the asymmetry in 'pyramid-shaped' industries, where there are few big buyers and a fragmented mass of sellers as in the car industry, the market is biased, favouring one side. They say that in these situations exchanges are likely to be set up by the big companies who have the finance, an established dominant position with the sellers and a large critical mass of transactions that will make the network viable. On the other hand, 'butterfly-shaped' industries that are highly fragmented on both sides are neutral markets and they lend themselves to the establishment of independent, third party exchanges. And it is here where there are opportunities for entrepreneurial intermediaries who could set up and manage market infrastructures.

Some of the biggest potential gains from B2B lie in small firms' purchases of indirect inputs such as telephone or office equipment, which together can easily account for up to 60 per cent of non-labour costs. If small firms start using the internet to pool their buying power, probably through intermediaries in these 'butterfly-shaped' industries, they could make enormous savings. However, the potential savings would come not only from bulk buying but also from efficiency savings associated with placing and processing orders online.

Business-to-consumer retailing

For the consumer the internet offers the opportunity to shop worldwide with greater choice, making it easy to compare price and specifications. However, websites do not replicate the social functions of shopping. Nor, because it usually depends on separate delivery, can it offer instant gratification. It is therefore not good for impulse buys or goods needed for instant consumption. Bulky or heavy goods may be expensive to deliver and therefore a price advantage is not always guaranteed. Indeed the type of goods that currently sell best on the internet are the 'low-touch' goods such as computer hardware or software, travel, financial services, books, music or video. It is best if these goods or services can also be delivered over the net. 'High touch' goods such as clothes and shoes do not sell well and still incur high storage and delivery costs.

At the moment the narrowband connections of the telephone line mean that only text, music and simple static images can be delivered on the internet and even these sometimes come through at a grindingly slow pace. Video and complex graphics cannot be delivered until broadband networks are in place. It is estimated by *Broadband Intelligence*, an industry newsletter, that only 1.5 million homes (1.5 per cent) in the USA had broadband connections in 2000. Many people feel that the retail side of e-commerce will really only take off when more homes have this, speeding access enormously and allowing high qual-

Boo.com was the most spectacular B2C failure of 2000. Founded by two young Swedes, **Earst Malmsten** and **Kajsa Leander**, the failure was greeted with many jibes about their high-spending personal and corporate lifestyles. Without doubt they failed on a grand scale to manage the cash flow. They were inexperienced and badly managed. However, at the heart of the problem was the fact that their website was just too high-tech.

Boo.com sold sports fashion goods. It was launched in seven languages and 18 countries. In theory you could span through 360 degrees to view clothes and shoes and dress a model in your intended purchases. However, only the most powerful computers could access the site and make it work. Even a radical simplification proved too cumbersome for many computers and by then a reputation had been made – for all the wrong things. Boo.com's vision of e-retailing will only come about with broadband connections and more powerful computers. It was a business before its time, and timing is everything for the successful entrepreneur.

ity video and graphics to be transmitted. Interactive video will allow customers to explore the features and benefits of these 'high touch' products or services more. It will also allow the firms that sell the product to advertise, promote and ultimately sell them more effectively in the customer's home. It will allow them to interact in real time and ask questions and get immediate answers.

Broadband connections could develop in a number of ways. Some cable networks already offer broadband connections, although it has been estimated that only a third of cable customers in the USA had access in 2000. Mobile WAP phones and digital television, delivered via satellite, allow broadband, two-way delivery systems. Telephone companies are testing digital-subscriber-line technology which turns telephone lines into broadband channels. With the arrival of broadband networks retail e-commerce will be transformed and will become a real threat to the traditional high street trader. The delivery of a broad range of entertainment will also be revolutionised. The big names on the high street are already starting to turn their attention to the internet and they bring with them a long standing reputation and customer loyalty. At the moment there is something of a 'chicken and egg' situation, with customers not rushing to existing networks because of a lack of content and, because there are so few customers, content providers are biding their time to enter the market. The decision is when to move.

At the moment as much as 75 per cent of B2C e-business is done through five sites: Amazon, eBay, AOL, Yahoo! and Buy.com. Most of the business on these sites is in 'low-touch', branded products where the features of the product are already understood, or for products or services such as books, CDs, airline or theatre tickets where, once again, customers understand precisely what they are buying. Amazon, and its rival Barnes and Noble, were among the top-10 online retailers in 1998. Amazon offers a vast number of book titles online, with many books heavily discounted. They also offer CDs and auctions and are now starting to use what may become their most valuable resource – their customer database that allows them to make product offerings to customers based on previous buying patterns.

Started in 1998, **Cold Fusion Sports Inc.** operates out of a ramshackle store and offices in insalubrious part of San Francisco, USA, surrounded by clubs and car-parts shops. Rooms are divided by corrugated metal sheeting and old doors. Packing cases and stock clutter up the rooms. But none of this matters because Cold Fusion is a virtual shop that sell its snowboards and accessories on the web. All that matters is their attractive, professional website on http:/www.thesnowboardshop.com. Customers were on the site within an hour of it being set up and sales were made on the very first day.

The company was set up with less than $50 000 and quickly took in revenue of $100 000. Turnover in its second year is expected be $800 000. The site also has a bulletin board where customers can post ideas about snowboarding. There are also weather updates and local resort travel information. Customers even send in photographs that are posted on the website. They can also get feedback on potential new product lines.

Data can be far more easily exploited on the internet than in the real world. Everything can be recorded from website visits to banners clicked onto, from time spent on pages to products purchased. All this really does create the possibility of the ultimate niche marketing – one-to-one – and on a mass, global basis, tailoring products and offerings to meet specific customer needs. The internet could overturn much of the traditional economics of retailing. Evans and Wurster (1999) propose three dimensions for assessing the effect of the internet on an industry:

1   *Reach* – the size of audience;
2   *Richness* – the intricacy and customisation of the services on offer;
3   *Affiliation* – the extent of perceived response to customer interests.

In the physical world these often have to be traded off against each other – mass audiences means loss of richness and affiliation. However, the internet means that you can achieve all three dimensions at the same time.

Many industries are facing major upheavals because of the arrival of the internet and the travel industry is just one. Online ticket sales for both planes and railways are growing fast. Click onto the website for easyJet.com and you can check schedules, ticket availability and then purchase your ticket online, at a small discount, with only a reference number required to turn up for your flight. EasyJet now sells more than half its tickets online. In 1998 the online leisure travel market in the USA was some $3 billion. Forrester Research estimate that it will grow to $29 billion by 2003 – 12 per cent of the total market.

Another innovative angle on ticket sales is the growth in the sale of late ticket deals for anything from holidays to theatre bookings by companies such as Lastminute.com. The internet is ideal for speedy, late bookings of this nature and could help establish a whole new industry.

The entertainment industry will be the next to feel the winds of change fanned by the internet as broadband connections become more commonplace. The digital downloading of music from the

Richard Downs set up **Iglu.com** with his French-born partner **Emmanuelle Drouet** in 1998, having just completed his MBA at London Business School. Emmanuelle Drouet has a Masters in Marketing and seven years experience in the travel industry. The company offers on-line skiing holidays. To attract interest it also provides information on ski resorts around the world, including maps, photographs and details of facilities, prices and accommodation. It also provides snow reports and live webcam views of resorts.

Iglu.com raised £500 000 to build the website and secure properties and suppliers, and launched the business in October 1998 at the London Ski Show. Within a year they had received over 1 million hits and took over 1000 people skiing in their first season. With the help of a further £5 million from venture capitalists their turnover increased 10-fold in the next season and they currently employ 30 people.

. . . to be continued

internet has sent shock waves through the music industry. The MP3 digital compression format makes it easy to download CD recordings from the internet and when agreement is reached on encryption and the secure transmission of music online it will revolutionise not only the way we buy music but also the type of music we will be able to buy because access to specialist music outlets and independent music labels will become so much easier as costs of distribution come down. The advent of broadband will mean that videos will be available for sale by downloading from the internet. It is no wonder the merger of AOL and Time Warner was seen as so important in 2000.

The growth of web retailing is driving the development of shopping agents. These are services that make product/price/performance comparisons easier. Services such as Mysimon.com and DealPilot.com enable speedy comparison of products and prices on offer. DealPilot.com gives users a piece of software that automatically informs them of the cheapest price on offer. If you intend to buy a book from Amazon, say, a box will pop up telling you if you can get it cheaper elsewhere. Frictionless.com enables you to rank products by the weighted performance criteria that you select. There are even shopping agents that rank websites.

Retailing on the web offers the opportunity to do business 24 hours a day, seven days a week. It offers the chance to build relationships and develop an understanding of individual customers' buying patterns. On the face of it, selling on the web seems to offer the attraction of dispensing with the major fixed costs of a retail business – the site and the shopfloor staff. For the entertainment business distribution costs will tumble. However, as we shall see, the costs of hardware and software, establishing the website and brand identity can be very high.

Ernesto Schmitt set up in 1998 **Peoplesound.com** when he was 27 years old, giving up his job with the Boston Consulting Group. The company offers free tracks of undiscovered artists and small independent record companies to consumers for downloading. If they like the tracks, they can order CDs at present. In the future these will be available for downloading. Half the royalties go to the musicians. Ernesto wants the site to become a massive meeting point for musicians, consumers, music journalists and A&R people. The ultimate aim of the company is not to make money from the music on the site but from the advertisements it carries.

In 1999 he raised venture capital backing that valued the company at £12.5 million.

Advoco is one of the few service markets that is already on line. The firm signs up experts who wish to give advice. Users then pick one of the advisers directly or post questions for them to answer on a bulletin board. Once the service is delivered and paid for, users evaluate the seller on a scale of one (lowest) to five (highest) and post comments about them.

Information and special interest sites

Not all websites are designed to sell you things. Some are just information providers. Estimates suggest more than one million pages are added to the world wide web every day. For example, there are many government.net and public service sites and much of the information you need to find out about customers and competitors can be obtained online. News and public affairs information is also available on line. For example, there is BBC On-line and many newspapers have their own websites. Universities have their own websites. Most of these are free of charge.

Getting people to pay for information content on the internet is a problem. The online editions of many newspapers started out charging subscriptions but have now deserted that model, relying instead on advertising revenue and therefore facing all the problems discussed earlier. The content that customers seem most willing to pay for is time-sensitive or data-driven. The *Financial Times* and the *Wall Street Journal* successfully run subscription models; and sport, which is often both time-sensitive and data-driven, also works well. One other product also sells – pornography – whose vulnerability to censorship always puts it in the vanguard of distribution technologies.

There are also a growing number of community interest websites. Benjamin Cohen set up sojewish.net at the age of 16, targeted at Britain's 300 000 Jews and sold it to AIM-listed Totally three years later in 2000. It includes synagogue listings and kosher recipes. Many of these sites do not appear to try to sell you anything but even these sites can make money if they contain advertisements and hyper-links to the advertiser's site where you can buy their products or services. You may log into the website of your favourite ski resort to find out how the snow is only to have an advertisement for a local hotel drop down ten seconds later. Many community sites also sell products or services, relying on the loyalty of a special interest group to visit and revisit the site and make purchases. IslamiQ.com offers financial advice and services based upon Islamic values which forbids the charging of interest and investment in sectors of the economy involving gaming, alcohol or conventional financing. Attractive content, promoting participation and building loyalty through close relationships are the keys to success for a community site.

Many special interest, information and even retail sites sell advertising space to earn revenue. Retail sites must ensure that the advertisers are not

Steve Burns launched **Totally** onto the Alternative Investment Market in 2000, raising £2 million and valuing the firm at £6 million.

The company aims to set up community-based websites such as totallyjewish.com, totallyasian.com and totallyblack.com as well as non-ethnic sites such as totally-dance.com and totallybald.com. In all it has registered some 170 site names.

Not only did the company buy out sojewish.net in 2000, it also bought the *London Jewish News*, a free community newspaper. It plans to break into the US by buying a Jewish newspaper or television station and has already had an offer for the *Jewish Post* turned down.

Table 7.1 E-business income

Type of e-business	Source of income
ISP	Subscription for service
	Subscription or charge for content
	Connection charges
	Advertising
B2B	Trade
B2C	Trade
	Advertising
C2B	Trade
Intermediaries	Charge for service
Information and special interest sites	Subscription
	Advertising
	Premium services fees
	Sale of membership information

competing against them and losing them custom. Advertisers are interested in the sites that receive the largest number of hits and many of these are not, overtly at any rate, selling you anything. For example, most of the daily newspapers have websites that contain advertisements. Too much advertising can, however, clutter a site and make it difficult to navigate which in turn leads to fewer hits and a declining ability to attract advertisers and charge premium rates. What is more, advertising rates on the internet are falling anyway.

Most pure internet firms are finding it difficult to trade profitably on the internet. Customers are increasingly reluctant to subscribe for services or pay for information. Advertising rates are falling and B2C customers are proving reluctant to buy certain types of goods. Only B2B is really thriving. However, many traditional bricks-and-mortar firms who use the internet as another route to market find it a worthwhile source of additional revenue. Table 7.1 summarises the sources of income available to the different types of e-businesses.

> **Student-net** is a sort of web version of the student union handbook. It was set up in 1999 by four Nottingham University students – **Alan Edmondson**, **Peter Atalla**, **Michael Haycock** and **John Woodcock** – whilst they were still at University. With the help of a £10 million capital injection from IMPG, a Nevada-based venture capitalist. The company now has two offices in Nottingham, two in London and has 15 employees.

Setting up a website

For a pure internet firm, start-up is about more than just setting up a website. There are systems, procedures and content to be developed. However, for a conventional bricks-and-mortar firm, developing a website may not be as daunting as you might expect. The first thing you need to set up a website is the hardware and software. Many companies such as IBM and Microsoft offer free business assessment guides on CD-ROMs or their own websites that allow you to 'walk through' what is needed and what they have to offer. IBM's interactive review looks at the full range of technology available for stock and debtor control as well as communication with vendors, plus web-based selling. A server plus fast internet connection are essential and all this technology will need regular maintenance. Not surprisingly therefore, many small firms rent space on a local host server, one permanently linked to the internet and serviced by the supplier.

Good web design is also essential. People may visit any website once, by accident, but the trick is to generate repeat business. That means that the essentials of any business are being met – that is, that the products or services on offer meet a genuine market need. However, even if this is the case, the design of the website can be very important. The site design must satisfy customer interest and needs, be easy to navigate and, for the retail sector particularly, be entertaining and fun. It must be easy to use – simple but stylish. It must be easy to place orders and make enquiries. It should be 'sticky' – keep customers' interest. The site will need to be constantly updated. Customer experience is the key driver of success online. In evaluating a site, four questions need to be addressed:

> **Shopcreator** is a small firm based in Tadcaster, North Yorkshire. It sells the software needed to set up an e-commerce trading site within an hour for only £199. It also provides maintenance, handling online orders and payments, registering products with internet search engines and sorting out stock control.
>
> One of its customers is another small Wetherby based firm called **Fox Saddlers**. The Shopcreator system allows potential shoppers to search for items such as 'saddle' and 'Yorkshire' to arrive at Fox Saddlers' website. In this way Monty Don, the famous 'horse whisperer', became a customer after he found out that the company stocked a specific type of bridle he was looking for. Fox Saddlers now has customers from as far away as Australia, thanks to e-commerce.

1　What are the company's objectives for the site?
2　Who are the target customers and what are their goals?
3　Does the site help customers achieve their goals as well as the company achieve its goals?
4　Do customers experience something quick and easy enough to bring them back, and keep them from going to competitors?

Whilst even children can design their own website these days, designing an effective one for commercial purposes is probably best left to professionals, The price of the designer's work can vary enormously and some people may feel sufficiently competent to undertake the design themselves. Indeed proprietary software is available to help with this.

Most retail sites have secure credit card transaction facilities. This means that personal financial data is encrypted in such a way that this is only intelligible by the supplier. This is essential if a firm is to be accepted by the major credit card firms.

A start-up must register their name with a portal and its search engine. They must also register key words describing their product or service. There is a fee for this and an annual charge for maintaining the registration. The choice of key words is important. One of the reasons for Cold Fusion's success was that early on it registered key words such as 'snowboards' and 'snowboarding' with Yahoo! and AOL.

The major problem facing small firms is getting customers to visit and then revisit their site. If they do not wish to rely just on search engines they might decide to advertise on other sites. By using a hypertext link, users can click onto certain words or images and jump to another website, even from the other side of the world. In addition there is also a growing number of Business Directories, just like the telephone's *Yellow Pages* directory, or Ukdirectories and Scoot.

Retail sites can also use the more conventional advertising media. This can be particularly important for the more innovative retail sites where they need to develop awareness amongst customers who may be unaware of the nature of the service they offer. What is more they must develop a market presence quickly before competitors react. The problem with any form of advertising is that is expensive and the sums involved can be enormous, particularly for start-ups, and this is one reason pure internet start-ups require so much capital.

Smaller firms can also join one of the many e-malls that have been set up for both retail and business-to-business traders. These are centralised websites with links to a range of other like-minded organisations. This can be particularly useful for companies wishing to export goods. In fact, not only does the internet make it easier for small firms to find customers overseas and for them to find the firm, it also makes it easier to do business. It smoothes time differences, eases communication. Secure payment transactions can minimise paperwork, charges, risks and the delays associated with currency exchange.

Sites can also build up buying profiles of the customers using it so as to speed their purchases or target them with special offers. For example, supermarket

Who said you could trade on the internet quickly? **Philip Evans** sells top quality glass, metal, jewellery, wood and ceramics made by British artists and designers from his shop in Chelsea. His business, **The Room,** has a turnover of some £180 000. In 1999 he decided to start selling his products on the internet, but he had not counted on the obstacles he would face.

The first was the price of designing the website. He was quoted between £3500 and £35 000. But how could he decide what met his needs and gave best value for money? He managed to sort that out by taking professional advice. The second problem was less expected. In order to trade on the internet you need authorisation to take credit card payments over the web. Even more important is the need for transaction security. Banks therefore carry out stringent credit checks on new internet trading companies, in the same way as they do with mail-order firms, as well as checks to ensure that customers are provided with net security before trading can start. And all of this takes time!

shopping via the internet is daunting to start with, but once you have built up a shopping list you only have to add or subtract from it every week, and you are always made aware of the special offers. It is only a matter of time before we start receiving the equivalent of e-commerce junk mail, based upon our buying habits.

A key factor in success is building a community interested in the site. This encourages visitors to revisit the site. Cold Fusion's website has a bulletin board for boarders where customers post ideas and even photographs. There is also weather and travel information. The 'community' can also act as an on-line market research tool, with visitors posting ideas about how the firm might improve or new products it might sell. Not only do communities build up web loyalty, they also build brand or company loyalty and a greater willingness to purchase from the company that developed the community.

Brady (1999) argues that success for a pure internet start-up depends on several factors, although, interestingly all but the last factor could apply to any business:

> **Mansfield Motors** in Manningtree, Essex was set up in 1993 as an independent Land Rover garage that sells parts as well as offering workshop facilities. It now sells parts worldwide via the internet and can boast a quicker delivery time than many overseas authorised Land Rover dealers.
>
> Its website, mansfield-motors.com, was developed by consultants who were also Land Rover enthusiasts. It provides information on the garage, an easy parts and accessory ordering service and also a 'tea room' with news, a bulletin and a discussion board, small ads as well as club news and information on recalls. Add to this the opportunity to give feedback and you also have a good community site.

> 'Creating a sense of community is what it is all about; getting a lot of like-minded people together.'
>
> **David Bowie**, rock star and co-founder of **UltraStar**, a web development company
> *Sunday Times* 11.06.00

- Providing something different;
- The business must be clearly focused but be sufficiently flexible to change quickly to sustain growth;
- The management must be good with a good plan, a grasp of critical issues and credibility in the eyes of financiers;
- The business must develop a strong brand and, on the back of this, create and maintain very high levels of service;
- Delivery must be on time;
- The site must be readily accessible, orders must be simple to place and easily tracked whilst they are in the system.

How e-business affects marketing strategies

For a conventional bricks-and-mortar business, the internet might be seen as just another communications tool to be added to the 5Ps of the marketing mix under the heading of 'promotion', or a new route to market or way of doing business that can be added under the heading of 'place'. However, potentially the internet is a dramatic and fundamental change in the way we do business which will increase competition and improve the competitive chances of small against large firms. It is worth revisiting some of the models we have developed to understand just what the effects might be.

Starting with Porter's Five Forces (Figure 4.4) that determine the degree of competition in an industry, it has been argued that e-business has now rendered this analysis obsolete because all markets will face intense competition. Whilst this may be an extreme generalisation, it is possible to imagine industries where the power of the buyers and the power suppliers may both increase because of the internet. At the same time e-commerce facilitates entry into a market, even for the smallest of firms. What is clear is that competition will intensify, in most industries. However, the analysis is still useful as factors other than the internet will remain more important in some industries.

Porter's generic marketing strategies (Figure 4.5) also need some reinterpretation. It has been argued that differentiation will no longer be an alternative strategy to price as firms will have to compete on both differentiation and price in order to survive in the new world of e-business. The reality, however, is that competition will become cut-throat for commodity suppliers whilst differentiation will become even more important, but more difficult to establish. At the

---

Lastminute.com was floated on the Stockmarket in 2000 at a valuation of more than £400 million. As we saw in Chapter 2, part of the reason for this high valuation was the strength of the management team **Brent Hoberman** and **Martha Lane Fox** were able to put together. However, there were four reasons for this exceptional valuation:

1 *Brand*: lastminute.com claims to be the second most recognised e-retailer in the UK after Amazon. This is partly as a result of a very 'old-media' advertising and promotion campaign.
2 *Timing*: it was first in the marketplace and, in 2000, there were few signs of real competition. First movers have a distinct advantage in e-commerce.
3 *Innovation*: the product/service it offers is tailor-made for the internet. Not only are its partners eager to sell off their products at a discount to customers who have forgotten to buy it in the first place, it is also attempting to create a last-minute marketplace in its own right, when people can leave decisions about holidays and so on until a time that suits them. It is not just selling on cheapness, it is about getting its partners to provide a sufficient supply to make buying at the last minute a viable and reliable option.
4 *Track record*: although young, the founders grew the company with determination and a clear vision – and a strong management team.

The company planned to use the floatation proceeds to expand into Asia and America as well as extend its range to include financial services, household services, consumer products and information services.

same time, the internet is offering firms new ways of creating differential advantage by developing new ways of trading. However, the e-customer will find it increasingly easier to see through claims of differentiation that are less than real and increased competition will make the price/performance decision easier for the customer as information becomes more readily available. Price differentials may therefore narrow in many markets.

Central to the success of a differentiation strategy is one of effective branding. E-commerce increases this imperative. Customers need to be able to find their way through the e-commerce maze quickly and may be asked to make buying decisions without seeing the product or experiencing the service. Branding can help them do these things. This is one reason why pure internet start-ups invest so much in advertising themselves using the internet and conventional media. Amazon.com has become a well-known, established e-retailer that others find difficult to compete with because the brand is so well-known.

E-commerce offers the opportunity to develop ever slimmer market segments, focusing on very narrow markets, but then targeting that focused market on a global basis. E-commerce will allow firms better to understand the buying patterns of these narrow market segments as they trade and their buying habits are recorded and analysed. So, although apparently paradoxical, you can have a narrow, focused market that is also global. Porter's 'broad market' terminology must be interpreted in marketing rather than geographic terms.

This raises the question of economies of scale. E-commerce brings with it the opportunity to be a 'niche player' and, because sales are global, also gain from economies of scale and make even higher profits. Perhaps the 'outstanding success' of Porter's model will cease to exist as markets are constantly fragmented once they prove to be successful. Indeed, the subversive nature of the internet is such that it helps bring down some of the key costs for many businesses, for example the costs of communicating with customers and distribution. Expensive distribution networks involving shops, wholesalers and so on can now be avoided. In Brazil it is quicker to get Land Rover parts delivered directly from Mansfield Motors in Manningtree, England, ordered via the internet, than it is to get them via the local Brazilian authorised dealer. This means that the 'no-man's-land' facing firms trying to grow with a competitive strategy based on price (Figure 4.6) becomes less daunting and more small firms making use of economies of small scale may now try to grow.

It is not just about combating existing large businesses where the internet is changing our thinking. The economics of the internet seem to offer powerful first-mover advantage. Because an e-commerce operation can be scaled up at a relatively low cost in a way that a traditional business cannot, there is a strong incentive to do so. That is not to say that the first mover automatically wins. Amazon and eBay were not the first in their marketplaces. However, if a first mover gets most things right – website, order fulfilment and distribution – it will be difficult to displace even by an established name in retailing.

Porter's generic marketing strategies do need to be reinterpreted with the advent of e-commerce. However, the resulting fierce competition is likely to create as many opportunities as threats, particularly for small firms. It does mean that even start-ups can prepare to trade in a worldwide market but speed is essential and careful planning is vital.

Help and advice

Under the Information Society Initiative (ISI) Programme for Business, a network of about 80 Local Support Centres, offers advice on e-commerce and can help businesses start trading on the internet. The DTI (1998) offers a free booklet which contains basic information as well as useful check-lists to help in the selection of ISPs. Sage, the small-business accounting software company, also has a national network of centres offering practical help and advice on a commercial basis. Virgin Biznet offers to get small companies online without requiring them to learn how to program.

However, it is one thing to set up webpages and it is quite another to start up a pure internet company. Pure internet companies face a very short window of opportunity. If they miss it, the idea will probably be taken up by somebody else. If they are late in the market, they start at a disadvantage and may have to fight it out with established competitors. Timing and speed of start-up is therefore vital.

Pure internet start-ups face technical and commercial problems that need to be sorted out quickly. They will probably have to launch and grow very rapidly, and that brings high risk. They will probably need large amounts of venture capital to develop their product or service and penetrate the market quickly through advertising and promotion. Retail sites in particular often need extensive advertising campaigns using traditional media to make the public aware of their existence and to persuade them to visit. They also need an excellent business plan if they are to convince venture capitalists to part with large amounts of money. But most of all they need a strong and experienced management team – and, like Lastminute.com, that probably means giving up some of the equity in order to attract them. All of which means internet start-ups need lots of advice, help and support.

At the turn of the millennium venture capitalists seemed to be queuing up to back internet start-ups. By 2000, the honeymoon seemed to be coming

> Iglu.com attracted its seed capital from the London Business School's Sussex Place Incubator Unit. They put someone on the Board of the company who took an active role in developing it, spending about a day a week there. By the time it was ready to attract its second round of finance from GEO Capital it had nine employees with three managers ready to join within a month of getting venture capital backing. These experienced managers were attracted by being offered equity in the business.

> 'The internet is going to disappear in the way that all technologies disappear. It is becoming ubiquitous and as taken for granted as air, gravity, the telephone or television. Everything will be connected to everything else. So instead of communicating to get things done – for example picking up the phone to track a package – we have things that communicate. The package will tell the world, via the web, where it is at any given moment.'
>
> **John Browning,**
> co-founder of **First Tuesday**
> *Sunday Times*, 11.06.00

> 'Everything will be connected to the web. You will be able to access the internet from your car, through your mobile, television, games console and your computer. Although I don't know what the net will be delivering, it will get there fast. Access to the internet means that everybody, no matter where they live, has equal opportunity – we must ensure it does not increase the divide between the haves and the have-nots.'
>
> **Chris Dedicoat**, VP and managing director of **Cisco UK and Ireland**
> *Sunday Times*, 11.06.00

to an end and a more hard-nosed commercial attitude seemed to be coming back. Oxygen is a venture capital company specialising in student internet start-ups. From an initial investment of £1 million in five start-ups, it floated itself on the Stockmarket in 2000 with a valuation of £240 million. John Browning co-founded First Tuesday, a global network club, in 1998 to help net entrepreneurs grow their companies more quickly, including raising money, hiring staff and finding premises, all via their website (www.firsttuesday.com).

Four of the world's most influential companies – Cisco Systems, Oracle, Sun Microsystems and Exodus Communications – came together in September 1999 to offer an incubator environment for entrepreneurs wanting to establish themselves on the internet. They are well-placed to do so; 80 per cent of internet traffic currently runs over Cisco hardware, 80 per cent on Sun servers and 69 per cent of the world's e-commerce sites are powered by Oracle software. The joint venture, called business-incubator.com, offers participants access to the four companies' technology – hardware, software, networking infrastructure and web-hosting facilities – at a discount price (currently £15 000) so that they can test e-commerce applications for three months before launching a full e-business. The intention is that companies come out of the incubator with proven technology and a business plan ready for venture capitalists. It allows the entrepreneurs to focus more on the business rather than the technological problems. The scheme can even put the company in touch with venture capitalists and consultants to help prepare a business plan. Entrepreneurs must apply to participate and it is not guaranteed that they will be accepted onto the scheme. Some firms are turned away because their business plan is too advanced, others because they are not ready for further development. By definition, the scheme also ties the incubator company into using the technologies supplied by the sponsors.

If this does not suit, then Andersen Consulting has set up Dot-com Launch Centres, in London, Dublin and 15 other cities around the world to help e-commerce start-ups and spin-offs from formation to an initial public offer. As remuneration for their services, Andersen will take up equity in the firms it helps. Other consultants have similar schemes.

Summary

E-commerce is the most important innovation affecting business in the twenty-first century; it creates three major opportunities for small firms:

1   The opportunity to establish the network and, like **Freeserve** become an ISP or portal through which traders gain entry to the new marketplace.

2   The opportunity to establish innovative trading businesses, like **QXL** or **EarthPort.com**, that exploit the unique characteristics of the internet;

3   The opportunity to compete in a global marketplace on price, the differentiated qualities of the products or service, or by being able to focus even more effectively on market segments – niche marketing.

Some ISPs will start to focus on specific target markets. Others will try to appeal to the mass retail market and for these the content they offer will become increasingly important, particularly as broadband networks are established. For all ISPs a fast and effective search-engine is vital. As demonstrated by **Fast Search & Transfer** and **Waysearch**, there are major entrepreneurial opportunities here. Similarly, **Virtual Internet** proved that there were major opportunities in registering domain names.

The lasting legacy that the internet gives us is the new routes to market that change the balance of power in the small versus large firm equation of competition. Almost any market on the planet is now accessible by the smallest of firms. With barriers down, competition is likely to intensify. To combat this, effective branding will become increasingly important. B2B trading on the internet has so far seen the major growth. Companies such as **Dell Computers** show the way forward with their 'information partnership' and 'fully integrated value chain' allowing stock to be delivered on a just-in-time basis. However, the increasingly symbiotic relationship between large assemblers and small suppliers carry many dangers for the suppliers.

B2C retail business will expand dramatically as broadband networks are established allowing interactive video to be transmitted. As demonstrated by **Cold Fusion Sports Inc.**, there are many opportunities for new companies on the internet that allow them to tap large markets without the overheads associated with the high street. However, the big high-street names are increasingly looking to establish themselves on the internet and they will capitalise on their established brand and a loyal customer base.

Selling on the web offers the opportunity to do business 24 hours a day, seven days a week and the chance to build relationships and develop an understanding of individual customer's buying patterns. It does not require the major fixed costs of a retail business – the site and the shopfloor staff. At the moment retail e-commerce is most successful for branded products where the features are already understood, or for 'low-touch' products or services such as books, CDs, airline or theatre tickets where, once again, customers understand precisely what they are buying. However, even here the nature of trading will change as broad band networks allow media to be delivered directly to customers via the internet rather than through the post.

The travel and leisure industries are seeing a major expansion of internet sales through established firms and pure internet firms such as **Iglu.com**. The entertainment industry will probably be the next industry feeling the winds of change as downloading CDs and videos from the internet becomes common practice. The giant **AOL Time Warner** and the much smaller **Peoplesound.com** are well-placed to exploit this. The retail sector has also seen many innovative approaches to doing business such as the auction site of **QXL** and **Avoco**. A variant on this is the bulk buying sites which pull together a consortium of buyers.

A successful website gets people to visit and then revisit it. Registration of both the firm and key words associated with the products or services it sells is important. Firms might also decide to advertise on related sites. Both B2B and B2C retail e-commerce business can join e-malls – centralised websites with links to similar organisations. Good web design is essential but you can purchase the software to set up your own site from companies such as **Shopcreator** and this is the low cost approach many small firms like **Fox Saddlers** have taken. Sites must also be secure if they are to take credit card transactions and, as **The Room** found out, checks by credit card companies can take a long time.

Many sites try to build community interest. This generates web loyalty and customer trust. **Mansfield Motors** develop a community for Land Rover owners with its 'tea room'. One angle on community, exploited by the start-up called **Totally**, is to set up community sites that make money from advertising and offering services. There is even a student site called **Student-net**. Membership information can be a valuable asset for these sites. Attractive content, promoting participation and building loyalty through close relationships are the keys to success for a community site.

E-business is not just a new element to be added into the marketing mix. It is a fundamental and dramatic change in the way we do business which increases the degree of competition and makes us reinterpret some of the fundamentals of marketing. However, as in the case of **Lastminute.com**, it is probably about reinterpreting rather than reinventing them.

A pure internet start-up faces commercial as well as technical problems. It will probably have to launch and grow very rapidly, and that brings high risk. It will probably need large amounts of venture capital to develop. All of which means it needs lots of help and support. Help and advice is available for all firms from the DTI through the ISI Programme. It is also available from Sage and Virgin Biznet. There are also incubator environments for pure internet start-ups such as **business-incubator.com**. Arthur Andersen offer help in exchange for equity through their **Dot-com Launch Centres**. There is even a venture capital company, called **Oxygen**, focusing on student internet start-ups and **First Tuesday** offers a global network of support.

⬛ Essays and discussion topics

1 Is the development of the internet really as significant as the development of railways in the last century?
2 What entrepreneurial opportunities does e-commerce create?
3 What are the likely effects of e-commerce on small retail firms?
4 What are the likely effects of e-commerce on small service firms?
5 What are the likely effects of e-commerce on small manufacturing firms?
6 What new developments have there been in the development of ISPs?
7 What are the advantages and disadvantages of being a small supplier to a large assembler linked through a fully integrated supply chain?
8 What are the advantages and disadvantages of e-commerce to a small retail business?
9 In the age of e-commerce, how important is branding?
10 What effect will the advent of broad band network have on retail e-commerce?
11 How is music (CDs) likely to be marketed and sold in five years' time?
12 What products or services will be the most difficult to sell through e-commerce?
13 Will the high street survive the advent of e-commerce? How might it change?

14 What are the problems of selling a service on the internet?
15 What do you consider to be important in designing a lively and interesting commercial website?
16 What are the most annoying things about bad websites?
17 What are the particular problems facing a small firm wanting to sell on the internet and how might they be overcome?
18 Do you still need business skills for an e-commerce start-up?
19 Do Porter's generic marketing strategies still apply in the new world of e-commerce?
20 What are the particular problems likely to be faced by an e-commerce start-up?

⬤ Exercises and assignments

1 Try the following search-engines by keying in the same search request. Evaluate them in terms of speed, ease of use and information produced.

All the Web	www.alltheweb.com	Considered the largest search engine with more than 300 million pages in 25 languages
AltaVista	www.altavista.co.uk	A large engine with its own translation service for searching and reading foreign sites
Ask Eric	http:/ericir.syr.edu	A research service specialising in educational requests
Ditto	www.ditto.com	Specialises in picture searches
Excite	www.excite.com	This has its own directory of over 50 million pages
Google	www.google.com	Ranks sites in order of relevance Good for company names
Ingenta	www.ingenta.com	Indexes academic journals and articles
Lycos	www.lycos.co.uk	Large system but tends not to trawl deeply
Northern Light	www.northernlight.com	Wide index including news and books and magazines
Yahoo!	www.yahoo!.co.uk	The biggest UK system covering 22 countries

2 Visit the website of easyJet on www.easyJet.co.uk and see how easy it is to book an airline ticket. easyJet are widely seen as having one of the easiest UK commercial websites to navigate and now generate most of their business from it. They have even pioneered ticketless flying through it.

3 Visit the website of Amazon books on www.amazon.co.uk and see how easy it is to buy a book. Amazon are probably the leading international commercial website.

4 The BBC website is widely held to be one of the best in terms of information content. Visit it on www.bbc.com and www.beeb.com.

5 Visit a community website (e.g. www.totallyjewish.com or www.davidbowie.com) and see what information it contains.

6 ZDNet on www.zdnet.com provides a 'top 10' of the best examples of e-commerce. Visit the site and find out which sites are in the 'top ten' and why. Visit each site and evaluate it yourself. Do you agree with the criteria ZDNet have used?

7 ZDNet on www.zdnet.com also provides a top 10 of the worst examples of e-commerce. Visit the site and find out which sites are in the top 10 and why. Visit each site and evaluate it yourself. Do you agree with the criteria ZDNet have used?

8 ZDNet on www.zdnet.com also provides evaluations of various types of sites and gives you the one it thinks is best. These include live chat, live audio, web directories, search-engines, web developer resources and even the best place for free webpages.

9 Find out the 50 UK websites that register the largest number of hits by visiting www.top50.co.uk. What does this tell you about e-commerce in the UK?

10 Visit the top 10 sites. Evaluate their web design by listing the positive and negative points of each.

11 Select a community that you know well (for example, students). Outline the information content for a website that would be of interest to the community as a whole. List potential advertisers on the site.

12 Repeat exercises 1 to 3 of the start-up exercise at the back of the book on your ideas for an e-commerce start-up. Consider whether you want to take the idea further.

● Websites to visit

1 Visit the website of the ISI Programme for Business on www.isi.gov.uk and see what the programme offers.

2 The Barclays Bank ebusiness website offers a range of help, advice and facilities. Visit it on www.businesspark.barcays.com/ebusiness and see what it offers.

3 Visit Sage's website on www.sage.com and Virgin Biznet on www.virginbiz.net and see what they can do to help a web start-up.

4 Visit the First Tuesday Club on www.firsttuesday.com and see what they can do to help internet firms grow.

● References

Brady, G. (1999) 'The New Rules for Start-ups', *e-business*, December.

DTI (1998) *How the Internet can Work for You: A Guide to Implementing the Internet and the World Wide Web in Your Business*, London: HMSO, December.

Evans, P. and Wurster, T. (1999) *Blown to Bits*, Boston: Harvard Business School Press.

Hagel, J. and Singer, M. (1999) *Net Worth*, Boston: Harvard Business School Press.

Kaplin, S. and Sawhney, M. (2000) 'B2B E-commerce Hubs: Towards a Taxonomy of Business Models', *Harvard Business Review*, May.

chapter eight

Developing a business plan

Contents

Learning outcomes

By the end of this chapter you should:

- Understand the importance of the business plan;
- Understand the business planning process;
- With practice, be able to develop your own start-up business plan to suite different purposes;
- Understand how it can be used to raise finance;
- Be able to critically analyse a business plan.

Why you need a business plan

One of the most important steps in setting up any new business is to develop a business plan. It allows the owner-manager to crystallise their business idea and to think through the problems they will face, before they have to cope with them. It allows them to set aims and objectives and thereby give themselves a yardstick against which to monitor performance. Perhaps of more immediate importance, it can also act as a vehicle to attract external finance.

Success, for businesses of all sizes, is positively correlated with planning. Timmons (1999) claims that the vast majority of *INC.* magazine's annually-produced 500 fastest growing companies had business plans at the outset. In a research study, Woo *et al.* (1989) found that those firms which claimed to spend time in planning activities were those that experienced rapid growth. Another study by Kinsella *et al.* (1993) concluded that 93 per cent of fast growth firms in his study had written business plans, compared to 70 per cent of matched firms. At a more pragmatic level, just try raising finance for your business without a plan and you will realise how essential it is.

Business plans do not have to be long and elaborate. In many ways the process of thinking through how to go about setting up the business is far more important than the final document and for that reason internal plans can be informal, working documents. Only when they are used to obtain external finance do they need to become a more elaborate 'selling document'.

The planning process

Planning is a three-stage process:

1   Understanding where you are;
2   Deciding where you want to go;
3   Planning how to get there.

The business plan is just like a road map and the planning process is just like map reading; decide on where you are, the town you want to go to and then you can start to plan your route. You might decide not go in a straight line because there are longer but faster routes; you might be forced to take diversions because unexpected road works upset you plans; you might not get to your destination as quickly as you expect because the car breaks down. Indeed it is just possible that you will never reach your destination at all because of an accident. If you cannot decide where you are or where you want to go, the map is of little use. If you know where you are and where you want to go, a good map increases the chance of getting there. And planning the route will also help you estimate the petrol you need and the money you will therefore need to buy it. The business planning process is simple but systematic.

1   *Understanding where you are:*

- Understanding your product or service and how it is better and worse than that of your competitors – your competitive advantage:
  - How do you compete in terms of price, quality and so on?
  - Is the product or service differentiated in any way?
  - How can this be reinforced?
  - Can the product or service be easily copied?
  - Can you discern any patterns in successful or unsuccessful competitors?
- Understanding who your customers are and why and how they will buy from you:
  - Can you identify market segments and can you get to them?
  - Are your existing customers happy with the product or service?
  - What is good and bad about your marketing mix?
  - Can more customers be found who are similar to your existing customers?
  - Are you selling to a niche market?
- Understanding your own and your firm's strengths and weaknesses:
  - What are your own aims, your own strengths and weaknesses?
  - How good are your people and your facilities?
  - Are you good at leadership and communication?

   – What are the critical success factors – those things that it is crucial that
     you get right if you are to grow?
   – What will be the critical problem areas if you grow?
   – Do you have money of your own to put into the business?
● Understanding the opportunities and threats that the market might present
  you with:
   – Are market tastes changing?
   – Is the market growing?
   – Are there changes in the social, legal, economic, political or technolo-
     gical environment that are likely to effect you in the future (see SLEPT
     analysis on page 292)?
   – How easy is it for competitors to come into your industry? Do you have
     new product or service ideas?

2   *Decide where you want to go:*

● Decide the general aims you have for your business and for you. Do you want
  a lifestyle or do you want to go for growth? For some firms, aims become
  'mission statements' – statements of what the owner-manager wants the
  business to become. For example, a medical general practice came up with the
  mission 'to provide the best possible healthcare for patients at all times by
  responding to needs, providing accessible medical and anticipatory care of the
  highest quality and doing all that is possible to improve the social
  environment of the community'.
● Set some specific objectives that signal you have achieved your aims.
  Objectives must be quantified, bounded in time and realistically achievable.
  They can then serve as useful goals and yardsticks against which to judge your
  performance. For example, an objective might be to achieve profit growth of 10
  per cent with a minimum return on capital of 15 per cent. Objectives are the
  milestones on your journey. They tell you where you are going and let you
  know when you have arrived.

3   *Planning how to get there:*

● Strategies need to be developed to enable you to achieve your objectives.
  Strategies are 'how to' statements. They are not complicated, they are just
  'joined-up' tasks. Their development involves co-ordination of the different
  management functions – marketing, operations, people and finance.
● In particular, you will need to develop a marketing plan that produces a
  consistent and coherent marketing mix to address how to sell the product or
  service to the different customers.
● You will need to draw up financial budgets – profit and cash flow forecasts –
  to see what financial resources are needed to undertake the plan. Do you need
  to attract investors? Can you? If not, your plans might have to be modified.

The whole process is shown in Figure 8.1. It starts with the aims of the owner-
manager and the mission for the business. It is vital that owner-managers are
truthful to themselves about their own aims – otherwise the rest of the plan will
be useless. The next element is a SWOT firm (strengths, weaknesses,
opportunities and threats) analysis which gives a realistic appraisal of the

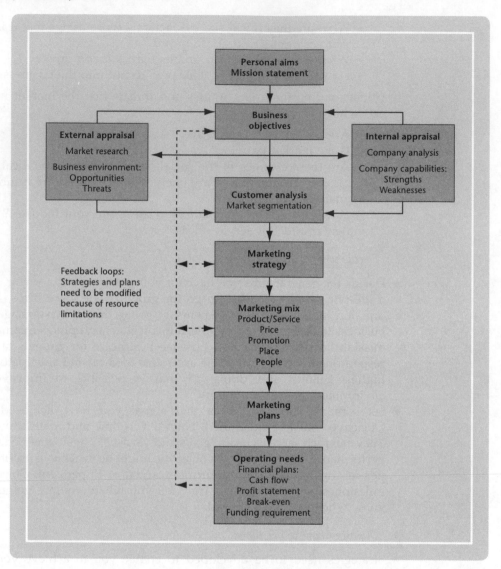

Figure 8.1 The business planning process

options open to the business. This feeds into both the business objectives and the analysis of customers (market segmentation). The marketing strategy is then developed into a detailed plan, which involves constructing a marketing mix to suit each of the different segments the firm is targeting. These are developed into detailed marketing plans for each product/market offering – who does what and when. These plans are then costed and developed into a detailed budget. However, there may be feedback loops where plans, strategies or even business objectives have to be modified because of resource limitations. It is worth spending a few minutes thinking through how Figure 8.1 works.

Figure 8.1 sets out what Chaston (2000) would call a 'conventional plan' – which is certainly what financial backers would be looking for. In the context of entrepreneurial marketing and the process he proposed for this (Figure 5.7), this marketing plan can be described as the 'detailed map' (step 7). The essential difference with Chaston's process is its emphasis on analysing the market, challenging conventional marketing approaches and trying to develop new approaches, within the capabilities of the business. This is a slightly different approach to the conventional SWOT analysis.

The great advantage of a business plan is that it forces you to think systematically and in detail about the future of the business. It forces you to think through the options that are open to you and justify the decisions you take, whilst thinking through the consequences of your actions. That is not to say you will anticipate all the problems you will face, but it will mean that you are better able to meet these challenges because you have a thorough understanding of the business and its market place. Remember, it is the process that is really important and a true entrepreneur is constantly refining or modifying their plan to meet changing opportunities and threats.

As we saw in Chapters 4 and 5, there are many sources of help and advice to assist in developing a business plan. Most banks provide free resource packs that include computer disks with pre-formatted cash flow forecasts. Once developed, it always pays to get feedback on your plan, particularly if you intend to use it to raise finance for the business. The more rapid the growth your business will face, the more likely you are to need advice. Indeed, evidence shows that fast-growth firms are more likely to seek out and use advice (Cosh and Hughes, 1998). However, it cannot be proved directly that the advice led to growth.

The SWOT analysis

The SWOT analysis is just a shorthand way of looking at you and the business – strengths and weaknesses – and the market environment in which it operates – opportunities and threats. As already stated, this is partly to do with your personal strengths and weaknesses, in relation to the business idea, but it is also to do with the business idea and its fit with the market place. We have covered some tools and techniques that can be applied to this. For example, the generic marketing strategies are relevant to the internal appraisal and market research, knowledge of economies of scale and Porter's Five Forces analysis of industry competitiveness are relevant to the appraisal of the external environment. There are some other techniques but they are more applicable to established businesses and are dealt with in Chapter 10. Because of their subjective nature, it is easily possible to under or overestimate the importance of elements of the SWOT and it is often a good idea to ask the opinion of a friend or colleague. But equally important is to remember always to challenge the conventions of the market place, to find ways of turning a weakness into a strength, of finding opportunities by being unconventional.

What the SWOT process is seeking to achieve is an overlap between the business environment and the firm's resources. In other words, a match between the firm's strategic or core competencies and a market opportunity. This match, as such, may not create sustainable competitive advantage – it may be copied – and may change over time. It is the continuing process of analysis, positioning and repositioning that is important. In other words the value of planning is really as a continuing process.

The process is an art rather than a science. The firm is looking for attractive business opportunities which, given the firm's capabilities, have a high probability of success. This probability is influenced by the firm's strengths, in particular how its distinctive competences match the key success requirements to operate in the market, given the existing competition. Threats may be classified according to their seriousness and probability of occurrence. A view of the overall attractiveness of a market is based upon the opportunities it offers balanced by the threats that it poses. In doing this it is often useful to list the factors – whether you control them or not – that are critical to the success of the venture.

The SWOT analysis itself should be short, succinct and easy to read. However, it is by definition a summary of the key issues emanating out of the marketing audit and should contain clear indicators of the key determinants of success rather than just being a smorgasbord of apparently unrelated points. A useful discipline in writing a SWOT is to continually ask yourself what each point means for the business.

As we have seen in previous chapters, developing a business plan was an important part of helping **Chris Hutt** decide what **Unicorn Inns** was doing right and how it could be developed. It set out his philosophy and approach, his marketing strategy and his financing requirements. However, it also identified five factors critical for the success of this strategy in 1991:

1 An extended recession: Chris recognised that, although they had so far avoided being hit, a longer recession would adversely affect profitability. He decided he could do little about this, but all the indicators at the time were positive.

2 Lack of suitable property: the plan depended on locating appropriate sites. An upturn in the property market might lead to rising prices, and inhibit suitable site acquisition. Again, Chris could do little about this, however, there was no indication that prices were about to rise.

3 Poor site evaluation: this was a high risk as the brand depended on good sites. Careful specification and a commitment to selling sites that proved unsuitable were intended to overcome this problem. Chris was confident that, having widely circulated a clear specification to appropriate estate and property agencies, they had the skills to recognise an ideal site.

4 Refurbishment delays or cost over-runs, always a possibility with the industry: Chris decided to take on a manager specifically with responsibility for opening and commercially developing new sites.

5 Poor performance by managers, an identified weakness in the industry: Chris decided to appoint a manager with specific responsibility for day-to-day management of new sites, once established.

. . . to be continued

What a business plan looks like

There are no set of rules that can be used to create a 'perfect business plan'. Each plan is particular to its business and will be different to others. Whilst later in the chapter we give a pro forma plan, even this will be adapted to say more or less about each heading, depending on the particular circumstances. The seven-page pro forma covers the following areas:

- Business details – name, address, legal form, business activity;
- Business aims and objectives;
- Market information – size, growth, competitors;
- The firm's strengths and weaknesses as well as competitive advantage;
- Customers;
- Marketing strategy – advertising, promotion, pricing and so on;
- Premises and equipment needs;
- Key people, their functions and background;
- Financial highlights – turnover, profit, break-even, funding details;
- Detailed profit forecast;
- Detailed monthly cash flow forecast.

This pro forma is intended for a relatively straightforward, small-scale start-up. For a large start-up, a proposal for development loans for an existing business or one seeking to attract equity finance would probably be longer, giving more detailed information and possibly covering forecasts for three years or more. Brochures and financial statements from past years might be appended. In these circumstances an executive summary at the front of the plan is essential – for a venture capitalist it may be all they ever read. The plan will also need a contents page.

Here are some further considerations:

1   When you write the plan have clearly in mind who it is intended for. If it is just for yourself, it can be brief, almost in check-list form. If you are trying to raise funds it may have to be longer. A proposal for venture capital funds may be 50 pages long, including appendices. Have clearly in your mind what your audience is looking for in the plan.
2   Keep it as short as possible. Do not pad it out. The plan should be sufficiently long to cover the subject adequately but short enough to maintain interest. Use appendices to provide necessary support information.
3   Check spelling, grammar, punctuation and, most important of all, financial accuracy. Errors damage your credibility and can throw you off when noticed as you present your plan. Word processors have grammar and spelling checks. A spreadsheet package can be used for the cash flow forecast and that will ensure arithmetic accuracy.
4   Ensure the plan is functional, clearly set out and easy to use. It does not have to be over elaborate or expensively produced. Modern word processing packages do an excellent job.

The investor's view

Whether you want to borrow money from a bank or seek equity finance you will need to do two things:

1 You will need to establish a relationship of trust and respect with the investor;
2 You will need to present them with a business plan.

The reality is that investors ultimately invest in individuals, not in businesses or plans. The plan is just one way, albeit very important, of communicating with the investor. It must therefore reinforce the perceptions the investor has of the individual(s) seeking finance. That perception must be that they know what they are talking about and that the business proposal has a good chance of success. However, banks and equity investors are looking for slightly different things and their approach to lending or investing is further explored in Chapter 12.

Banks

Banks are in the business of lending money; in that respect they are just like any other supplier of a commodity. However, about two-thirds of external finance for small firms comes from banks, which makes them an important supplier. The lending criteria banks adopt are set out in Chapter 12. The thing to remember about them is that they are not in the risk business, they are looking to obtain a certain rate of interest over a specified period of time and see their capital repaid. They do not share in the extra profits a firm might make, so they do not expect to lose money if there are problems. What is more, the manager stands to lose a lot if he lends to a business that subsequently fails.

Bank managers represent a set of values and practices alien to many owner-managers. They are employees, not independent professionals. They often talk 'a different language' and are subject to numerous rules and regulations that an owner-manager would probably find very tedious. Since they trade in money, they often cannot make decisions on their own without getting approval from 'up the line'. In these circumstances the business plan is an essential weapon in helping them get authorisation for a loan. Any manager will only be able to lend within the bank's own policies, at acceptable levels of risk and with adequate security to cover the loan. However, each of these three constraints requires the exercise of judgement and can therefore be influenced, not least through the style and content of the business plan.

A business plan prepared for a bank needs to demonstrate how the interest on the loan can be paid, even in the worst possible set of circumstances, and the capital can be repaid on the due date. In this respect the cash flow forecast is something that the bank manager will be particularly interested in. As well as cash flow, they are also particularly interested in two important financial ratios:

● Break-even – which tells him about the operating risk the business faces;
● Gearing – which tells him about the financial risks the business faces from borrowing.

In an ideal world, they would like both of these to be as low as possible.

Bank managers are trained to examine business plans critically. So expect to be questioned. Make explicit any assumptions that the plan is based on. The plan should seek to identify and then reassure the bank manager about the risks the business faces. All businesses face risks, so the manager will expect them to see them identified. Bank managers tend to dislike plans that they see as over-ambitious, since they will not share in the success, so the plan needs to be conservative. Bank managers will always ask questions about some of the claims in the plan, so you must always be able to back them up. Avoid any tendency to generalise in order to disguise a weakness in your knowledge.

For a start-up it is particularly important to establish the credibility of the owner-manager and other key managers. This can be done by summarising skills and previous experience, particularly in a related field. For an existing business the bank manager will be more interested in the firm's track record, particularly its financial performance, so previous financial statements will need to go with the plan. Where a long-term loan for R&D or capital expenditure is being sought, where there is little prospect of loan repayment in the short term, the plan must emphasise the cash-generating capacity of the business and take a perspective longer than one year.

Equity investors

Individuals and institutions investing in unquoted companies are becoming increasingly sophisticated. Who these individuals and institutions are and their investing criteria are set out in Chapter 12. Most businessmen submit investment proposals to more than one institution for consideration. However, on the other side of the coin, most investment institutions are inundated with proposals. It has been estimated that less than one in 20 will ever reach negotiation stage. To a large extent, therefore, the decision whether to proceed beyond an initial reading of the plan will depend crucially on its quality. The business plan is the first and often the best chance that an entrepreneur has to impress prospective investors with the quality of their investment proposal. A good executive summary is, therefore, vital.

Because of this and the likelihood that the sums involved are higher than would be sought from a bank manager, business plans tend to be longer – more comprehensive and going into greater depth – and better presented. An equity investor needs to be convinced of two things:

1   That a business opportunity exists which has the potential to earn the investor the high return that they need, within a time frame that is acceptable. They are likely to be seeking a return in excess of 25 per cent per annum, including capital gains, and an exit route (sale of their investment) within five to ten years.
2   That the company proposing to exploit this opportunity can do so effectively. This depends on the firm's competitive advantage and the quality of management.

Any business plan must therefore address both issues. This requires a careful balance between making the proposal sufficiently attractive, on the one hand, while realistically addressing the many risks inherent in the proposal, in particular how rapid growth will be handled. To do this the plan needs to emphasise the strengths of the business, particularly compared to the competition. Behind all plans there are people, and equity investors, like bank managers, need to be convinced that the entrepreneur and key managers can deliver what they are promising. Venture capitalists often say that the single most important element in the decision whether or not to invest is the credibility and quality of the firm's management.

The most difficult aspect of any deal is deciding on the split of equity between the various partners. The simple answer is that there is no set of rules and the final result will depend on the attractiveness of the proposal and the negotiating skills of the individuals concerned. However, *Venture Capital Report*, a monthly publication of investment opportunities, suggests the following rough starting point:

- 33 per cent for the idea;
- 33 per cent for the management;
- 33 per cent for the money.

It is also advisable to consider the objectives of the investing individual or institution. They will be interested in taking money out by way of dividends or interest and, over a longer period, through capital gains. What are they looking for and over what period? It may not be in the interests of the business to see cash going out in the first few years. Are there any tax implications to their preferred strategy? Are they looking to sell their investment? If so, when and to whom (their 'exit route')? This may be an opportunity for the entrepreneur to increase their share of the business by buying out the investor. It may also be an opportunity for the entrepreneur to dilute their share of the business or exit completely themselves, by encouraging a merger with, or buy-out by, another company. Exit routes and time scales need to be considered and agreed upon before any deal is done.

A related issue is how much control the entrepreneur is willing to surrender. Most want to part with as little as possible. Indeed few investors would want the entrepreneur's share to fall below 50 per cent, otherwise they might lose their sense of ownership and this might affect their motivation. Some equity investors prefer a 'hands-on' approach to managing their investment whereby they have a non-executive director on the Board, visit the firm monthly and keep in regular phone contact with the entrepreneur. Others have a 'hands-off' approach,

Ben Hayman now owns just under 50 per cent of **Mediasurface**, a company set up in 1996 to provide software and support to help companies update information on their websites instantaneously. However, in that time he has raised £8.5 million.

In 1996 he took £1 million from 3i Group in exchange for 15 per cent of the business. A year later he raised a further £1 million from Elderstreet Investments, using the money to open offices in California and France. In 1999 he raised a further £6.5 million from existing backers and Amadeus, Dresdener Kleinwort Benson and Index Ventures in order to triple the size of the offices.

The company has not yet made a profit. Sales in 1998 were only £260 000 but took off in 1999 and are expected to be £10 million in 2000. Without the venture capital backing this could not have happened.

preferring not to interfere once they have invested, perhaps meeting once a year to review the progress of the business. Further details are given in Chapter 12.

Whereas a bank loan will probably take weeks to arrange, an equity investment will take months. It will involve numerous meetings, interviews and presentations. The investors, or their accountants, will undertake their own investigations into the business (called 'due diligence'). The development of the legal documentation will involve lengthy, detailed work. The sheer scale of the work is one reason for the continuing belief that it is difficult to raise equity sums below £100 000 from institutions, leaving the investment of sums less than this to 'business angels' who will either be willing to do much of the work themselves, or just 'take a risk'.

Presenting a case for finance

At some point the owner-manager can expect to be asked to 'present' their case for finance. Part of the reason for this will be to support and elaborate on details contained in the business plan but part of it will be to allow the potential backer to form judgements about the owner-manager, and possibly other managers in their team. They will be looking for motivation, enthusiasm and integrity but most of all the managerial ability to make the plan actually happen.

To get a business to grow successfully requires a genuine desire – amounting almost to a need – to succeed against all adversity. Owner-managers need to be able to motivate themselves and their team. They must be willing to take risks, but only moderate ones that can be overcome, and show to potential backers how this will be achieved. However, enthusiasm and drive must be tinged with a strong sense of realism in taking a market view of the business and its potential. Most successful companies are run by people who understand the market. The technician who has a good product idea but really only wants to build modified prototypes and is not interested in production, let alone selling and marketing, will not find anybody willing to back him without teaming up with others who have the qualities he lacks.

The presentation is an opportunity to demonstrate these personal qualities. First impressions are important, but an in-depth knowledge of the key areas in the business plan will go a long way towards generating the confidence that is needed. There are ways of enhancing a presentation. It is important to rehearse it thoroughly. Always stress the market and the firm's competitive advantage. Stress the competencies of all the managers. In terms of style, it is important to demonstrate the product and, in Western culture, to make frequent eye-to-eye contact. The owner-manager should manage the presentation with respect to any co-presenters. They should try to involve the investor and turn the presentation into a discussion or dialogue, responding to questions thoughtfully and honestly. Trying to weasel your way out of questions you do not know the answers to rarely works, so the best advice is to say you do not know but will get back with the answer in a few days.

A leading venture capitalist once admitted that, whilst discussions with the owner-manager centred on the business plan, the final decision whether or not to invest really was a result of 'gut feel' – a personal 'chemistry' between them and the owner-manager. At the end of the day, that chemistry must lay the foundation for a long term relationship based, as with all relationships, on trust and respect.

Pro forma business plan

The business plan is a description of the business and what the owner-manager wants it to become over the next 12 months. It should contain targets, estimates and projections and describe how they will be achieved. It should help the owner-manager think ahead systematically and raise finance. It is an invaluable route map to help their business succeed.

The pro forma plan on the following pages is meant as a guide for how one should look. It is intended for a modest start-up. Notes are included in the relevant sections. It is one devised by the author and used by a number of Training and Enterprise Councils and subsequently Business Links for a number of years. Specimen business plans based on this pro forma are shown in the Appendices. They are intended to be used for discussion only and not as examples of good or bad plans.

Business plan

> **Business name and address:**
>
> **Proprietor's name and address:**
>
> **Business form:**　[Sole trader/partnership/limited company]
>
> **Business activity:**
>
> [Enter here a description of the business, including product/service details. Obviously this is the core around which the plan revolves. It should describe it as thoroughly as possible, but can be supplemented with samples, photograph and so on. It should also give details of any intended future product/service developments.]
>
> **Aims:**
>
> [Aims for the business and the owner-manager should go here. For example, the aim might be to provide secure employment and an adequate income for the owner-manager and their spouse. The aims are broader than the objectives.]
>
> **Objectives:**
>
> [The objectives are the specific targets. For example, the objective might be to achieve sales of £150 000 in the first year and a gross profit margin of 40 per cent.]

Market size and growth:

[Market research information can go here. Try to estimate the size of the market the business is aiming for (either locally or nationally) and the share it hope to capture, the growth in the last few years and any other characteristics. For example, it could be that there are many small competitors without the competitive advantage you have. A good product/service will sell only if a market for it exists or can be created.]

Competitors:

Names	*Strengths*	*Weaknesses*

[List major competitors together with their strengths and weaknesses. For example, there may be a major national competitor but they cannot deliver the personal service this firm offers. The aim is then to develop these advantages but also to counter any advantages competitors might have.]

Your business:

Strengths	*Weaknesses*

[In listing the strengths and weaknesses, the aim is to build on the strengths, particularly when they generate a competitive advantage. Weaknesses will need to be addressed in the marketing plan.]

Competitive advantages:

[Competitive advantage should come from the business strengths and weaknesses. This section also needs to address how the advantage will be maintained. For example, is there a patent or copyrights? Remember that if a new idea proves successful others will copy it.]

Proposed customers:

[This should describe the customers the business intends to sell to, if possible, naming names. For example, the business might intend selling to farmers in a particular geographic area. Try to quantify the number of customers.]

Advertising and promotions strategy:

[This should describe how the business will communicate with the proposed customers. For example, by telephone or mail shot. Will it be by advertising? If so what form might it take (for example, notice-board, newspapers, radio and so on).]

Pricing strategy:

[This should explain what the pricing policy is and why. Does the firm intend to be cheapest, most expensive or just take the 'going rate'. If relevant, it might describe how the price for a customer is arrived at.]

Premises:

[This should describe (size, location and any other special characteristics) the type of premises the business will operate from – private home, shop, workshop and so on. Note should be made of planning permissions required and cost – lease, rent or purchase.]

Equipment

[Any special equipment needed should be described here together with cost and proposed method of acquisition – lease, hire or purchase. Will more equipment be needed in the future?]

Key people and job functions:

[Key people, including the owner-manager, and their roles and responsibilities should be described here.]

Background details of key people:

[The background of the key people should be described here – qualifications, training, previous industry experience and personal strengths and weaknesses. If the plan is used to obtain finance, the owner-manager may need to give fuller background details. This helps establish credibility.]

Financial highlights

12 months to:

Turnover:

[This section summarises information from the profit and loss account.
Sales are the value of goods or services estimated to be sold in the year. It represents the value invoiced to customers and NOT the amount of cash received.]

Profit:

[Net profit (or loss) represents the difference between sales and direct variable and fixed costs. Out of this a sole trader would take drawings. On the other hand, the owner-manager of a limited company will pay themselves a wage or salary (shown in costs) but if they want to take more out of the business they might decide to do so by way of dividends.]

Break-even:

[The break-even calculation should be shown here. This is a measure of the operating risk facing the business. It should be as low as possible.]

Funding requirement:

[This should disclose any funding required and the months it is required, taken from the cash flow forecast. Remember, always to add something as a contingency against the plan going wrong. It should also describe where these funds are expected to come from.]

Source of funds:

[Here indicate the expected source and nature of funding (for example, overdraft for 8 months).]

Forecast profit and loss account

Business:

Period:

Sales: £ (A)

Less direct (variable) costs:

materials £

direct wages £

other £

Total direct (variable) costs: £ _____

Gross profit/contribution: £ (B)

Fixed costs (overheads):

wages/salaries (including taxes) £

rent £

heat/light/power £

advertising £

insurance £

transport/travel £

telephone £

stationery/postage £

repairs/renewals £

depreciation £

local taxes £

other _____ £

other _____ £

Total fixed costs £ _____ (C)

Net profit £

Less drawings or dividends £ _____

Profit retained in the business £ _____

Break-even point $= \dfrac{(C) \times (A)}{(B)}$

Direct (variable) costs are the costs of materials, labour and other expenditures that vary directly with sales activity. It represents the costs associated with the goods or services sold. It does not necessarily represent the total goods or services purchased, since some of these might have been purchased for stock. Nor does it represent the cash spent, as some goods might have been purchased on credit terms.

Fixed costs are the overhead costs of the business that do not vary with sales activity. For example, rent of premises. They do not represent the cash spent, as goods might be purchased on credit or services might be paid for in advance. Furthermore, items like depreciation represent an allocation of the cost of a fixed asset, not the cash spent on it.

Cash Flow Forecast

Month:													
SALES													
Volume:													
Value:													
RECEIPTS													
Sales – cash													
Sales – debtors													
Capital introduced													
Grants, loans etc													
Total (*A*)													
PAYMENTS													
Materials													
Wages/salaries													
Rent													
Heat/light/power													
Advertising													
Insurance													
Transport/travel													
Telephone													
Stationery/postage													
Repairs/renewals													
Local taxes													
Other _____													
Other _____													
Capital purchases													
Loan repayments													
Drawings/dividends													
Total (*B*)													
CASH BALANCES													
Cash flow (*A*)−(*B*)													
Opening balance													
Closing balance													

Cash flow is the lifeblood of a business. The cash flow forecast shows where the cash will be coming from and where it will go. Each monthly column should show the actual amounts the business expects to receive and pay out. But remember, sales made in January may not generate cash until February or later if terms of trade are 30 days. Cash receipts, therefore, show cash coming in, including capital introduced and any loans or grants. Similarly, cash payments include loan repayments, withdrawals or dividends. They do not include depreciation, which is an allocation of the capital cost of an asset over its expected life.

The cash increase (or decrease) is the difference between total cash receipts and total cash payments. This is added (or subtracted) from the opening balance to give the closing balance that month – that is, the surplus of cash in any month – which is carried forward into next month's column as the opening balance.

Summary

Developing a business plan is important to help you crystallise your business idea, think through the problems you might face and to develop a yardstick against which to measure your performance. It also is essential if you need to raise external finance. The planning process is more important than the written business plan itself and a true entrepreneur is constantly refining their plan to meet changing opportunities and threats – even if this is not written down. Planning is a three stage process:

1 Understanding where you are;
2 Deciding where you want to go;
3 Planning how to get there.

Starting with your personal aims and ambitions, you develop business objectives that are quantifiable, realistic and bounded in time. These are based upon an internal appraisal of your business capabilities (strengths and weaknesses) and an external appraisal of the business environment (opportunities and threats). This is called a SWOT analysis. You go on to identify your customers and develop a marketing strategy based upon your marketing mix (product, price, promotion, place and people) that will enable you to sell your product or service in the appropriate volumes to meet your business objectives. This is detailed in a marketing plan with can be translated into financial and operating budgets. **Chris Hutt** and **Unicorn Inns** found the process invaluable and refined it further by determining what might be the factors that were critical to the success of the plan.

There is no standard format for a business plan; however, a typical one might contain the following:

- Business details – name, address, legal form, business activity;
- Business aims and objectives;
- Market information – size, growth, competitors;
- The firm's strengths and weaknesses as well as competitive advantage;
- Customers;
- Marketing strategy – advertising, promotion, pricing and so on;
- Premises and equipment needs;
- Key people, their functions and background;
- Financial highlights – turnover, profit, break-even, funding details;
- Detailed profit forecast;
- Detailed monthly cash flow forecast.

The business plan should only be as long as it needs to be. Keep it as short as possible, whilst delivering all relevant information.

A business plan presented to a bank needs to demonstrate how interest on the loan can be paid and the capital repaid on the due date. Particular attention, therefore, needs to be paid to the cash flow forecast. Bank managers are risk averse. To obtain a loan you need to gain their trust and develop their respect in your business ability. Credibility is vital.

A business plan developed for an equity investor needs to demonstrate that a business opportunity exists that can earn a high return (in excess of 25 per cent) in a five to ten-year time frame and that the management team are capable of exploiting the opportunity. Issues of control and ownership need to be thought through though. But, as was the case with **Mediasurface**, it is often better to have 50 per cent of something rather than 100 per cent of nothing.

Essays and discussion topics

1   List the contents of a business plan that is drawn up:

    (1)   For planning purposes within the firm;
    (2)   For raising external finance.

    How are they different?

2   Draw up a report for your superior in a bank outlining the criteria you recommend the bank to use in making a loan to:

    (1)   A start-up business;
    (2)   An established firm.

    How are they different? How much of the necessary information can come from the business plan?

3   How can computer based systems help develop a business plan? What advantages do they offer? Are there any drawbacks?
4   What form do you think a business plan should take for your own, internal use?
5   In a rapidly changing world, is planning really of any use?
6   In a world 'turned upside down' and in chaos, full of uncertainty, how can you plan?
7   Are entrepreneurs congenitally incapable of planning?
8   Every business graduate can produce a good business plan, but not even one per cent are entrepreneurs. Discuss.
9   How can you write a business plan for an e-commerce business when the market will have changed within one month?
10   The best business plan is a short business plan. Discuss.

Exercises and activities

1   Select one of the three specimen business plans in the Appendix to this chapter and review them. Critically evaluate the business proposition.
2   Visit any of the main banks and obtain a business start-up pack. Many of these contain pro forma business plans on disk. Do the specimen business plans they contain differ in any significant way from the ones we have looked at?

Start-up exercise

Undertake steps 12 to 15 of the start-up exercise at the back of the book.

Websites to visit

1   The following websites contain downloadable business tools, including business plans. Visit each one and see whether the tools are worth using to help develop your business plan.

    ● Barclays Bank: www.smallbusiness.barclays.co.uk
    ● NatWest Bank: www.natwest.co.uk
    ● Department for Education and Employment resources for small business: www.business-info.org.uk/resources
    ● Master Planner www.masterplanner.co.uk
    ● Wall Street Journal (US): www.startup.wsj.com

2 Barclays Bank website contains a Business Opportunities Profiles Service which gives information such as potential customers, competition and start-up costs for selected business sectors. Visit the site and see if there is any information relevant to your business. The site is on: www.smallbusiness.barclays.co.uk.

3 The following websites contain business and management information which may be relevant to your business. Visit each one and see whether there is information that might be helpful in developing your business plan.

● Start-ups www.startups.co.uk
● Bnet www.bnet.co.uk
● Enterprise Zone www.enterprisezone.org.uk

● Appendix 1: Business plan for Sport Retail

Business name and address:

Sport Retail
14 Lower Street
Bedford

Proprietor's name and address:

John Bull
Address as above

Business form: Sole trader

Business activity:

The shop will sell general sportswear, clothing, footwear and sports accessories from a good secondary retail location close to the main shopping area of Bedford. Sports covered will include football, cricket, golf, tennis, archery, skiing and other sports, as appropriate to the season. In addition, the shop will sell general sports clothing and footwear such as track suits, trainers and so on. Suppliers will include major names such as Adidas, Nike, and so on.

Aims:

The aim of the business is to provide an adequate income for myself and my wife. We shall be living above the shop.

Objectives:

1. Sales of £250,000 in the first year
2. Gross profit margin of 40%
3. Net profit margin of 16%
4. Drawings at least £25,000

Market size and growth:

The last decade has seen a substantial increase in the popularity of sport and consequently the growth of the sportswear market. It is estimated that two-thirds of time spent on leisure pursuits is devoted to sport. The estimated size of the sport clothing and footwear market is some £1 billion. The market for sport equipment is about the same size and the market for swimwear and beachwear is over £200 000. These estimates are very approximate because the demarcation between sportswear and fashionwear is becoming increasingly blurred.

Competitors:

Names	Strengths	Weaknesses
Olympus Sports Silver St. (400 yards away)	Located in main shopping area Very price competitive National promotion Shop layout appeal to young	Lack of expert advice Lack of personal service Limited range Lower end of market
2 Seasons Harpur St	Skiing and tennis equipment Good service Well known brands	Poor location Cramped shop, poor displays
Market stall	Cheap	No service Only open market day Poor quality low end of market

Your business:

Strengths	Weaknesses
Personal, expert service	Secondary location (better than 2 Seasons)
Wide range of equipment	Limited merchandising opportunities
Quality equipment	Cannot afford expensive promotions
Well-known brands	

Competitive advantages:

1. Personal, expert service
2. Football links – proprietor local football celebrity
3. Links with local sports clubs, schools and so on will enable equipment and sportswear to be purchased to meet their specific requirements
4. Wide range of quality merchandise

Proposed customers:

General public   Typical market segments: School age (male and female)*
                                                 Teenage and twenties
                                                 Middle age (mainly male)*
                                                 Impulse shopper
                                                 Dedicated buyer*

Sports clubs and schools*

* These are the groups we expect to attract

Advertising and promotions strategy:

1. Very limited advertising in local paper: shop opening and seasonal sales. It is proposed to get a well-known sportsman to open the shop.
2. Extensive promotion to sports clubs and schools offering special equipment and sportswear and 'discounts'. Displays may be mounted at Clubs and so on or special evenings could be arranged.
3. In-store seasonal promotions of particular sportswear or equipment. This could include special displays, promotional signs and, perhaps, a discounted 'loss-leader' to get customers into the shop.
4. Store displays would emphasise the professional football links.

Pricing strategy:

We cannot compete against Olympus on price and will not attempt to do so. We will offer good quality branded merchandise at recommended retail prices. We will attempt to stock alternative merchandise and brands to Olympus. We will offer good value for money but not lowest price.

Premises:

1000 square foot retail premises on Lower Street, Bedford. This is a prime secondary site close to the main shopping area of Bedford. Bedford itself offers a good location and is the main shopping centre for the north of the county. The premises are leasehold with 18 years to run, let on a full repairing and insuring basis with rent reviews every 5 years. There is a two-bedroom flat above the shop in which I intend to live with my wife.

Equipment

Shop display equipment only.

Key people and job functions:

Mr and Mrs Bull – Proprietors
There may be other part-time counter staff, as required for Saturday work and so on.

Background details of key people:

Mr Bull
Formerly professional footballer (joined from school). Retired 4 years ago. Worked as a salesman with Rank Xerox selling photocopiers to large companies. Made redundant 6 months ago.
Still maintains good links with local sports clubs and, in particular, old football club.

Mrs Bull
Housewife. No work experience since marriage.
Prior to marriage was employed as counter staff with Marks & Spencer.
Currently Parent Governor of Priory School and on organising committee for local Youth Club.

Financial highlights

12 months to: 30 April 2002

Turnover:

£250,000

Profit:

£40,000 before drawings

Break-even:

$$\frac{£60,000 \times 250,000}{100,000} = £150,000$$

Funding requirement:

Lease purchase	£20,000
Redecoration	5,000
Fixtures and fittings	15,000
Total	£40,000

+ Overdraft facility as required (see cash flow)

Source of funds:

Own funds	£25,000
Bank loan	15,000

We shall be seeking a 10 year, fixed interest rate loan.

Forecast profit and loss account

Business: Sport Retail

Period: Year to 30 April 2002

Sales:		£250,000 (A)
Less direct (variable) costs:		
materials	£150,000	
direct wages	£	
other	£	
Total direct (variable) costs:		£150,000
Gross profit/contribution:		£100,000 (40%) (B)
Fixed costs (overheads):		
wages/salaries (including taxes)	£ 12,000	
rent	£ 18,000	
heat/light/power	£ 3500	
advertising	£ 2500	
insurance	£ 1500	
transport/travel	£ 6000	
telephone	£ 3000	
stationery/postage	£ 2000	
repairs/renewals	£ 500	
depreciation	£ 4000	
local taxes	£	
other Professional fees	£ 5000	
other _____	£	
Total fixed costs		£ 60,000 (16%) (C)
Net profit		£ 40,000
Less drawings or dividends		£ 25,000
Profit retained in the business		£ 15,000

$$\text{Break-even point} = \frac{(C) \times (A)}{(B)}$$

Cash Flow Forecast

Month:	May	Jun	Jul	Aug	Sept	Oct	Nov	Dec	Jan	Feb	Mar	Apr	Total
SALES													
Volume:													
Value:	–	20.0	25.0	15.0	20.0	25.0	30.0	30.0	15.0	20.0	25.0	25.0	250.0
RECEIPTS													
Sales – cash		20.0	25.0	15.0	20.0	25.0	30.0	30.0	15.0	20.0	25.0	25.0	250.0
Sales – debtors													
Capital introduced	25.0												25.0
Grants, loans etc.	15.0												15.0
VAT on sales		3.5	4.4	2.6	3.5	4.4	5.3	5.3	2.6	3.5	4.4	4.4	43.9
Total (A)	40.0	23.5	29.4	17.6	23.5	29.4	35.3	35.3	17.6	23.5	29.4	29.4	333.9
PAYMENTS													
Materials	30.0	–	12.0	15.0	9.0	12.0	15.0	18.0	18.0	9.0	15.0	15.0	168.0
Wages/salaries	–	1.0	1.0	1.0	1.0	1.0	1.0	1.0	1.0	1.0	1.0	1.0	11.0
Rent	9.0	–	–	–	–	–	–	–	–	–	–	–	9.0
Heat/light/power	–	–	–	4.5	–	4.5	–	–	4.5	–	–	–	13.5
Advertising	–	0.5	–	0.2	0.2	0.2	0.3	0.2	0.2	0.3	0.2	0.2	2.5
Insurance	1.5	–	–	–	–	–	–	–	–	–	–	–	1.5
Transport/travel	0.5	0.5	0.5	0.5	0.5	0.5	0.5	0.5	0.5	0.5	0.5	0.5	6.0
Telephone		0.75	–	–	0.75	–	–	0.75	–	–	0.75		3.0
Stationery/postage	1.0					0.5						0.5	2.0
Repairs/renewals						0.25						0.25	0.5
Local taxes			0.5			0.5			1.0			1.5	3.5
Other _____													
Other _____	0.6	0.4	0.4	0.4	0.4	0.4	0.4	0.4	0.4	0.4	0.4	0.4	5.0
Capital purchases	20.0	20.0											40.0
Loan repayments													
Drawings/dividends													
VAT on purchases	5.3	–	2.1	2.6	1.6	2.1	2.6	3.2	3.2	1.6	2.6	2.6	29.5
VAT paid to C & E			0.5			4.2			4.2			5.5	14.4
Total (B)	67.9	22.4	17.75	24.2	12.7	22.4	24.3	23.3	29.25	17.3	19.7	28.2	309.4
CASH BALANCES													
Cash flow (A)–(B)	(27.9)	1.1	11.65	(6.6)	10.8	7.0	11.0	12.0	(11.65)	6.2	9.7	1.2	
Opening balance	–	(27.9)	(26.8)	(15.15)	(21.75)	(10.95)	(3.95)	7.05	19.05	7.4	13.6	23.3	
Closing balance	(27.9)	(26.8)	(15.15)	(21.75)	(10.95)	(3.95)	7.05	19.05	7.4	13.6	23.3	24.5	24.5

● Appendix 2: Business plan for Jean Young (Consultancy)

Business name and address:

Ms. Jean Young
New House, West Street,
St Albans

Proprietor's name and address:

Ms. Jean Young
As above

Business form: Sole trader

Business activity

Management consultancy and training for the health care market.

Consultancy assistance with business planning, financial control and marketing will be offered. This will involve working with managers with responsibilities in these areas, to help them develop and use the necessary skills. Associated services will be the provision of standard or bespoke management training, developed to suit clients' needs and delivered at the clients' convenience. A range of standard training modules has already been assembled which can be used directly or tailored to suit client needs. The work will be carried out in association with one or more larger consultancy firms.

Aims:

To provide an independent income based upon my broad business skills and experience and to allow me to plan for the future.
My husband is also bringing in an income to the family that is sufficient to support us.

Objectives:

1. Income over £17 000
2. Profit over £12 000
3. To work with at least four separate organisations during the year
4. To obtain repeat work from them whenever it is available

Market size and growth:

The main market will be the four regions of the NHS in the south east of England: Oxford, North West Thames, North East Thames and East Anglia. Within these four regions there are 45 District Health Authorities, 29 Family Health Associations, approximately 100 NHS Units (mainly hospitals) and 81 NHS Trusts. In addition there are approximately 50 fundholding general practices. The regional and district structure of the NHS is undergoing massive change, with responsibilities being devolved to semi-independent organisations. All these organisations need to develop new management skills to cope with the changes and need help and advice to cope with the constant restructuring.

Competitors:

Names	Strengths	Weaknesses

Consultancy:
- Numerous small consultancies but the Directory of Management Consultancies in the UK lists only 14 in the relevant geographical area specialising in services for the health market.
- Large consultancies such as KPMG, PWC and Harvest usually take on major restructuring projects rather than work in the area I have targeted.

Training:
- Numerous sole traders, mainly ex-NHS employees with special connections. They tend to specialise in narrow, non-'business' fields and are often steeped in NHS tradition and practice. This is now often seen as inappropriate.
- Small consultancies are the greatest threat. They understand the NHS and are cheap. I can identify 10 small consultancies operating in the area.
- Large consultancies and education centres do not offer great competition in this area.

Your business:

Strengths	Weaknesses
NHS experience of training and consultancy	Small; could get overstretched
Small business experience	Possible perceived lack of credibility
Small, so flexible and responsive to customer needs	
Low cost business to run	
Only need to cover business expenses	
for first 4 months	

Competitive advantages:

The main success factor for consultants is good client relationships. Being small, these can be developed on a personal basis and services can be adapted to meet quite specific client needs. Some good relationships are already established and will be built on.

Also, I have worked in Trusts and hospitals applying for Trust status and am keenly aware of the issues they face. I have assisted business planning in a regional headquarters, worked with GPs and carried out training programmes for districts.

Proposed customers:

See section on 'Market size and growth'.

Buyers of my consultancy and training services will be at a number of levels within the NHS. There is no standard form of approach as each region, district, unit and Trust is different. However, there are a large number of discrete buyers, purchasing on an individual basis.

Advertising and promotions strategy:

1 Personal approaches, as appropriate, within the organisations. Brochures, advertising and so on are inappropriate.
2 Personal approaches will also be made to a number of the established small consultancies with a view to being taken on as an associate. This is an established mode of work, offering significant advantages to the firm and to the associate.

Pricing strategy:

Consultancy and training charges in the NHS range from £300 to £1200 per day (Health Service Journal).
I shall charge between £300 and £500, depending on circumstances.

Premises

Working from home as there will be no client visits. The local authority has confirmed that planning permission is not required. Consultancy will be at clients' premises and training at suitable venues.

Equipment

I already own a VW Golf and have an office at home with good quality PC, telephone and fax (value approximately £3600)
I need a laserjet printer, business software and overhead projector, flip charts and so on – cost approximately £2000.

Key people and job functions:

Background details of key people:

Ms Jean Young, BSc.(2i in computer science, Leicester University), MBA (South Bank University).
Age 34, married, one child
Work experience includes:

- 3 years as Senior Consultant with Talbot Hawkins, a small consultancy specialising in working for the NHS, including Trusts and GPs. Work undertaken included training and consultancy in the areas of business strategy, planning and marketing.
- 2 years as Business Development Manager with Saatchi & Saatchi, working with a range of public and private sector clients.
- 3 years as Business Development Manager with Medical IT, a small company providing software solutions to the NHS. My job was related to financial control and planning.

Financial Highlights

12 months to: 31 October 1999:

Turnover:

£17,200

Profit:

£12,018 (before drawings of £6600)

Break-even:

$$\frac{5,182 \times 17,200}{17,200} = £5,182$$

= approximately 13 days at a fee of £400 per day

Funding requirement:

Printer	£1500	
Software	£300	
Other	£200	
Total	£2000	including VAT

Source of funds:

Own funds

Forecast profit and loss account

Business: J. Young, Consultant

Period: Year to 31 October, 1999

Sales:		£ 17,200	(A)
Less direct (variable) costs:			
materials	£		
direct wages	£		
other	£		
Total direct costs		£ –	
Gross profit/contribution:		£ 17,200	(B)
Fixed costs (overheads):			
wages/salaries (incl. taxes)	£ 330		
rent	£		
heat/light/power	£		
advertising	£		
insurance	£ 100		
transport/travel	£ 430		
telephone	£ 450		
stationery/postage	£ 570		
repairs/renewals	£ 350		
depreciation	£ 2667		
local taxes	£		
other Prof. fees	£ 175		
other Sundry	£ 110		
Total fixed costs		£ 5182	(C)
Net profit		£ 12 018	
Less drawings or dividends		£ 6600	
Profit retained in the business		£ 5418	

$$\text{Break-even point} = \frac{(C) \times (A)}{(B)}$$

Cash Flow Forecast   1998/99

Month:	Nov	Dec	Jan	Feb	Mar	Apr	May	Jun	Jul	Aug	Sept	Oct	Total
SALES													
Volume: days	1	1	2	2	3	4	5	5	5	5	5	5	43
Value:	400	400	800	800	1200	1600	2000	2000	2000	2000	2000	2000	17200
RECEIPTS													
Sales – cash													
Sales – debtors		470	470	940	940	1410	1880	2350	2350	2350	2350	2350	17860
Capital introduced	2000												2000
Grants, loans etc.													
VAT on cap. expend.		299											299
Total (A)	2000	769	470	940	940	1410	1880	2350	2350	2350	2350	2350	20159
PAYMENTS													
Materials													
Wages/salaries Sec	10	120	20	20	20	20	20	20	20	20	20	20	330
Rent													
Heat/light/power													
Advertising													
Insurance		100											100
Travel Petrol	10	10	20	20	30	40	50	50	50	50	50	50	430
Telephone	120			100			100			100			420
Stationery/postage	130	40	40	40	40	40	40	40	40	40	40	40	570
Repairs/renewals		200						150					350
Local taxes													
Other Prof. fees	50											125	175
Other _____													
Capital purchases	2000												2000
Loan repayments													
Drawings/dividends						820	850	970	860	730	770	875	785	6660
VAT on purchases													
VAT paid to C & E		70			350			840			1050		2310
Total (B)	2320	550	90	190	1270	960	1190	1970	850	990	2045	1030	13455
CASH BALANCES													
Cash flow (A)−(B)	(320)	219	380	750	(330)	450	690	380	1500	1360	305	1320	
Opening balance	-	(320)	(101)	279	1029	699	1149	1839	2219	3719	5079	5384	
Closing balance	(320)	(101)	279	1029	699	1149	1839	2219	3719	5079	5384	6704	6704

⬤ Appendix 3: Business plan for Dewhurst Engineering Ltd.

Business name and address:

Dewhurst Engineering Ltd.
Unit 7
Highgrove Industrial Estate
Coventry

Proprietor's name and address:

Nitin Shah
11 Prospect Place
Kineton
Warwickshire

Business form: Limited company

Business activity

The company specialises in undertaking high quality, high added value engineering work for local technology based companies. Such work is usually for prototypes, one-off projects or specialist requirements. The company was established in 1972 and is now offered for sale with its existing customer base by the owner who is retiring because of ill health. Excluding the owner, there are three full-time shop floor employees plus one part-time secretary/bookkeeper. The, as yet, unaudited accounts for the year ending 31 March 2000 show a turnover of £140 000 and a net profit of £10 000.
The company is offered for sale as a going concern for £50 000.

Aims:

To become a major supplier of specialist engineering services for technology based and other companies in the area (20 mile radius) within five years.

Objectives:

For year to March 2001:   Turnover £187 000, after tax profit £18 000.
For year to March 2002:   Turnover of £270 000, after tax profits of £30 000.

All of this to be financed through retained earnings and using the existing premises.

Market size and growth:

There are an estimated 250 technology based companies within a 20 mile radius of Coventry. The company currently sells to only about 30 of them. About 150 of the remaining companies are potential customers, judging from the Chamber of Commerce Directory of Companies.

Competitors:

Names   *Strengths*   *Weaknesses*

There are few direct competitors in the area who offer the same range of services. Most engineering firms concentrate on batch or production line engineering work in order to warrant the use of their expensive CNC machinery. The major competition comes from the potential use of in-house facilities by customers.

Your business:

Strengths

1. Good reputation for quality work
2. High level of repeat work
3. High level of service provision
4. Competent, loyal workforce

Weaknesses

1. Owner has let things drift during his illness

Competitive advantages:

No direct competition in the area.

Proposed customers:

The majority of existing customers are situated within 20 miles of Coventry. Typically, they are commercial companies or other organisations involved in R&D and/or design and manufacturing. They are technology based and include welding equipment, printing technology and new product R&D companies. Some work comes from motor manufacturers such as Jaguar. They value quality of work and service, including speed of delivery. A list of current customers is attached to this plan.

The marketing plan envisages doubling the customer base to approximately 60 companies within one year.

Initial orders, however, are likely to be relatively small.

Advertising and promotions strategy:

In the past, promotion has been mainly by personal selling. Over the last year, because of illness, the company has relied heavily on repeat business from existing customers.

Personal visits will be reinforced by direct mail to generate new customers. It is intended to mail 15 companies per month, which should result in 7 visits, from which it is hoped to generate 2 new customers.

Pricing strategy:

The component is usually a small part of the total product cost and therefore not subject to intensive price scrutiny. Currently pricing is based on 'cost +': a standard hourly labour charge + cost of materials + 40% mark-up. Sometimes the mark-up is increased when the job can stand it. However, sometimes jobs are taken on with a lower mark-up, to help contribute to overheads.

Premises

The company operates out of a 1000 sq foot unit leased from the City Council on the outskirts of the city. The lease runs to the end of 2002 at a cost of £6400 pa. This is very low. It is anticipated that the rent review will increase this by 50%.

Equipment

Existing: 2 × lathes   2 × milling machines   2 × gear shapers
           1 × gear hob   1 × milling machine, horizontal   1 × surface grinder
           Various other low value machines

All are fully paid for other than the milling machine on which payments finish this year. No new machinery is needed this year.

Key people and job functions:

Nitin Shah	Managing Director
	Responsible for sales and organisation of production
Monty Young	Foreman
John Goody	Shop floor worker
Brian Johns	Shop floor worker
Sue Brown	Secretary/bookkeeper

Background details of key people:

Nitin Shah   Age 38
Formerly Production Manager at Hunting Engineering (a customer of Dewhurst).
17 years in the engineering industry, starting as a toolmaker and working up from the shop floor.
Experience and contacts in the industry.

Monty Young   Age 47
Foreman. Trained and qualified toolmaker. Been with the company 12 years.

John Goody   Age 38
Trained and qualified toolmaker. Been with the company 15 years.

Brian Jones   Age 43
Trained and qualified instrument maker. Been with the company 2 years.

Sue Brown   Age 27
Been with the company 4 years.

Financial highlights

12 months to: 31 March 2001

Turnover:

£187,380 (excluding VAT)

Profit:

£18,138, after tax
This represents a 48% per cent return on the £50 000 invested

Break-even:

$$\frac{118 \times 187.4}{143.8} = \text{Approximately } £153,800 \text{ turnover}$$

This treats all wage costs (other than overtime) as fixed.
If wages were treated as variable, the break-even drops to £116,300.

Funding requirement:

The company is offered for sale as a going concern for £50,000.
This is not shown in the cash flow as it will be used to purchase the shares from the present owner.

Source of funds:

£3,000 own money
£20,000 loan for 10 years, plus overdraft facility of £15,000

Forecast profit and loss account

Business: Dewhurst Engineering

Period: 31 March 2001   £'000

Sales: (excluding VAT)   £ 187.4   (A)
Less direct (variable) costs:

materials	£ 28.4	
direct wages Overtime	£ 15.2	
other	£	

Total direct costs   £ 43.6
Gross profit/contribution: £ 143.8   (B)
Fixed costs (overheads):

wages/salaries (including taxes)	£ 75.1	
rent	£ 8.0	
heat/light/power	£ 1.2	
advertising	£	
insurance	£ 0.9	
transport/travel	£ 9.4	
telephone	£ 1.8	
stationery/postage	£ 1.2	
repairs/renewals	£	
depreciation	£ 16.1	
local taxes	£	
other Professional fees	£ 1.9	
other	£ 2.4	

Total fixed costs   £ 118.0   (C)
Net profit   £ 25.8
Less   Interest   1.9
Net profit after interest   23.9
Less: Tax   5.7
Profit retained in the business   £ 18.2

Break-even point $= \dfrac{(C) \times (A)}{(B)}$

Cash Flow Forecast

2000/2001, £'000   *includes VAT   A schedule of debtor payments is attached

Month:	May	June	July	Aug	Sept	Oct	Nov	Dec	Jan	Feb	Mar	Apr	Total
SALES													
Volume:													
Value: *	16.4	15.3	16.5	16.5	21.5	16.5	16.5	22.6	11.8	23.7	20.4	20.4	218.1
RECEIPTS													
Sales – cash													
Sales -debtors *	8.0	13.2	16.4	15.5	16.3	17.4	19.9	16.9	17.6	19.8	15.1	21.8	197.9
Capital introduced													
Grants, loans etc													
VAT on sales													
TOTAL (A)	8.0	13.2	16.4	15.5	16.3	17.4	19.9	16.9	17.6	19.8	15.1	21.8	197.9
PAYMENTS													
Materials *	1.4	2.1	3.7	5.6	3.6	3.0	4.0	5.3	2.3	5.0	5.4	4.4	45.8
Wages/salaries	7.0	7.0	7.0	7.0	7.0	7.4	7.4	8.1	8.1	8.1	8.1	8.1	90.3
Rent			2.0			2.0			2.0			2.0	8.0
Heat/light/power													
Advertising													
Insurance				0.9									0.9
Transport/travel	0.7	0.7	0.8	0.8	0.8	0.8	0.8	0.8	0.8	0.8	0.8	0.8	9.4
Telephone			0.5			0.5			0.5			0.3	1.8
Stationery/postage	0.1	0.1	0.1	0.1	0.1	0.1	0.1	0.1	0.1	0.1	0.1	0.1	1.2
Repairs/renewals													
Local taxes												1.2	1.2
Other Prof. fees							1.9						1.9
Other	0.2	0.2	0.2	0.2	0.2	0.2	0.2	0.2	0.2	0.2	0.2	0.2	2.4
Capital purchases													
Loan repayments	0.1	0.2	0.2	0.2	0.2	0.2	0.2	0.2	0.1	0.1	0.1	0.1	1.9
Drawings/dividends													
VAT on purchases													
VAT paid to C&E	2.5			4.2			5.1			4.7			16.5
TOTAL (B)	12.0	10.3	14.5	19.0	11.9	14.2	19.7	14.7	14.1	19.0	14.7	17.2	181.3
CASH BALANCES													
Cash flow (A) - (B)	(4.0)	2.9	1.9	(3.5)	4.4	3.2	(0.2)	2.2	3.5	0.8	0.4	4.6	
Opening balance	(8.2)	(12.2)	(9.3)	7.4	(10.9)	(6.5)	(3.3)	(3.1)	(0.9)	2.6	3.4	3.8	

References

Chaston, I. (2000) *Entrepreneurial Marketing: Competing by Challenging Convention,* Basingstoke: Macmillan – now Palgrave.

Cosh, A. and Hughes, A. (1998) *Enterprise Britain: Growth, Innovation and Public Policy in the Small and Medium-Sized Enterprise Sector 1994–1997,* ESRC Centre for Business Research, University of Cambridge.

Kinsella, R.P., Clarke, W., Coyne, D., Mulvenna, D. and Storey, D.J. (1993) *Fast Growth Firms and Selectivity,* Dublin: Irish Management Institute.

Timmons, J. A. (1999) *New Venture Creation: Entrepreneurship for the 21st Century,* Singapore: McGraw-Hill International.

Woo, C.Y., Cooper, A.C., Dunkelberg, W.C., Daellenbach, U. and Dennis, W.J., (1989) 'Determinants of Growth for Small and Large Entrepreneurial Start-ups', paper presented at Babson Entrepreneurship Conference.

chapter nine

From entrepreneur to leader

Contents

- Change or die
- Entrepreneurial organisations
- Changing skills
- Coping with crises
- The role of leader
- Creating culture
- Leadership style
- Building the management team
- The board of directors
- Summary

Learning outcomes

By the end of this chapter you should:

- Understand how the entrepreneur must change as the business grows;
- Understand the implications of growth models of business development for the entrepreneur, their style of management, the organisation of the firm and the practical application of the functional aspects of management;
- Understand how an entrepreneurial organisation is likely to be structured, the advantages and disadvantages of this structure and appreciate how it might have to change as the firm grows;
- Understand what the job of a leader entails;
- Appreciate the importance of culture for the success of a firm and understand the elements of culture that go towards making a successful entrepreneurial firm;
- Appreciate the roller coaster of emotions the entrepreneur faces as they go through the inevitable crises they will face as the firm grows;
- Understand the influences on leadership style and what is appropriate for a growing firm;
- Be able to evaluate the leadership style of individuals;
- Understand the factors that make an effective team;
- Be able to evaluate the effectiveness of team working;
- Appreciate the role and importance of the board of directors and the skills they need to undertake their job effectively.

Change or die

As the business grows the entrepreneur needs to change and adapt. The more rapid the growth, the more difficult this is. It is not just that the role of the founder and the qualities and skills needed to manage the business successfully change, it is also that the application of the functional disciplines of marketing, accounting and people management change. The entrepreneur superhero needs to metamorphosise into a leader. The business needs to change the way it operates and become more formal without becoming more bureaucratic. And all of these changes need to be properly managed if the firm is to grow successfully. It is little wonder that so few firms grow to any size.

Chapter 2 gave some clues about the background of the entrepreneurs who make this metamorphosis successfully. Research shows what their antecedent influences generally are:

● They were well-educated;
● They start the business for positive motivations;
● They leave a managerial job in an established company to start the business;
● Historically they tend to be middle-aged but there is some evidence that there is a new generation of very young entrepreneurs, particularly in the e-business sector;
● They are willing to share ownership of the business with other key managers.

These qualities impact upon the process of change and how the entrepreneur handles them. There are a number of growth models that seek to describe the changes that the entrepreneur faces and, by inference, how the changes need to be managed. One of the most widely used models was developed by Greiner (1972). This is shown in Figure 9.1; it offers a five-stage framework for considering the development of a business, but more particularly the managerial changes facing the founder. Each phase of growth is followed by a crisis that necessitates a change in the way the founder manages the business if it is to move on and continue to grow. If the crisis cannot be overcome then it is possible that the business might fail. The length of time it takes to go through each phase depends on the industry in which the company operates. In fast-growing industries, growth periods are relatively short; in slower growth industries they tend to be longer. Each evolutionary phase requires a particular management style or emphasis to achieve growth. Each revolutionary period presents a management problem to overcome. Only phases one to four really apply to smaller firms.

> 'You start the business as a dream, you make it your passion for a while and then you get experienced managers to run it because it's not as much fun as starting. I think there's a lot to be said about starting a business and lot to be said about running a business when its mature. I think I'm capable of making the distinction and coping with both.'
>
> **Stelios Haji-Ioannou**
> founder, **easyJet**
> *Sunday Times* 29.10.00

● **Phase 1** Growth comes through entrepreneurial creativity. However, this constant seeking out of new opportunities and the development of innovative ways of doing things leads to a crisis of leadership. Staff, financiers and even customers increasingly fail to understand the focus of the business – where it is going, what it is selling – and resources become spread too thinly to follow through effectively on any single commercial opportunity.

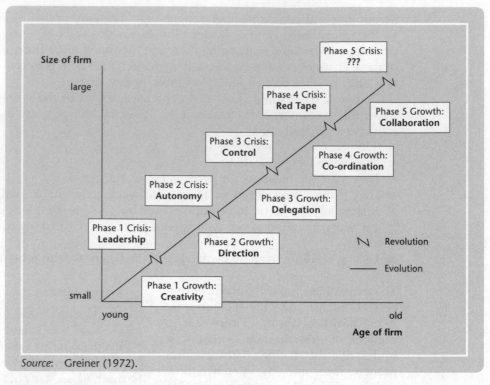

Source: Greiner (1972).

Figure 9.1 The Greiner growth model

- **Phase 2** Growth comes from the direction given by effective leadership in this phase. The entrepreneur must become more of a leader and give the business the direction it needs. However, entrepreneurs have a strong internal locus of control, which means that there is a danger that they will be unable to delegate responsibility to their management team. The leader then faces a crisis of autonomy that will only be addressed by putting that management team in place and delegating work to it.

- **Phase 3** Growth in this phase comes because the team is in place and effective delegation is taking place. The business is no longer a one-man-band. However, there is always the danger that delegation becomes abdication of responsibility and, as the firm continues to grow, there is a loss of proper control. Entrepreneurs are notorious for not being interested in the detail of controlling a business.

- **Phase 4** Growth now comes from effective co-ordination of management and its work force. Controls are in place and are working effectively. By this stage the firm will have ceased to have many of the characteristics of an owner-managed firm because there are set procedures and policies for doing things. The danger now is that it might lose its entrepreneurial drive and the next crisis it might face is one of red tape or bureaucracy. Greiner says this can only be overcome by collaboration – making people work together through a sense of mission or purpose rather than by reference to a rule book. In other words, creating an appropriate culture in the business.

To address each of these crises the entrepreneur needs to adapt and change. In particular, they need to develop into a leader. They need to put in place a management team and work as part of this team – difficult when you consider many of the strong personal characteristics exhibited by entrepreneurs. Alongside this the organisational structure of the firm will need to adapt and change, and an appropriate business culture will need to be created. These then are the four challenges entrepreneurs face as the business grows:

- Leadership;
- Team-working;
- Organisation structure;
- Culture.

> **Richard Branson** now runs the **Virgin** empire from a large house in London's Holland Park. Although there does not appear to be a traditional head office structure, Virgin employs a large number of professional managers. It has a devolved structure and an informal culture. Employees are encouraged to come up with new ideas and development capital is available. Once a new venture reaches a certain size it is launched as an independent company within the Virgin Group and the intrapreneur takes an equity stake.
>
> *. . . to be continued*

Entrepreneurial organisations

Entrepreneurial organisation structures, seen most clearly at the start-up phase, have been likened to the spider's webs shown in Figure 9.2a. The entrepreneur sits at the centre of the web with each new member of staff reporting to them. The management style tends to be informal, one of direct supervision. Just as entrepreneurs prefer informal marketing techniques, building on relationships,

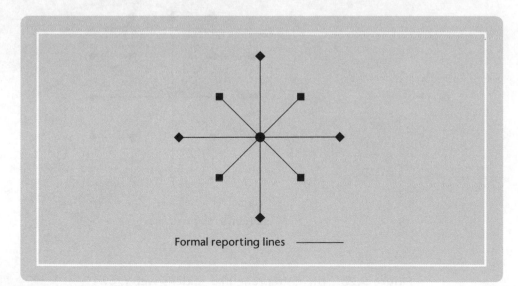

Formal reporting lines ————

Figure 9.2a The entrepreneurial spider's web

they prefer informal organisation structures and influences rather than rigid rules and job definitions. They persuade and cajole employees, showing them how to do things on a one-to-one basis, rather than having prescribed tasks. They rely on building personal relationships. After all, the business is growing rapidly and there are no precedents to go by. The future is uncertain, so flexibility is the key. The pace of change probably means that rigid structures would be out of date quickly. What is more, in a small firm everybody has to be prepared to do other people's jobs because there is no cover, no slack in the system if, for example, someone goes off sick. It is also perfectly flat and therefore efficient – overheads are reduced – and it is responsive – communication times are minimised. This is the typical small, entrepreneurial structure with the entrepreneur leading by example and communicating directly.

The entrepreneurial structure works quite well up to a couple of dozen employees. However, around this point it starts creaking at the seams as the entrepreneur tries to do everything themselves. Even when they try to delegate and introduce new staff who report to existing members of staff, the entrepreneur tends to meddle and the new employees soon find an informal reporting line to the entrepreneur, short circuiting the manager or supervisor they are supposed to report to, as in Figure 9.2b. It is no wonder that this creates frustration, resentment and an unwillingness to accept responsibility in the manager. Why should they take responsibility when their decisions are likely to be questioned or reversed, or when staff supposedly reporting to them are constantly being checked up on by the entrepreneur?

The root cause of these problems lie in the entrepreneurial character and, in particular, the strong need for control that can exhibit itself in some entrepreneurs. Derek du Toit (1980), an entrepreneur himself, said that 'an

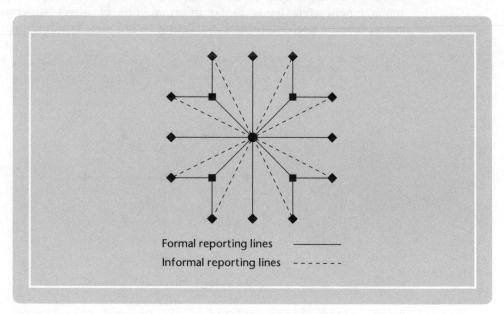

Formal reporting lines ——————
Informal reporting lines - - - - - - -

Figure 9.2b The entrepreneurial spider's web grows

entrepreneur who starts his own business generally does so because he is a difficult employee'. He probably finds it difficult to be in the alternating dominant and then submissive role so often asked of middle management. He hates being told what to do and wants to tell everybody what to do. He also believes he can do the job better than others, which may be true, but he must find a way of working through others if the business is to grow successfully.

Kets de Vries (1985) was probably the first to argue that these traits can lead to entrepreneurs wanting to over-control their business – becoming 'control freaks'. This is not such a problem in a micro business, where the owner-manager does everything themselves anyway, where their business is their life and their life is the business. Indeed it can be a virtue – making certain everything gets done properly. However, as the business grows this characteristic starts to be a problem. For example, in a fruit juice bottling plant with about 200 employees the owner-manager could not bear to relinquish any control to senior managers and insisted that copies of all external correspondence came to him. In this way he believed he still had some control. De Vries says employees in these situations become 'infantilised', expected to behave as incompetent idiots, taking few decisions and circulating little information. The better ones just do not stay.

There is no single 'correct' organisation structure, but the entrepreneurial structure must evolve to become more formal, although not bureaucratic. Whilst keeping levels of management to a minimum, there needs to be a hierarchy of some sort that gives managers confidence that they have the authority to manage. The traditional hierarchical structures of the kind shown in Figure 9.3a are most suited to organisations that require security and stability. The matrix or task structure shown in Figure 9.3b is often seen in organisations undertaking project work, for example consultancies. It can be combined very effectively with the hierarchical structure.

Traditional hierarchical structures as in Figure 9.3a are most appropriate where firms are tackling simple tasks with extensive standardisation, in stable environments, where security is important. As the environment becomes more liable to change, standardisation becomes less viable and responsibility for

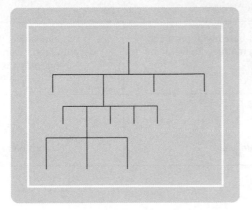

Figure 9.3a
The hierarchical structure

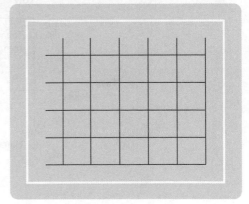

Figure 9.3b
The matrix structure

coping with unexpected changes needs to be pushed down the hierarchy. Complex tasks in stable environments mean that it becomes worthwhile developing standard skills to tackle the complexities. Whilst the matrix organisation shown in Figure 9.3b is appropriate, teams work within set protocols – as they do, for example, in a surgical operation.

The appropriate organisation structure therefore depends upon the complexity of the task and the degree of change in the environment. This is shown in Figure 9.4. The main characteristic of the entrepreneurial environment is that it is one of change. In a changing environment where there is high task complexity an innovative, flexible, decentralised structure is needed. Authority for decision-making needs to be delegated. Team-working is likely to be the norm with matrix structures involved somehow in the organisation. Decentralisation often involves having structures within structures. Clear job definitions should never lead to a narrowing of responsibilities so that new tasks that emerge are ignored. In many ways, far more important than the formal organisation structure for a firm of this sort is the culture of the organisation that tells people what needs to be done and motivates them to do it.

Where there is low task complexity in a changing environment there is scope for greater centralisation but the structure needs to be responsive to change, probably through central direction and supervision from the entrepreneur. The structure, although hierarchical, should be relatively flat with few middle management positions. However, culture is still important because the workforce still need to be motivated to make these frequent changes to their work practices. A business is a little like a house. If people are the bricks that are used to build it, the organisation structure is the plan for the house and the culture is the cement that holds the bricks together. Ignore any one element at your peril.

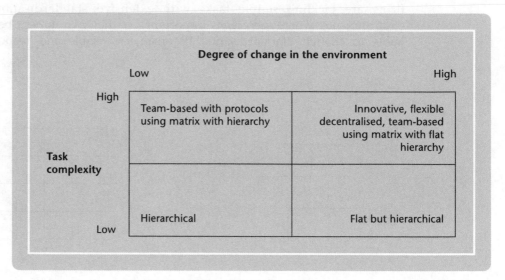

Figure 9.4 Organisation structure based upon task complexity and change in the environment

Changing skills

As the business grows and the scale of activities increases, the entrepreneur has to learn to delegate. The business will need to take on a more formal hierarchical structure and the structure will need to be adhered to, by everybody. The entrepreneur has to learn to control the business by monitoring information rather than by direct physical intervention – which is their preferred approach. They have to rely on collecting information in different ways, at appropriate times. This information comes in different forms but it generally relates to the business functions of people management, marketing and financial control. Information then has to be translated into action, and again the processes have to become more formalised. In other words, at the same time as the role of the founder is changing, so too are the skills they require.

David Poole set up his direct-marketing agency **DP&A** in 1995. By 1999 turnover was £25.1 million, profit £349 000 and cash reserves totalled £1.2 million. Although it ranks 15th in its industry, it is still a small player compared with the top five. Dan Douglas, creative director, and Tony Appi, commercial director, each own 20 per cent but David Poole maintains 60 per cent. He wants to expand rapidly but a newspaper article on the firm highlighted the issue of control. Here are some quotes from David Poole:

I have got to do things my way and prove I've got what it takes . . . I love my business and find it massively stimulating, but I guess it all boils down to ego.

I haven't spent a lot of time on strategic planning . . . I have an open and honest relationship with my fellow directors, but they haven't yet been involved in strategic planning. I don't want to distract them from their core work. I'm capable of taking the decisions myself.

A venture capitalist will have a strategy that is not necessarily in line with the best interests of the company and will always be looking towards a profitable exit, so effectively I would not be in charge.

[Going to the stock market] would give access to funding for development and provided I continued to perform well then I would keep control [but] quite simply we are too small.

Sunday Times 20.02.00

The Churchill and Lewis (1983) model, shown in Figure 9.5, is often used to link marketing, people and financial management issues. The five stages are identified as follows:

1 *Existence* The business strategy is to stay alive, and the company needs to find customers and deliver products/services. Everything has a short-term time horizon. The organisation is simple, typically the spider's web in Figure 9.2a, with one-to-one relationship management and direct supervision. The owner does everything, or at least is involved in doing everything. Planning is minimal, sometimes non-existent.

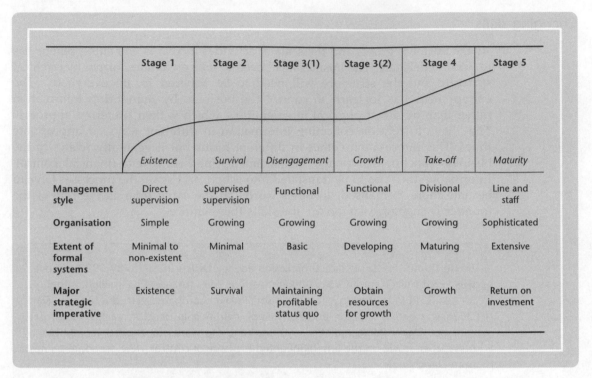

	Stage 1	Stage 2	Stage 3(1)	Stage 3(2)	Stage 4	Stage 5
	Existence	*Survival*	*Disengagement*	*Growth*	*Take-off*	*Maturity*
Management style	Direct supervision	Supervised supervision	Functional	Functional	Divisional	Line and staff
Organisation	Simple	Growing	Growing	Growing	Growing	Sophisticated
Extent of formal systems	Minimal to non-existent	Minimal	Basic	Developing	Maturing	Extensive
Major strategic imperative	Existence	Survival	Maintaining profitable status quo	Obtain resources for growth	Growth	Return on investment

Figure 9.5 The Churchill and Lewis growth model

2 *Survival* The business imperative is to establish the customer base and product portfolio. The company has to demonstrate that it has sufficient products and customers to be a viable business. It has to control its revenues and expenses to maintain cash flow. The organisation is still simple and planning is, at best, short-term involving cash flow forecasting. The owner is still 'the business'. The spider's web still exists, with one-to-one relationship management and direct supervision.

3 *Success* By this stage the company is big enough and has sufficient customers and sales to establish itself with confidence. The owner has supervisors or managers in place and basic marketing, financial and operations systems are operating. Planning is in the form of operational budgets. This company has two strategic options:

● Option 1 is disengagement. If it can maintain its market niche or adapt to changing circumstances, it can stay like this for a long time. If not, it will either cease to exist or drop back to the survival stage. This is what we described in an earlier chapter as a lifestyle business.

● Option 2 is growth. If this is a viable and desirable option then the entrepreneur must consolidate, clarify their vision and ensure that resources are diverted into growth. This is where they must start to give clear leadership, based upon the vision they have for the firm and a clear strategy as to how the vision might be achieved. However, throughout all this the business must remain profitable.

4 *Take-off* This stage is dangerous and therefore critical. The entrepreneur must ensure that satisfactory financial resources and good management are in place to take the company through it. If this stage is handled properly the company can become very successful and large.

5 *Maturity* The business now begins to develop the characteristics of a stable, larger company with professional management and formal information systems, and will have established strategic planning.

Churchill and Lewis also developed a simple summary of the key factors which affect the success or failure of a business in the different stages of its life. These are split between the attributes of the owner-manager and resources. Figure 9.1 shows the factors and their relative importance. The important point is the move from the owner's operational ability to their strategic ability as the business grows. This is one of the key qualities of leadership. Lifestyle businesses can survive on high levels of operational ability and relatively lower levels of managerial and strategic ability. This changes at the take-off stage. Even when the business is mature, in the final stage, the ability of the owner to think strategically is still critical to its development. The other point to notice is the increasing importance of personnel and systems resources at the take-off stage. In lifestyle businesses these are less important, although some lifestyle businesses do have strong systems that allow them to 'tick over' with the minimum intervention of the owner-manager.

Drawing heavily upon the work of Greiner and Churchill and Lewis, there have been a number of other growth models. Scott and Bruce (1987) proposed a five-stage model, summarised in Table 9.2. This shows the appropriate management role, style and organisational structure at different stages. As can be seen, once into the expansion phase the firm loses many of the characteristics of the entrepreneurial firm.

A four-stage model proposed by Burns (1996) summarises the main business imperatives as a firm grows in terms of the orientation of the firm and then the main functional disciplines of management, marketing, accounting and finance. This is shown in Table 9.3. It also emphasises the drift from informal to more formal structures. In this model, lifestyle businesses that never go beyond the

Table 9.1 Churchill and Lewis's growth stages imperatives

	Stage 1 Existence	Stage 2 Survival	Stage 3 Success	Stage 4 Take-off	Stage 5 Maturity
Owner's attributes					
Own goals	☆☆☆	☆	☆☆☆	☆☆☆	☆☆
Operational ability	☆☆☆	☆☆☆	☆☆	☆☆	☆
Management ability	☆	☆☆	☆☆	☆☆☆	☆☆
Strategic ability	☆	☆☆	☆☆☆	☆☆☆	☆☆☆
Resources					
Financial	☆☆☆	☆☆☆	☆☆	☆☆☆	☆☆
Personnel	☆	☆	☆☆	☆☆☆	☆☆
Systems	☆	☆☆	☆☆☆	☆☆☆	☆☆
Business	☆☆☆	☆☆☆	☆☆	☆☆	☆

Critical ☆☆☆   Important but manageable ☆☆   Not very important ☆

Table 9.2 The Scott and Bruce growth model

	Top management role	Management style	Organisational structure
Inception	Direct supervision	Entrepreneurial and individualistic	Unstructured
Survival	Supervised supervision	Entrepreneurial and administrative	Simple
Growth	Delegation and co-ordination	Entrepreneurial and co-ordination	Functional and centralised
Expansion	Decentralisation	Professional and administrative	Functional and decentralised
Maturity	Decentralisation	Watchdog	Decentralised and functional/product

Table 9.3 The Burns growth model

	Existence	Survival	Success	Take-off
Orientation	◼ Tactical	◼ Tactical	◼ Strategic	◼ Strategic
Management	◼ Owner is the business and is 'jack of all trades' ◼ Spider's-web organisation ◼ Informal, flexible systems ◼ Opportunity driven	◼ Owner is still the business ◼ Still spider's web organisation ◼ Some delegation, supervision and control	◼ Staff start to be recruited ◼ Organisation starts to become formalised ◼ Staff encouraged and motivated to grow into job ◼ Delegation, supervision and control ◼ Strategic planning	◼ Staff roles clearly defined ◼ Decentralisation starts ◼ Greater co-ordination and control of staff ◼ Emergence of professional management ◼ Operational and strategic planning
Marketing	◼ Get customers ◼ Undertake market research ◼ Develop relationships and networks	◼ Generate repeat sales ◼ Develop unique selling proposition (USP) and select market segmentation ◼ Use relationships and networks	◼ Generate repeat sales and find new customers ◼ Develop competitive advantage based upon USP and target markets ◼ Use relationships and networks	◼ Select new customers and generate repeat sales ◼ Aggressively attack competition ◼ Use relationships and networks
Accounting	◼ Cash flow	◼ Cash flow ◼ Accounting controls ◼ Break-even and margin of safety	◼ Cash flow ◼ Accounting controls ◼ Break-even and margin of safety ◼ Balance sheet engineering	◼ Cash flow ◼ Accounting controls ◼ Break-even and margin of safety ◼ Balance sheet engineering
Finance	◼ Own funds ◼ Creditors, HP, leasing ◼ Bank loans	◼ Own funds ◼ Creditors, HP, leasing, factoring ◼ Bank loans	◼ First phase venture capital ◼ Creditors, HP, leasing, factoring ◼ Bank loans	◼ Venture capital ◼ Creditors, HP, leasing, factoring ◼ Bank loans

survival stage can exist using an informal, tactical orientation on a day-to-day basis. Once they go into the success phase they need to take on a far more strategic orientation, with more formalised procedures and structures. At this phase they also start to recruit managers to the business. Managers coming from other, often larger, firms is associated with successful growth companies. Perhaps this is related to the changes in culture that are taking place in the firm at this stage.

An interesting feature of this model is the way it describes the changes in the functional disciplines. For example, marketing changes from simply getting customers, developing relationships and finding out why they buy from you into developing a unique selling proposition (USP) based upon what is working (called 'emergent strategy formulation'), and then using relationships and networks to get repeat sales. In the growth phase this becomes the basis of defining and developing some form of competitive advantage which will allow the firm to attack the competition.

These models are often used as predictors of the problems that the firm is likely to face as it grows. However, they have four problems associated with them:

1 Most firms do not experience growth and never get beyond the first stage, many dying shortly after start-up.
2 If they do experience growth, it is not quite in the way or sequence as the models predict. There are so many variables that it is unlikely all will come together at the same time. For example, the owner-manager's managerial style might be inherited from their previous employment and be out of phase with the organisational structure.
3 Often firms reach a plateau in their development at certain stages of the model – particularly survival – and do not progress beyond that phase, preferring to remain a lifestyle business. Indeed most firms do not survive the recurrent crises they face.
4 The actual sequence of issues or imperatives predicted by the models is not supported by empirical research. This is particularly true of Greiner's model.

Because of these issues the models are probably best used as checklists of the imperatives that an entrepreneur and a firm ought to face up to if they wish to grow through the different stages of development. The models should not be applied mechanistically, but rather with judgement and discretion, particularly in relation to sequence and timing. However, they provide an invaluable description of the changing role of the entrepreneur and the skills they need. Whatever you may think of these models, there is a well documented process of growth to crisis to consolidation that many surviving firms follow (shown in Figure 9.6).

Figure 9.6 The growth process

Coping with crises

Figure 9.6 glosses over the considerable problem of coping with successive crises. As the company passes through each crisis, the entrepreneur faces a rollercoaster of human emotions as they find themselves facing a different role with new demands. The classic change/denial curve shown in Figure 9.7 illustrates these changes very well and can offer insights into the attitude of the entrepreneur at each stage (Kakabadse, 1983). At each stage in the growth curve the entrepreneurs must learn to become more effective in their new roles and to adopt new attitudes and skills. As with any change, this can take time.

● *Phase 1*   The unfamiliarity of entrepreneurs with their new roles makes them feel anxious about their contribution and so their effectiveness drops slightly. They need to get used to the new circumstances. Within a short time, having become used to the role using previously successful skills, and finding support to help them, their effectiveness improves and they start to believe that they do not have to change. This is the denial phase.

● *Phase 2*   Real demands are now being made and entrepreneurs experience real stress as they realise that they do have to develop new skills to keep up with the job. They need to relearn their role. Although they may eventually learn how to do their new job, a period of anxiety makes them less effective because they can no longer rely on their old skills and they may believe that they can no longer cope. In fact this 'low' indicates that the person is realising that they have to change and then, at some point, they abandon the past and accept the future. However, it is the most dangerous point in the change cycle as the entrepreneur feels really stressed and may be tempted to give up.

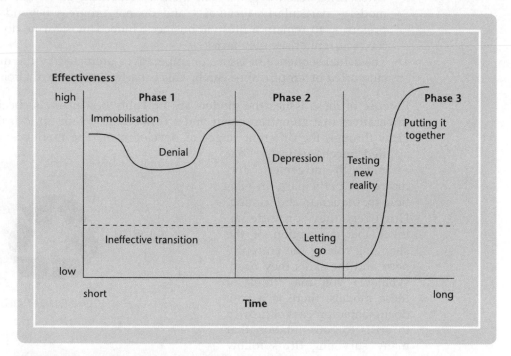

Figure 9.7   Work effectiveness through change

● *Phase 3* This testing period can be as frustrating as it can be rewarding. Mistakes can recreate the 'low', but, as the newly learnt skills are brought into play effectively, the entrepreneurs' performance improves and they achieve a higher level of effectiveness than at the beginning of the stage. They now have a set of new skills alongside their old ones. However, this transition is not inevitable and some people fail to acquire new skills or cannot pull themselves out of the 'low'. The risk is that entrepreneurs may give up.

The role of leader

The challenge for the entrepreneur as the firm grows is to become an effective leader of a cohesive management team. Timmons (1999) says that successful entrepreneurs are 'patient leaders, capable of instilling tangible visions and managing for the long haul. The entrepreneur is at once a learner and a teacher, a doer and a visionary.' He talks about six dominant themes for successful entrepreneurs:

1   Leadership;
2   Commitment and determination;
3   Opportunity obsession;
4   Tolerance of risk, ambiguity and uncertainty;
5   Creativity, self-reliance and ability to adapt;
6   Motivation to excel.

If ever the job definition for a leader were written it would probably include five elements:

1   *Having vision and ideas*   It is this that gives people a clear focus on the key issues and concerns facing the firm, the values it stands for, where it is going and how it will get there. Entrepreneurs, typically, find this part of the job definition easiest. They have vision and ideas in abundance, indeed often too many ideas and the problem is persuading them to focus on any one at a time.
2   *Being able to undertake long-term, strategic planning*   It is one thing to know where you want to go, it is quite another to know how you get there. The heart of leadership is about being able to chart a course for future development that steers the firm towards the leader's business aims. Most text books talk about strategies being deliberate, consciously intended courses of action. Entrepreneurs often believe they are bad at this. However, strategies can also emerge as consistent patterns that lead to success over a period of time or course of events. They 'emerge' without advance deliberation. The trick for entrepreneurs is to spot the successful patterns, capitalise upon them and use them as part of future strategy. Body Shop's characteristic green-painted pine decor was as much born out of lack of cash as anything else, yet it came to symbolise its 'no-frills' approach to retailing. Any start-up needs some luck to survive, but the skill for the entrepreneur is to recognise what works and what is needed to build upon that success.

Born in 1965, **Michael Dell** is the ninth richest man in the world with a fortune in excess of £12.5 billion. He started **Dell Computers** in 1984 with just £620. Today the company is worth billions and employs some 37 000 people, globally.

His entrepreneurial career started early. At the age of 12 he made £1200 by selling his stamp collection. At the age of 14 he devised a marketing scheme to sell newspapers which earned him over £11 000. From the age of 15 his interest in calculators and then computers started to grow. He started buying microchips and other bits of computer hardware in order to build systems because he realised that he could buy, say, a disk drive for £500 which would sell in the shops for £1800. In 1983 he began a pre-med degree at the University of Texas but dropped out fairly quickly to set up his own business selling computers direct to end-users.

From the start Michael Dell knew what was the critical success factor for his business. He used an expert to build prototype computers whilst he concentrated on finding cheap components. The firm grew at an incredible pace, notching up sales of £3.7 million in the first nine months. The company has gone on to pioneer direct marketing in the industry and, more lately, integrated supply chain management. At all times focusing clearly on a low-cost/low-price marketing strategy.

Michael Dell has moved from being an entrepreneur, wheeling and dealing in cheap components, then innovating in direct marketing techniques, to being a visionary leader, understanding where his competitive advantage lies and then putting into place the systems and processes to keep his company two steps ahead of the competition.

. . . to be continued

3   *Being able to communicate effectively*   Even if the entrepreneur has a vision and a strategy, they still have to communicate it to the stakeholders in the business. This is about inspiring and motivating staff, customers and financiers so that they understand where the business is going, how it is going to get there and motivating them to make it happen. It is about persuading them that the firm can deal with an uncertain environment and manage that most difficult thing of all, rapid change.

4   *Creating an appropriate culture within the firm*   We defined culture in Chapter 2 as 'the collective programming of the mind which distinguishes one group of people from another.' At a firm level we might simply call it 'how it is around here' – that pattern of taken for granted assumptions. Creating an appropriate culture in the firm is the single most important thing a leader has to do.

5   *Monitoring and controlling performance*   This is the routine task that entrepreneurs like least and are probably worst at doing. Typically, entrepreneurs prefer informal systems which involve direct, personal supervision and control, rather than formal systems which involve checking information and dealing with paperwork. However, as the firm grows the informal systems start to break down and need to be replaced by regular, routine procedures and some elements of a hierarchical organisation structure are bound to appear.

Nevertheless control information can be tailored so as to be the minimum needed to manage the firm on an exception basis. For example, rather than poring over detailed financial statements every month the entrepreneur could monitor the six financial drivers covered in Chapter 6. Only when these are out of line with the budgets will further investigation be necessary. In a later chapter we shall look at how larger firms are controlled and how budgets can be used to help entrepreneurs delegate.

Creating culture

The culture of an organisation affects strategy. Bowman and Faulkner (1997) talk about culture being formed from three influences:

● *Organisational processes* These can be deliberate or emergent, evolving organically from within the organisation and may not be intended. There are many influences on this:

- The organisational structure can influence culture. Hierarchical organisations can discourage initiative. Functional specialisation can create parochial attitudes and sends signals about which skills might be valued.
- The power to make decisions is an important dimension for entrepreneurial organisations. Flat, decentralised structures send signals about encouraging decision-making, although sometimes informal power can lie outside formal hierarchies.
- Controls and rewards send important signals about what the firm values. People take notice of what behaviour gets rewarded – as well as what gets punished – and behave accordingly. Status, praise and public recognition are powerful motivators.
- Management and leadership styles, as we shall see later in the chapter, are an important influence. They send signals about appropriate behaviour. How managers allocate time sends signals about priorities.
- Routines and rituals can have a strong subconscious influence. They form the unquestioned fabric of everyday life, but they say a lot about the organisation. 'Guarded' or 'open' management offices, reserved or unreserved parking spaces, dress codes, normal methods of communication all influence the culture of the organisation.
- Stories and symbols have a part to play in preserving and perpetuating culture. Who are the heroes, villains and mavericks in the firm? What do staff talk about at lunch? Are there symbols of status that are important such as car or office size? How do staff talk about customers? How do staff talk about the entrepreneur and other senior managers?

● *Cognitive processes* These are the beliefs, assumptions, values and attitudes staff hold in common and take for granted. They are likely to be strongest in firms that have a long history and where staff join young and stay on in the firm for most of their careers. Therefore in a new, entrepreneurial firm they can be moulded and developed by the enthusiasm and personality of the entrepreneur. Even in larger firms this can be developed through training processes.

The **Body Shop** brand is inexorably linked with its culture, which in turn is based firmly in its ethical and environmental beliefs and values. Based very much around the charismatic **Anita Roddick**'s views that business can be a vehicle for social and environmental change, the firm has championed numerous causes. These not only show themselves in window displays and PR activities, they also underscore everything the company does. Franchisees are selected partly upon their 'fit' with her ideas. Employees receive regular newsletters and videos concentrating on Body Shop campaigns. Employees are given time off to work on local social projects. In 1995 the firm introduced in-store satellite transmitted radio. Body Shop takes every opportunity to put forward its values and beliefs which it believes sets it out as distinctive and different to its high street competition.

. . . to be continued

◼ *Behaviour* This is what actually happens in an organisation. Behaviour in organisations normally reflects and reinforces culture. However behaviour can also be influenced by a wide variety of external influences, within society as a whole, within a profession or within a sector or industry. Behaviour that becomes routine can be difficult to change. However, attitudes can be influenced over time by getting people to behave in certain ways.

Most small firms start life with a 'task culture' – getting the job done. If the entrepreneur finds it difficult to delegate that may turn into a 'power culture' – where people vie to have power and influence over the entrepreneur. As this sort of firm grows, especially if the delegated authority is not genuine, there is a danger of developing a 'role culture' whereby job titles become too important. These cultures are not conducive to success and are to be avoided. Timmons (1999) says that a successful entrepreneurial culture can be described along six dimensions:

◼ The degree of organisational clarity in terms of goals, tasks, procedures and so on;
◼ The degree to which high standards are expected;
◼ The extent to which employees are committed to the firm's goals;
◼ The extent to which they feel responsible for these goals without being constantly monitored;
◼ The extent to which they feel they are recognised and rewarded for high performance;
◼ The extent to which there is a sense of cohesion and team working within the firm.

An entrepreneurial culture needs to motivate people to do the right things, in the right way, for the organisation as well as for themselves. Entrepreneurs are good at doing this by example – 'walking the talk' – but as the firm grows they need to find different ways of communicating with more people. Anita Roddick now sends out a monthly video to all employees giving news of what has been happening, new business initiatives as well as reinforcing the values the firm stands for. Equally simple things can tell you a lot about the culture of the firm. What impression does a firm with reserved parking spaces and managers in offices 'guarded' by secretaries give you? If salaries are based mainly on sales bonuses and there is a monthly league table of the best sales people, what does this tell you about the firm, its values and its goals? The culture of a firm comes from the entrepreneur, it reflects their personal values, but it is made up of a lot of small items of detail. Cultures can come about by chance, but if an entrepreneur wants to plan for success, they need to plan to achieve the culture they want.

Leadership style

The role of leader is normally based on some sort of authority. Authority can derive from role or status, tradition, legal position, expert skills or their charismatic personality. Timmons (1999) believes that in successful entrepreneurial ventures leadership is based on expertise rather than authority and this then means there is no competition for leadership. Many of the best known, successful entrepreneurs clearly also have charisma.

It is a myth to think that leaders are born, not made. Like entrepreneurship, leadership is a skill that can be developed. However, it is a complex thing. As represented in Figure 9.8, it depends upon the interactions and interconnections between the leader, the task, the group being led and the situation or context. A leader may prefer an informal, non-directional style, but faced with a young apprentice working a dangerous lathe he might be forgiven for reverting to a fairly formal, directive style with heavy supervision. In that situation the change in style is appropriate. Try the same style with a group of senior creative marketing consultants and

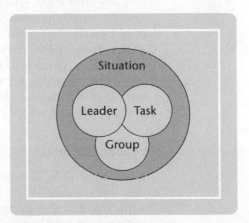

Figure 9.8 Leadership style

there would be problems. Many different styles may be effective, with different tasks, different groups and in different contexts. What is more, there is no evidence of any single leadership style characterising successful businesses.

Leader and task

The leadership grid shown in Figure 9.9 was developed by Blake and Mouton (1978). It shows style as dependent upon the leader's concern for task compared to their concern for people. Entrepreneurs are usually more concerned with completing the task but, as the firm grows, must become more concerned with people if the tasks are to be accomplished. Task leadership may be appropriate in certain situations, for example emergencies, but concern for people must surface at some point if effective, trusting relationships are to develop. Low concern for both people and task is hardly leadership at all. High concern for people – the

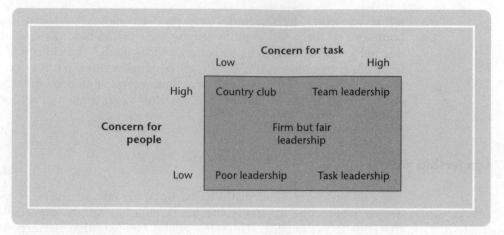

Figure 9.9 Leader and task

country-club style – is rare in business but can be appropriate in community groups, small charities or social clubs where good relationships and high morale might be the dominant objectives.

Timmons (1999) believes that the emphasis in successful entrepreneurial ventures is more on performing task orientated roles although 'someone inevitably provides for maintenance and group cohesion by good humour and wit'. If this is the case then it is even more important to ensure that there is an appropriate and effective management team in place.

Leader and group

Leadership style also depends on the relationship of the leader with the group they are leading. Figure 9.10 shows this in relation to the leader's degree of authority and the group's autonomy in decision-making. If a leader has high authority but the group has low autonomy, they will tend to adopt an autocratic style, simply instructing people what to do. If they have low authority, for whatever reason, they will tend to adopt a paternalistic style, cajoling the group

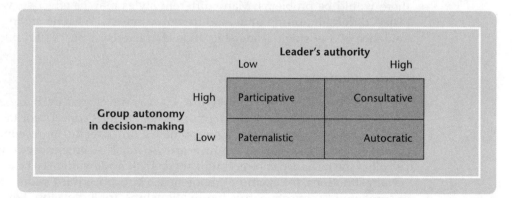

Figure 9.10 Leader and group

into doing things, picking off individuals and offering grace and favour in exchange for performance. If the leader has low authority and the group has high autonomy, then they will tend to adopt a participative style, involving all the group in decision-making and moving forward with consensus. If the leader has high authority then they will seek opinions but make the decision themselves using a consultative style.

A survey of small-business managers in Britain, France, Germany, Spain and Italy showed that most used a consultative style (Burns and Whitehouse, 1996). However, 20–30 per cent of managers in all countries other than Germany used an autocratic style. It has been said that growth orientated companies are initially characterised by an autocratic or dictatorial style, but as the company grows, a more consultative style develops (Ray and Hutchinson, 1983). The survey confirmed this. Leadership styles also seem to be influenced by national culture. The survey revealed that a significant (35 per cent) proportion of German managers use a participative style, despite the fact that none of them thought their subordinates liked it. This probably reflects cultural differences at a national level, where consultative or participative decision-making is the norm, particularly when unions are involved. However, this mismatch between actual style, dictated by cultural norms, and desired style must create tension for German entrepreneurs.

Leader and situation

John Adair (1984) put forward the view that the weight the leader should put on these different influences depends on the situation or context they find themselves in. In an entrepreneurial firm that situation can be characterised as one of uncertainty, ambiguity and rapid change. What does that tell us about the context? Timmons (1999) observed that:

> There is among successful entrepreneurs a well-developed capacity to exert influence without formal power. These people are adept at conflict resolution. They know when to use logic and when to persuade, when to make a concession, and when to exact one. To run a successful venture, an entrepreneur learns to get along with different constituencies, often with conflicting aims – the customer, the supplier, the financial backer, the creditor, as well as the partners and others on the inside. Success comes when the entrepreneur is a mediator, a negotiator, rather than a dictator.

How a good entrepreneurial leader approaches any task, with any group, therefore, depends on the situation they face. The implications of the entrepreneurial situation are:

- Entrepreneurial leaders should not use an autocratic or dictatorial leadership style.
- Entrepreneurial leaders must be adept at using informal influence. Their powers of persuasion and motivation are important. They should meet and influence people.
- Entrepreneurial leaders must be adept at conflict resolution. In these situations Timmons (*ibid.*) observes: 'Successful entrepreneurs are interpersonally supporting and nurturing – not interpersonally competitive.'

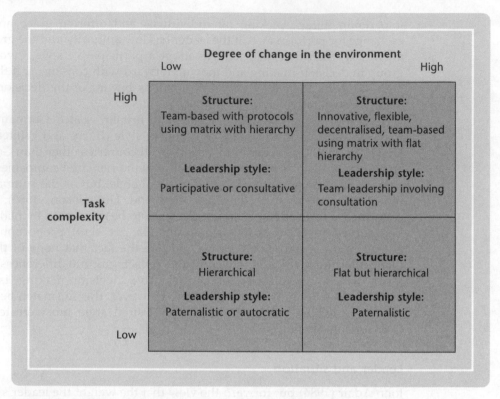

Figure 9.11 Organisation structure and leadership style based upon task complexity and change in the environment

We can now start to combine these leadership styles with the organisation structures discussed earlier and, in particular, link them to the changing environment faced by the entrepreneurial organisation. Figure 9.11 is based upon Figure 9.4 with the addition of the appropriate leadership style. The assumed linkage is that increasing complexity of task requires greater group autonomy in decision-making. Where task complexity is high, a team leadership style involving consultation in an innovative, flexible, decentralised, team-based structure using a matrix organisation within a flat hierarchy is likely to be effective. Where complexity is low, a paternalistic style within a flat hierarchy is likely to be effective but strong controls will be necessary.

This means that entrepreneurial leaders have to be flexible and adapt their leadership style to suit different and changing circumstances. Because flat structures are important for rapid response, they must attract good quality management to lead in the first place – possibly giving up equity to do so – and learn to delegate to them whilst still maintaining control of the business. If they face complex tasks, they need to become leaders of a team and that means becoming a team player themselves. These changes are a lot to ask of anybody and many entrepreneurs cannot make the transition. Some learn that they are best at start-ups and sell the business at the point where proper controls and procedures need to be put in place and management teams developed, recognising their strengths but equally their weaknesses.

How do you behave in situations involving conflict?

Often in business you find yourself at odds with others who hold seemingly incompatible views. For a leader to be effective they need to understand how they handle these conflict situations and be able to modify their behaviour to obtain the best results from others. Based on research by Kenneth Thomas and Ralph Kilmann, the Thomas–Kilman Conflict Modes questionnaire published by Xicom shows how a person's behaviour can be classified under two dimensions:

● Assertiveness – the extent to which individuals attempt to satisfy their own needs;
● Cooperativeness – the extent they attempt to satisfy the needs of others.

These two dimensions lead the authors to identify five behavioural classification which the questionnaire can identify in individuals:

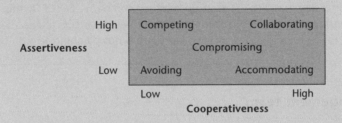

1. *Competing* is assertive and uncooperative. Individuals are concerned for themselves and pursue their own agenda forcefully, using power, rank or ability to argue to win the conflict. This can be seen as bullying with less forceful individuals or, when others use the same mode, it can lead to heated, possibly unresolved, arguments.
2. *Accommodating* is unassertive and cooperative, opposite of competing. Individuals want to see the concerns of others satisfied. They might do so as an act of 'selfless generosity' or just because they are 'obeying orders', either way they run the risk of not making their own views heard.
3. *Avoiding* is both unassertive and uncooperative. It may involve side-stepping an issue or withdrawing from the conflict altogether. In this mode any conflict may not be even addressed.
4. *Collaborating* is both assertive and cooperative, the opposite of avoiding. Issues get addressed but individuals are willing to work with others to resolve the conflict, perhaps finding alternatives that meet everybody' concerns. This is the most constructive approach to conflict for a group as a whole.
5. *Compromising* is the 'in between' route, the diplomatic, expedient solution to conflict which partially satisfies everyone. It may involve making concessions.

Each style of handling conflict has its advantages and disadvantages and can be effective in certain situations. However, management teams or Boards of Directors, if they are to get the most from each member over a longer period of time, work best when all members adopt the collaborating or compromising modes. A team made up of just competers would find it difficult to get on and, indeed to survive. A team made up of just accommodaters would lack assertiveness and drive.

Jim Clark is worth about $3 billion. He is now a cross between a serial entrepreneur and a venture capitalist because he realised that he is better at start-ups than running the business in the longer term. He discovered this with his first company, **Silicon Graphics (SGI)**, which he built around a graphic chip called the Geometry Engine that he invented in the 1970s. He spent 13, mainly unhappy, years at SGI where he found he just did not like the discipline of running a successful growing business.

He left in 1994 and invested $3 million of his own money in a primitive web browser called Mosaic and a 22-year-old who helped develop it called Marc Andreesen. **Netscape** went public 18 months later and made Jim Clark a billionaire.

In 1995 he moved on and founded another company called **Healtheon**, which uses the internet to share patient and administrative information between doctors, hospitals, insurance companies and the patients themselves. Again the business was run by somebody else, Mike Long.

Jim Clark has now started up another company, **MYCFO**, this time using the internet to help the wealthy manage their financial affairs. It also satisfies a necessary condition for success: Jim Clark is not planning to run it.

Building the management team

An entrepreneur will only succeed in growing their company if they get a good management team to work with. Attracting good staff is always difficult for small firms because of perceived lack of job security, uncertainty about promotion prospects and the fact that it is often difficult for new people to fit into an existing team. Hence the need, often, to offer shares in the company.

Selecting a team will depend upon the mix of functional skills and market or industry experience required in the firm, as well as the personal chemistry between its members. For a team to be effective individuals need to have the right mix of a certain set of personal characteristics. Dr Meredith Belbin (1981) identified nine clusters of personal characteristics or attributes which translate into 'team roles'. Individuals are unlikely to have more than two or three of them, yet all nine clusters of characteristics need to be present in a team for it to work effectively.

The leader's role is to select the team and then to build cohesion and motivation. In most cases this involves building consensus towards the goals of the firm, balancing multiple viewpoints and demands. However, too great a reliance on achieving consensus can lead to slow decision-making, so a balance is needed that will strain the interpersonal skills of the leader. However, in the best entrepreneurial firms leadership seems to work almost by infection. The management team seem to be infected by the philosophies and attitudes of the entrepreneur and readily buy into the goals set for the firm, something that is helped if they share in its success.

All personal relationships are based upon trust and this is the cornerstone of a good team. It is imperative that the management team trust the entrepreneurial leader. For the leader this involves being firm but fair, flexible but consistent in values and in dealings with individuals and always placing the interests of the firm first, also being supportive for individuals and having their interests at

What sort of team player are you?

Developing a successful team depends not just on the range of professional skills it has, but also on the range of personal characteristics – the chemistry of the team. Based upon research into how teams work, Dr Meredith Belbin (1981) identified nine clusters of personal characteristics or attributes which translate into 'team roles'. The roles are:

The Shaper: This is usually the self-elected task leader with lots of nervous energy. They are extrovert, dynamic, outgoing, highly strung, argumentative, a pressuriser seeking ways around obstacles. They do have a tendency to bully and are not always liked. However, they generate action and thrive under pressure.

The Plant: This the team's vital spark and chief source of new ideas. They are creative, imaginative and often unorthodox. However, they can be distant and uncommunicative and sometimes their ideas can seem a little impractical.

The Coordinator: This is the team's natural chairman. They are mature, confident and trusting. They clarify goals and promote decision-making. They are calm with strong interpersonal skills. However, they can be perceived as a little manipulative.

The Resource Investigator: This is 'the fixer' – extrovert, amiable, six phones on the go, with a wealth of contacts. They pick other people's brains and explore opportunities. However, they can be a bit undisciplined and can lose interest quickly once initial enthusiasm has passed.

The Monitor-Evaluator: This is the team's rock. They are introvert, sober, strategic, discerning. They explore all options and are capable of deep analysis of huge amounts of data. They are rarely wrong. However, they can lack drive and are unlikely to inspire or excite others.

The Team-Worker: This is the team's counsellor or conciliator. They are mild mannered and social, perceptive and aware of problems or undercurrents, accommodating and good listeners. They promote harmony and are particularly valuable at times of crisis. However, they can be indecisive.

The Implementer: This is the team's workhorse. They turn ideas into practical actions and get on with the job logically and loyally. They are disciplined, reliable and conservative. However, they can be inflexible and slow to change.

The Completer-Finisher: This is the team's worry-guts, making sure things get finished. They are sticklers for detail, deadlines and schedules and have relentless follow-through, picking up any errors or omissions as they go. However, they sometimes just cannot let go and are reluctant to delegate.

The Specialist: This is the team's chief source of technical knowledge or skill. They are single-minded, self-starting and dedicated. However, they tend to contribute on a narrow front.

Most individuals are naturally suited to two or three roles. However, to work effectively a team must comprise elements of all nine roles. If a team lacks certain 'team roles' it tends to exhibit weaknesses in these areas.

heart. Trust also has to be built up between other members of the management team. It takes time to build and needs to be demonstrated with real outcomes.

Effective teams, therefore, do not just happen, they have to be developed, and that can take time. It is said that teams go through a four-stage development process:

> 'I can't remember a single day when I didn't want to go to work. I had such a good team. There was an incredible feeling of trust. None of the boys would let me down.'
>
> **Tom Farmer**
> founder of **Kwik-Fit**
> *Daily Mail* 11.05.99

1 The group tests relationships. Individuals are polite, impersonal, watchful and guarded.
2 Infighting starts in the group and controlling the conflict is important. However, whilst some individuals might be confrontational, others might opt out and avoid the conflict altogether. Neither approach is good. Collaboration is best. This is a dangerous phase from which some groups never emerge.
3 The group starts to get organised, developing skills, establishing procedures, giving feedback, confronting issues.
4 The group becomes mature and effective, working flexibly and closely, making the most of resources and being close-knit and supportive.

The whole process of team formation and development has been likened to courtship and marriage, involving decisions based partly on emotion rather than logic. For that reason it is important that the team shares the same values and is committed to the same goals. They may disagree on tactics but they all agree on the destination and how they are going to get there. It is also important that team roles are clearly defined, although given the uncertainty involved with rapid growth, it is also important that flexibility is maintained.

The board of directors

In many firms the management team will also function as the legal board of directors of the company. The legal duties and responsibilities of directors arise out of common law and statute. Directors have a fiduciary duty to act honestly and in good faith, exercise skill and care and undertake their statutory duty. The broad functions of the board are summarised in Figure 9.12 along the dimensions of inward/outward looking and past/future orientation. The prime function of the board is to establish corporate strategy and policy:

● Overall strategic planning;
● Approval of strategies in key areas;
● Changes in the scope or nature of operations;
● Changes in organisational structure;
● Major company decisions.

The other responsibilities include:

1 Monitoring and supervising management performance;
2 Planning for management succession;
3 Setting remuneration levels;

4   Providing proper accountability to other stakeholders in the firm, for example, by appointing auditors and approving the annual financial statements, as well as ensuring that the company complies with all aspects of the law.

Whilst establishing corporate strategy and policy is the most important job for the board, it is unlikely that it will be given the appropriate weighting in terms of time allocation. Most boards spend too much time on the other functions, particularly monitoring management performance.

Whilst corporate governance and business ethics are high on the agenda of many high-profile public companies, that is not necessarily the case for smaller firms. There are, of course, exceptions. 'Green' issues were always high on the agenda of Body Shop, even as a start-up. Research shows that business ethics for smaller firms tends to take the form of informal codes of practice and an understanding of acceptable and unacceptable behaviour rather than standardised, formal procedures, which are a feature of the larger firm (Spence, 2000).

A strong management team and board of directors is invaluable and their worth is no more evident than in the criteria venture capitalists use for investment; management, management and management. To help boards develop and operate more effectively, the Institute of Management has published a useful set of best practice checklists based upon a model of board-level competencies (Allday, 1997). Twenty-three board-level skills were identified grouped together under the four key headings shown in Figure 9.13. These generic competencies need to be balanced and tailored to particular circumstances and specific functional board roles.

More than 90 per cent of the *Financial Times* Stock Exchange (FTSE) companies comply with the recommendation that they have non-executive directors. However, in small unquoted companies the proportion is much, much smaller. Often non-executive directors are imposed by financial backers to oversee their investment. However, non-executive directors have a valuable role bringing different skills, an independent and objective perspective and a new network of contacts. They should act as an early warning system for potential future difficulties, and as we shall see, their role can be particularly valuable in family firms.

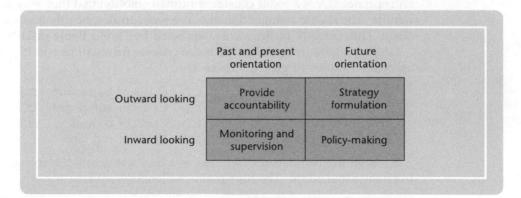

Figure 9.12   The role of the board of directors

Strategy: Guiding strategic direction	People: Practising 'human' skills
Strategic thinking Systems thinking Awareness of external environment Entrepreneurial thinking Developing the vision Initiating change Championing causes	Communicating Creating a personal impact Giving leadership Promoting development of others Networking
Culture: Developing organisation culture	Operations: Exercising executive control
Customer focus Quality focus Teamwork focus People resource focus Organisational learning focus	Governance Decision-making Contributing specialist knowledge Managing performance Analysing situations Awareness of organisational structure

Figure 9.13 The Institute of Management model of board-level competencies

Summary

As firms grow the role of the founder needs to change. Like **Michael Dell**, founder of **Dell Computers**, they need to metamorphosise into a leader; this change is not easy. Some, like **Stelios Haji-Ioannou**, founder of **easyJet**, can make the change, others cannot. Some, like **Jim Clark**, founder of **Silicon Graphics**, **Netscape**, **Healtheon** and **MYCFO**, choose to only do what they enjoy and are good at – start-ups.

As they develop, firms typically go through a period of growth, followed by crisis and then a period of consolidation. In going through each crisis the entrepreneur faces a roller coaster of human emotion that they may not be able to handle. The classic change/denial curve seeks to describe their emotions at each stage. This range of feelings was expressed by **David Poole** of **DP&A**.

Greiner's growth model predicts the crises a firm will face as it grows and the associated causes of growth. These are:

Growth through creativity	⇨	Crisis of leadership	⇨
Growth through direction	⇨	Crisis of autonomy	⇨
Growth through delegation	⇨	Crisis of control	⇨
Growth through coordination	⇨	Crisis of red tape	⇨

Richard Branson has realised that as a business grows the entrepreneur needs to change and adapt. The four main challenges they face are:

- Leadership;
- Team-working;
- Organisation structures;
- Culture.

An entrepreneurial organisation structure is a spider's web, with the entrepreneur at the centre. They prefer informal structures and management styles relying on building personal relationships and influence. They lead by example. However, this can lead to over-control and, whilst it may be flat and efficient, it only works up to a certain size. What is more, managers can find that it undermines their authority and that leads to frustration, even 'infantilisation'. Whilst avoiding bureaucracy, more formal structures need to be introduced as a business grows. The entrepreneur needs to recruit managers from outside and learn to delegate. In a changing environment innovative, flexible, decentralised, team-based groupings using matrix and flat hierarchical structures are likely to be most effective for entrepreneurial firms facing a high level of task complexity. Where task complexity is low, a simple flat but hierarchical structure is most likely to be effective.

The Churchill and Lewis growth model summarises management style, organisational characteristics, formality of systems and major strategies at different stages of the firm's life. It distinguishes between lifestyle and growth firms, at the 'success' stage and highlights the changes that take place at this point for the different types of firm. It emphasises the importance of the entrepreneur's strategic abilities, compared to their operating abilities, as the firm grows. The changes in the entrepreneur's role and style as well as the organisational structures are emphasised by the Scott and Bruce model. The Burns model emphasises the drift from informal to formal structures in many aspects of how the firm is managed, including the main functional disciplines.

A job definition for a leader would include five elements:

1   Vision and ideas;
2   Strategic planning;
3   Effective communication;
4   Creation of culture;
5   Monitoring and controlling performance.

Creating an appropriate culture in the firm is the most important, and probably the most difficult, task. Culture is influenced by organisational and cognitive processes and behaviour. As in the case of **Body Shop**, it can be based upon the entrepreneur's strongly held beliefs and values. It can be deliberate or emerge organically. Entrepreneurs 'infect' staff with a culture that motivates them to do the right things, in the right way. They create culture by example. However, as the firm grows culture can be influenced through training. Most firms start with a 'task culture' which can easily evolve into a 'power' or 'role' culture if care is not taken. An effective entrepreneurial culture involves:

- Clear goals;
- High standards;
- Commitment;
- Recognition;
- Team cohesion.

Leadership stems from authority. Entrepreneurial authority, in the main, comes from expertise. There is no single best leadership style. The appropriate style depends upon the leader, the group, the task and the situation or context they are in. In the context of a growing firm, an autocratic or dictatorial style is unlikely to be appropriate. Entrepreneurial leaders must be adept at using informal influence to get their way. In firms with low task complexity this is likely to lead to a paternalistic management style and, when there is high complexity, a consultative style. Entrepreneurs must also be adept at resolving conflict, through a collaborative or compromising approach.

Building the management team is not just about appropriate skills. It is about assembling a mix of different personalities. Belbin identified nine characteristics that need to be present to form an effective team: shaper, plant, coordinator, resource investigator, monitor-evaluator, team-worker, implementer, completer-finisher and specialist. Teams have strong interpersonal relationships and, as **Tom Farmer** founder of **Kwik Fit** points out, all relationships are based upon trust. Building this up takes time and the team is likely to go through a four stage process in its development:

1 Testing;
2 Infighting;
3 Getting organised;
4 Mature effectiveness.

The board of directors becomes an increasingly important team as a company grows. Its most important functions are strategy and policy formulation. It also has to monitor the performance of management and provide accountability to stakeholders. Members therefore need to be able to give that strategic direction, develop organisational culture, practice 'human' skills and exercise effective executive control. Non-executive directors are valuable in providing different skills, objectivity and a new network of contacts. They can be particularly valuable for family firms.

⬛ Essays and discussion topics

1 How does the role of and skills required by the founder change as the business grows?
2 Is the Greiner growth model an accurate predictor of the growth process?
3 How are the antecedent influences on an entrepreneur likely to improve their chances of successfully growing the firm?
4 What are the advantages and disadvantages of an entrepreneurial organisation?
5 What are the possible negative consequences of the internal locus of control that is characteristic of so many entrepreneurs.
6 Discuss how the typical entrepreneur's preference for physical intervention and informal, personal controls shows itself. Is this a good thing?
7 Discuss David Poole's comments. What insights do they give you into his priorities and personality?
8 Critically evaluate the three growth models by Churchill and Lewis, Scott and Bruce, and Burns.
9 Is operational capability more important than strategic capability at start-up?
10 How is the marketing function likely to change as the firm grows?
11 As long as a small firm is not homogeneous, growth models will not work. Discuss.
12 How are the recurrent crises facing the growing firm likely to affect the entrepreneur and how they react to them?
13 How does the role of leader differ from that of entrepreneur?
14 What is vision?
15 Has Michael Dell made the transition from entrepreneur to leader?
16 What is culture and how can it be developed?

17 What is an entrepreneurial culture? Do Timmons' six dimensions adequately describe it?
18 What is the relationship between an entrepreneurial culture within a firm and an entrepreneurial national culture? Can one exist without the other?
19 Is there such a thing as an effective leadership style for a growing business?
21 Why is an ability to handle conflict important in the growing firm?
21 How do you build an effective team?
22 How do you generate trust?
23 What is the role of the non-executive director? How important are they for the growing firm?
24 Leaders are born not made. Discuss.

⬤ Exercises and assignments

1 List the questions you would ask an entrepreneur who has successfully grown their business to try to assess how they and the skills they have needed have changed as the firm grew.
2 Based upon these questions, interview a successful entrepreneur and write an essay describing the changes they have faced and how they coped.
3 Based upon a small firm with about a dozen employees, draw the formal organisation chart and then, based upon interviews with employees, draw the informal organisation.
4 Answer the Leadership Styles Questionnaire overleaf and plot your score on the Leadership Grid at the end of this chapter.
5 Obtain the Thomas–Kilman Conflict Mode questionnaire from Xicom and evaluate how you handle conflict.
6 Using the questionnaire in Meredith Belbin's book, evaluate your preferred team roles.

⬤ Growth audit exercise

Undertake steps 1 and 2 of the growth audit exercise at the back of the book.

⬤ Websites to visit

The Department of Education and Employment sponsor an excellent site for people who work with managers, entrepreneurs and small firms on www.business-info.org.uk. The *Highlights* section is a fortnightly publication of articles and news items publicising current initiatives, signposting items of interest, ideas and opinions, case studies and opinions about good practice. The *Resources* section provides a range of free downloadable management tools and advice notes together with articles of interest on small business issues. The *Projects* section provides details of various Business School projects that have occurred over the past few years.

⬤ References

Adair, J. (1984) *The Skills of Leadership*, London: Gower.
Allday, D. (1997) *Check-a-Board: Helping Boards and Directors become More Effective*, London: The Institute of Management.
Belbin, R.M. (1981) *Management Teams – Why They Succeed and Fail*, London: Heinemann Professional Publishing.
Blake, R. and Mouton, J. (1978) *The New Managerial Grid*, London: Gulf.
Bowman, C. and Faulkner, D.O. (1997) Competitive and Corporate Strategy, London: Irwin.
Burns, P. (1996) 'Growth', in P. Burns and J. Dewhurst (eds), *Small Business and Entrepreneurship*, London: Macmillan – now Palgrave.

Leadership Style Questionnaire

For each of the following statements, tick the 'Yes' box if you tend to agree or the 'No' box if you disagree. Try to relate the answers to your actual recent behaviour as a manager. There are no right and wrong answers.

		Yes	No
1	I encourage overtime work	☐	☐
2	I allow staff complete freedom in their work	☐	☐
3	I encourage the use of standard procedures	☐	☐
4	I allow staff to use their own judgement in solving problems	☐	☐
5	I stress being better than other firms	☐	☐
6	I urge staff to greater effort	☐	☐
7	I try out my ideas with others in the firm	☐	☐
8	I let my staff work in the way they think best	☐	☐
9	I keep work moving at a rapid pace	☐	☐
10	I turn staff loose on a job and let them get on with it	☐	☐
11	I settle conflicts when they happen	☐	☐
12	I get swamped by detail	☐	☐
13	I always represent the 'firm view' at meetings with outsiders	☐	☐
14	I am reluctant to allow staff freedom of action	☐	☐
15	I decide what should be done and who should do it	☐	☐
16	I push for improved quality	☐	☐
17	I let some staff have authority I could keep	☐	☐
18	Things usually turn out as I predict	☐	☐
19	I allow staff a high degree of initiative	☐	☐
20	I assign staff to particular tasks	☐	☐
21	I am willing to make changes	☐	☐
22	I ask staff to work harder	☐	☐
23	I trust staff to exercise good judgement	☐	☐
24	I schedule the work to be done	☐	☐
25	I refuse to explain my actions	☐	☐
26	I persuade others that my ideas are to their advantage	☐	☐
27	I permit the staff to set their own pace for change	☐	☐
28	I urge staff to beat previous targets	☐	☐
29	I act without consulting staff	☐	☐
30	I ask staff follow standard rules and procedures	☐	☐

Adapted from J. Pfeiffer and J. Jones, (eds) (1974) *A Handbook of Structured Experiences from Human Relations Training*, Vol. 1 (rev.), University Associates, San Diego, California.

Burns, P. and Whitehouse, O. (1996) 'Managers in Europe', *European Venture Capital Journal,* no. 45, April/May.

Churchill, N.C. and Lewis, V.L. (1983) 'The Five Stages of Small Business Growth', *Harvard Business Review,* May/June.

Du Toit, D.E. (1980) 'Confessions of a Successful Entrepreneur', *Harvard Business Review,* November/December.

Greiner, L.E. (1972) 'Evolution and Revolution as Organisations Grow', *Harvard Business Review,* July/August.

Kakabadse, A. (1983) *The Politics of Management,* London: Gower.

Kets de Vries, M.F.R. (1985) 'The Dark Side of Entrepreneurship', *Harvard Business Review,* November/December.

Ray, G.H. and Hutchinson, P.J. (1983) *The Financing and Financial Control of Small Enterprise Development,* London: Gower.

Scott, M. and Bruce, R. (1987) 'Five Stages of Growth in Small Businesses', *Long Range Planning,* vol. 20, no. 3.

Spence, L.J. (2000) *Priorities, Practice and Ethics in Small Firms,* London: The Institute of Business Ethics.

Timmons, J.A. (1999) *New Venture Creation: Entrepreneurship for the 21st Century,* Singapore: Irwin/McGraw Hill.

● Exercise 4 scoring

To obtain your leadership orientation rating, score 1 point for the appropriate response under the each heading, then total your scores. If your response is inappropriate you do not score. As a guide, a score of 5 or less is low, and 12 or more is high.

PEOPLE SCORE (maximum score 15)
'Yes' for questions 2, 4, 8, 10, 17, 19, 21, 23, 27.
'No' for questions 6, 13, 14, 25, 29, 30.

TASK SCORE (maximum score 15)
'Yes' for questions 1, 3, 5, 7, 9, 11, 15, 16, 18, 20, 22, 24, 26, 28.
'No' for questions 12.

Next plot your position on the Leadership Grid below.

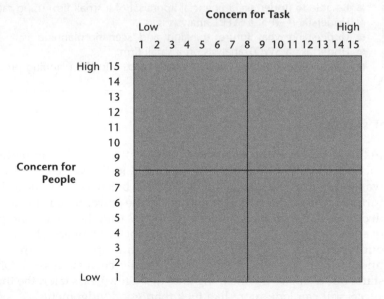

chapter ten

Growth: success

Contents

- Ingredients of success
- Barriers to growth
- Securing competitive advantage
- Value chains
- Product life-cycles

- Product portfolios
- Financial analysis
- The SWOT analysis revisited
- Summary

Learning outcomes

By the end of this chapter you should:

- Understand what are the ingredients of success for a growing firm;
- Appreciate what small firms consider to be barriers to their growth;
- Understand what is needed to be able to secure competitive advantage and be able to analyse how it is derived in a small firm;
- Understand the concept of a value chain;
- Understand the marketing implications of product life-cycles;
- Understand the marketing, financial and managerial implications of product portfolios;
- Be able to use the Boston Matrix to analyse product portfolios and decide on product/market strategies;
- Understand the meaning of key financial ratios;
- Be able to undertake a financial appraisal of a small firm using ratio analysis;
- Understand what a SLEPT analysis is;
- Understand what 'futures thinking' and 'scenario planning' is;
- Undertake a SWOT analysis on a small firm;
- Understand how the SWOT analysis feeds into the planning process.

Ingredients of success

In the turbulent world of business, survival – over a longer period – is a badge of success. The growth models we looked at in the last chapter indicated that this was something of a watershed. Should the business continue as it is or grow even further? This is the critical point where the entrepreneur makes some important decisions. Do they want the firm to grow? Can they make the personal changes needed to make the firm successful in the next phase? Notwithstanding these questions, the basis for a successful transition through this phase is an understanding of why the firm has actually been successful. Often the business starts out trying to do one thing and, just a few years later, the things that made it successful can look more like luck than good judgement.

Entrepreneurs like Bill Gates and Richard Branson managed to do more than just survive, they managed to grow their businesses and grow them extremely quickly and with enormous success. Despite being few in number, high-growth businesses – companies that go on to the take-off phase in our growth models – are important to national economies. Harrison and Taylor (1996) claim that in the USA it has been estimated that, whilst 15 000 medium-sized businesses represent just 1 per cent of all businesses, they generate a quarter of all sales and they employ a fifth of all private sector labour. For the UK, Storey *et al.* (1987) have asserted that 'out of every 100 small firms, the fastest growing four firms will create half the jobs in the group over a decade.'

So, is there such a thing as a recipe for success? The answer is that we know the ingredients, but the precise recipe can vary from situation to situation. The ingredients of success are shown in Figure 10.1; they comprise:

- *The entrepreneurial character* This is the vital ingredient. Growth rarely happens by chance. The owner-manager must want it and possess all the characteristics of the entrepreneur. Previous chapters have shown how this needs to adapt and change over time, as the business grows.
- *The business culture* Previous chapters have shown how this is an important tool for effective leadership of an entrepreneurial firm. Having the right culture is probably more important than the right structure. What is more, part of the culture must be the ambition to grow. Companies which have risen to positions of global leadership over the last 20 years invariably began with ambitions that were out of proportion to their size or resources. They maintained an obsession with winning long enough to succeed.
- *Company strengths* For successful growth a company needs a good management team and good financial control systems. It needs to understand who its customers are and why they buy from them rather than competitors. Previous chapters have shown how to undertake a SWOT analysis at start-up. The SWOT analysis needs to be more comprehensive and sophisticated for an established firm. This chapter will develop the frameworks needed to undertake this.

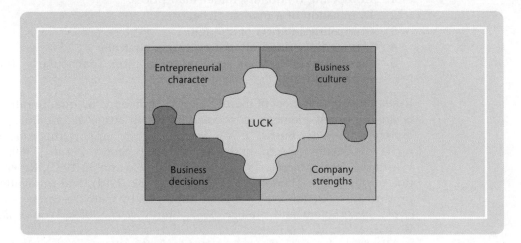

Figure 10.1 The ingredients of success

Perween Warsi's parents arranged for her to marry a doctor at the age of 16 in India. The couple moved to Britain in 1975 with their two sons. Bored, with time on her hands, she decided to try producing high quality, authentic Indian food and set up **S&A Foods** (named after her sons Sadiq and Abid), working from her kitchen with six staff, selling to neighbourhood takeaways. Within six months she had moved to a unit on a local industrial estate and within a year was selling to Asda, followed by Safeway, Waitrose, Budgen, Morrisons and even Welcome Break and Scottish & Newcastle. S&A now has four factories in Derby, a workforce of 1100 and an annual turnover of £100 million. Warsi is the second richest Asian businesswoman in Britain and her husband, Talib, gave up being a GP in 1995 to become S&A's marketing manager.

The target market for the food is 'cash-rich, time-poor' consumers. The firm has to keep on top of a rapidly developing market and launches some 300 new products each year, developing thousands more. S&A is expanding into Europe and already sells to supermarkets in France.

I knew my products could be marketed nationwide before I had sold a single samosa. There was a huge gap in the market for quality Indian and Thai food . . . When the business started I was very busy. In the mornings I would take the boys to school, then come home and make food all day . . . My husband was very supportive, but I still feel very guilty that I wasn't always there for my beautiful sons . . . I can't imagine retiring. What would I do? Our future is bright and we are always looking to innovate.

Boss Women, BBC1, 24.07.00

● *Business decisions*   Making no business decisions can be just as disastrous as making bad decisions. So what are the right strategic decisions that ensure growth? In their survey of 179 supergrowth companies, Harrison and Taylor's (1996) entrepreneurs identified five 'winning performance factors:

1 Competing on quality rather than prices;
2 Domination of a market niche;
3 Competing in areas of strength;
4 Having tight financial and operating controls;
5 Frequent product or service innovation (particularly important in manufacturing).

Research supports most of these findings. Competing on quality rather than price is an important element of success for small firms across Europe (Ray and Hutchinson, 1983; Burns, 1994). Many surveys support the conclusion about niche marketing (Solem and Steiner, 1989; Storey *et al.*, 1989; Birley and Westhead, 1990; Macrae, 1991; Siegel *et al.*, 1993 and 3i, 1993). Researchers often link strong financial control with planning (3i:, 1991), and innovation and new product introduction is also seen as important by many researchers (Dunkelberg *et al.*, 1987; Solem and Steiner, 1989; Storey *et al.*, 1989; Woo *et al.*, 1989 and Wynarczyk *et al.*, 1993).

All of which leaves the question of luck. Whether success was due to luck or good judgement or good timing is a difficult question to answer. Timing is

Specialist cereals producer **Jordans** is a family company tracing its origins back to 1855 with milling and the supply of animal feed. In the 1960s the company switched from producing white to wholemeal flour in the face of fierce price competition from big conglomerates. It also started producing small quantities of oat-based cereals, which it sold to health food stores.

By the 1970s health foods had really caught on and Jordans were selling to the supermarkets. Two keys to their growth since then have been product quality and innovation. Quality, backed with a respected brand identity, have allowed them not to be drawn too far into the vicious food price wars. Innovation has kept them one step ahead of the big-company competition. They were among the first to introduce 'food on the run' cereal bars. They were also amongst the first to introduce freeze-dried fruits to their breakfast cereals, even innovating in the packaging by introducing cellophane bags. They pioneered the introduction of 'conservation grade' ingredients which are cheaper than organically grown but contain few pesticides.

However, Jordans has also entered the own-brand market and 20 per cent of its £50 million turnover comes from this source. Even here it trades on its 'brand integrity' – its ability to produce tasty and nutritious cereals in an environmentally-friendly way. But it has had to control costs. It is also entering the adult savoury market with its low-fat cereal-based oven-crisped chips. It now plans a major expansion into Europe. Bill Jordan explains the key to his strategy:

The company needs to differentiate its products rather than slog it out on price. We need to sustain advertising support to develop customer demand, which is the key to getting our goods placed on the supermarket shelf.

Sunday Times 12.03.00

everything and a good product or service, launched before its time, with insufficient demand is likely to fail. Cecil Duckworth wanted to manufacture self-service petrol pumps but at the time petrol stations did not have self-service. He went on to set up Worcester Engineering and to manufacture direct-water-feed central heating boilers, a company he eventually sold to Bosch for some £40 million. How many of the factors that made for Body Shop's success – the ethical and environmentally friendly emphasis, the cheap, green painted pine decor, the plastic reusable bottles – were luck? When David Bruce opened his first Firkin pub, brewing its own beer, with bare floorboards and seating from an old church, having forgotten to order a juke box or gaming machine, was it luck that he had stumbled onto a successful formula?

Chapter 12 will go on to provide an insight into how to make the right business decisions to take growth forward – the options available and the risks associated with them. The rest of this chapter will develop an understanding of how the firm has survived and prospered to this point.

Barriers to growth

Another approach to the issue of growth in small firms is the so-called 'barriers to growth' literature. Table 10.1 shows the barriers to growth reported in a survey of

Table 10.1   Barriers to growth

Barrier	Nature	1997	1990
Increased competition	External	2.67	2.40
Availability and cost of finance for expansion	External	2.63	2.75
Marketing and sales skills	Internal	2.53	2.29
Availability and cost of overdraft finance	External	2.38	2.72
Growth of market demand	External	2.35	2.59
Management skills	Internal	2.31	2.14
Skilled labour	Internal	2.25	1.90
Acquisition of new technology	?	1.95	1.29
Difficulty implementing new technology	Internal	1.89	1.20
Availability of appropriate premises	External	1.75	1.16
Access to overseas markets	?	1.60	1.05

Key: 1 = insignificant, 5 = crucial.
Sources: For 1997, A. Cosh and A. Hughes (eds) (1998), *Enterprising Britain: Growth, Innovation and Public Policy in the Small and Medium-Sized Enterprise Sector 1994–1997*, ESRC Centre for Business Research, Cambridge. For 1990, Small Business Research Centre (1992), *The State of British Enterprise: Growth, Innovation and Competitive Advantage in Small and Medium-Sized Firms*, Cambridge.

some 2500 UK small firms in 1997 by the ESRC Centre for Business Research at Cambridge University, probably the most authoritative recent survey. Only a factor score of over 2.5 indicates any real problem, therefore only the top three factors are significant. It is interesting that the top two are both external factors, increased competition reflecting the intensification of competitive pressures in the 1990s. The issue of raising capital is a perennial problem for small firms and is dealt with in a subsequent chapter, but the barrier is likely to reflect cost and issues of collateral rather than general availability. Even in the 1990 survey, when Britain was in recession, availability and cost of finance and market conditions – although this time growth of market demand – were the two most important barriers.

The survey also showed that manufacturing small firms faced greater constraints in more areas than did service firms, larger (that is, medium-sized) firms faced greater constraints than did micro-firms and innovating small firms faced higher levels of constraints than did non-innovating firms. Medium-sized firms tended to rate inadequate management skills, and to a lesser extent marketing and sales skills, more highly as a constraint. Newer and fast-growing firms rated financial constraints more highly and faster growing ones also rated management skills and skills shortages more highly.

Much has also been said by lobby groups and in the press of government regulation and general 'red tape'. However, this is probably a greater burden for the smallest companies rather than medium-sized ones. The survey of super-growth companies by Harrison and Taylor (1996) cited 'barriers to entry' when penetrating new markets as the biggest obstacle to growth, followed by 'establishing a reputation' and 'intense competition and monopoly practises'. The reality seems to be that, whilst competition and finance are general problems, many of the others are specific to the firm and need to be overcome in different ways, which comes down to understanding the business through reworking the SWOT analysis.

Securing competitive advantage

The debate about entrepreneurial skill or good luck can go on for ever. But the distinguishing feature of entrepreneurs is that they recognise what works and replicate it quickly before competitors can react. So, the first thing that a growing firm needs to understand is why it has been successful so far. It needs to revisit the generic marketing strategies and the SWOT analysis in order to be certain it can answer four key questions that enable it to understand the basis of its competitive advantage and capitalise on the relevant factors:

1 Who are our customers?
2 What benefits are they looking for when they buy or products or services?
3 Why do they buy from us rather than our competitors?
4 What strengths do we have and how can they be used to build advantage?

Each of the generic marketing strategies (reproduced in Figure 10.2) has certain strategic decision-making implications. These are actions that you would expect the firm to be undertaking in order to secure its competitive advantage for as long as possible. After the initial success of a start-up it is good to just pause to consider how this will be achieved.

A company that is selling on price needs to maintain cost leadership. This means imposing tight cost controls and being aware of how cost savings might be achieved, for example through economies of scale, the introduction of more efficient ways of working or the introduction of new technology. To be market leader implies being the lowest cost provider and doing whatever it takes to achieve this. This means constantly moving down the cost curve and keeping all costs as low as possible, for example by moving production to countries with low cost labour, changing the materials used in manufacture or minimising sales and distribution costs. To sustain cost leadership can be a constant struggle and to help in this, wherever possible, companies develop patents and copyrights on

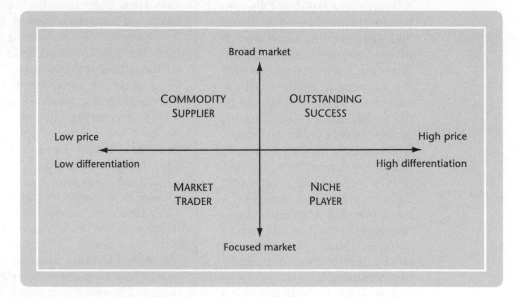

Figure 10.2 Generic marketing strategies

Dell Computers' market place is highly competitive. Dell prides itself on good marketing of quality products but, most important, speedy delivery of customised products. Nevertheless, whilst it might not sell the cheapest computers in the market place, the price it asks must always be competitive and that means costs must be kept as low as possible.

Dell decided early on that its competitive advantage lay in the computer-based processes it used to keep costs low and to build-to-order, quickly. In the 1990s, in order to sustain these competitive advantages, Dell started applying for patents, not for its products, but for different parts of its ordering, building and testing processes. It now holds about 80 such patents. However good, the machines it sells have become commodities using homogenous components from hard disk drives to microprocessors – mostly from Intel – but the processes Dell uses to build them allow the company to achieve competitive advantage and to sustain it.

their processes and procedures. Accountants play an important part in running this sort of company. The commodity supplier needs to have a strategy for doing all these things.

As we discussed in previous chapters, it is vital for a company following a policy of differentiation that it understands the basis of its differential advantage very clearly and then does whatever is needed to reinforce and build it. Differentiation involves being different and distinctive in some way. It often involves innovation. Branding has a vital role to play for a company trying to differentiate itself. A brand should be the embodiment of the product or service offering to customers. It takes time to build as it is based upon trust that the product or service will consistently deliver what it promises. A good brand is a valuable business asset and a firm following a differentiation strategy will need to invest time and money in developing it.

If a firm is focusing on a narrow market, then it needs to

'Basically any brand is an assurance to customers. It is an assurance of quality, an assurance of consistency. There is an immediate recognition, when you see the Cadbury signature on the front of the chocolate bar or box of Milk Tray, all those things are guaranteed.'

Sir Adrian Cadbury,
The Times 8.07.00

Gary Frank understands the importance of image and branding, particularly for a small firm trying to carve a niche in the market for itself. The company he set up in 1989, the **Delicious Doughnut Company**, was turning in lacklustre performance. It did not even produce doughnuts any more. So in 1997 he decided to create a new image and re-brand the company with the name **Fabulous Bakin' Boys**. He invested £300 000 in the name change and recruited a marketing manager.

Sales increased instantly by 6 per cent. They have now become one of Europe's leading muffin makers and their eye-catching products can now be seen on the shelves of Tesco, Sainsbury and Safeway. Profits have grown to £400 000 on sales of £7 million.

be undertaking regular market research to monitor changes in that market segment. Are tastes changing? Should the firm be adapting its offering to reflect these tastes, after all, the strength of the business should be its knowledge and close relationship with the narrow market segment that it sells to. One danger is that the smaller the number of customers in a segment, the greater the risk that the changing buying patterns of just a few will have a dramatic impact on the firm. However, these days focusing on a narrow market segment can go hand in hand with having a global market of millions of customers.

Value chains

There is one further framework that is useful in understanding competitive advantage. Real advantages in cost or differentiation need to be found in the chain of activities that a firm performs to deliver value to its customers. Porter (1985) says that the value chain, shown in Figure 10.3, should be the start of any strategic analysis. He identified five primary activities – inbound logistics (receiving, storing, disseminating inputs), operations (transforming inputs into a final product), outbound logistics (collecting, storing and distributing products to customers), marketing and sales and service – and four secondary activities – procurement (purchasing consumable and capital items), human resource management, technology development (R&D and so on) and firm infrastructure (general management, accounting and so on). Porter argues that each generic category can be broken down into discrete activities unique to a particular firm.

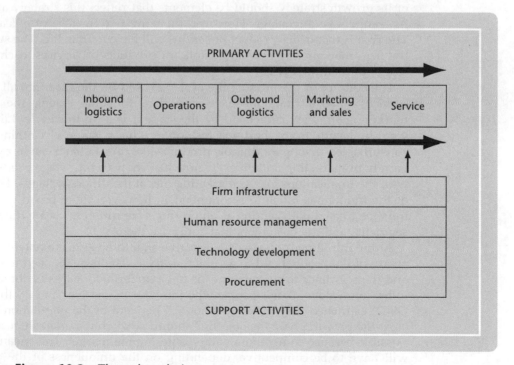

Figure 10.3 The value chain

The firm can then look at the costs associated with each activity and then try to compare it to the value obtained by customers by the particular activity. By identifying the cost or value drivers – the factors that determine cost or value for each activity – and the linkages which reduce cost or add value or discourage imitation, the firm can develop the strategies that lead to competitive advantage.

This is a way of focusing on the drivers of value in a business that ought to influence the strategy of the firm. For example, the low cost supply situation may be linked to being close to a key supplier and could therefore disappear if the firm decides, as part of its expansion plans, to move to another location. The value chain is also a useful way of thinking about how differentiation might be achieved. For example, a high-quality product might be let down by low quality after-sales service – the value to the customer not being matched by the investment. In other words, differentiation is likely to be achieved by multiple linkages in the value chain – a consistent marketing mix. If multiple compatible linkages can be established, they are more difficult to imitate than single linkages. Similarly, building switch costs into the value chain can also enhance competitive position. However, the advent of e-commerce has generally made it easier to disaggregate the value chain, establishing markets at different points along it, allowing firms to radically rethink or 're-engineer' the way their product-market offering is put together.

Product life-cycles

Whichever of the generic marketing strategies the firm is following, at the centre of its growth strategy should be elements that reflect this strategy and reinforce its competitive advantage. However, there are two further complicating factors. The first is that every product or service will have a finite life. The second is that the firm may already have a portfolio of products or services, each at different stages in their life-cycle.

The concept of the product life-cycle is based on the idea that all products or services have a finite life-cycle and that, to some extent, the appropriate marketing strategy, is dictated by the stage it is at in this cycle. Life-cycles can vary in length from short for fashion products, such as clothing and other consumables, to long for durable products like cars. Often it can be extended by a variety of marketing initiatives. Figure 10.4 shows a four stage product life-cycle with the implications for the marketing mix at the different stages. The simplicity of the model has much to recommend it; however, these broad generalisations must be treated with caution as all products are different, as are different market segments and the customers that comprise them.

At the introductory phase the objective should be to make potential customers aware of the product and to get them to try it. The benefits need to be explained and the relevance to customer needs to be underlined. Early customers are likely to be 'innovators', that is people who think for themselves and try things. Rogers (1962) estimated they make up some 2.5 per cent of the population.

At the growth phase the objective should be to grab market share as quickly as possible because competitors will be entering the market. This means that prices will have to be competitive, depending on the uniqueness of the product and how well it can be differentiated. The promotion emphasis should shift to one of promoting the brand and why it is better than that of competitors. 'Early adopters' will now be buying the product. These tend to be people with status in their market segment and opinion leaders. They adopt successful products, making them acceptable and respectable. These are estimated to represent some 13.5 per cent of the population. The product range should start to be developed at this stage so as to give customers more choice and gain advantage over competitors. A professional marketing approach at this stage is vital.

The 'middle and late majority' now start buying the product and take it into the mature phase of its life-cycle. The early majority (comprising some 34 per cent) are more conservative, with slightly higher status and are more deliberate. They only adopt the product after it has become acceptable. The late majority (also comprising some 34 per cent) are typically below average status, are sceptical and adopt the product much later. In this phase competitors are becoming established as some fall by the wayside. In order to maintain market share, pricing tends to be defensive at, or around, the level of competitors. There should be an emphasis on cost reduction so that profits are as high as possible. The accountant's influence should be evident at this stage in the life-cycle. It is at this point that products tend to get revamped – by changing designs, colours, packaging and so on – in order to extend their life-cycle. Towards the end of this period, price reductions may be hidden by offering extra elements to the product for the same price. Cars, for example, often get this treatment with limited edition models offering many extras for the same price.

Reliant Motors, makers of the Reliant Robin three-wheeler, is a company that has had to cope with a product at the end of its life-cycle. 350 vehicles a week were sold in 1973, 25 a week in 1995 and less than 10 a week in 2000. It has been in receivership three times, the last time in 1996. The unique selling point for three wheelers was that they were classed as mopeds and drivers did not need a full driving licence. Most buyers were aged between 60 and 65 and had never passed a car driving test – but this was, quite literally, a dying market. What is more, because of the small production runs, the price of the Robin was higher than many conventional cars – and that despite the fact that the company lost money on every one sold.

The company was bought by the venture capitalist **Kevin Leech** in 1996 largely because it had a profitable spares trade, with more than 120 000 Robins still in use each, given their galvanised chassis and plastic body, with a life expectancy of 35 years. In 1998 **Stewart Halstead** was appointed Managing Director. He decided to switch assembly to a smaller site and subcontract much of the production. However, despite cutting costs it was still not profitable and in 2000 production was stopped. His answer was to switch from being a vehicle assembler to a vehicle importer, selling the French Liger and Italian Piaggio vehicles – also legally classed as mopeds and therefore selling to the company's established markets. Profits for 2001 are forecast at £0.5 million on sales of £9.3 million (plus profits of £120 000 on sales of £1.2 million for Robin spares). However, Kevin Leech is particularly keen to preserve Reliant's car-maker status and the company is currently looking to buy the rights to manufacture vehicles developed by other companies.

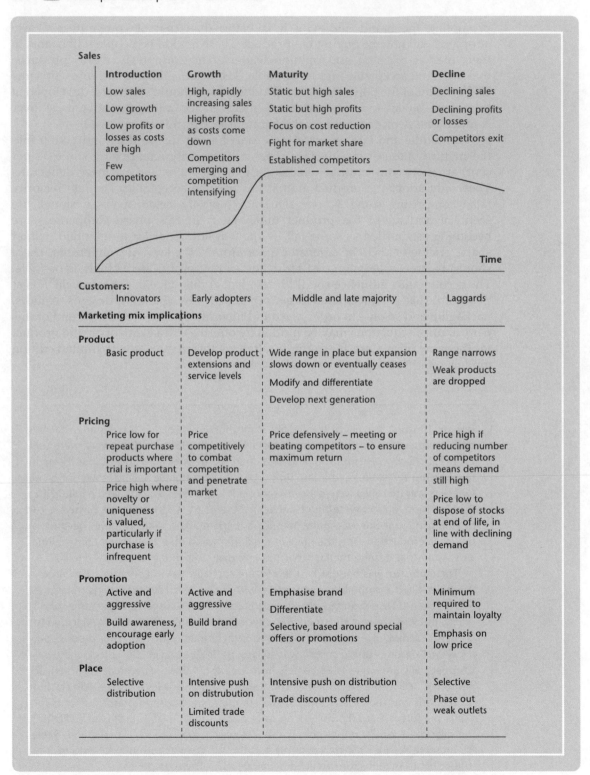

Figure 10.4 The product/service life-cycle

'Laggards' (comprising some 16 per cent) tend to view life through the rear view mirror and will continue buying products because of habit. The interesting thing about the decline phase of the life-cycle is that there may still be the opportunity to charge high prices and make good profits, at least in the short term, because competitors may be exiting the market quicker than demand is tailing off. Exactly when to exit is therefore a matter of careful judgement.

The problem with this concept is one of trying to establish where a product might actually be. Firms plotting their own product sales are not recording the product's life but their ability to manage it. Bad management can lead to an early downturn in sales which is not necessarily the mature phase of the life-cycle, and vice versa. What is more, products can be in the mature phase of their life-cycle in one market but at the introductory phase in another. You only have to see the queues and check the prices for McDonald's hamburgers in Russia to realise that the product has a long way to go in that market. Whereas in the USA it is clearly a successful but mature product.

Culmark first started manufacturing shaving brushes some two hundred years ago. The process may not have changed much over the years but the market certainly has. In 1900 Culmark sold 1 million brushes. During the two World Wars soldiers were issued with Culmark saving brushes and took them around the world.

It was the advent of shaving foam, and then shaving gel, that signalled the product might be coming to the end of a long life cycle. Now, only 10 per cent of shavers use a brush and in 2000 Culmark sold only some 300 000 brushes, albeit to dozens of countries throughout the world. 25 years ago the firm employed 50 workers, today it employs only four.

However, **John Chapman**, who now runs the firm, intends to fight back. He has just introduced a new 'Autofoam' brush. You just inject the foam into the brush and then apply it to your face without getting your hands wet. Whether this will further extend the life of the shaving brush remains to be seen.

The point about the product life-cycle is that it demonstrates clearly that the marketing mix must change over time, as the product or service matures. For the entrepreneur, what has been a successful marketing strategy at start-up, may need to be changed at the growth phase and beyond. They cannot afford to assume that, just because a certain approach has worked in the past, it will continue to work in the future.

One final point to consider about the product life-cycle is its influence on organisational culture. Johnson and Scholes (1993) summarise the key influences in Table 10.2. In many ways this mirrors Greiner's growth model discussed in Chapter 9 and highlights how situational factors influence many aspects of management. They point out that it is the growth phase that involves the greatest variety of cultural change and, by implication, is therefore the most difficult to manage.

Table 10.2 The influence of life-cycle on organisational culture

Life-cycle stage	Key cultural features	Implications for strategic choice
Introduction	▪ Cohesive culture ▪ Founders dominant ▪ Outside help not valued	▪ Try to repeat success ▪ Related developments favoured
Growth	▪ Less cultural cohesion ▪ Mismatches and tensions arise	▪ Diversification often possible ▪ Vulnerability to take-over ▪ Structural change needed for new developments ▪ New developments need protection
Maturity	▪ Culture institutionalised ▪ Culture breeds inertia ▪ Strategic logic may be rejected	▪ Related development favoured ▪ Incrementalism favoured
Decline	▪ Culture becomes a defence	▪ Readjustment necessary but difficult ▪ Divestment may prove necessary

Source: G. Johnson and K. Scholes (1993) *Exploring Corporate Strategy*, Hemel Hempstead: Prentice Hall International.

Product portfolios

The second complication is that if a company has more than one product or service, then it might be following different generic strategies for the different products or services. Indeed it might be following different generic strategies in order to sell the same product in different markets. Because of this complication with products and markets, marketers talk about different product-market offerings, so you can have the same product with a different marketing mix in another market. One obvious reason for this is that each of these product-market offerings might be at different stages of its life-cycle. So, for example, McDonald's may have a slightly different marketing mix for its products in Russia compared to the USA. The added complexity of having a portfolio of product-market offerings can be handled using a technique adapted from the 'Boston Matrix', which derives its name from the Boston Consulting Group that developed it. The original matrix was adapted by McKinsey so as to have more realistic multidimensional axes. Figure 10.5 shows the adapted matrix.

The matrix is best used as a loose conceptual framework. Market attractiveness is measured on the vertical axis, by such features as:

▪ Size of the market;
▪ Growth in the market;
▪ Profitability of the market;
▪ Level of price that might be charged;
▪ Degree of competition in the market (Porter's Five Forces);
▪ Customer loyalty or reliability of the market.

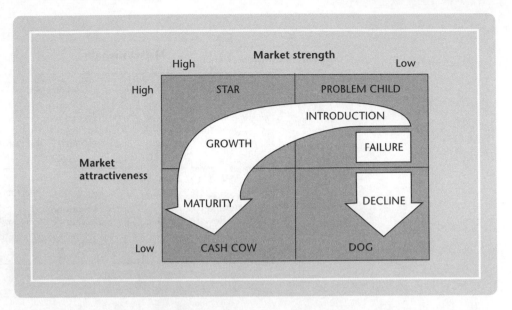

Figure 10.5 The Boston matrix

The strength of product or service offering in the market is measured on the horizontal axis, according to, for example:

- Market share;
- Reputation and image;
- Base of loyal customers;
- Technical expertise;
- Production or delivery expertise.

When a product or service offering is first developed it will be launched into an attractive market (otherwise why do it?), but the firm is unlikely to have a great deal of strength. This is called a Problem Child and is equivalent to the introduction phase of the life cycle. Sometimes the market proves to be unattractive – the life-cycle is very short. This is called a Dog. More often, if the market is attractive, sales will grow and the product or service offering will become more established and will strengthen in the market. This is called a Star. Eventually, however, the market will mature and the product or service will become a Cash Cow. These are market leaders with a lot of stability but little additional growth.

Figure 10.6 links the concept with cash flow. The Problem Child consumes cash for development and promotional costs at a rate of knots, without generating much cash by way of revenues. The Star might start to generate revenues but will still be facing high costs, particularly in marketing, to establish its market position against new entry competitors. It is therefore likely to be cash neutral. Only as a Cash Cow are revenues likely to outstrip costs and cash flow likely to be positive. There are two kinds of Dogs. One is a Cash Dog that covers its costs and might be worth keeping, for example if it brings in customers for other products or services or it shares overheads. The other is the Genuine Dog which is losing money and should be scrapped. It is from this model that phrases like 'shoot the dog', 'invest in stars' and 'milk the cow' came from.

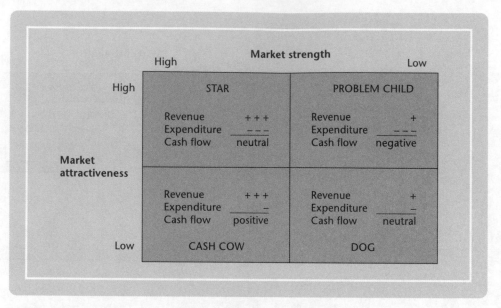

Figure 10.6 The Boston matrix: cash flow implications

Ideally, companies need a balanced portfolio of product–service offerings so that surplus cash from Cash Cows can be used to invest in the Problem Children. At start-up this is clearly not the case, but as the firm grows and more products or services are developed, an understanding of the product life-cycle allows it to engineer its portfolio to be more balanced. If this is not possible, then at least it can plan to manage its cash flow requirements.

There are problems with the framework at an operational level. For example, defining the market a firm is in so that market share or market growth can be measured. Just one factor on each axis can be used or, indeed, a number of them weighted appropriately using some sort of simple scale. However, it is probably best used as a loose conceptual framework. Treated with caution, it can be extremely valuable. In a complex world, anything that simplifies, and therefore helps our understanding, must be of value. For example, it allows us to make some broad generalisations about marketing strategy for product–service offerings in different quadrants. These are shown in Figure 10.7.

The Boston Matrix also allows us to present complex information more understandably, particularly when linked to forecasting future market positions and strategies involved in getting there. For example, Figure 10.8 represents the hypothetical three-product portfolio for a company. The size of each circle is proportionate to the turnover each achieves. The lighter circles represent the present product positions, the darker circles represent the positions projected in five years' time. The portfolio looks balanced and the diagram can be used to explain the strategies that are in place to move the products to where they are planned to be. However, one essential added complexity is the generic marketing strategies. If products A and B are commodities, selling mainly on price, with low margin under intense pressure, it has implications not only for strategy but also for the cash flow available to invest in product C, particularly if this is a niche market product needing heavy investment.

Market attractiveness / Market strength	High	Low
High	STAR **Objective** Invest for growth **Elements of strategy** ■ Penetrate market ■ Expand geographically ■ Sell and promote aggressively ■ Differentiate ■ Promote brand, if possible ■ Accept moderate short-term profits ■ Extend product range	PROBLEM CHILD **Objective** Develop opportunities **Elements of strategy** ■ Be critical of prospects ■ Invest selectively in products or services ■ Specialise in strengths ■ Shore up weaknesses
Low	CASH COW **Objective** Maintain market position and manage for earnings **Elements of strategy** ■ Maintain market position with successful products or services ■ Prune less successful ones in range ■ Differentiate ■ Promote brand, if possible ■ Stabilise prices, except where temporary aggressive pricing is required in the face of competition	CASH DOG **Objective** Maintain but monitor carefully to decide when to kill off **Elements of strategy** ■ Reduce costs ■ Improve productivity ■ Live with declining sales GENUINE DOG **Objective** Kill off as soon as appropriate **Elements of strategy** ■ Maximise cash flow ■ Minimise expenditure ■ Judge when is the best time to kill off

Figure 10.7 The Boston matrix: strategy implications

Financial analysis

No SWOT analysis would be complete without an analysis of the company's financial position. Chapter 6 set out many of the elements of this – break-even and margin of safety remain important measures of risk. However, once established, investors, and other backers of a firm start to look for other things and make use of a technique called 'ratio analysis'.

This starts by assuming that the owner (shareholder) of the firm wants to maximise their investment. Whatever they invest in, an investor is ultimately

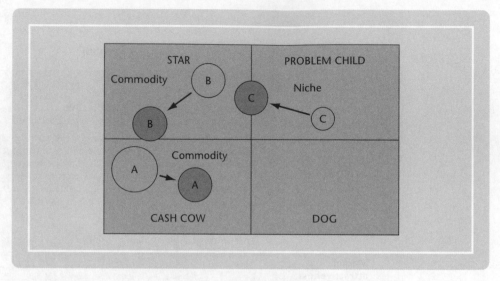

Figure 10.8 Boston matrix for hypothetical company

interested in the final return they receive, after all expenses, in relation to their investment. If they invest £10 and receive £1, after all expenses, they receive a 10 per cent return which can then be compared to other investment opportunities. A shareholder, who owns all the profits of the firm, wants to maximise the return they receive on the shareholders funds they have invested (share capital + retained profit). The critical performance ratio, that must be kept as high as possible, is therefore:

$$\text{Return to shareholders (\%)} = \frac{\text{Profit after interest (and all other costs)}}{\text{Shareholders' funds}}$$

This is expressed as a percentage. To maximise it means operating profit should be as high as possible, interest should be as low as possible and shareholders' funds should also be as low as possible. And here lies the dilemma. One way of keeping shareholders' funds low is to borrow (shareholders' funds = total assets – loans), but this increases interest payments. So the question is, how much to borrow? The following example should provide the answer. The business makes a return on all the money invested in it, both shareholders funds and loans. Let us say that the shareholder puts £50 into the business and then obtains a bank loan of £50 on which interest of 10 per cent is payable. The business makes a return of 25 per cent on the total £100 invested in it. The situation is set out below:

Investment:		Return:	
Total assets	£100	Business @ 25%	= £25
comprising:		less:	
Loans	£ 50	Interest @ 10%	= £ 5
Shareholders' funds	£ 50	Balance for shareholder	= £20

The shareholder therefore gets to keep £20 – a 40 per cent return on their investment. This is above the 25 per cent return the business is making because the shareholders are willing to take the risk of borrowing money on which they only pay a 10 per cent rate of interest. They get to keep the additional 15 per cent. However, this is a risk. If the business were only able to make a 5 per cent return (return = £5) then all the money would go to pay interest, leaving nothing for the shareholder. Similarly, in the unlikely event of interest rates rising above 25 per cent, the return to the shareholder would suffer.

As long as the return the business is making is above the rate of interest charged, the shareholders' return will be increased by maximising borrowing. However, in doing this the riskiness of the business increases because fixed interest costs increase. The appropriate level of borrowing, called gearing or leverage, is the classic risk/return trade-off decision – it is a question of judgement. However, bankers do have some benchmark ratios to inform their lending decisions, as we shall see later.

Therefore, as far as the business is concerned, the critical performance ratio, that must be kept as high as possible, is:

$$\text{Return on total assets (\%)} = \frac{\text{Operating profit (before interest)}}{\text{Total assets}}$$

This is also expressed as a percentage. It is a measure of the operating efficiency of the business, the return operations make as opposed to the way the business is financed. It should be as high as possible, but be aware that the owner will also be taking a salary out of the business which is deducted in arriving at operating income. The measure can therefore be distorted if salaries are unrealistically low or high. The ratio, in turn, depends on two further ratios that when multiplied together yield the above ratio:

$$\text{Profit margin (\%)} = \frac{\text{Net Profit}}{\text{Sales}}$$

This measures the profit margin the firm is able to command and is expressed as a percentage. The ratio should be as high as possible.

$$\text{Asset Efficiency} = \frac{\text{Sales}}{\text{Net assets}}$$

This measures how efficiently the assets are being used in relation to the level of activity, measured by sales, and is expressed as a number. It should be as high as possible.

This ratio in turn depends upon how its constituent parts perform:

$$\text{Gross profit margin (\%)} = \frac{\text{Gross profit}}{\text{Sales}}$$

Gross profit is the difference between sales or turnover and the costs to produce the goods sold. The ratio should be as high as possible.

This ratio in turn depends upon how its constituent parts perform:

$$\text{Debtor turnover} = \frac{\text{Sales}}{\text{Debtors}}$$

This number tells you how many times debtors turn over each year. If sales are £3.0 million and debtors are £0.6 million, they turn over 5 times a year, equivalent to every 1.2 months. You can compare this to the credit terms offered to customers.

There are also some key cost ratios, also expressed as percentages, that should be kept as low as possible:

$$\frac{\text{Cost of materials}}{\text{Sales}}, \quad \frac{\text{Cost of labour}}{\text{Sales}},$$

$$\frac{\text{Overhead costs}}{\text{Sales}}$$

There may be other costs that are high and sensitive to changes in the market place that can be usefully measured against sales in this format.

$$\text{Stock turnover} = \frac{\text{Sales}}{\text{Stock}}$$

$$\text{Fixed asset turnover} = \frac{\text{Sales}}{\text{Fixed assets}}$$

These ratios are expressed as numbers and should be as high as possible.

Ratios are useful because they measure one number against another – they therefore allow for growth. So, for example, debtors are bound to increase as the business grows and sales increase, but what is important is not the absolute value of debtors but rather its relationship to sales, measured by debtor turnover. Similarly, there is no way of knowing whether a £2 million profit in one company is better than a £1 million profit in another unless you know how much was invested in each to achieve it.

To obtain a high return to the shareholder, a firm needs effective profit management and efficient asset management. Put crudely, margins need to be as high as possible and assets should be kept as low as possible. Systematic calculation of these ratios can give you clues about how profit might be increased and where assets might be reduced. Of course to do this you need some benchmarks. One fundamental benchmark is the rate of interest. The return on total assets should never fall below this, otherwise you are better off closing the company and putting the money in the bank. Another benchmark is your payment terms against which debtor turnover can be judged. All the others are a question of judgement, but you can judge them against:

- *Projected budgets*: ratios can be based on projected as well as actual financial information. Comparing actual to budgeted financial performance is part of effective financial control.
- *Trends over time*: ratios do change over time and trends can give both good and bad news.
- *Industry norms*: industry based ratios, often based on published financial statements, are produced by organisations like The Centre for Interfirm Comparison and ICC Business Ratios.

There are also two ratios that measure the liquidity of a business. These are of particular interest to people offering credit to the business as they measure the firm's ability to repay them. These ratios are all expressed as numbers:

$$\text{Current ratio} = \frac{\text{Current assets}}{\text{Current liabilities}}$$

This is expected to be greater than 1, indicating that current assets exceed current liabilities.

$$\text{Quick ratio} = \frac{\text{Current assets excl. stock}}{\text{Current liabilities}}$$

This is expected to be near to 1, perhaps as low as 0.8.

The level of borrowing is called gearing or leverage. High gearing or leverage is risky. It is measured by a number of ratios that are of particular interest to bankers:

$$\text{Gearing } (\%) = \frac{\text{All loans} + \text{overdraft}}{\text{Shareholders funds}}$$

Bankers like this ratio to be under 100%, indicating that shareholders have put in more money than the banks. Frequently for growing firms this is not the case. Above 400 per cent is considered very high risk and the business likely to fail. However, some management buy-outs can have gearing above this level.

$$\text{Short-term borrowing } (\%)$$
$$= \frac{\text{Short-term loans} + \text{overdraft}}{\text{All loans} + \text{overdraft}}$$

Long-term loans give greater security than short-term loans. Therefore the higher this ratio, the riskier the firm. The ratio must be read alongside gearing. Low gearing means the percentage short-term borrowing can be higher.

$$\text{Interest cover} = \frac{\text{Operating profit}}{\text{Interest}}$$

This measures how secure interest payments are. The higher the number the better.

The margin of safety remains an important ratio measuring the riskiness of the business due to its level of fixed costs. A financial ratio checklist which includes the margin of safety is shown as Figure 10.9. You may wish to revisit Chapter 6 where many of these terms and some of these ratios were explained.

J. J. Cash, a Coventry-based textile manufacturer with 138 staff, put the company in for the UK Benchmarking Index and got some surprising results. They knew they had good product quality and thought they had excellent labour relations. However, the Index showed that the customer satisfaction rate was not good. Despite good product quality, the speed of response, vital in the fashion-led clothing industry, was not fast enough. Where they had lead times of four to six weeks, other firms could manage two. What is more, a set of key indicators such as accident rates, absenteeism and staff turnover revealed that the workers were suffering a lack of motivation.

What followed was nothing short of a complete culture change in the company. The old assembly-line production methods were dropped and new team-working structures were implemented across the entire organisation, underpinned with a generous training budget. Teams were given more authority and new 'two-way' communications procedures were put in place. As a result delivery-on-time rates increased from 60 per cent to 90 per cent, prototypes leave the factory in 48 hours, stock waste has fallen from 6.5 per cent to 2 per cent, stock turnover has increased and staff absenteeism and turnover rates have gone down.

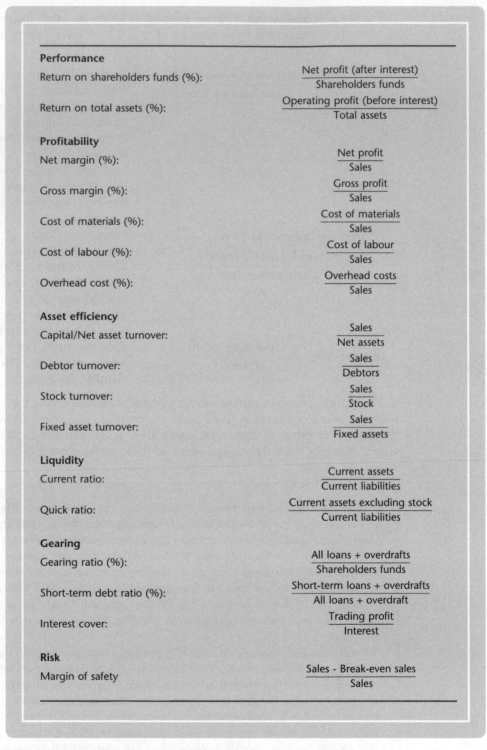

Performance

Return on shareholders funds (%): $\dfrac{\text{Net profit (after interest)}}{\text{Shareholders funds}}$

Return on total assets (%): $\dfrac{\text{Operating profit (before interest)}}{\text{Total assets}}$

Profitability

Net margin (%): $\dfrac{\text{Net profit}}{\text{Sales}}$

Gross margin (%): $\dfrac{\text{Gross profit}}{\text{Sales}}$

Cost of materials (%): $\dfrac{\text{Cost of materials}}{\text{Sales}}$

Cost of labour (%): $\dfrac{\text{Cost of labour}}{\text{Sales}}$

Overhead cost (%): $\dfrac{\text{Overhead costs}}{\text{Sales}}$

Asset efficiency

Capital/Net asset turnover: $\dfrac{\text{Sales}}{\text{Net assets}}$

Debtor turnover: $\dfrac{\text{Sales}}{\text{Debtors}}$

Stock turnover: $\dfrac{\text{Sales}}{\text{Stock}}$

Fixed asset turnover: $\dfrac{\text{Sales}}{\text{Fixed assets}}$

Liquidity

Current ratio: $\dfrac{\text{Current assets}}{\text{Current liabilities}}$

Quick ratio: $\dfrac{\text{Current assets excluding stock}}{\text{Current liabilities}}$

Gearing

Gearing ratio (%): $\dfrac{\text{All loans + overdrafts}}{\text{Shareholders funds}}$

Short-term debt ratio (%): $\dfrac{\text{Short-term loans + overdrafts}}{\text{All loans + overdraft}}$

Interest cover: $\dfrac{\text{Trading profit}}{\text{Interest}}$

Risk

Margin of safety: $\dfrac{\text{Sales - Break-even sales}}{\text{Sales}}$

Figure 10.9 Financial ratio checklist

Performance ratios need not always be financial; benchmarking performance has been around in one form or another since the 1960s. However, in 1996 the DTI launched the UK Bench-marking Index aimed at smaller firms. The index gathers data on a wide range of performance indicators including customer satisfaction rates, profitability, earnings per worker, productivity and stock turnover. It can be accessed via local Business Links and Training and Enterprise Councils and costs from about £400. It has now gathered data on over 2500 companies. *Closing the Gap*, a recent report based on this data shows that companies in the top quartile achieve profit margins five times higher than those in the bottom quartile. They achieve 98 per cent supplier accuracy and delivery reliability against 60 per cent accuracy and 85 per cent reliability for companies in the bottom quartile. Also in these companies spending on training is ten times higher and staff absenteeism 75 per cent lower. The initiative is now being extended to the continent and the EC is funding its use in some 1500 middle-sized firms across nine European countries. It is also now being used in the USA, Singapore, South Africa and Australia.

The SWOT analysis revisited

At this point it would be a good idea to revisit the whole planning process, outlined in Chapter 7, and in particular the SWOT analysis. Figure 10.10 shows the overall business planning process. The SWOT analysis is the basis for undertaking customer analysis and deciding on market segmentation as well as setting business objectives. It informs marketing strategy.

The internal appraisal of the company is to do with identifying its strengths and weaknesses in relation to its market place. There is no prescriptive approach to this. Sometimes a strength may also be a weakness, for example, in relation to different market segments. The techniques developed to help in the appraisal include:

- Generic marketing strategies;
- Life-cycle analysis;
- Portfolio analysis;
- Financial ratio analysis;
- Benchmarking;
- Culture evaluation.

The external appraisal of the environment is to do with identifying the threats and opportunities that the firm faces. Again there is no prescriptive approach, and again an opportunity can often be a threat; for example, if you do not make the most of it. The techniques developed to help in this include:

- Market research;
- Porter's Five Forces Industry Analysis;
- Economies of scale.

However, these techniques are curiously based in the present. What is needed is a framework to think about the future and just what might happen. One such framework is known by the acronym SLEPT and looks at the changes that are likely to occur in the following areas:

Social   Social changes such as an ageing population, increasing work participation often from home, 24-hour shopping, increasing crime, increasing participation in higher education, changing employment patterns, increasing number of one-parent families and so on.

Legal   Legal changes such as Health and Safety, changes in employment laws, food hygiene regulations, patent laws and so on.

Economic   Economic changes such as entry into the Euro currency area, changes in interest rates, growth, inflation, employment and so on.

Political   Political changes like local or central government elections; political initiatives, for example on competitiveness in car prices or at supermarkets, new or changed taxes, merger and take-over policy and so on.

Technological Technological developments such as the internet, increasing use of computers and chip technology, increasing use of mobile phones, increasing use of surveillance cameras and so on.

The trick is to brainstorm and think outside the square about how these developments might affect the business. For example, the development of the internet and broadband networks might be thought to dramatically bring into question the future viability of shops selling CDs or videos. The development of teleconferencing might be seen as a threat to those firms providing business travel over long distances, such as airlines. The development of internet shopping might cause developers to rethink the purpose and structure of our town centres as well as individual shops to re-engineer the way they meet customer needs. The future may be uncertain, but it cannot be ignored.

Another technique used sometimes to help think about the future in a structured way is called 'futures thinking'. Futures thinking tries to take a holistic perspective, avoiding a rigid approach to strategic planning. With it a vision about a desired future state is developed and planning then takes place, backwards, from that state to where the firm is at the moment. Current constraints to action are ignored and in this way the barriers to change are identified. Some barriers may be permanent, but some might not be.

Similar to this is 'scenario planning' which can be a valuable tool for assessing a firm's environment in conditions of high uncertainty over a longer term, say five years or more. With this technique, views of possible future situations that might impact on the firm are constructed. Often major trends in the environment are identified from the SLEPT analysis and built into scenarios. These situations must be logically consistent possible futures, usually an optimistic, a pessimistic and a 'most likely' future, based around key factors influencing the firm. Optional courses of action or strategies are then matched to these scenarios. In effect, the scenarios are being used to test the sensitivity of possible strategies. They also allow assumptions about the status-quo of the environment in which a firm operates to be challenged. So, for example, a company planning overseas

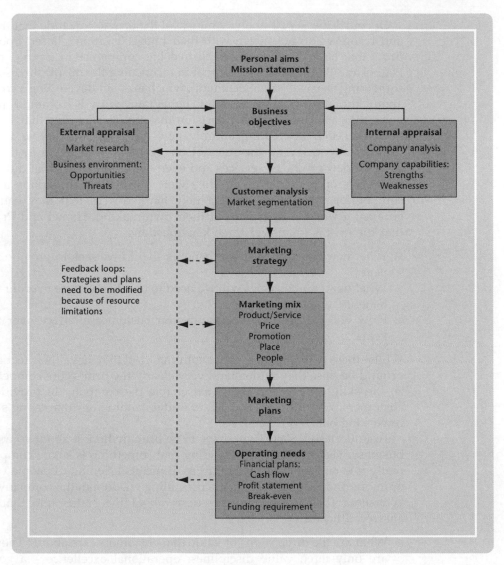

Figure 10.10 The business planning process

expansion may be uncertain about factors like exchange rate fluctuations or tariff barriers and might construct possible futures that help it decide whether to manufacture in the UK and export or to set-up a manufacturing base in the country.

Scenario planning takes the firm away from the short-term, day to day imperatives and helps it think about long-term trends and changes in its environment. Most entrepreneurs, however, prefer to learn by doing and take a short-term, incremental approach to decision-making, reacting to events as they occur. However, in a risky environment, or one where high capital costs are involved, scenario planning has a lot to recommend it – and it is a lot cheaper than making mistakes.

Of course the SWOT analysis may lead the firm to conclude that their strengths and resources do not match with their high aspirations. Based upon a study of firms that have challenged established big companies in a range of industries, Hamel and Prahalad (1994) say that in reconciling the misfit, successful firms use something they call 'strategic intent', which is about developing a common vision about the future, aligning staff behaviour with a common purpose and delegating and decentralising decision-making. They argued that 'the challengers had succeeded in creating entirely new forms of competitive advantage and dramatically rewriting the rules of engagement'. Managers in these firms can imagine new products, services and even entire industries that did not exist and then went on to create them. They were not just benchmarking and analysing competition, they were creating new marketplaces that they could dominate because it was a marketplace of their own making. Hamel and Prahalad claim that the trick is to answer three key questions:

● What new types of customer benefits should we seek to provide in 5, 10 or 15 years?
● What new competencies will we need to build or acquire in order to offer these benefits?
● How will we need to reconfigure our customer interface over the next few years.

Whilst these managers may be revolutionaries, they have their feet firmly on the ground because they understand very clearly the firm's core competencies – that is, the skills and technologies that enable the company to provide benefits to customers. Which brings us back to understanding our marketing strategies and reworking our SWOT analysis.

To undertake a SWOT you have to be brutally honest about yourself and your business. That means not pretending that something is a core competence when really it is not. As Gary Hamel urges, it means listening to people with different opinions and judging what is the prevailing wisdom in the company. Treacy and Wiersema (1995) pose five questions about the status quo that need to be answered honestly:

● What are the dimensions of value that customers care about? They claim there are only three value disciplines: operational excellence – a good product-market offering (for example, McDonald's or Dell), product leadership – the best quality, most innovative product (for example Dyson or Morgan Motor Company), customer intimacy – understanding and developing a relationships with customers (for example, Body Shop).
● For each dimension, what proportion of customers focus on it as their primary or dominant decision criterion?
● Which competitors provide the best value in each of these value dimensions?
● How does the firm compare to the competition on each dimension?
● Why does the firm fall short of the value leaders in each dimension of value?

From the answers to these questions realistic options can be listed and choices made. But, once again, honesty is essential because this means being realistic about the options even if some of them are not very pleasant.

So, Porter wants you to select cost leadership, differentiation or focus. Hamel and Prahalad want you to focus on core competencies. On the other hand, Treacy and Wiersema want you to select operational excellence, product leadership or customer intimacy. Which do you select? The key theme is that strategy should emphasise something that makes the firm as unique as possible and delivers as much value to the customer as possible today, and more importantly, tomorrow.

Summary

The ingredients of successful growth, as shown by the experience of **S&A Foods**, are:

● An owner-manager who is an entrepreneur;
● The right business culture;
● A strong company;
● Making the right decisions;
● Luck.

Successful firms tend to innovate, compete on quality rather than price, dominate their market niche, compete in areas of strength and have good financial controls. **Jordans** is a good example of a firm that fits this profile.

Barriers to growth vary according to the economic conditions of the time and many company-specific factors. However, consistent general barriers are market conditions and cost or availability of finance. Securing competitive advantage involves understanding who customers are, what benefits they are looking for and why they buy from us rather than competitors. What are our core competencies? How do we add value to customers? Which strategies have worked in the past? Future strategy should build upon these strengths. An understanding of the generic marketing strategies and the value chain can inform these judgements. **Dell** understands where its competitive advantage lies and uses patents to secure it. **The Fabulous Bakin' Boys** use image and branding to secure their competitive advantage.

The product life-cycle has important implications for marketing strategy. Strategy needs to change as a product or service progresses through the life-cycle – introduction, growth, maturity and decline. As **Culmark** have found, all products come to the end of their life-cycle and it can be difficult to extend. Often, like **Reliant Motors**, companies have to move into new areas of business.

The Boston Matrix is a useful way of conveying complex information about product portfolios. It provides an insight into marketing as well as financing strategies and how a balanced portfolio might be achieved.

Financial ratio analysis is an important part of a SWOT analysis. Based on the premise that shareholders want to maximise the return they make on their investment, it provides information on how profit might be increased and assets reduced. It also provides information about liquidity and gearing or leverage. As **J. J. Cash** found, other non-financial performance ratios can also be calculated and used to benchmark performance via local Business Links.

A SLEPT analysis looks at the social, legal, economic, political and technological changes that might occur in the future. Scenario planning is about trying to identify key environmental influences on the firm and then see how changes in their current state might affect it. Future thinking tries to envisage a desired future state and work back to see how it might be achieved.

A SWOT analysis is the cornerstone of strategic analysis. In developing it, honesty is essential. There is no prescriptive approach, however, techniques that can be applied include:

Internal analysis:
● Generic marketing strategies
● Life cycle analysis
● Portfolio analysis
● Financial ratio analysis
● Bench-marking
● Culture evaluation

External analysis:
● Market research
● Porter's Five Forces analysis
● Economies of scale
● SLEPT analysis
● Scenario planning
● Futures thinking

Whilst Porter emphasises cost leadership, differentiation or focus, Hamel and Prahalad highlight core competencies and Treacy and Wiersema emphasise operational excellence, product leadership or customer intimacy; the unifying theme to come from these theorists is that strategy should emphasise something that makes the firm as unique as possible and delivers as much value to the customer as possible today and, more importantly, tomorrow.

● Essays and discussion topics

1   Most small firms will not grow to any size. It is therefore not worthwhile trying to 'pick winners'. Discuss.
2   How much luck is involved in successfully growing a business?
3   Are there any real barriers to growth or are there only excuses?
4   Porter wants you to select cost leadership, differentiation or focus, Hamel and Prahalad want you to focus on core competencies and Treacy and Wiersema want you to select operational excellence, product leadership or customer intimacy. All these strategies are just fad and fancy. Nobody really knows how to generate competitive advantage. Discuss.
5   Value chains are an elegant concept but cannot be operationalised. Discuss.
6   Some products – basic necessities such as food and water – do not have a life-cycle. Discuss.
7   How useful are the labels of 'innovators', 'early adopters', late adopters and 'laggards' to customers at different stages of the life-cycle?
8   In practical terms it is impossible to find out where a product is at in its life-cycle. Discuss.
9   What are the factors that influence the culture of a business?
10 How useful is the Boston Matrix?
11 How would you go about creating a scale for each axis of the Boston Matrix that reflects a range of factors? Give a practical example.
12 In what circumstances might you not want to 'shoot a dog'?
13 You cannot determine profit in a small firm because there are too many ways for the entrepreneur to manipulate it. Any form of financial analysis will therefore not work. Discuss.
14 How might you go about determining the profitability of a small firm so that financial analysis can be undertaken?
15 Death Valley just goes on and on for the growing firm. Explain why.
16 What should a small firm do to ensure that debtors pay promptly?
17 We can only guess what the future might hold, so there is no point in trying to predict it. Discuss.
18 How do you think music will be sold in the future? How can firms make profit?

19 A firm needs two plans – one for the provider of capital that 'sells' the business idea to them and a second that is a true evaluation of how the firm might perform. Discuss.
20 How would you go about undertaking a SWOT on an established small firm?

⬤ Exercises and assignments

1 Select a successful entrepreneur, like Bill Gates or Richard Branson, and research their backgrounds, show how their business developed and analyse why they have been so successful.
2 Select a well-known product that is now in the mature phase of its life-cycle and chart how the marketing mix has changed over that life-cycle.
3 Consider the case of **Reliant Motors**; what do you consider to be the main challenges now facing the business?
4 Consider the case of **Culmark**; do you think the firm has a future?
5 For your University, College or Department, try to analyse their course portfolio using the Boston Matrix. What are your conclusions?
6 For a selected company, try to analyse their product portfolio using the Boston Matrix. What are your conclusions?
7 Use Small Business Audit Checklist 5, in the Growth Audit and the back of the book to undertake as comprehensive a financial analysis as you can on the three firms in the Appendix to Chapter 8 – Sport Retail, Jean Young and Dewhurst Engineering. Why can you not undertake a full analysis? Try estimating any numbers you are not given in the business plans.
8 For a selected set of published financial statements, undertake a financial analysis using Small Business Audit Checklist 5.
9 Undertake a SLEPT analysis on your University, College or Department. Based upon this try scenario planning on one major trend that you identify.
10 Undertake a SLEPT analysis on a selected firm. Based upon this, try scenario planning on one major trend that you identify.
11 Undertake a SWOT analysis on your University, College or Department. Draw up a list of action points that follow from your analysis.
12 Undertake a comprehensive SWOT analysis on your course. Draw up a list of action points that follow from your analysis.
13 Consider the case of **Dell Computers**; where does its competitive advantage lie and how can it secure it?

⬤ Growth audit exercise

Using the appropriate Checklists, undertake steps 3 to 6 of the growth audit exercise at the back of the book.

⬤ Websites to visit

1 The following websites provide help, support and advice for growing firms. Visit each one to see what it has to offer.

   ⬤ Small Business Service: www.businessadviceonline.gov.uk
   ⬤ Business Links: www.businesslink.co.uk
   ⬤ Forum for Private Business: www.fpb.co.uk
   ⬤ 3i: www.3i.com
   ⬤ Trade Partners UK: www.tradepartners.gov.uk

2 The following websites provide business and management information. Visit each one to see what it has to offer.

- Bnet: www.bnet.co.uk
- Start-ups: www.startups.co.uk
- Enterprise Zone: wwwenterprisezone.org.uk

⬤ References

Birley, S. and Westhead, P. (1990) 'Growth and Performance Contrasts Between "Types" of Small Firms', *Strategic Management Journal*, vol. II.

Burns, P. (1994) *Winners and Losers in the 1990s*, 3i European Enterprise Centre, Report no. 12, April.

Dunkelberg, W.G., Cooper, A.C., Woo, C. and Dennis, W.J. (1987) 'New Firm Growth and Performance', in N.C. Churchill, J.A. Hornday, B.A. Kirchhoff, C.J. Krasner and K. H. Vesper (eds), *Frontiers of Entrepreneurship Research,* Boston, Mass: Babson College Press.

Harrison, J. and Taylor, B. (1996) Supergrowth Companies: Entrepreneurs in Action, Oxford: Butterworth-Heinemann.

Hemel, G. and Prahalad, C.K. (1994) *Competing For the Future: Breakthrough Strategies for Seizing Control of your Industry and Creating the Markets of Tomorrow*, Boston, Mass: Harvard Business School Press.

Johnson, G. and Scholes K. (1993) *Exploring Corporate Strategy*, Hemel Hempstead, Herts: Prentice Hall International.

Macrae, D.J.R. (1991) 'Characteristics of High and Low Growth Small and Medium-Sized Businesses', paper presented at 21st European Small Business Seminar, Barcelona, Spain.

Porter, M.E. (1985) *Competitive Advantage: Creating and Sustaining Superior Performance*, New York: Free Press.

Ray, G.H. and Hutchinson, P.J. (1983) *The Financing and Financial Control of Small Enterprise Development,* London: Gower.

Rogers, E.M. (1962) *Diffusion of Innovation,* New York: Free Press.

Siegel, R., Siegel, E. and MacMillan, I.C. (1993) 'Characteristics Distinguishing High Growth Ventures, *Journal of Business Venturing*, vol. 8.

Solem, O. and Steiner, M.P. (1989) 'Factors for Success in Small Manufacturing Firms – and with Special Emphasis on Growing Firms', paper presented at Conference on SMEs and the Challenges of 1992, Mikkeli, Finland.

Storey, D.J., Keasey, K., Watson, R. and Wynarczyk, P. (1987) *The Performance of Small Firms: Profits, Jobs and Failures,* London: Croom Helm.

Storey D.J., Watson R. and Wynarczyk, P. (1989) *Fast Growth Small Business: Case Studies of 40 Small Firms in Northern Ireland,* Department of Employment, research paper no. 67.

3i European Enterprise Centre (1991) *High Performance SMEs: A Two Country Study,* Report no. 1, September.

3i European Enterprise Centre (1993) *Britain's Superleague Companies,* Report no. 9, August.

Treacy, M. and Wiersema, F. (1995) *The Discipline of Market Leaders,* Reading, Mass: Addison-Wesley.

Woo, C.Y., Cooper, A.C., Dunkelberg, W.C., Daellenbach, U. and Dennis, W.J. (1989) 'Determinants of Growth for Small and Large Entrepreneurial Start-Ups', paper presented to Babson Entrepreneurship Conference.

Wynarczyk, P., Watson, R., Storey, D.J., Short, H. and Keasey, K. (1993) *The Managerial Labour Market in Small and Medium-Sized Enterprises,* London: Routledge.

chapter eleven

Growth: take-off

Contents

- Growth options
- Existing products/services and existing markets
- Product/service development
- Market development
- Diversification
- Risk
- Mergers and acquisitions
- Strategy development
- Planning and control
- Summary
- Appendix: Forecasts and budgets – a comprehensive example

Learning outcomes

By the end of this chapter you should:

- Understand what are the growth options facing a firm, the reasons for pursuing them and the advantages and risks associated each one;
- Understand the consequences of selecting appropriate strategies and the factors that are important to make each strategy work;
- Understand the different types of diversification and their risks;
- Understand what synergy is and how it might be achieved;
- Appreciate the degrees of risk that are built up in a growth strategy;
- Understand the different types of mergers and acquisitions, the reasons for following this strategy and the risks involved;
- Understand the way strategy develops in a small firm;
- Be able to critically evaluate a growth plan;
- Appreciate the importance and advantages of planning and control at the take-off stage;
- Understand how a detailed budget for a medium-sized business is drawn up.

Growth options

The move from the success to take-off stage in the growth models outlined in Chapter 9 is dangerous. It can take, well, as long as it takes. Without a clear understanding of what has made the business successful, there is no sound foundation for the move forward. Some entrepreneurs understand what they are doing, what works and what does not, as they do it, sometimes almost instinctively. Others are more reflective and need time to analyse the situation. Getting the right people and putting the right systems in place can take time. Some situations are more complex than others. Once the entrepreneur understands the basis for their successful survival, so far, they can start to plan their take-off, the growth that will eventually make them leaders of the very small number of high-growth businesses upon which whole economies are so dependent for their growth. This is the point where the small business caterpillar, having become a butterfly, will try to fly.

In general terms, to achieve growth a company should build on its strengths and core competencies, shore up its weaknesses and develop a marketing strategy for each product-market offering that reflects:

- the appropriate generic marketing strategy;
- the stage a product-market offering is at in its life-cycle;
- all placed in the context of its portfolio of product-market offerings.

In that context, research tells us that product/service innovation leading into a niche marketing strategy, involving selling a differentiated product or service not selling primarily on price, that allows the company to dominate its market niche, is the strategy that is most likely to lead to success. Although firms following other strategies do, of course, succeed, the importance of this research-based finding cannot be under-emphasised. Business, like life, is about playing the odds. You ignore these odds at your peril.

In order to start planning the take-off phase, there is one further tool that we need. It helps analyse how growth can be achieved in a systematic fashion. It is called the Product/Market Matrix, was originally devised by Igor Ansoff (1968), and is shown in Figure 11.1. This simple conceptual framework uses existing/ new products on one axis and existing/new markets on the other. It then goes on to explore the options within the four quadrants of the matrix and how the options might be achieved. Like all useful business frameworks it is attractively simple and intuitively logical. To achieve growth a company has four options:

1 Stay with existing products/services and existing markets and customers;
2 Product development;
3 Market development;
4 Diversification.

To use this framework we need to explore each option systematically in greater detail, find out what it entails and weigh up the risks and returns associated with each one. Empirical research tells us a lot about which are likely to work and which are not.

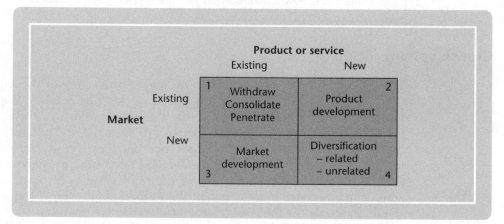

Figure 11.1 The product/market matrix

Existing products/services and existing markets

Within this option there are a number of possible courses of action. Firstly, the entrepreneur might decide to withdraw, perhaps selling the business to capitalise on the growth so far. Richard Branson did this in 1982 when he sold his original business, Virgin Records, to concentrate on the airline business. It might also be just the right time to get a very good deal, for example because of consolidation in the industry. Alternatively the entrepreneur might not see themselves as being able to change and develop in the way that is needed to lead a growing firm. They might prefer to go into another start-up.

Secondly, there is the option to consolidate, that is keeping products/services and markets the same, but changing the way the firm operates. Often this is not a sensible option in a growing market as it leaves competitors free to take market share, which might then affect the firm's competitive cost base. In a mature market it is common for companies to place increasing emphasis on quality, marketing activity or reducing their cost base so as to create barriers to entry for new competitors. In a declining market, consolidation may involve cost reduction, volume reduction and ultimately selling off part or all of the business.

Finally, there is the option of further market penetration. This involves selling more of the same product/service to the same market

Body Shop's initial roll-out owes much to the clear focus **Anita** and **Gordon Roddick** had on where their competitive advantage lay. They realised that the idea they had could be easily copied and success would only come from developing the brand and a rapid expansion. Unfortunately they had little cash to do either. It was Gordon who had the idea of a franchise, which meant that franchisees paid to become part of Body Shop and managed the shop themselves. The Roddicks decided not to manufacture their products or even invest in a distribution system, but rather to concentrate on getting the franchise formula right, developing the brand and protecting it from imitators. The franchisees generated sufficient cash to finance early expansion until 1984 when the company went to the stock market.

Body Shop could not afford to advertise. Developing the brand was heavily reliant upon the personality of Anita and her ability to get free PR for the environmental causes associated with the firm. Indeed, advertising would have been very much against the firm's image. In those early days her outspoken, controversial views – concerning just about anything – guaranteed her media coverage and helped her win the Businesswoman of the Year award just before the stock market launch.

. . . to be continued

– just selling more to existing customers or finding new customers from the same market segment. The best way of finding new customers is to understand your existing customers and try to find more of the same. This involves understanding why they buy the product or service and being able to describe the customers' common characteristics – effectively describing the market segment(s) buying the product or service. This is what a start-up will have been doing and, with increased marketing activity, in a growth market there may be ample opportunity to achieve further growth in this way. However, the ease which a business can pursue this policy will depend on the nature of the market and the position of competitors. In a static or declining market it is much more difficult to pursue this option, unless competitors are complacent or are leaving the market.

These options can be attractive for a number of reasons. Essentially they involve staying very much the same so there are none of the risks associated with developing new products or markets. This allows the firm to focus on what it is doing and to do it better, rather than always having to run in order to stand still. Customers may appreciate better service and may even be willing to pay for it. Staying the same also allows the firm to develop its reputation. It might allow the firm to do what it is doing more efficiently and therefore cut costs. It is said that it costs five times less to sell to existing customers than it does to new ones. However, there are also dangers with this approach. As we have seen, the strategy is operationally difficult in a static or declining market where there is the additional question of how much life is left in the product/service. Similarly, it may be risky in a growing market when it may be important to grab market share as quickly as possible. There is also the danger of complacency in just doing the same thing and perhaps ignoring changes in the market.

> **Noto Catering** was set up in 1986 to offer Japanese lunches to a largely Japanese customer base. However, with the mushrooming popularity of sushi, its fortunes have been transformed largely because it was a pioneer in the UK market.
>
> The company was founded by Japanese, including, of course, a sushi chef, and takes its name from the Noto region on Japan's West Coast, which is noted for its sushi. The company has a number of sushi bars in London including one in Harrods. It also supplies a number of supermarkets and the Prêt à Manger chain, which now accounts for one-third of its turnover.
>
> It had turnover of £4.5 million in 1998 and employs a workforce of 92, including seven sushi chefs working in its London factory.

Product/service development

We have already seen that product-service innovation is one of the key characteristics of successful growth companies. In Ansoff's framework its first option is to do this for its existing market. It may be that completely new products are introduced into the portfolio because market opportunities are spotted. These might be completely new, innovative products to either replace or sell alongside the existing product range. It might involve product development or extension of existing products where the changes are small and evolutionary, or it might entail developing 'me-too', copied products where another firm has successfully pioneered the product in the market. This may be necessary when a product is in its growth phase – through product extension. It may also be necessary at the mature phase when the product is nearing the end of its

Established in 1900, the family bakery business of **Wilson & Son** has had to adapt to some radical market changes in order to stay in business. A hundred years ago families would buy two or three crusty loaves each day from one of a dozen bakers in close proximity to their shop. **Charles Wilson** introduced doorstep delivery to combat that competition The First World War saw bread rationing, which at least made demand very predictable, and government subsidies to cushion prices. But it was the arrival of low-priced, factory-produced bread that did most to threaten the business.

Today, families often shop only once a week and prefer soft bread. Competition comes from supermarkets who offer loaves for as little as 20 pence. And the economics of breadmaking have changed. Today's loaf costs 94p, equivalent to 10 minutes work in the bakery. In the 1950s the loaf cost 6 pence, equivalent to 15 minutes work, and in the 1920s the loaf cost only 2 pence, but this was equivalent to 30 minutes work.

Today **Andrew Wilson** runs the bakery helped by his sister, brother and wife. They offer a wide variety of bread including sunflower, seeded and wholemeal, all baked in the traditional way, free of chemical additives. However, they rely far more for their profits on cakes, fresh sandwiches, pizzas and other take-away food.

life-cycle – product replacement. It may also be necessary as other firms produce a 'better' product and the firm is forced to react. This can be a particular problem for small firms pioneering a product in a market with low barriers to entry, especially if the product develops into a commodity.

One justification for following this growth path is that the company's existing customers are loyal and demand is growing. However, probably the most important reason for following this path is that the firm has a close relationship with customers – a customer focus – and a good reputation for quality or delivery that can be built upon. If there is a relationship of trust, customers are more likely to try the new product, provided of course they perceive a need for it and that means the company must also be good at communicating with customers in whatever way is most appropriate. In developing new products the customer focused firm will have an advantage because, if it understands how its customers' needs are changing, it ought to be able to develop new products that meet them. The key to this strategy, therefore is building good customer relationships, often associated with effective branding. Virgin is a good example of a brand that has been applied to a wide range of diverse products, mainly successfully, linking customers and their lifestyle aspirations.

One advantage of this approach is that is often far more cost-effective to increase the volume of business with existing customers than it is to go out looking for new ones. What is more, good relationships often result in customers bringing in new customers through word of mouth or referral. However, developing new products, even for existing customers, can be expensive and risky. Development must be grounded firmly in the needs of the existing market. And even then, if done too rapidly, it can mean resources are spread too thinly across an unbalanced portfolio.

Virgin is one of the best-known brands in Britain with 96 per cent recognition and is well-known worldwide. It is strongly associated with its founder, **Sir Richard Branson** – 95 per cent can name him as the founder. The company has pioneered the concept of a branded venture capitalist, mirroring a Japanese management structure called 'keiretsu', where different businesses act as a family under one brand. The Virgin Group is made up of more than 20 separate umbrella companies, operating some 200 companies worldwide with a global turnover of over £3 billion in 1999.

Virgin now uses its brand as a capital asset in joint ventures. Virgin contributes the brand and Richard Branson's PR profile, whilst the partner provides the capital input – in some ways like a franchise operation.

The brand has been largely built through the personal PR efforts of its founder. However, between January 1997 and November 1999 the Group spent £137 million on advertising. According to Richard Branson,

Brands must be built around reputation, quality and price . . . People should not be asking 'is this one product too far?' but rather, 'what are the qualities of my company's name? How can I develop them?'

According to Will Whitehorn, director of corporate affairs at Virgin Management:

At Virgin, we know what the brand name means, and when we put our brand name on something, we're making a promise. It's a promise we've always kept and always will. It's harder work keeping promises than making them, but there is no secret formula. Virgin sticks to its principles and keeps its promises.

Market development

It is one thing to find new customers in a market that you are familiar with, but it is quite another to enter new markets, even when you are selling existing products or services that you are familiar with. Nevertheless, if a firm wants to grow it will have to seek out new markets at some stage. These might be new market segments or new geographical areas. In seeking new overseas markets the lowest risk option is to seek out segments similar to the ones the firm already sells to. Of course, market development and product development might go hand-in-hand, since the move into a new market segment may involve the development of variants to the existing product offering by altering the marketing mix or even changes to the product range. However, we are talking about incremental changes rather than brand-new products.

One reason for finding new markets is if there are economies of scale of production to be had – particularly important if the product is perceived as a commodity and cost leadership is dependent upon achieving economies of scale. It might also be that a company's core competence lies with the product rather than the market, for example with capital goods like cars, and therefore the continued exploitation of the product by market development is the preferred route for expansion. Most capital goods companies follow this strategy, opening

Tim Slade and **Julian Lever** originally set up the clothes retailer **Fat Face** in 1993 in order to finance their lives as 'ski bums'. Seven years later it had developed into a cult brand for sports enthusiasts and enjoys a profitable niche with sales of £8.5 million from 28 stores across Britain and three in the French Alps. Julian Leaver explains:

> When you buy a Fat Face product, you are not just buying the fleece, you are buying the experience – the chat in the shop about the snow in Val d'Isère – or surfing in Cowes. Staff are selected because they are passionate about the lifestyle.

In 2000 it raised £5 million expansion capital from Friends Ivory & Sime Private Equity. The challenge the company faces is to expand globally but to manage the brand as it does so. Julian Leaver explains:

> We could easily wholesale the hell out of it and be in every ski and surf shop and department store inside a year. Within two years, we would have trashed the brand.

Slow, planned expansion will come through increasing the number of shops in Britain and Europe and eventually the rest of the world, making certain that the right sort of staff, with the right sort of personality, are recruited. In the past Fat Face has entered new markets based upon intuition and on a experimental basis. In the future they intend to undertake more professional market research. So, for example, in Scandinavia where computer penetration is high it is researching an internet-based market-entry strategy. Like Virgin, Julian Leaver believes the Fat Face brand is transferable to drinks, surfboards or even four-wheel drive vehicles and therefore expansion is ultimately about brand management.

Sunday Times 27.02.00

up new overseas markets as existing markets become saturated because of the high cost of developing new products. By way of contrast, many service businesses such as accounting, insurance, advertising and banking have been pulled into overseas markets because their clients operate there. Finally, another reason to find new markets for a product or service might be simply that it is nearing the end of its life-cycle in the existing market. This was the case with McDonalds and its entry into the East European markets.

Two important factors in deciding which markets to attach are entry and exit barriers. These are shown in Figure 11.2. The most attractive market from the point of view of profitability is likely to be one with high entry barriers and low exit barriers – few firms can enter but poor performers can easily exit. With high entry barriers but high exit barriers, poor performers are forced to stay on making the returns more risky as they fight for market share. Unfortunately, a firm seeking to enter these markets has to overcome the high entry barriers, whatever they be. For example, this could involve overcoming legal barriers or high investment costs. If entry barriers are low returns are likely to be low, but stable if exit barriers are low and unstable if exit barriers are high and poor performers are forced to stay on if the market worsens.

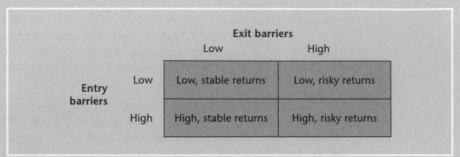

Figure 11.2 Barriers, profitability and risk

Body Shop's rapid growth owes much to its successful global roll-out. Overseas expansion followed the same model as in the UK. In most countries a head franchisee was granted exclusive rights as user of the trade mark, distributor and, after an initial trial of running a few shops themselves, the right to sub-franchise. In this way the firm built upon local market knowledge and minimised its risks. This model was not always followed because of the quality of the head franchisee. For example, the firm took back control of the franchise in France because the head franchisee was not delivering the volume of sales expected.

. . . *to be continued*

The Eggparka is an inflatable jacket that help reduce injury to motorcyclists when they are involved in an accident. The jacket inflates automatically in under a second to support the rider's back and neck if they fall off the bike, deflating after 30 seconds.

The Eggparka is made by a small Japanese company called **Mugen Denko** but in 1999 it was sold only in Japan. In order to sell into Europe the company needed a distributor who knew the local markets. Selling such a new idea, particularly to a market that is so resistant to innovation, was never going to be easy; nor was finding a distributor when the company had no local contacts. But they hit on a bright idea. They decided to use the product's novelty and uniqueness to gain free PR. In July 1999 they 'placed' an article about the jacket on the Innovations page of *Sunday Times*. The result was customer interest and numerous inquiries about distribution. However, despite this, you'll be lucky to see an Eggparka on British roads.

> **P&M Products Ltd** holds the worldwide licences to Blitzer and Blowpen, children's pens that create airbrush effects. It was set up in 1992 by **Doug Eaton** and now has sales of over £10 million, 80 per cent coming from exports to over 45 countries. This sales growth was derived from a simple strategy of selling the product into these countries through distributors, thus reducing the financial risk of expansion abroad. P&M simply exhibited and signed up distributors at overseas Toy Fairs.
>
> In 1999, its own growth and the emergence of global retailers influenced by mergers and the demand for consolidation of suppliers forced it to rethink its strategy. In particular, a benchmarking exercise underlined the differing performance of distributors. Whilst a highly committed Finnish distributor achieved a 60 per cent penetration amongst its target market of 5 to 13-year-olds, its US distributor achieved only 3 per cent and its average was 20 per cent. Upon investigation it emerged that the US distributor had many other products in his portfolio and viewed P&M's products as marginal. After a six-month search P&M could not find a distributor that might be more committed to their products and decided to change strategy and set up its own subsidiary in this vital market. It adopted a strategy of direct response television promotions and spent some £650 000 on 'infomercials', which appeared at prime time on kids' channels giving an 0800 telephone number and web-site address. The campaign was successful and big retailers like Toys 'R' Us and Wal-Mart started to take interest. US sales rose from $1 to $5.5 million in 1999.
>
> *. . . to be continued*

Exporting is one example of market development. In fact, few small firms export. Exporting presents the small firm with the risk of currency fluctuations, lengthy payment terms, the possibility of bad debts as well as the problems of finding out how to market their product effectively in the country they are exporting to. Perhaps it is little wonder that one survey suggests that only some 6 per cent of UK small firms, across all sectors of the economy, do so (Carson, 1990). There are a number of schemes providing help and assistance for those firms wanting to follow this route. For example, the Department of Trade and Industry (DTI) provides information on trading with most countries through their various country desks; the British Chambers of Commerce issue export documentation and often, together with the local Business Link, provide advice; the Central Office of Information offers export publicity information and the Export Credits Guarantee Department of the DTI can arrange insurance against the possibility of non-payment. This can be assigned to a bank or other lending institution in order to obtain export finance.

For many small firms, exporting often means finding a distributor in the country they wish to export to that understands the local distribution channels and variations in customer needs. In such situations the firm is very dependent upon the distributor. The distributor might influence changes in the product or other elements of the marketing mix to suit local needs. They might be expected to finance advertising and promotion themselves, and with no certainty of a profitable return. Finding a distributor can be difficult enough, but if, for whatever reason, the distributor does not push the firm's products, then there is little the firm can do other than change distributors, unless they are willing to take on the job of marketing in the country themselves – and that can be both expensive and risky. To be effective the firm and their distributor must have a symbiotic relationship, one based upon mutual trust and with effective incentives to ensure success.

Diversification

The final growth option is to sell new products into new markets – called diversification. The rationale for this is normally one of 'balancing' the risk in a firm's business portfolio by going into new products and new markets. However, since this strategy involves unfamiliar products and unfamiliar markets, it is actually a high-risk strategy, with too many unknowns in the equation. Nevertheless, it is worth distinguishing between two types of diversification, each with different degrees of risk.

1 **Related diversification** where development is beyond the present product and market, but within the confines of the 'industry' or 'sector' that the firm operates in. There are three variants of this:

- *Backward vertical integration*, where the firm becomes its own supplier of some basic raw materials or services or provides transport or financing. When Anita Roddick first set up Body Shop is was purely as a retail business. After a few years the firm started manufacturing its own products, and recently it has started to move away from this and concentrate on its core retailing activity.
- *Forward vertical integration*, where the firm becomes its own distributor or retailer, or perhaps services its own products in some way. In this way Doc Martens have opened a number of prominently sited retail outlets selling Doc Martens branded products.
- *Horizontal integration*, where there is development into activities which are either directly complimentary or competitive with the firm's current activities, for example, where a video rental shop starts to rent out video games. In this way Ford now earn more from financial services related to car purchase than from the manufacture of the vehicles themselves.

All strategies entailing new product or service technologies and new customers or markets are relatively risky but not as risky as the second form of diversification.

In the 1980s **Body Shop** started its own warehousing and distribution network, based upon a sophisticated stock control system, and built up a substantial fleet of lorries. Products could typically be delivered within 24 hours. It also started manufacturing many of its cosmetics mainly in the UK, although many of the ingredients came from overseas under its 'trade-not-aid' policy. These two elements of strategy initially worked well for it and generated substantial sales and profit growth but the manufacturing policy was reviewed in the late 1990s.

. . . to be continued

David Poole believes his direct-marketing agency **DP&A** must grow just to survive and resist acquisition. Fuelled by the internet and other digital media the industry is seeing rapid growth and is becoming dominated by acquisitive advertising companies. Organic growth might be too slow, but David Poole is loath to obtain outside finance which might dilute his ownership and end up with him losing control.

In 1999 direct marketing accounted for 57 per cent, press 19 per cent, television 14 per cent, radio 6 per cent and magazine inserts 3 per cent of DP&A's turnover. David laid out his growth ideas in a newspaper article:

> We could diversify horizontally into fields such as advertising and design. With a strong, effective management team and particularly effective financial management, we would be well placed to cross-sell and generate additional business from existing customers. Alternatively, we could diversify vertically into other areas such as data mining or maybe look further ahead and invest in new areas.

> Digital media such as mobile phones, interactive TV and the web need to be stitched into everything we do. These new channels will generate a lot of new business and expand the direct marketing business, so maybe this is where our attention should be focused.

Sunday Times 20.02.00

2 **Unrelated diversification** where the firm develops beyond its present industry or sector into products and markets that, on the face of it, bear little relationship to the one they are in.

'Synergy' is often used as a justification for both related and unrelated diversification, particularly when it involves acquisition or merger. Synergy is concerned with assessing how much extra benefit can be obtained from

Wing Yip came to Britain from Hong Kong in 1958 with only £10 in his pocket and got a job as a waiter in a Chinese restaurant. Within a few years he had his own small chain of Chinese restaurants but he had trouble getting the food supplies he needed. Nobody stocked everything he needed and he had to spend valuable time travelling to a number of different suppliers. This led him to realise that other Chinese restaurants were facing the same problem. And so, in 1970, he decided to set up a cash-and-carry business for Chinese restaurants with his brother Sammy, based in Birmingham.

By 1998 **W. Wing Yip & Brothers** supplied more than 2000 outlets and made profits of £2.9 million on sales of £65 million. Based in Nechells, Birmingham, their main site now houses the head office, a Chinese medical practice, a travel agency, a law firm serving the Chinese community and a 250-seater restaurant called Wing Wah. The company acts as agents for Hong Kong suppliers and sells to other cash-and-carries such as Booker. They also make their own range of Chinese sauces which they sell to most of the big supermarket chains.

providing linkages between activities or processes which have been previously unconnected, or where the connection has been of a different type, so that the combined effect is greater than the sum of the parts. It is often described as 'one plus one equals three'. Synergy in related diversification is mainly based upon core product or market characteristics. The claimed synergy in unrelated diversification is normally based on financing – the positive cash flows in one business being used for the funding requirements of another. Another often claimed synergy is based on the managerial skills of the head office.

Whilst Johnson and Scholes (1993) claim that attempts to demonstrate the effects of diversification on performance are inconclusive, they also admit that successful diversification is difficult to achieve in practice. However, many researchers have found that more focused firms perform better than diversified ones (Wernerfelt and Montgomery, 1986). This is reflected in their low share price. Diversified conglomerate manufacturing companies are valued at some 20 per cent less on average, than the sum of their parts (*Economist*, 7 July, 2001). What is more, it has been demonstrated that smaller firms that diversify by building on their core business – related diversification – do better than those who diversify in an unrelated way (Ansoff, 1968). This was established for a broader range of firms in the 1970s (Rumelt, 1974) and used as part of Porter's (1987) argument for firms that build on their core business doing better than those who diversify in an unrelated way. The conclusion must be that diversification generally is risky and therefore requires careful justification. Nevertheless one of the companies that has adopted a strategy of diversification most successfully is Lonrho, and its strategy has been one of unrelated diversification. Its interests range from hotels in Mexico to freight forwarders in Canada, from motor distribution in Africa to oil and gas production in the USA.

In 1934 Reg Bott, a German chemist, fled the Nazis and set up **Standard Photographic** in Leamington Spa. It is a family firm now run by **Gordon Bott**. By 1999 it had sales of £23.5 million and employed 185 staff.

Standard stopped making photographic film in 1967 and instead now buys film from the big producers and repackages it as 'own-brand' film for firms such as Boots, Dixons, Tesco and Truprint. It also converts photographic paper by cutting it to the size used by mini-laboratories, publishing houses and X-ray laboratories. It has also diversified into film processing, handling mail-order processing for Fuji slides. Because these elements of the business require good logistics – a 36-hour nationwide delivery of replacement film stock is guaranteed – the firm also diversified into delivering similarly high value products such as floppy disks and printing and publishing products. Based on this success, the firm now wants to diversify into order delivery for dotcom businesses – a growing market, but one in which it has no expertise or track record. Standard will be competing against firms like Exel, Business Express, Securicor Omega and many others and will be delivering not just to business but also home addresses. The question is whether this is one diversification too far.

Risk

Ansoff's analysis gives us a valuable insight into the risks associated with growth. The lowest risk strategy of all is market penetration. For companies whose core competence lies in production, market development is the second lowest risk strategy. For those whose competence lies in their closeness to the customer, particularly if they are not involved in manufacturing the product themselves, the second lowest risk strategy is product development. The highest risk strategy of all is diversification, with unrelated diversification being extremely high risk.

Figure 11.3 takes this a little further by distinguishing between the different types and degrees of market and product development. Risk gets progressively higher as the firm moves to the bottom right-hand corner in terms of its strategy. Of course, this is not to say that a company should not take risks, but rather that growth involves risks and it is as well to understand the degrees of risk associated with different strategies. Research indicates that successful small firms follow a strategy of incremental, mainly internal, growth (Burns, 1994). They move carefully into new markets with existing products or sell new products to existing customers. The strategy of diversification is high-risk and only to be adopted after careful consideration. Smaller firms must consider carefully whether this is really appropriate to their needs. If it is to be followed, the safest routes are through joint ventures or strategic alliances, particularly in overseas markets, where the risks can be compartmentalised and failure will not therefore endanger the whole business.

One further important point; for a small firm with limited resources, pursuing all four strategies within any one time frame is likely to be extremely risky. Assuming market penetration will always continue, it is best advised to follow only one other strategy at a time, perhaps alternating the strategy over time.

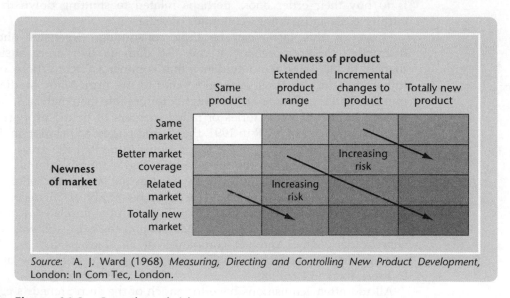

Source: A. J. Ward (1968) *Measuring, Directing and Controlling New Product Development*, London: In Com Tec, London.

Figure 11.3 Growth and risk

Making the right choice is an important decision, but one that has to be made by a conscious choice rather than by drift or force of circumstance.

One very practical application of these techniques is to help evaluate sales projections or targets. The projections can be broken down into the constituent elements of the product/market matrix (Figure 11.1) or the growth and risk matrix (Figure 11.3). Probabilities of achieving these projections or targets can then be attributed to each constituent element of the matrix. Any projection based largely on market penetration, *a priori* unless the market is saturated, has a high probability of being achieved. Any projection heavily dependant on diversification is, *a priori*, not only highly risky, but also has a low probability of being achieved.

Sales people can also use these matrices to have sales targets set with commission rates in the various elements of the matrix reflecting the different levels of risk, for example, basic commission for sales of existing products to existing customers, higher rates for further market penetration and higher rates still for sales of new products. As the probability of achieving sales targets decreases, sales commissions can be increased.

Mergers and acquisitions

Mergers and acquisitions are frequently used by entrepreneurs as a tool for achieving rapid growth and also as a short-cut to diversification. The compelling reason for this tactic is the speed at which it allows the entrepreneur to enter a new product/market area. Another reason might be that the firm lacks a resource, such as R&D or a customer base, to develop a strategy unaided. Often, particularly when a market is static, it is seen as the easiest way to enter a new market, for example overseas. Sometimes the reason for buying out a competitor is to buy their order book, perhaps related to shutting down their capacity, cutting costs and gaining economies of scale.

However, this tactic can be time consuming, expensive and risky. By distracting the entrepreneur, it can also damage short term business performance. In fact there is no evidence that commercial acquisitions or take-overs (other than in a distress sale) add value to the firm. Many studies show that mergers and acquisitions suffer a higher failure rate than marriages, and business history is littered with stories of failed mergers of titanic proportions such as AT&T's purchase of NCR in 1991, the second largest acquisition in the history of the computer industry. The evidence seems to be that the great conglomerate-merger wave of the 1960s did not generally lead to improvements in performance for those firms involved, and was reversed by the large-scale selling of unrelated businesses in the 1980s. Porter (1987), in his study of 33 major corporations between 1950 and 1986 concludes that 75 per cent of unrelated acquisitions were subsequently sold-off rather than retained, and the net result was dissipation of shareholder value. And yet companies of all sizes persist in following this strategy. In 1999 the global value of mergers and acquisitions rose by over a third to more than $3.4 trillion.

All too often acquisitions have too much of the entrepreneur's ego tied up in the deal and that can lead to a loss of business logic. It is important that there is a clear logic to the acquisition, related to the product/market matrix; for example:

- As a defensive acquisition to maintain market position, perhaps to gain economies of scale, or as a result of aggressive competitive reaction from rivals;
- As part of a strategy to develop new products when the firm does not have the capability to do so, for example because of R&D or technology;
- As part of a strategy to develop new markets, for example overseas;
- As part of a strategy of diversification, although this must be seen as the highest of high risk growth strategies.

In searching for companies to acquire, it is first necessary to decide on the industry. Related diversification will normally be into the same industry. If it is unrelated diversification, then the industry should be one where the acquiring company has the core competencies required for success in the sector and, where there is a deficiency, they should be addressed by being present in the target company. The attractiveness of the industry will depend to some extent on the strategic direction of the company, informed by an analysis of the industry (perhaps using Porter's Five Forces and a SLEPT analysis). The acquisitions that are most likely to succeed are those where an attractive market presents itself to a company with a good 'mesh' between the acquiring company's core competencies and the sector's required key competencies.

The Northamptonshire based **R. Griggs Group** produces the world-famous Dr Martens boots. The family-owned shoemaker was set up in 1901, but its real growth came in the 1960s. At each phase of the company's expansion the firm bought other local shoemakers until it now comprises over twenty firms in the group. Each has a distinct product role: producing laces, soles or limited edition footwear. For this company, knowledge of local opportunities to buy existing shoemakers was an essential ingredient in its growth and success.

The experience **P&M Products Ltd** had in the USA forced it to realise that, as large retailers rationalised their suppliers, they would continue to be squeezed as they did not offer a range of products that was large enough to be attractive. Consequently P&M decided to reposition itself as a pan-European supplier that could also sell products from other, smaller producers. Part of this strategy involved acquiring other, smaller firms so as to increase its product range. It now intends to get to a position where 25 per cent of sales are generated from new lines.

Of course, some acquisitions are simply opportunistic. For example, when a rival firm or a firm in a related area goes into receivership, the temptation to buy it out cheaply and quickly from the receiver might be irresistible and might also make sound commercial sense. Most acquisitions take three to nine months to complete but a sale from a receiver can be completed in as little as three weeks. Whether buying a trading company or one in receivership, it is always important to take professional advice although fees can amount to 5–7 per cent of the value of the business. Accountants undertake what is called 'due diligence' work, which ensures that the assets on the balance sheet are as stated, there are no undisclosed liabilities and that profit projections are put together in a logical and consistent way, based upon reasonable and explicit assumptions. Accountants can also undertake searches for acquisition prospects and most of the major firms keep informal 'books' of companies that they believe might be available for purchase.

The major reason mergers and acquisitions fail is because of failure of implementation. Claimed synergies may not be achieved, perhaps rationalisation is insufficiently ruthless, possibly because clear management lines and responsibilities are not being laid down. However, one of the major reason for this failing boils down to the clash of organisational cultures that does not get resolved. This can arise because of many factors, but it results in the merged organisations being unable to work together effectively. That

> **NCR** had always been a conservative, tightly controlled, top-down company. **AT&T** was politically correct and decentralised. After the take-over by AT&T in 1991, NCR's hierarchy was 'flattened' and the firm 'downsized'. Employees became 'associates', managers became 'coaches', executives' office doors were removed, home phone numbers were given out and international employees came under AT&T regional directors giving them, effectively, two bosses. The company was renamed AT&T Global Information Solutions.
>
> By 1995 only five of the 33 top NCR managers in place at the time of the take-over were still there, and the company had moved from being a profitable company to one making losses of $720 million, excluding a $1.6 billion write-off for restructuring. In 1997 it was made independent again, having lost some 50 per cent of its value in six years.

was the major reason for the seemingly logical, but ultimately disastrous, take-over of NCR by AT&T in 1991, which nearly brought down both companies. For whatever reason, one common outcome of mergers or acquisitions is that many managers in the acquired company will leave within a short space of time. They may, of course, be 'pushed' rather than leave by their own volition, but nevertheless this means that the time scale for proactive management of change can be very short.

Company valuation in mergers and take-overs is crucial but problematic for smaller firms, especially if they operate in new areas of business such as e-commerce. A company with a high value placed on its current level of earnings can use this to its advantage in buying out a company with a low valuation, particularly if the deal is based upon shares rather than cash. This is dealt with in a subsequent chapter.

Strategy development

The last two chapters have talked very much as if strategy can be developed in a systematic, logical way. This process is shown in Figure 11.4. To a large extent strategy can be developed in this way. However, many entrepreneurs develop

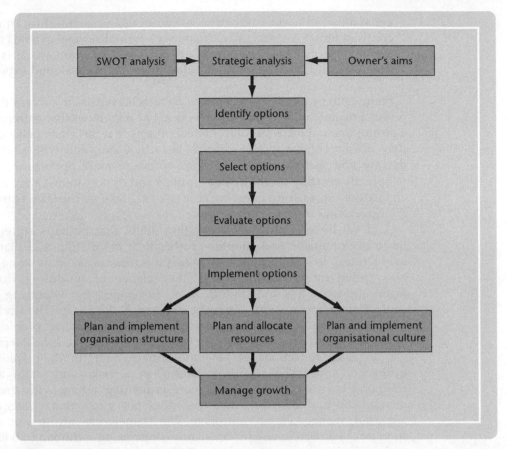

Figure 11.4 Strategy development – the systematic approach

strategy instinctively – often they call it 'gut feel'. They do not know the jargon, do not use the frameworks we have developed – and justified with empirical evidence – but instinctively they arrive at the right decision. There is nothing wrong with this. These words and frameworks give meaning and logic to what they do. Many excellent musicians or athletes were not taught what they do. They picked up the skills instinctively. Explaining why they do what they do can give confidence to replicate their successes and even improve.

Strategic frameworks replicate what is good practice. They ought to be logical, common sense. They are not in the nature of a scientific discovery. They are, to quote a colleague, 'a glimpse of the blindingly obvious', something you knew all along but were never quite able to express it in that simple way. As John Kay (1998) explained:

An organisational framework can never be right, or wrong, only helpful or unhelpful. A good organisational framework is minimalist – it is as simple as is consistent with illuminating the issues under discussion – and is memorable . . . The organisational framework provides the link from judgement through experience to learning. A valid framework is one which focuses sharply on what the skilled manager, at least instinctively, already knows. He is constantly alive to strengths, weaknesses, opportunities, threats which confront him . . . A successful framework formalises and extends their existing knowledge. For the less practised, an effective framework is one which organises and develops what would otherwise be disjointed experience.

Some entrepreneurs may claim to have achieved their success through luck. Never underestimate luck, we all need it, but remember that entrepreneurs have a strong internal locus of control which means that they may believe in luck, but they do not believe in fate. They believe they can, and will, shape their own destiny and that may mean working to create more opportunities than most people. By creating more strategic options and opportunities, they improve their chances of successfully pursuing at least one. Make no mistake, entrepreneurs to a large extent create their own luck.

And yet there is always the nagging doubt that perhaps entrepreneurs are more opportunistic and adaptive, rather than calculating and planning in the way strategy is laid out in books. In fact this view is as old as strategy itself and was called by Lindbolm (1959) 'the science of muddling through'. The implications of this for strategy were developed by Mintzberg (1978) who contrasted deliberate with emergent strategy. As he put it: 'The strategy-making process is characterised by reactive solution to existing problems . . . The adaptive organisation makes its decisions in incremental, serial steps.' And here we do catch reflections of how the entrepreneur, in their spider's web of influence, approaches decision-making in a risky, uncertain and rapidly changing environment. But then there is nothing wrong with strategy that is incremental and adaptive, and that does not mean that strategy cannot be analysed, managed and controlled. The frameworks are just as useful. And successful entrepreneurs are constantly strategising – thinking about the future and analysing their options. Indeed, Sir George Mathewson, Executive Deputy Chairman of the very entrepreneurial Royal Bank of Scotland Group (which includes NatWest, Direct Line and even Coutts Bank) has gone so far as to propose that formalised strategic planning is inappropriate in today's changing environment. What is needed instead is more strategising and the development of strategic options – options that lead the firm in the general direction it wants to go – with decisions on which option to select depend upon market conditions and opportunities (Mathewson, 2000). The greater the number of strategic options open to the firm, the safer it is in an uncertain environment.

So, for some firms, strategy development may be systematic and deliberate but for many entrepreneurial firms it is likely to be emergent. It is likely to be incremental and adaptive. 'Strategic intent' is still needed to give the firm clear direction, only the path to achieve these goals is not always clear. In these circumstances the process of strategising or strategy development is vital. The development of multiple strategic options is the key to success, with decision-making based upon opportunistic circumstances at the time. Thus the entrepreneur needs to know the goal they are ultimately seeking and needs to have the frameworks to make those incremental, adaptive decisions. There is nothing wrong with having a map with a planned route, but it makes sense to find a way around any road blocks you encounter rather than going headlong into them.

These road blocks are the crises that the firm will inevitably encounter as it passes through the predictable cycle of growth–crisis–consolidation. Just as many of these crises originate from predictable causes and lead to changes in the entrepreneur's style of management, one research study indicates that they might lead, not only to changes in strategy, but also to changes in the strategy development process, causing shifts from the emergent to the deliberate style, at least for a period (McCarthy and Leavy, 2000). The study suggests that the strategy development process in small firms is *both* deliberate and emergent in nature and the degree of deliberateness in the foundation phase is influenced most by the personality of the entrepreneur and the nature of the business context. Over time, strategy-formation follows a phase pattern, moving from an early fluid phase to a more defined phase, usually triggered by a crisis or defining episode, so that the degree of deliberateness is also a function of history, with firms oscillating between emergent strategy development, when learning is taking place, and deliberate planning modes over time. Rather than small firms having only one style, they would seem to adopt both, depending on circumstances.

Planning and control

Rapid growth can be every bit as dangerous as start-up. It can lead to the danger of over-trading – the Death Valley curve getting longer and deeper. Proper planning and management of cash flow is therefore vital. If cash is needed to finance growth, bankers like to be forewarned so that facilities can be made available in advance. It also makes sense to negotiate from a position of strength rather than weakness. Planning and good management might also allow a firm to minimise its cash flow requirements. Just as the preparation of financial plans was important at start-up, they are important for a growing firm.

Plans and budgets are an invaluable tool to control and monitor performance of the business. By comparing actual financial results to budget on a timely basis, the entrepreneur can 'manage by exception', only intervening when performance deviates from plan. This can free up time to concentrate on strategy or dealing with real problems. The budget provides a framework against which the performance of the firm can be judged. For a larger firm, the detail involved in pulling together a complicated budget can be time consuming, but by this stage it is certain that the firm will have its own accountant who can undertake the task. Nevertheless the appendix to this chapter contains a detailed example of how to go about drawing up a budget for a medium-sized firm – cash flow forecast, profit statement and balance sheet.

As the firm grows, budgets can be prepared at the department and division level, rather than just at the company level. This has the advantage of encouraging the entrepreneur to delegate responsibility for planning and decision-making to other managers, whilst at the same time providing them with sufficient information to satisfy themselves that everything is running as planned. The budgeting process can then be used as a tool for communicating and coordinating the activities of responsible managers It can become a systematic tool for establishing standards of performance, providing motivation and assessing the results managers achieve. An essential element in this process of making managers accountable is that each knows exactly what they are held responsible for, and each does indeed control this aspect of the firm's operations. Responsibility cannot be assigned without authority. A fundamental necessity is to have a clear management structure. The principle is to make every manager responsible for the costs and revenues they control, even if they, in turn, delegate responsibility down the line.

Of course, if managers are going to be held responsible for the costs and revenues they control, they are going to want to be involved in the budgeting process. The advantage of this is that often they may know more about certain aspects of the business than the owner. Also, if budgets are to motivate staff, they have to 'buy-into' them and believe that they are realistic and achievable. Once they accept the standards of performance against which they are to be judged, they will normally try hard to achieve them. Imposing budgets from above normally causes resentment and leads to a lack of commitment.

The basics of sound financial control remain the same as outlined in Chapter 6. Financial drivers are just as useful for a medium-sized firm as for a start-up. Perhaps the difference is one of scale. But also, most medium-sized firms now operate computerised accounting and budgeting systems. The most popular is produced by Sage. These speed the processing of transactions and the production of financial information. They also help with the management of trade credit. Almost all business transaction are on credit terms and it has been estimated that trade debtors represent 28 per cent of total assets in small firms whilst trade creditors are equivalent to 11 per cent, and yet managing trade debtors seems to be the Achilles heel of most small firms – they are just bad at it (Chittenden, Poutziouris and Michaelas, 1998).

Before embarking on a growth path a company needs to have in place robust financial planning and control mechanisms. It needs to have a strategy and to plan how it will grow, not just in terms of the Product/Market matrix, but also by producing detailed budgets that reflect the consequences of the growth and indicate any financing needs. In other words, it probably needs to prepare another business plan.

Summary

To achieve growth, a company should build on its strengths and core competencies, shore up its weaknesses and develop a marketing strategy for each product-market offering that reflects:

● the appropriate generic marketing strategy;
● the stage the product-market offering is at in its life-cycle;
● all placed in the context of its portfolio of product-market offerings.

It has four options:

1   Stay with existing products/services and existing markets and customers;
2   Product development;
3   Market development;
4   Diversification.

Any start-up must focus initially on market penetration (option 1). **Body Shop** understood this and focused all its efforts on a rapid roll-out coupled with brand development. If a company wants growth, staying with the existing products/services and existing customers usually means further market penetration – selling more to existing customers and finding new customers in the marketplace – like **Noto Catering**. The best way of finding new customers is to understand your existing ones and then try to find more of the same. This can be difficult in a static or declining market but also, if the market is growing, you run the risk of being left behind.

Product/service development involves developing new products or services and selling to your existing market, like **Wilson & Son** have done. This is often a successful strategy for firms that have a strong relationship with their customers – a customer focus – and a strong reputation. The firm can develop products that customers want and their loyalty means they will try them. Getting existing customers to buy more is also often very cost effective. Often associated with this strategy is a strong brand identity. **Virgin** is probably the best-known brand in Britain today, but the company has evolved into a branded venture capitalist, using its brand as a capital asset in joint ventures.

Market development is about finding new markets for existing products or services, thus benefiting from economies of scale or capitalising on the firm's product knowledge competence. In deciding on which markets to enter, consideration should be given to entry and exit barriers. The classic example of market development is into overseas markets, either opening overseas ventures like **Fat Face** are doing or by exporting. **Body Shop** used its franchise model to help it become a global retail chain whilst minimising its risk exposure. Exporting is risky and most small firms do not try it. Most exporters go through an agent but, as **Mugen Denko** discovered, finding one can be difficult. Then, as **P&M Products** discovered, not all agents perform equally well. To succeed there needs to be a symbiotic relationship, based on trust and effective incentives.

Diversification is the riskiest of the four options. Related diversification is about staying within the confines of the industry through either backward vertical integration – becoming your own supplier (like **Body Shop**); forward vertical integration – becoming a distributor or retailer (again, like **Body Shop**); or horizontal integration – moving into related activities, of the sort being considered by **DP&A**. Unrelated diversification is the riskiest strategy of all and involves developing beyond the firm's present industry, normally because of the claimed benefits of synergy. **W. Wing Yip & Brothers** may be seen as doing this, but in fact their growth into new markets and new products is more incremental; for example, the sauces they now sell to supermarkets were developed originally for the cash-and-carry business. However, this incremental approach to diversification can go too far and this might be the case for **Standard Photographic** as they go into an unfamiliar market. As well as being a risky strategy, researchers have found that focused firms perform better than diversified ones.

The Product/Market matrix is a useful tool to help evaluate the risks associated with a growth strategy and the probabilities attached to the related sales estimates. For a small firm with limited resources pursuing all four strategies within any one time frame is likely to be extremely risky. Assuming market penetration will continue, they should select only one other strategy within any time frame, otherwise they risk spreading themselves too thinly.

Mergers and acquisitions are frequently used as a means of achieving rapid expansion. However, the tactic can be time consuming, expensive and risky. The frequent failure of mergers, like that of **NCR** and **AT&T** arise because of failure of implementation, with claimed synergies not being realised. However, **R. Griggs Group** has bought out local Northamptonshire shoemakers and now has over 20 firms in the group, each with their own distinct product role. **P&M Products** were forced to buy other toy-makers to develop its range to a size that allowed it to stay in business.

Strategy development in most growing small firms is likely to be incremental and adaptive – emergent rather than deliberate – with strategic intent giving direction. The process of strategising and the generation of strategic options are therefore important. However, small firms do adopt both types of strategy development, depending upon circumstances, with shifts from one mode to another precipitated by some form of crisis.

Effective planning and control is essential for the risky take-off stage of growth. Growth eats into cash and the financing needs of the firm during its growth need to be anticipated and arranged. Comprehensive budgets need to be prepared – cash flow, income and balance sheet. These help in the management of the firm and can be a useful tool to encourage the entrepreneur to delegate control to the managers they have recruited. Increasingly from here the firm will start to look more professional with formal organisation and control systems. It is about to stop being a 'small firm' – by any definition.

◼ Essays and discussion topics

1 Penetrating the market is just about selling more. Discuss.
2 Penetrating the market is a low-risk option and therefore always the most attractive option. Discuss.
3 In what circumstances might product development be a lower-risk strategy than market development, and vice versa?
4 How might a small firm go about exporting so as to minimise the risks that it faces?
5 Exporting is expensive and risky. It is therefore not an attractive growth option. Discuss.
6 How do you go about minimising your exposure to currency fluctuations?
7 What business is Virgin in?
8 Diversification is the 'Wally Box' of the product/market matrix. Discuss.
9 Under what circumstances might diversification be an attractive option?
10 Do you think the latest diversification for Standard Photographic will work?
11 Diversified companies underperform 'focused' companies. Discuss.
12 Why might a small firm be looking for another to acquire?
13 Under what circumstances might an acquisition or merger be attractive?
14 What is synergy and how might it be achieved?
15 Why do so many mergers or acquisitions fail? Give examples.
16 What advice would you give to a company taking over another?
17 In an uncertain world, planning is a waste of time and developing strategy a meaningless activity. Discuss.
18 How do entrepreneurs develop strategy? Explain and give examples.
19 Are entrepreneurs lucky?
20 Why is budgeting so important at the take-off stage?
21 Budgeting helps entrepreneurs to delegate effectively. Discuss.

Exercises and assignments

1 For your own Department in your University or College, use the Product/Market matrix to list the growth options that it faces for the courses on offer.
2 Select a country and find out what help there is available in order to export to it.
3 Research the history of a merger or acquisition such as AT&T and NCR or Daimler Benz and Chrysler and analyse the reasons for its success or failure.
4 Interview an entrepreneur and find out how they develop strategy.
5 Work through the budget setting process for the PC Modem company in the Appendix to this chapter. Make certain you understand the calculations and processes.
6 Using Small Business Audit Checklist 5 in the Growth Audit at the back of the book analyse the projected performance of the PC Modem company in the Appendix. How much finance will it need. Do you think it will obtain it?

Growth audit exercise

Undertake steps 7 to 10 of the growth audit exercise at the back of the book.

Appendix: Forecasts and budgets – a comprehensive example

Preparing forecasts or budgets can be complicated, particularly for a manufacturing company. This is a comprehensive example for just such a company. This company is already in business, producing two specialist PC modems (A and B). The year-end (31 December 2004) balance-sheet for the company is shown as Table A1 (see p. 322) We shall prepare the budget for 2005 only. The budgeting process would be easier for a start-up company, since there would be no balance-sheet at the beginning of the period, and easier for a service business, since there would not be a manufacturing process to complicate the costing.

The company has been fairly successful so far and the owner is looking for a return (profit before interest and tax) on his net assets of 15 per cent per annum. So far it has funded its fairly rapid expansion by a long-term loan of £100 000, which is not due for repayment until 2012, and an overdraft which, this year, reached its maximum permissible level of £30 000. Because of the highly cyclical nature of demand, the company has experienced difficulty with supplies of modems at certain times of the year. Since the modems are always required for immediate delivery, if an order cannot be met within a few days, it will be lost. The company would like to rectify this problem by increasing its stock of finished modems.

Sales budget

The sales manager sees the 2005 market as continuing to be extremely good for the company. He is aware that this is an expanding market but equally aware that costs are going up ahead of inflation. He feels that a 5 per cent increase in selling price can easily be accommodated and sales volume would still increase by an estimated 20 per cent. Looking at the pattern of last year's sales and noting the requirements of existing major customers, he arrives at his first estimate of sales, broken down by month, as shown in Table A2 (see p. 322). Since he knows that his budget exceeds the productive capacity of existing plant, before proceeding further he passes it on to the managing director and the production manager for consideration.

Table A1 Balance sheet, 31 December 2004

	£	£	£
FIXED ASSETS			484 000
CURRENT ASSETS:			
Stock			
– Finished goods: modem A (400)	30 400		
modem B (360)	19 800		
	50 200		
– Raw materials base stock	10 000		60 200
Debtors		VAT	
– estimated payment January	66 000	11 550	
– estimated payment February	78 000	13 650	169 200
			229 400
CREDITORS DUE WITHIN ONE YEAR:			
Overdraft			(30 000)
Creditors		VAT	
– due for payment January	20 880	3654	
– due for payment February	20 880	3654	(49 068)
Corporation tax (due September)			(27 500)
			(106 568)
NEW CURRENT ASSETS (WORKING CAPITAL)			122 832
NET ASSETS (FIXED ASSETS *less* NET CURRENT ASSETS)			606 832
CREDITORS DUE AFTER MORE THAN ONE YEAR:			
Long-term loan			(100 000)
			506 832
CAPITAL AND RESERVES:			
– Share capital			10 000
– Profit-and-loss account			492 832
			506 832

Table A2 Preliminary sales budget

Units	Jan	Feb	Mar	Apr	May	June	July	Aug	Sep	Oct	Nov	Dec	Total
Modem A	400	400	440	280	100	100	80	80	200	360	360	440	3 240
Modem B	600	660	520	320	160	160	120	120	360	660	780	780	5 240

Production budget

The company would like to be able to meet both the tentative sales budget and to build up finished modem stocks. However, demand is cyclical, whereas production needs to be kept fairly stable throughout the year, since skilled labour cannot be hired and fired at will. Also, even if new machinery were to be purchased in January, it could not be installed and working effectively until March. An added problem is works holidays: one week in December and January and two weeks in August. In those months production is always down, *pro rata*.

Based upon the production schedule, the production manager decides how many new machines to purchase. These machines will cost £120 000 (+ VAT @ 17½% = £21 000) and can be installed in January. Like all creditors, payment can be delayed two months. These machines will increase production of modem A from the normal 240 to 320 per month and of modem B from 400 to 520 per month from March onwards.

Table A3 Production budget

Units	Jan	Feb	Mar	Apr	May	June	July	Aug[3]	Sep	Oct	Nov	Dec	Total
Modem A													
Start stocks	400	180	20	0	40	260	480	720	800	920	880	840	
+ production	180	240	320	320	320	320	320	160	320	320	320	240	3380
− sales	400	400	340	280	100	100	80	80	200	360	360	440	3140
= End stock	180	20	0	40	260	480	720	800	920	880	840	640	
Modem B													
Start stocks	360	60	0	0	200	560	920	1320	1460	1620	1480	1220	
+ production	300	400	520	520	520	520	520	260	520	520	520	390	5510
− sales	600	460	520	320	160	160	120	120	360	660	780	780	5040
= End stock	60	0	0	200	560	920	1320	1460	1620	1480	1220	830	

[1] lower of budgeted sales or stock on hand.
[2] $\frac{3}{4}$ production.
[3] $\frac{1}{2}$ production.

The budgeted production schedule is shown in Table A3. Opening stocks of value A were 400 and of value B 360. The new production schedule will indeed result in higher year-end stocks of 640 and 830 respectively. The lower production in January, August and December reflects the works holidays. Monthly stock levels were computed to compare with the provisional sales budgets to ascertain whether demand will be met. Unfortunately this is not always so, and it is estimated that sales of 100 A modems and 200 B modems will be lost in March and February respectively. However, our investment appraisal tells us it is not worth installing extra productive capacity to satisfy demand in these months. Thus budgeted annual production, sales and stock figures are agreed:

	Units	Modem A	Modem B
	Stock 31 Dec. 2004	400	360
plus	Production	3380	5510
minus	Sales	−3140	−5040
	Stock 31 Dec 2005	640	830

The cost of production, after taking into account inflation in material prices and wage increases, are shown below. These are derived from the company's detailed costing record.

Cost per unit (£)	Modem A	Modem B
Direct labour (fixed cost)	24	15
Direct materials (variable cost)	22	18
Variable factory overheads	15	12
Fixed factory overheads (depreciation)	15	10
	76	55

Workers are on fixed weekly wages. The current wage bill is £10 290 per month. With wage increases due in March and the new operatives needed in that month, this will jump to £14 319 per month (a total of £163 770 for the year). This level of direct labour will be sufficient to meet the planned range of production. Direct material and variable overheads are paid under normal trade terms, on average delaying payments by two months. Fixed factory overheads is depreciation of plant and equipment. This totals £105 800 (£15 ×3380 + £10 ×5510). These unit costs give the following estimates of production costs, cost of sales and stock costs:

		Modem A		Modem B	
		Units	£	Units	£
	Stock 31 Dec. 2004	400	30 400	360	19 800
plus	Production (costs)	3380	256 880	5510	303 050
minus	Sales (costs)	−3140	−238 640	−5040	−277 200
	Stock 31 Dec. 2005	640	48 640	830	45 650

The company keeps a tight control over raw material stocks, and the current base stock of £10 000 will be maintained in value terms.

Purchasing budget

The next task for the company is to prepare the monthly purchasing budget. This is shown in Table A4. The unit variable costs of direct material and overheads and fixed direct labour costs are applied to the production schedule shown in Table A3 to arrive at estimated purchases each month.

Notice that VAT at 17½ per cent has been added to purchases of materials and overheads, assuming all purchases are chargeable. A company acts as a collector of VAT for

Table A4 Budgeted purchases, overheads and wage payments

	Jan	Feb	Mar	Apr	May	June	July	Aug	Sept	Oct	Nov	Dec	
Modem A Production (units)	180	240	320	320	320	320	320	160	320	320	320	240	
Direct materials @ £22　£	3960	5280	7040	7040	7040	7040	7040	3520	7040	7040	7040	5280	
Variable overheads @ £15　£	2700	3600	4800	4800	4800	4800	4800	2400	4800	4800	4800	3600	
Labour @ £24　£	4320	5760	7680	7680	7680	7680	7680	3840	7680	7680	7680	5670	
Modem B Production (units)	300	400	520	520	520	520	520	260	520	520	520	390	
Direct materials @ £18　£	5400	7200	9360	9360	9360	9360	9360	4680	9360	9360	9360	7020	
Variable overheads @ £12　£	3600	4800	6240	6240	6240	6240	6240	3120	6240	6240	6240	4680	
Labour @ £15　£	4500	6000	7800	7800	7800	7800	7800	3900	7800	7800	7800	5850	
Totals Direct materials & variable overheads　£	15 660	20 880	27 440	27 440	27 440	27 440	27 440	13 720	27 440	27 440	27 440	20 580	**Totals** 290 360
Related VAT @ 17½%　£	2241	3654	4802	4802	4802	4802	4802	2401	4802	4802	4802	3602	50 814
Quarterly VAT totals　£		11 197			14 406			12 005			13 206		
Labour　£	10 290	10 290	14 319	14 319	14 319	14 319	14 319	14 319	14 319	14 319	14 319	14 319	163 770

the Customs and Excise. Although it will have to pay VAT on purchases and charge VAT on most sales, it can reclaim the VAT paid and must repay the VAT it collects to the Customs and Excise on a quarterly basis. Therefore, while VAT does not affect a business's profitability (except in so far as it may deter customers), it can cause cash-flow problems, as the business pays and collects VAT at different times from its payments to the Customs and Excise.

Revised sales budget

The original sales budget could not be met and therefore it will have to be revised, in line with Table A3. The revised sales budget is shown in Table A5. Modem A is priced at £90, and modem B at £75, excluding VAT. Notice that, once more, VAT chargeable is shown separately. This will only affect the cash-flow budget.

To achieve this level of sales it is estimated that selling, distribution and general costs will have to rise to £24 000. Let us assume, for simplicity, that these costs incur VAT at 17½ per cent (£4200), they accrue evenly over the year, and that they are paid monthly.

Table A5　Final sales budget

		Jan	Feb	Mar	Apr	May	June	July	Aug	Sep	Oct	Nov	Dec	Total
Modem A	units	400	400	340	280	100	100	80	80	200	360	360	440	3 140
@ £90														
each	£	36 000	36 000	30 600	25 200	9 000	9 000	7 200	7 200	18 000	32 400	32 400	39 600	282 600
Modem B	units	600	460	520	320	160	160	120	120	360	660	780	780	5 040
@ £75														
each	£	45 000	34 500	39 000	24 000	12 000	12 000	9 000	9 000	27 000	49 500	58 500	58 500	378 000
Total	£	81 000	70 500	69 600	49 200	21 000	21 000	16 200	16 200	45 000	81 900	90 900	98 100	660 600
Related VAT @ 17½%	£	14 175	12 338	12 180	8 610	3 675	3 675	2 835	2 835	7 875	14 333	15 908	17 168	115 607
Quarterly VAT totals				38 693			15 960			13 545			47 409	

Budgeted income statement

The budgeted income statement is shown in Table A6. Sales are as shown in Table A5 and cost of sales was calculated from the costing records detailed previously. The budgeted profit before interest and tax payments is £120 760: a margin of 18 per cent on sales. Notice that this calculation excludes VAT.

Table A6　Budgeted income statement, 2005

	Modem A	Modem B	Total
Sales	£282 600	£378 000	£660 600
Cost of sales	238 640	277 200	515 840
GROSS PROFIT	£43 960	£100 800	£144 760
Selling, distribution and general costs			24 000
PROFIT BEFORE INTEREST AND TAX			£120 760
Estimated corporation tax			18 000
Profit before interest but after tax			£102 760

Cash-flow forecast

The cash flow forecast is shown in Table A7. This shows the cash-flow surplus or deficit each month and the resulting effect on the cash balance or overdraft of the business. Sales receipts and related VAT are lagged by two months. In other words, sales in January (see Table A5) do not generate cash receipts until March. Obviously this means sales in November and December will not have been collected by the year-end. Similarly, purchases and related VAT are lagged by two months. January purchases (see Table A4) are not paid until March, and November and December purchases are not paid for by the year end. Selling, distribution and general costs and related VAT are paid in the month incurred, as are direct labour costs. The capital expenditure and related VAT is paid in March, and the corporation tax bill shown in last year's balance-sheet is paid in September.

VAT payments to the Customs and Excise are quarterly, at the end of March, June, September and December. These are normally based, not as you might expect, upon VAT received *less* VAT paid, but instead upon the VAT you have charged *less* the VAT charged to you during the period, irrespective of whether or not you have received or paid it. Budgeted VAT payments have been calculated in Table A8. VAT receivable is taken from Table A5 and VAT payable on materials and variable overheads from Table A4. Selling and general costs and capital expenditures are as detailed. This complication is unfortunate, but essential, since VAT can make an enormous difference to the cash flows of any business and often a small business can experience difficulty meeting these quarterly bills.

Table A7 Cash flow forecast 2005

£		Jan	Feb	Mar	Apr	May	June	July	Aug	Sept	Oct	Nov	Dec	Total
RECEIPTS														
Sales receipts		66 000	78 000	81 000	70 500	69 600	49 200	21 000	21 000	16 200	16 200	45 000	81 900	615 600
Related VAT		11 550	13 650	14 175	12 338	12 318	8 610	3 675	3 675	2 835	2 835	7 875	14 333	107 731
Total receipts	**A**	77 550	91 650	95 175	82 838	81 780	57 810	24 675	24 675	19 035	19 035	52 875	96 233	723 331
PAYMENTS														
Direct materials and overheads		20 880	20 880	15 660	20 880	27 440	27 440	27 440	27 440	27 440	13 720	27 440	27 440	284 100
Related VAT		3 654	3 654	2 741	3 654	4 802	4 802	4 802	4 802	4 802	2 401	4 802	4 802	49 718
Selling, general etc.		2 000	2 000	2 000	2 000	2 000	2 000	2 000	2 000	2 000	2 000	2 000	2 000	24 000
Related VAT		350	350	350	350	350	350	350	350	350	350	350	350	4 200
Direct labour		10 290	10 290	14 319	14 319	14 319	14 319	14 319	14 319	14 319	14 319	14 319	14 319	163 770
Capital expenditure				120 000										120 000
Related VAT				21 000										21 000
VAT payments				5 446			504			490			3 315	339 593
Corporation tax										27 500				27 500
Total payments	**B**	37 174	37 174	181 516	41 203	48 911	49 415	48 911	48 911	76 901	32 790	48 911	82 064	733 881
CASH FLOW	**A – B**	40 376	54 476	–86 341	41 635	32 869	8 395	–24 236	–24 236	–57 866	–13 755	3 964	14 169	–10 550
Brought forward		–30 000	10 376	64 854	–21 489	20 146	53 015	61 410	37 174	12 938	–44 928	–58 683	–54 719	–30 000
CASH BALANCE		10 376	64 854	–21 489	20 146	53 015	61 410	37 174	12 938	–44 928	–58 683	–54 719	–40 550	–40 550

Table A8 VAT quarterly returns summary

	Mar	June	Sep	Dec	Total
VAT receivable	£38693	£15960	£13545	£47409	£115607
minus					
VAT payable					
Materials and overheads	−11197	−14406	−12005	−13206	−50814
Selling and general	−1050	−1050	−1050	−1050	−4200
Capital expenditure	−21000	—	—	—	−21000
Quarterly payments	£5446	£504	£490	£33153	£39593

The budgeted cash-flow statement is essential for short-term planning. The business started the year with an overdraft of £30000, which was the maximum facility offered by the bank. This overdraft limit will not be exceeded until September, when an overdraft of £44928 will be required. This will increase to £58683 in October, and even at the end of the year will be £40550. Obviously the business must either arrange to increase its overdraft facility in advance for these months or arrange for a term loan to inject the needed cash. But would the banks lend to the business? To find this out, we need to look at the business's profit and its balance-sheet.

Budgeted balance-sheet

The budgeted balance sheet is shown in Table A9. Debtors and related VAT represent November and December sales, and creditors and related VAT represent November and December purchases of materials and overheads. Finished-goods stock was calculated in the production schedule and the raw materials base stock is maintained at £10000. The overdraft was calculated from the budgeted cash-flow statement. Corporation tax is estimated at £18000.

Fixed assets are calculated below:

	brought forward 31 Dec. 2004 (net)	£484000
plus	purchases	120000
minus	depreciation	−105800
	carried forward 31 Dec. 2005 (net)	£498200

Depreciation is calculated by writing off assets over an estimated 10-year life. The company does this by charging depreciation of 10 per cent on the gross cost of the asset over a 10-year period.

Net assets for the company total £709592, an increase of £102760 over last year, which represents the profit the business has made this year since our budget shows no increase in share or loan capital. For those readers with a more detailed knowledge of accounts, Tables A9 and A10 analyse the movement on key balance-sheet accounts.

The business is making a return on net assets of:

$$\frac{120760}{709592} \times 100 = 17\%$$

This is well above the target set by the owner, and above current interest rates. However, this return does exclude interest and taxation. The capital gearing is:

$$\frac{(40550 + 100000)}{609592} \times 100 = 23\%$$

This is well below the maximum level of security that many lenders require. That maximum gearing level of 10 per cent would be reached with outside loans of £609 592 on the same capital base. In other words, the business would probably be able to support more loan capital to enable it to meet the cash-flow deficit. The owner now has all the information he requires either to approach the bank manager or another source of funds.

Table A9 Budgeted balance sheet, 31 December 2005

	£	£	£
FIXED ASSETS (NET)			498 200
CURRENT ASSETS:			
Finished goods: modem A (640)	48 640		
modem B (830)	45 650		
	94 290		
Raw material base stock	10 000		104 290
Debtors		VAT	
– November sales	90 900	15 908	
– December sales	98 100	17 168	222 076
			326 366
CREDITORS DUE WITHIN ONE YEAR:		VAT	
Overdraft			(40 550)
Creditors			
– November materials and overhead purchases	(27 440)	(4 802)	
– December materials and overhead purchases	(20 580)	(3 602)	(56 424)
Corporation tax (estimate)			(18 000)
			(114 974)
NET CURRENT ASSETS			211 392
NET ASSETS			709 592
CREDITORS DUE AFTER MORE THAN ONE YEAR:			
Long term loan			(100 000)
			609 592
CAPITAL AND RESERVES:			
Share capital			10 000
Profit-and-loss account			
– brought forward 2004	496 832		
– 2005 profit	102 760		599 592
			609 592

Table A10 Analysis of accounts

Debtors

brought forward 2004	£144 000
+ sales	660 600
− cash received	− 615 600
carried forward 2005	£189 000

Creditors

		Stock	
brought forward 2004	£ 41 760	brought forward 2004	£ 60 200
+ purchases	290 360 →	+ purchases	290 360
− cash paid	− 284 100	+ depreciation allocation	105 800
carried forward 2005	£ 48 020	+ labour costs	163 770
		− cost of sales	− 515 840
		carried forward 2005	£ 104 290

VAT

Brought forward 2004: debtors (Nov & Dec)	£25 200	
− creditors (Nov & Dec)	− 7 308	£ 17 892
− collected from sales		−107 731
+ paid on purchases (materials and overheads)		49 718
+ paid on selling and general costs		4 200
+ paid on capital expenditure		21 000
+ VAT paid quarterly to C & E		39 593
Carried forward 2005: debtors (Nov & Dec)	£33 076	
− creditors (Nov & Dec)	− 8 404	£ 24 672

References

Ansoff, H.I. (1968) *Corporate Strategy*, London: Penguin.

Burns, P. (1994) *Winners and Losers in the 1990s*, 3i European Enterprise Centre, Report no. 12, April.

Carson, D. (1990) 'Some Exploratory Models of Assessing Small Firms Marketing Performance', *European Journal of Marketing*, vol. 24, no. 11.

Chittenden, F., Poutziouris, P. and Michaelas, N. (1998) *Financial Management and Working Capital Practices in UK SMEs*, Manchester Business School.

Johnson, G. and Scholes, K. (1993) *Exploring Corporate Strategy*, Hemel Hempstead: Prentice-Hall International.

Kay, J. (1998) *Foundations of Corporate Success*, Oxford: Oxford University Press.

Lindblom, L.E. (1959) 'The Science of Muddling Through', *Public Administration Review,* vol. 19, Spring.

Mathewson, Sir G, (2000) Keynote address, British Academy of Management Annual Conference, Edinburgh.

McCarthy, B. and Leavy, B. (2000) 'Strategy Formation in Irish SMEs: A Phase Model of Process', British Academy of Management Annual Conference, Edinburgh.

Mintzberg, H. (1978) 'Patterns in Strategy Formation', *Management Science*, 934–48.

Porter, M.E. (1987) 'From Competitive Advantage to Competitive Strategy', *Harvard Business Review*, vol. 65, no. 3.

Rumelt, R.P. (1974) *Strategy, Structure and Economic Performance*, Boston, Mass: Harvard University Press.

Wernerfelt, B. and Montgomery, C.A. (1986) 'What is an Attractive Industry?, *Management Science*, 32, 1223–9.

chapter twelve

Financing small firms

Contents

- Money
- Bank finance
- The banker's perspective
- Banking relationships
- Venture capital
- The Alternative investment Market (AIM)
- Is there a financing gap?
- Summary
- Appendix: Sources of venture capital under £100 000

Learning outcomes

By the end of this chapter you should:

- Understand the principles of prudent financing;
- Understand the range of finance available to small firms and its appropriate use;
- Understand how small firms in the UK actually are financed;
- Appreciate the problems of lending to small firms and monitoring the loan;
- Understand the basis of the lending decision;
- Appreciate why and how collateral and security decisions are made;
- Be able to critically evaluate a lending opportunity;
- Appreciate the importance of the banking relationship and understand both how it can be enhanced and undermined;
- Appreciate the importance of venture capital funds and the uses to which they are put;
- Understand what venture capitalists are looking for when they make an investment;
- Understand what is meant by the 'financing gap' and whether it exists;
- Be able to critically appraise an application for finance.

Money

We saw in Chapter 10 that the availability and cost of finance is often cited by owner-managers as a barrier to growth. This is not new. Back in 1931 the Macmillan Committee believed it was extremely difficult for smaller firms to obtain long-term capital in amounts of less than £200 000 (a figure probably equivalent to about £5 million today; Macmillan, 1931). Since then there has been much debate about whether a 'financing gap' really does exist.

The adequate provision of finance is vital if small firms are to grow and make the most of their potential, but the topic raises paradoxes resulting from the ambiguous attitudes owner-managers have towards its provision. On the one hand they want outside finance in order to grow but, on the other hand, they do not want to lose independence or control. At the same time they want both the maximum flexibility and maximum security – objectives that are not easily reconciled – at the lowest price.

The first thing to realise is that not all money is the same. Different sorts of money ought to be used for different purposes and not all types of money are available to all small firms. In fact many owner-managers, particularly at start-up, try to avoid using money at all by borrowing or using other people's resources wherever possible. Where this fails, they might borrow money from friends or relatives. Many owner-managers make extensive use of personal credit cards, particularly at start-up, because of the problems they face in securing other sources of finance. Inevitably, however, most firms will need to obtain some form of external finance at some point in their life.

> **David Moulsade** trained as a dispensing optician through a correspondence course. In 1993, aged 24, he opened his first shop in Glasgow. Soon after he opened his third store in Edinburgh cash-flow problems hit and he had to borrow from his parents to pay the wages. They re-mortgaged their home. **Optical Express** is now one of Britain's fastest growing companies, having taken over the Specialeyes chain in 1997.

Table 12.1 summarises the major forms of finance and how they ought to be used, in theory. The principle is that the term-duration of the source of finance should be matched to the term-duration of the use to which it is put. Fixed or permanent assets should be financed by long-term sources of finance and only working capital should be financed by short-term finance.

The owner-manager is likely to have to put some personal equity into the business, whatever its size. For a limited company this takes the form of share capital. Over time these funds grow as profits are retained in the business. The majority of small firms rely on internal funds to finance their business; 79 per cent use retained profits and 72 per cent cash flow to fund activities according to one survey (Bank of England, 1998). According to another, one-third of small firms across Europe do not borrow at all from banks with most preferring to use internal funds to finance growth and development; another third move into and out of overdraft regularly; and the final third are consistent borrowers (Burns and Whitehouse, 1995b). For a growing company, there may also be the opportunity to get a venture capital institution or a private individual (called 'business angels') to invest. This is also the permanent capital of the firm which can be used

Table 12.1 Sources and uses of finance

	Source of finance	Use of finance

Long-term	▪ Equity
	  – personal investment.
	  – other people's money.
	▪ Medium and long-term bank loans.
	▪ Leasing.
	▪ Hire purchase.
		Fixed or permanent assets (land, buildings, furniture, equipment, plant, vehicles and so on)

Short-term	▪ Factoring. ▪ Short-term bank loans and overdraft.	Working capital (debtors and stocks)

to finance long-term, permanent assets. These shareholders expect dividends and stand to see the value of their shares increase if the firm does well. They might also expect to exercise some degree of directorial control over the business.

Alongside this, a firm is likely to be able to borrow medium- or long-term funds from a bank which again can be used to finance medium- or long-term assets. The principle is to try to match the term of the loan to the life of the asset. Loans are serviced by regular interest payments and the capital will, ultimately, have to be repaid. Interest may vary with base rate or be fixed for the term of the loan. Agreeing to a fixed rate may involve a certain amount of crystal-ball gazing, but it does ensure that a small firm knows what its financing costs will be for some time to come. As we shall see in the next section, bankers are likely to look for the security of assets to act as collateral against the loan and, if they cannot get this, they may ask for personal guarantees from the owner-manager.

Where a firm cannot provide a bank with the required security or does not have the track record to convince the bank to lend, then the Small Firms Loan Guarantee Scheme might be another way of getting finance. With this the government provides a guarantee to the bank against default by the borrowers. First introduced in 1981, terms and conditions have varied over the years. Currently the guarantee is against 70 per cent of the loan (85 per cent if the firm has been trading for two years) for a period of between 2 to 10 years. In exchange for this there is a premium of 1.5 per cent a year on the amount guaranteed (0.5 per cent if the loan is at a fixed rate of interest). The scheme is administered through the banks, who continue to make all commercial decisions. The DTI (1995) produces a free booklet on the scheme.

> **Drive Assist UK** may have been the fastest growing company in the *Sunday Times* 1999 Fast Track 100 companies but its growth was constrained by lack of capital in its early years. It was founded in 1992 by **Steve Birch** and **John Sherwood** after the car rental firm they worked for went into receivership. With £30 000 gathered from family and friends, they took no salary for the first 18 months, relying on their working wives to cover living costs. Eventually they secured two Small Firms Guarantee Scheme loans totalling £100 000.
>
> The company provides replacement cars for drivers whose cars have been in an accident. It has recently diversified into repairs and maintenance as well as car sales. Sales were £35.8 million in 1998 and it employs over 100 staff.

There are two other ways of financing the purchase of equipment:

- Lease – which allows the firm to use the asset without owning it by making regular lease payments;
- Hire purchase – which allows the firm to purchase the asset over a period of time, again, by making regular payments with the asset acting as security in the case of default.

The main practical difference between the two methods is their tax treatment. The DTI (1998) also produces a free booklet on this source of finance. Interest rates on lease and hire purchase schemes may be higher than on loans, but for a firm with little security to offer a banker they might be the only way to secure finance.

Short-term loans and overdrafts are most prudently used to finance working capital, like debtors and stock. However, most UK small firms make extensive use of overdraft finance. Most firms will use overdraft finance at some point in their life, but small firms in the UK have a far greater dependence on it as a source of finance than other firms in other European countries – 42 per cent of debt for UK small firms is overdraft compared to 17 per cent in Germany (Burns and Whitehouse, 1995b). What is more, they often imprudently use the overdraft to finance long-term investment. Whilst overdrafts are ultimately flexible and cheap – you only pay interest on the outstanding amount – firms relying on this run the risk of the bank calling-in the overdraft at any time and the high level of dependence seen in the UK may be linked to short-time horizons and pay-back periods for investment (Burns and Whitehouse, 1995a).

Nick Probett left the army in 1976 wanting to set up his own airborne taxi service, having learnt to fly whilst stationed in Nicosia, Cyprus. He worked as a car chauffeur for four years as he trained to obtain his CAA license. The problem was that left him £12 000 in debt and none of the banks would lend him the money to buy his first plane. But when a aircraft finance house that had initially refused him money repossessed a two-seater aircraft from a businessman, they decided to allow Nick to lease it.

Nick managed to get landing slots that enabled him to operate at London Heathrow airport and **Chauffair** was set up in 1980. The firm offers a 24 hour air-taxi service that can travel to anywhere in the world at a moment's notice – but the service is not cheap. Now it employs 50 staff of whom 21 are pilots and has sales of £4.7 million.

Factoring is a form of finance particularly suited to undercapitalised, growing firms, where the major asset on their balance sheet is debtors. The factoring company advances 75–80 per cent of the invoice when it is issued and the balance, less charges, when the invoice is settled. Interest is charged on the funds advanced at a rate of 2–4 per cent above base rate with a further administrative charge depending on the service required (they can take complete control of the debtors ledger and cover bad debts, if required), turnover and average size of invoice. It is therefore expensive, but for a firm growing rapidly it may, again, be the only way to raise funds. Factors do impose certain conditions such as minimum turnover, invoice value and maximum concentration of debt with a single customer. They will also insist on certain credit checks being undertaken on new customers. Where the firm retains control of its debtors ledger, this is more correctly called invoice discounting.

Most firms use a range of financing to suit their differing needs and circumstances. The flowchart in Figure 12.1 attempts to guide the small firm through the process of deciding upon a suitable financing package. It includes grants which, since free, and if available, should always be taken. It is taken from the free DTI (1997) booklet on sources of finance.

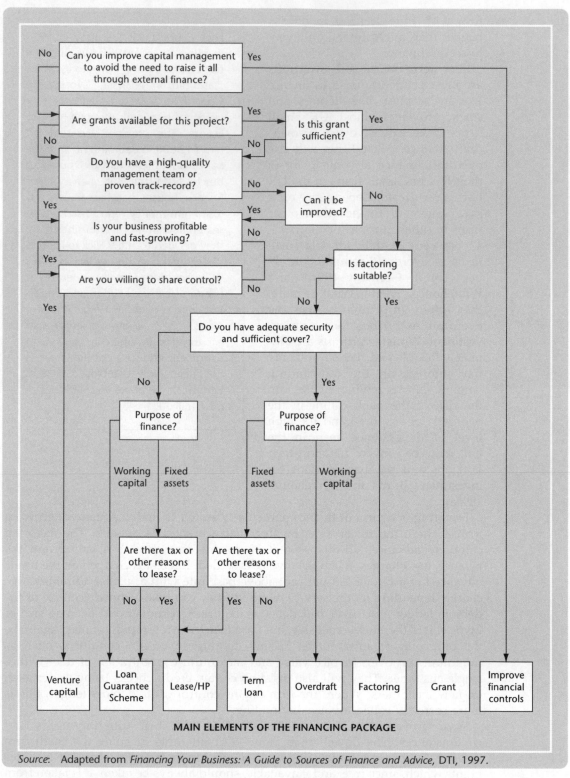

Source:　Adapted from *Financing Your Business: A Guide to Sources of Finance and Advice*, DTI, 1997.

Figure 12.1 How to finance the entrepreneurial business

NDT (Non-Destructive Testing) is located in Strood, Kent and undertakes inspection and testing for the engineering industry – welding and crack inspection, ultrasonic and radiography inspection as well as destructive tests, material analysis and hardness surveys. This involves both on-site and laboratory work. NDT operates in a very specialised market with only about a dozen competitors in the UK. Its clients include many blue-chip companies and about 80 per cent of its turnover comes from 20 per cent of its clients. It started life as a management buy-out from Royal Insurance, who decided it was not part of its core business. The 12 owner-directors each owns 5000, £1 shares (total share capital £60 000). The buy-out was financed by a two-year, interest free debenture loan of £50 000 from Royal Insurance, repayable in two annual instalments and secured by a floating charge on the assets of the company.

NDT were successful in securing a contract from Aiton, of Derby, to test pipework in a power station. The contract was initially only for 10 weeks and the managing director, **Roy Davenport**, expected to finance this by using NDT's overdraft facility. Aiton was a large engineering firm and typically paid creditors in about six weeks. However, the initial work disclosed some major problems which resulted in the need to test all the pipework in the power station. Staff on site were doubled after the first week, doubled again in the third week and doubled again two weeks later. NDT realised that the contract value would be over £3 million – ten times their current level of turnover.

The problem for Roy was how to finance this extremely lucrative work. Initially he relied on overdraft but within three weeks he had exceeded his modest overdraft facility of £20 000. The bank were very supportive but insisted that it could not provide the necessary funds without personal guarantees from the directors and not all of the 12 directors would agree to this. Roy decided to factor NDT's debts. Initially with some 80 customers on their books this worked well but the factoring company started to notice the heavy concentration of debt with Aiton. They agreed to a 40 per cent concentration, then a 59 per cent concentration and finally a 70 per cent concentration, but still the size of Aiton's debts kept mounting. When the concentration came to an unagreed 99.8 per cent the factoring company refused to accept any more invoices to Aiton.

Roy now had a major problem since Aiton currently owed NDT over £200 000 and, despite this extremely lucrative contract, there were no funds to pay salaries this month. He decided that he would go to Aiton and request a £100 000 advance on the work being undertaken plus a revision to the payment terms, which would mean that NDT received weekly payments one month in arrears. Aiton agreed to the revised terms but not the advance. Looking at the cash-flow projections Roy realised that there was no way that the firm could undertake the work and survive without the advance. He decided to forego the extra profit and withdraw from the contract.

Within 24 hours of him taking his men off site Aiton agreed to make the advance to NDT. What had not been meant as a threat, had the same effect. Aiton realised that NDT was willing to walk away from the highly profitable contract because it could not finance the large cash flow deficit it created. Profit is not the same as cash flow.

Other sources of 'soft' finance include:

● The Prince's Youth Business Trust which provides finance and advice to help younger people set up their own business. It is supported by funds from the EU, national and local government, as well as private companies and individuals.
● EU funds are available in certain areas affected by industry decline and closures.
● Regional Selective Assistance is available in designated Assisted Areas.
● The Rural Development Commission has limited funds to help rural firms.
● The Small Firms Merit Award for Research and Technology (SMART) and Support for Products Under Research (SPUR) are awards and grants administered by the DTI.
● Tourist Boards may also offer grants and loans.

Bank finance

Bank finance is the main source of external finance for the vast majority of small firms in the UK. What is more, it is a constant cause for complaint about unwillingness to lend, high charges and poor service. The 2000 survey by the Federation of Small Business of 22 000 of its UK members found that more than 70 per cent were dissatisfied with the charges levied by banks. Earlier in the year, the Cruickshank Report (Cruickshank, 2000) had found that more than a million small businesses were being overcharged by their banks to the extent of £500 million a year. Despite this, few customers actually change banks (perhaps as few as 5 per cent each year), although this might be because they do not perceive another bank as being any better than the one they are at or because of the high switch costs associated with changing banks. All of which begs the question of the degree of competition between banks in the UK.

However, banks face significant problems in lending to small firms. Banks lend a sum of money in return for agreed interest payments and the repayment of the sum borrowed. They do not share in the profits of a highly successful firm. And if a firm fails, the bad debt is expensive to recoup. So, if banks make a 4 per cent margin on a loan (the difference between the rate they can borrow at and the rate they can lend at), then every £100 lost as a bad debt will need a further £2500 to be lent for the margin to cover it ($100 \div 0.04$). Put another way, the bank has to make a further 25 loans to cover this one bad debt. Not unsurprisingly therefore bankers are risk averse and will do all they can to avoid a bad debt. What is more, they are all too aware of the failure statistics for business start-ups, which explains why it is often difficult to obtain start-up finance.

Even existing firms seem a risky lending proposition to a banker looking for security against their loan. Table 12.2 summarises the balance sheets of small and large companies in the UK. As pointed out by Burns (1985), comparison of the two would lead you to conclude that small firms, compared to large firms:

1 Overinvest in debtors and stock;
2 Underinvest in fixed assets;
3 Are overreliant on creditor finance – money that is probably due for payment in the very near future;
4 Are overreliant on short-term, particularly overdraft, finance;
5 Have insufficient capital and reserves and are undercapitalised.

Table 12.2 Balance sheet structures – small and large companies

	Small companies	Large companies
Fixed assets	32	57
Stock	20	14
Debtors	39	19
Cash	9	10
	100	100
Overdraft	13	8
Creditors	47	24
Long-term loans	9	15
Shares and reserves	31	53
	100	100

Sources: *Business Monitor MA3 Company Finance*, various issues, and Burns (1985).

As a banker you would see the small firm as the riskier lending proposition – higher, mainly short-term, gearing (particularly if creditors are taken into account) and fewer fixed assets to offer you security in the event of a bad debt. What is more, there is evidence of wide variability in gearing. Putting this in a European context, one survey in 1995 found that 56 per cent of small firms in Britain, France, Germany, Spain and Italy (52 per cent in Britain) had gearing levels of 50 per cent or less (gearing defined here as all loans divided by shareholders' funds) but 21 per cent had levels over 100 per cent (21 per cent also in Britain) (Bank of England, 1998). This had changed little since a previous survey in 1992 (Burns, 1992). Gearing levels tended to be lowest in Germany and highest in Spain, with Britain about average, although Britain was notable for its heavy reliance on overdraft finance – 42 per cent of debt compared to 17 per cent in Germany.

However, banks do not just lend on the strength of the balance sheet, they are interested in the general prospects of the business they are lending to and here the issue of information asymmetry – one party having better information than the other – arises. Where asymmetric information favours the small firm – the owner-manager having more or better information than the bank – the bank is likely to be more wary about lending because of greater uncertainty. This is less of a problem with larger firms because there is so much more public information about them and many independent analysts reviewing it for investment purposes. For the owner-manager it means that they have an uphill task convincing the bank manager of the viability of their project. It underlines the importance of effective communication. For the bank, it means that they are likely to incur extra costs in getting the information they need to make and then monitor a loan, and it is worth noting that these costs do not rise or fall pro rata with the size of the loan. This is one reason why banks so often ask for collateral against a loan. Where sufficient collateral can be made available, the bank may feel that less information is required because the debt is more likely to be recovered in the event of default. What is more, bankers may also feel that the provision of collateral gives the owner-manager a strong incentive to see the business succeed. If the firm's balance sheet cannot provide it, the owner-manager may be asked to guarantee the loan, secured on their personal assets.

Interestingly, it has been argued that information asymmetry favours the bank for a start-up (Jovanovic, 1982). The bank manager may have a broader experience on which to base a judgement of whether a start-up will succeed or not than the owner-manager, who will probably learn mainly from their experience of trading. It is only by surviving that the successful owner-manager distinguishes themselves from the less successful one.

One of the things that banks do to deal with the problem of information asymmetry is to create a portfolio of loans, combining a spectrum of different risk–return lendings across all the sectors of industry. The portfolio will always have firms that will fail but they will be more than balanced by those that survive and the risks the portfolio faces reflect those facing the whole economy.

The natural response of banks to the problem of information asymmetry is likely to be to charge higher rates of interest and to ask for collateral. However, it can be shown that charging higher rates of interest may not be to a bank's advantage because this discourages low-return but low-risk businesses (Stiglitz and Weiss, 1981). High-return but high-risk firms may continue to borrow but the banks do not share in their success – only their failure. The rational response to information asymmetry should therefore be to ration credit in some way rather than to raise interest rates, indeed whilst small firms typically do pay higher interest rates than larger firms, the difference is typically only a couple of points. If credit rationing is indeed taking place, then it leads to the question whether some borrowers are being excluded from access to credit, even though they might be willing to pay higher rates of interest. It therefore raises the question once more of the existence of a financing gap for riskier, growing firms.

In valuing collateral the bank assumes that the assets will be sold on a second-hand market and this typically leads to far lower prices being put on assets than many owner-managers would expect. Table 12.3 gives a guide to what to expect. Given these asset security values, it is clear that growing firms wishing to purchase new plant and equipment will have to spend more than the assets add to their collateral base. Because the business collateral base is insufficient for their needs they may well turn to lease, hire-purchase and factoring as ways of financing their growth and, if all else fails, the owner-manager may have to provide personal guarantees, perhaps using their house as collateral. However,

Table 12.3 Asset security values

Asset	% value that can be borrowed	
Freehold land and buildings	70	
Long leasehold	60	
Specialist plant and machinery	5–10	100% can be obtained by leasing but APR may be more
Non-specialist plant and machinery	30	100% can be obtained by leasing but APR may be more
Debtors	30–50	Depends on age and quality
Stock	25	Depends on age and quality and the significance of any retention of title clauses. Raw materials will be worth more than part processed stock.

Source: Financing Your Business: A Guide to Sources of Finance and Advice, DTI (1997).

this once more raises the question of debt gaps, particularly for growing firms, as it has been argued that a heavy reliance on collateral, particularly personal collateral, may effectively create such a gap because of the resultant erosion of limited liability status (Binks, Ennew and Reed, 1990). Many owner-managers observe that this frequent requirement to give personal guarantees means that the separation between a limited liability company and their own finances is little more than theoretical.

One solution to this problem, widely used in Europe but little seen in the UK, is the mutual guarantee scheme. Hughes (1992) points to their extensive use in Europe in 'pooling their private information about project riskiness and entrepreneurial quality, and developing mutual schemes to guarantee individual loan applications to banks by members of the group, after group screening based upon pooled information'. The problem is that, whilst the individual may benefit by easier access to finance and lower rates of interest, they also face the possibility of having to make good the bad debts of others in the mutual guarantee scheme.

> **Peter Kelly** started **Software Catalogue**, his mail-order software business, in 1993. It is now one of the main suppliers of Microsoft products in Britain and in 1999 made a £500 000 profit on sales of £18 million. However, success brought unexpected problems early in its life. Initially Peter drew up a business plan, put in £35 000 of his own money and found two external investors willing to each put in a further £10 000. The market of mail-order software was virtually untapped at the time and it was the firm's success that caused the problem. Within a year the firm had run out of cash and had reached the end of its ever-increasing overdraft limit as debtors were increasing at an alarming rate. The firm was overtrading – the classic example of success causing Death Valley to go on and on. Peter's response was to factor his debts – relying on the one asset in his balance sheet for security. It might have been more expensive than overdraft finance, but it helped the company survive, grow and become the success it is today.

The banker's perspective

Banks are in business to make as much money as possible with the least risk. Above all they want to avoid bad debts; they do not share in the profits of a successful firm, so they do not want to share in the risks. Bank managers are employees and they work in a highly regulated environment, and they have limited discretion. Two high-street banks use a computer-based expert-system which produces a lending recommendation for existing firms based upon historic and projected financial data and evaluations of various measures of competitive advantage and management capabilities. Lending decisions are heavily influenced by bank lending policies and procedures, and this can also reflect general economic conditions and the balance of the bank's lending portfolio. One bank can turn down an applicant that another will accept.

Having said that, bankers are likely to be interested in similar things to the providers of equity finance, albeit with different emphasise. Making a judgement about the ability of management is central to the lending decision. To this end they will want to understand the fundamentals of the business and to ask for financial information to enable them to measure management performance. The Business Plan is an excellent vehicle for providing this. Bankers are interested primarily in the ability of the business to generate sufficient cash to pay interest and, in due course, repay the capital sum. They are interested in minimising short-term risks and are very keen to see good financial controls in place – tight debtor and stock control should lead to strong cash flow. They also expect to come first when interest has to be paid and that can mean delaying capital expenditures and reducing or delaying drawings from the firm.

One acronym often used by bankers as a framework for making lending decisions is **CAMPARI**. This spells out the criteria on which the decision is based:

Character	What is the business track record of the owner-manager and their personal credit history? Honesty and integrity are difficult to judge, but most bankers still think lending is a very personal thing and making a judgement on the character of the owner-manager is vital.
Ability	How able is the owner-manager to make the plan happen? This is about their management ability and their financial and business acumen.
Management	Is the management team adequate? The quality of management can be judged by relevant business experience, education and training, and proven track record.
Purpose	What is the purpose of the loan? Is it consistent with bank policy? Is it legal? Is it in the best interest of the business?
Amount	Is the amount requested correct? Have all associated costs for the project been included? Has the borrower put money in themselves? Is there a contingency?
Repayment	Will the business generate sufficient cash to make the interest payments and repay the capital? Is the repayment term realistic?
Insurance	Is security necessary? Is the security properly valued? Is personal as well as business collateral required?

Bankers are keen to look at certain financial information and ratios – based both on projected and past financial data (Table 12.4). The cash flow forecast is a vital document for them because it shows whether interest payments can be made. They are particularly keen to look at the break-even point and the margin of safety – this tells them about the operating risk of the business in terms of the overheads it faces and the margin it is able to command. They will work out the range of gearing ratios discussed in Chapter 10, which tell them whether the lender is over-borrowed and the financial risk they face. They will also look at the asset management ratios to reassure themselves that debtors and stocks are being properly managed. This is not to say that they will not look at the performance and profitability ratios discussed in Chapter 10, just that they are less important.

Table 12.4 Financial data of particular interest to bankers

Cash flow forecast

Risk

Break-even point (£)

$$\frac{\text{Fixed costs}}{\text{Contribution margin}}$$

Margin of safety (%)

$$\frac{\text{Sales} - \text{Break-even sales}}{\text{Sales}}$$

Gearing

Gearing ratio (%):

$$\frac{\text{All loans} + \text{overdrafts}}{\text{Shareholders funds}}$$

Short-term debt ratio (%):

$$\frac{\text{Short-term loans} + \text{overdrafts}}{\text{All loans} + \text{overdraft}}$$

Interest cover:

$$\frac{\text{Trading profit}}{\text{Interest}}$$

Asset efficiency

Debtor turnover:

$$\frac{\text{Sales}}{\text{Debtors}}$$

Stock turnover:

$$\frac{\text{Sales}}{\text{Stock}}$$

Liquidity

Current ratio:

$$\frac{\text{Current assets}}{\text{Current liabilities}}$$

Quick ratio:

$$\frac{\text{Current assets excluding stock}}{\text{Current liabilities}}$$

Even after the loan is granted they will continue to monitor these figures, expecting to see annual audited accounts and budgets for the next year. What is more they will also monitor the bank account itself, looking out for irregularities and checking that throughput is in line with turnover expectations.

Banking relationships

The owner-manager and the banker need to have a good working relationship. A close relationship has the potential to provide the banker with the information they need about the firm and thus avoid the problem of information asymmetry. Like any relationship, this must be based on two elements, both of which have been weak between the banker and owner-manager:

● *Trust* – that both the owner-manager and the banker will honour the terms of the loan;
● *Respect* – that both the owner-manager and the banker are good at what they do.

Like any relationship, it is a personal thing that is developed by keeping in regular contact. That means visits and the provision of information. These days bankers like to make regular visits to their clients. They like to feel they know the firm and the individuals in it. More than anything, bankers do not like surprises.

These are some of the things that start to make them worry that all is not well in a firm:

● Frequent excesses on the bank account beyond the agreed overdraft facility. This makes the banker start to think cash flow is not being properly controlled.
● Development of hard-core borrowing on an overdraft facility. This makes the banker believe that a term-loan would be more appropriate.
● Lack of financial information. If the accounts and other information does not arrive regularly, they worry about the firm's ability to produce control information and, *in extremis*, can become suspicious that all is not well.
● Unavailability of the owner-manager. If the owner-manager is never available for a meeting or even a telephone conversation, bankers will start to believe something is wrong. Most people do not want to give bad news and avoiding is one way of not having to.
● Inability to meet forecasts. The banker will eventually start to question the credibility of the forecasts and the owner-manager's understanding of the market.
● Continuing losses, declining margins and rapidly diminishing or even increasing turnover. At the end of the day the banker is really only interested in the ability of the firm to service its loan.
● Overreliance on too few customers or suppliers. The loss of just one customer or supplier can then create a disproportionate problem for the firm.

The relationship between bank, or more particularly the bank manager, and small business owner-manager is an essential ingredient in addressing the problem of information asymmetry. Put succinctly, good relationships help the owner-manager obtain and maintain finance and bridge any financing gap. Also, as you might expect, there is evidence that the closer the relationship, the greater the owner-manager's perception of the quality of banking service and the less likely they are to want to change banks (Binks and Ennew, 1996). It would therefore appear that working to improve the banking relationship benefits both sides. In recent years the banks have invested enormous amounts in training managers about both the problems facing small-firms and how to analyse them, but also how to approach the issue of developing relationships. There are grounds for believing that a better relationship would prevail if owner-managers showed a greater willingness to participate in it (Hughes, 1992).

Venture capital

Venture capital funds provide equity and loan finance to businesses with growth potential. According to the British Venture Capital Association (BVCA, 1999/2000), the UK has the most developed venture capital industry in Europe and is second only to the USA in the world. Since the inception of the BVCA in 1983, its members have invested almost £25 billion in thousands of companies. About half of all investments goes to help established companies expand and about a third goes into management buy-outs (the management of a firm buying it) or buy-ins (external managers buying a firm and normally replacing the management). There are over 100 venture capital funds and investments range from as little as £5000 to over £100 000 million. The best known firm is probably 3i, originally established by the Bank of England and the clearing banks in 1945 to provide finance to growing firms.

Venture capitalists provide risk finance and the annualised rate of return they expect on their investment is high – from 30 per cent to 60 per cent, depending on the risk involved (Murray and Lott, 1995). They are therefore looking primarily for high growth firms to invest in. They reject some 95 per cent of the approximately 5000 applications made to them each year (Bannock, 1991 and Dixon, 1991). The financing structure they put together varies from deal to deal. Usually they do not want to take control of the business away from the entrepreneur, so the deal usually involves a mixture of equity (less than a 50 per cent stake), preference shares and loans. Preference shares are normally non-voting, allowing the venture capitalist to take equity without taking control of the business. They give a preferential claim over the profits and assets of the business over ordinary shareholders. The dividend on them is limited to a fixed percentage of the face value and there is no right to a dividend if the directors do not declare one, but they always have priority over ordinary shareholders if dividends are paid. Most preference shares are 'cumulative' which means that unpaid dividends must be accumulated and made good before ordinary shareholders are paid. They also have preference over ordinary shareholders in the event of a liquidation. Some preference shares are 'redeemable', normally at their face value at some specified future date. Others are 'convertible' into ordinary shares, normally at the shareholder's option.

A 'convertible preferred ordinary share' is a hybrid form of share capital much loved by some venture capitalists, such as 3i. They carry the right to either fixed or variable dividends and allow the company to pay dividends on them without obliging the ordinary shareholder to take a dividend which might, for tax reasons, be unattractive to them. When converted into ordinary shares, the right to these fixed dividends is lost and the shares become 'ordinary'.

Some 85 per cent of venture capital investment is in amounts over £100 000 and the average size of financing is about £3 million. Start-up investments therefore usually involve an investment in excess of £100 000 in a business capable of generating profits in excess of £250 000 within four or five years. There are relatively few institutions that regularly invest less than £100 000. A list is given in the Appendix. The BVCA produces a free annual directory which gives a full list of venture capital institutions and their investment criteria (British Venture Capital Association, Essex House, 12–213 Essex Street, London WC2R 3AA. Tel: 0207 240 3846. Website: www.bvca.co.uk.) The BVCA also produces a very useful *Guide to Venture Capital* which explains and offers advice on the venture capital raising process and outlines what should be included in a business plan intended for venture capitalists.

Smaller amounts of equity, between about £10 000 and £100 000, are also available from individual investors – called 'business angels' – either on their own or as part of an informal syndicate. Often this investment helps take the investee business to a point at which it is attractive for a venture capital firm. The typical UK business angel makes only one or two investments a year. Many have preferences about sectors or stages (seed, start-up, early stage, expansion, management buy-out or buy-in) of investment. Most prefer local investments in companies within, say, 100 miles from where they live or work. Most also prefer to stay anonymous. However, over the past few years a number of business angel

Andrew Barber and Robin Hall left Rover, where they were design engineers, to set up their own company producing a specialist sports car – but only after they had taken the advice of their local Business Link. Originally they thought the car would sell to a mass market at a competitive price, but advisors convinced them to pitch it to a specialist market niche and charge £30 000 for the vehicle. In this case lower volume also meant higher price and lower capital needs. The Business Link also advised them where to get finance – the pair did not even have equity in their houses to offer a bank – and helped them develop and present a business plan.

Now the company has secured £240 000 from a Business Angel which it invested in premises in Brackley, Northamptonshire and tooling for the first car. Called Census, the first one is due to roll off the production line in 2001.

networks have been established which act as 'introduction services'. Some of the networks can also provide help in raising finance from other sources and in preparing a business plan for a fee. The BVCA produce a free annual list of sources of business angel capital (BVCA, 2000b). Local business angels can also be contacted through the local Business Link or Enterprise Agency, who also have their own Local Investment Network Company (LINC) that seeks to match small firms seeking funds with potential investors. Investors receive a monthly bulletin of opportunities available, submitted to LINC as business plans from small firms seeking finance.

Larger companies may also invest in smaller businesses – called corporate venturing – although this may involve a take-over or a partnership. The reasons

Julian Metcalfe and Sinclair Beecham opened their first Prêt à Manger sandwich bar in Victoria Street, central London, in 1986. They made sandwiches in the basement from fresh ingredients bought every morning at Covent Garden market. They built Prêt on the simple concept of providing gourmet, fresh and organic fast-food in modern, clean surroundings. The formula proved successful. By 2001 Prêt had 103 stores in the UK and one in New York, producing a turnover of £100 000 million and profits of £3.6 million.

But the pair had ambitious plans to expand Prêt overseas, particularly in Asia, and the experience in New York had taught them how difficult, time consuming and expensive this could be. They also wanted to launch 'Family Prêt', a similar concept but with larger, less urban shops especially for children. The problem was that they needed both cash and worldwide contacts and expertise.

Nevertheless it came as a surprise to analysts when they sold a 33 per cent stake in Prêt to McDonald's in 2001 for an estimated £26 million. The motives were, however, simple enough. McDonald's could provide not only cash but also the support for Prêt's global expansion plans and they were happy not to change the Prêt formula in any way. McDonald's, who also own the Aroma coffee-bar chain, saw this as a strategic purchase that would advance their long term strategy of gaining a greater share of the diverse informal eating-out market.

for doing so rarely involve short-term financial gain but more normally relate to issues of innovation and strategic foresight. Small firms are often good at innovation and larger firms therefore have to buy them out to capitalise on their 'first mover advantage' in a critical area of new technology development. This happens far more in the USA than in the UK with firms like General Electric, Monsanto, Xerox, Apple, IBM and Kyocera particularly active. However, there are some funds run by large companies who have other investment criteria, such as creating jobs in areas where the company has made redundancies. Corporate venturing is also be used to spin-out non-core, but still very profitable, opportunities coming from in-house research, whilst still maintaining an equity stake in the new technologies. Monsanto, Apple, 3M and Xerox have used independent venture capital conduits for this purpose. However, as Murray (1996) observes, 'corporate venturing is noteworthy by its absence rather than its popularity'.

Venture capital is a cyclical business. In the UK, the 1980s saw recession followed by several years of increased economic growth, only to be replaced by recession at the start of the 1990s. The increasing economic growth of the late 1990s led to the massive investment in technology and in particular dot.com businesses in the late 1990s only to be followed by a shake-out in 2000. Specialist dot.com venture capitalists, such as Oxygen, have evolved alongside networks, such as First Tuesday, for finding venture capital for high-technology firms (see Chapter 7). Whilst the overall provision of venture capital has grown more rapidly than the economy as a whole, its provision is highly cyclical. One effect of this is that the time at which a fund is raised and starts investing has a major impact on its profitability. Irrespective of this cyclicality, Murray (1996) has argued that the industry in the UK is reaching its maturity, which means that competition is intensifying and profitability will increasingly be squeezed, whilst the 'big players', like 3i, will consolidate their position.

Most venture capital firms will want to appoint a non-executive director to the board. Some, particularly business angels, may also expect a more a 'hands-on', day-to-day involvement in the business. However, others such as 3i, the largest venture capital provider in the UK, take a far more 'hands-off' approach and will only intervene in the management of the firm in exceptional circumstances. This is because they take a portfolio approach to their investments, diversifying the

---

Julie Meyer and **John Browning** set up **First Tuesday** in 1998. The company brings together net entrepreneurs seeking funding and venture capitalists looking to invest on the first Tuesday of each month. It started as an informal network based in London and now spans 98 cities around the world with close to 250 000 members, and has helped raise more than £100 million in seed finance. The business has been franchised around the world. First Tuesday charges a membership fee but the bulk of its income comes from a 'marriage fee' of 2 per cent of the capital raised. The average deal size is £2.5 million.

In 2000 First Tuesday was bought by Yazan, an Israeli investment company, for £34.5 million.

In 1990 **Fred Turok** remortgaged his house to buy a loss-making private gym in a basement in Victoria in London's West End for £150 000. In the first year he turned a £30 000 loss into a £150 000 profit. Two years later he bought his second club in Kingston-upon-Thames and then a third in the Minories on the fringes of the City. The fourth club that he bought in Isleworth gave him the name for his business, **LA Fitness**. He paid for that in cash, but it used up every penny he had. So far all the acquisitions had been paid for by cash flow or borrowings but the business was doing very well and the fourth gym, a new-build in Golders Green, was also funded from cash flow.

At this point Fred saw an opportunity to raise some money for growth by going to the stockmarket but the £3 million float (valuing the firm at £8 million) was only 50 per cent subscribed because another firm, Fitness First, floated just two weeks before it. Fred pulled the float and instead went to 3i who put in £1.5 million in exchange for 30 per cent of the equity.

By the time LA Fitness had secured a full stockmarket listing in October 1999, 3i had put in another £1.5 million enabling the firm to grow to 15 clubs. The float valued LA Fitness at £55 million, including £15 million of new money. In 2000 the firm made a £10 million rights issue with a view to increasing the number of clubs from 25 to 70 by 2003. It also secured new bank facilities of £15 million with a further £25 million promised.

LA Fitness made profits of £3.2 million on turnover of £15.2 million in 2000. Fred Turok is now a paper millionaire, worth over £20 million.

risks they face across industries and sectors. The role of the venture capitalist has been described as (Sapienza and Timmons, 1989):

● Offering support;
● Providing a strategic overview;
● Providing access to a larger network of business contacts.

As with bank managers, it is important to develop a close personal relationship with venture capitalists. Since they only make money if the firm succeeds, they are highly committed to helping the growing firm through the inevitable problems it will face. Many have valuable business experience, sometimes in the same business sector, and they can bring with them a wealth of business contacts. In short, used properly they can be a real asset to the firm.

The alternative investment market (AIM)

Venture capitalists may expect high returns but they realise that their main reward will come in the form of a capital gain, rather than dividend or interest payments. Consequently they normally seek to realise their investment within 10 years. Often this means going for a public listing on a stock exchange such as the Alternative Investment Market (AIM). This was launched in 1995 by the London Stock Exchange with the aim of giving smaller firms access to the stockmarket without imposing on them the rigorous reporting and control requirements demanded for a full stockmarket listing. An increasing number of companies are seeking a floatation on AIM and a recent survey claimed that it was now the most popular market for those considering floatation, with the main market suffering a significant drop in popularity (HLB Kidson, 2000).

AIM now has more than 550 quoted firms with an average market value of £29 million. To obtain a listing a firm simply needs to be incorporated and have a broker and nominated advisor who must be available at all times. Typically it takes at least six months to obtain a listing. Brokers ideally want two non-executive directors on the board to ensure a system of checks and balances. They also want some evidence of a track record that can assure them of good corporate governance. They are looking for quality of earnings – assurance that earnings will continue in the future with some degree of predictability – and prefer firms that offer some unique selling proposition rather than 'me too' companies.

> **Mears Group** floated on AIM in 1996 when it raised £950 000 and had a market capitalisation of £3.6 million, based on profits of £400 000. **Bob Holt** is Chairman and Chief Executive of the firm which provides councils with a range of building maintenance services, such as window replacement and kitchen refurbishment. He drew up a prospectus with his advisor, appointed a non-executive director and, after unsuccessfully approaching a number of brokers, found a sponsoring broker. The money raised was used to fund organic growth and acquisitions.

The costs of an AIM floatation vary widely. However, with lawyers, accountants and brokers fees plus commission together with AIM joining fee and annual charge, firms with a valuation of below £1 million are likely to find membership costs prohibitive. The disadvantage of membership is the exposure to greater outside scrutiny and the dilution of control and decision making. Any owner-manager looking for an AIM quotation simply as a badge of success must realise that there is a high price to pay for it.

The two key reasons cited in the survey for floating on AIM were to raise funds for growth and to give investors and the entrepreneur the opportunity to release personal equity. This underlines the fact that AIM can also act as the first stage in the exit route that an entrepreneur may put in place to harvest the return from their years of personal investment in their business. AIM is the first step on the route to a full stock market listing and once that happens the firm probably will have become large by any criteria.

Is there a financing gap?

The question remains as to whether there is a financing gap – defined as an unwillingness on the part of suppliers of finance to supply it on terms and conditions that owner-managers need. Owner-managers who are unsuccessful in obtaining finance will always say there is. Survey after survey of owner-managers will reveal this to be a major 'barrier to growth'. However, just because the owner-manager might want finance – on specific terms – does not necessarily mean that it should be provided – either for the good of the owner-manager, the financier or the economy as a whole.

Economists would criticise the use of the word 'gap' and prefer to use the term 'market failure' or 'credit rationing' because there may be a 'gap' even in a perfect market simply because, for example, an owner-manager is unwilling to pay higher rates of interest or investors judge a project to be too risky. The preceding analysis has shown that 'gaps' can easily arise, largely as a result of information asymmetry, the fixed costs of providing small amounts of capital, in terms of assessing the project and monitoring the investment, and the requirement of bankers for small firms or owner-managers to provide collateral. Also there is the inherent reluctance of the owner-manager to share equity in their business. The question is, however, whether there is evidence that the gap actually exists.

On the one hand there is the evidence of the numerous surveys which ask owner-managers what they perceive to be barriers to the growth of their firm. Almost inevitably lack of appropriately priced finance will be cited as a major constraint, particularly for fast-growing and newer firms. However, this proves nothing – perception is one thing and reality another. Even if accurate, the lack of appropriately priced finance for certain projects may actually indicate that the market is working perfectly well.

The fact is that numerous surveys have been unable objectively to establish that a 'gap' exists in any systematic way. A survey of 1095 small, albeit mainly innovative and growing firms by Aston Business School (1991) into growth constraints concluded that 'small firms in Great Britain apparently face few difficulties in raising finance for their innovation and investment proposals in the private sector. Most authors agree. For example, Cosh and Hughes (1994) conclude that it is 'difficult to argue that there were financial constraints on business formations as a whole in the 1980s or that there is a more pervasive market failure for small firms in the availability of funds at least in quantitative terms'. Similarly, in his review of the literature, Storey (1998) concludes that 'the major empirical studies of the UK small business sector do not suggest the existence either of market failure or credit rationing on a major scale'. He adds that 'although there are instances where small firms are unable to obtain finance in the quantities and at the price they would like, the financial institutions in the provision of both loan and equity capital have increased their involvement with the small firm sector over the last ten years'.

Summary

The basic principle of prudent financing is to match the term-duration of the source of finance with the term-duration of the use to which it is put. Fixed or permanent assets should be financed with equity, medium- and long-term bank finance, leasing or hire purchase. Working capital should be financed by short-term loans and factoring, with fluctuations financed by overdraft.

Start-ups and fast-growing firms have particular problems raising finance. To get round this, they often 'borrow' resources and, where all else fails, like **David Mulsade** and **Optical Express**, they borrow cash from family and friends. Where they do not have the track record or security to obtain bank finance they may, like **Drive Assist UK**, be eligible for the Small Firms Loan Guarantee Scheme. However, most small firms prefer to rely on their own internally generated funds to finance their growth and development rather than to seek outside finance.

As **Chauffair** found, leasing can be a particularly effective way for growing firms to finance fixed assets, matching finance with the security of the asset it purchases. Similarly, as **Software Catalogue** found, factoring, although expensive, can sometimes be the only way a growing firm can finance its way through Death Valley. **NDT** realised that if there is insufficient finance available to undertake a contract, then the company may have to walk away from it, however lucrative.

Bankers are very risk-averse. They do not share in the success of the business but stand to lose all their capital if the business fails, and therefore they will do all they can to avoid a bad debt. Small firms present a riskier lending proposition than larger firms because they have higher, mainly short-term, gearing and fewer fixed assets to offer as security in the event of a bad debt. Information asymmetry is where one party in the lending transaction has more information than the other. Where this exists, it can be expensive for banks to get the information they need to make the lending decision and then monitor the loan. Banks' reaction to this problem is to seek collateral from small firms so as to offer them security in the event of default. Since the asset base of a small, growing firm is unlikely to be able to provide this, bankers often ask for personal guarantees from the owner-manager. Financing gaps can arise as a result of information asymmetry, the fixed costs of providing small amounts of capital and the requirement of bankers for small firms or owner-managers to provide this collateral.

Bankers look at a range of financial indicators in arriving at their investment decisions but they are particularly interested in the cash flow forecast because this shows the ability of the firm to make its interest payments and repay capital. However they are also interested in a range of business and personal factors, summed up in the acronym **CAMPARI**. It is important to have a good working relationship with the banker – it helps the owner-manager obtain and maintain finance and bridge any financing gap that might exist.

Venture capital is a mix of equity and loan finance for businesses with growth potential. Whilst the UK industry is the largest after the USA, it mainly invests in established companies and management buy-outs and buy-ins. Generally, it rarely invests sums of less than £100 000 and is not keen on start-ups unless they are capable of generating profits in excess of £250 000 within four or five years. There are some venture capital organisations investing smaller sums, but most of these investments come from 'business angels'. There are also specialist dot.com investment firms such as **Oxygen** and dot.com investment networks such as **First Tuesday** – which is a successful entrepreneurial start-up in its own right. Finally, larger firms might be persuaded to invest in a small growing business if there is some strategic reason to do so. This is what happened when McDonald's bought 33 per cent of **Prêt à Manger**.

Venture capitalists rarely take a controlling interest in the firm. Typically they are looking for a 30 per cent to 60 per cent annualised return on their investment, normally taken as a capital gain in about ten years' time. As in the case of **LA Fitness**, often the capital gain is realised by taking the business to a stockmarket such as AIM and then on to a full stockmarket float. Venture capitalists typically ask to place a director on the board but some ask for a more 'hands-on' involvement in terms of day-to-day management than others.

Despite numerous 'growth constraints' surveys, it has been impossible to objectively establish that a financing gap – indicating market failure or credit rationing – exists in any systematic way in the UK.

● **Essays and discussion topics**

1 Does the financing gap still exist? If so, why? What are the likely consequences? If not, explain why.
2 What can or should the government do to improve the provision of finance to small firms?
3 How can banks improve the service they offer small firms?
4 If there is a financing gap, it is more the fault of the owner-manager than the banker. Discuss.
5 How can banking relationships be enhanced and how can they be hindered?
6 It is not fair to ask the owner-manager for personal guarantees. Discuss.
7 There is no such thing as limited liability for the owner-manager. Discuss.
8 What are venture capitalists looking for from their investments?
9 Why are MBOs and MBIs such attractive investments for venture capitalists?
10 Why do venture capitalists not invest more in start-ups?
11 Why were venture capitalists so keen to invest in dot.com start-ups?
12 Is the venture capital industry in the mature phase of its life-cycle?

● **Exercises and assignments**

1 As an owner-manager, list the pros and cons of raising equity finance.
2 As an owner-manager, list the pros and cons of raising other sources of finance.
3 Interview an owner-manager and find out how the growth and development of their firm was financed and the problems they faced in securing finance.
4 As a bank manager, list the things that you would be looking for in lending to a small firm.
5 Interview a bank manager and find out how they go about making lending decisions and monitoring outstanding loans.
6 As a venture capitalist, list the pros and cons of investing in a start-up, other early stage and expansion stage ventures.
7 Investigate the provision of bank finance for small firms in Germany. Why is the system so different to the UK? Should the UK system be changed? If so, how?
8 Investigate the provision of venture capital in the USA. Is the provision different to the UK? Should the UK system be changed? If so, how?
9 Revisit the three business plans in Chapter 8 – Sport Retail, Jean Young (Consultancy) and Dewhurst Engineering Ltd. Evaluate these lending opportunities as a banker.
10 Visit the BVCA website on *www.bvca.c.uk* and update the information on venture capital investment in the UK.
11 Visit the DTI website on *www.dti.gov.uk* and see whether there are any new initiatives to help small firms finance their growth and development.
12 Visit the DTI sponsored Enterprise Zone on *www.enterprisezone.co.uk* to see what additional sources of finance might be available.
13 Consider the case of **NDT**. In the year before the Aiton contract the company had made a profit of only £4327 on turnover of £352 516. The 12 directors were paid £182 622. NDT's balance sheet from that year is shown opposite.

   (1) Was NDT right to take the contract?
   (2) Was the bank right to do what it did?
   (3) Was the factoring company right to do what it did?
   (4) Was NDT right to pull out of the contract?
   (5) Was there any other course of action open to NDT?

FIXED ASSETS (incl. vehicles: £56 000 and building: £40 000)		£116 032
CURRENT ASSETS		
Stocks	£ 4 350	
Debtors	53 334	
Cash	9 348	67 032
CREDITORS DUE WITHIN ONE YEAR		
(incl. debenture loan: £37 700 and vehicle HP: £32 441)		(103,395)
NET CURRENT LIABILITIES		£(36 363)
TOTAL ASSETS LESS CURRENT LIABILITIES		£ 79 669
CREDITORS DUE IN MORE THAN ONE YEAR		(15 342)
		£ 64 327
Share capital		£ 60 000
Retained profit		4 327
		£ 64 327

● Start-up exercise

Undertake step 16 of the start-up exercise at the back of the book.

● Websites to visit

The following websites provide information about different sorts of financing. Visit each one to see what it contains and whether the information is relevant to your start-up or growth exercise.

- Barclays Bank: www.smallbusiness.barclays.co.uk
- NatWest Bank: www.natwest.co.uk
- HSBC: www.banking.hsbc.co.uk
- Lloyds TSB: www.lloydstsb.co.uk
- Department for Trade and Industry: www.dti.gov.uk
- Business Angels: www.businessangels.co.uk
- 3i: www.3i.com
- First Tuesday Club: www.firsttuesday.com

● References

Aston Business School (1991) *Constraints on Growth of Small Firms*, Department of Trade and Industry, London: HMSO.

Bank of England (1998) *Finance for Small Firms*, 5th Report, January.

Bannock, G. (1991) *Venture Capital and the Equity Gap*, National Westminster Bank.

Binks, M. and Ennew, C. (1996) 'Financing Small Firms', in P. Burns and J. Dewhurst (eds), *Small Business and Entrepreneurship*, Basingstoke: Macmillan – now Palgrave.

Binks, M.R., Ennew, C.T. and Reed, G.V. (1990) 'Finance Gaps and Small Firms', Royal Economics Society Annual Conference, Nottingham.

British Venture Capital Association (BVCA) (1999/2000) *Directory*.

British Venture Capital Association (2000a) *A Guide to Venture Capital*.

British Venture Capital Association, (2000b) *Sources of Business Angel Capital 1999/2000*.

Burns, P. (1985) 'Financial Characteristics of Small Firms in the UK', 8th National Small Firms Policy and Research Conference, Belfast, November.

Burns, P. (1992) *Financing Enterprise in Europe*, 3i European Enterprise Centre, Report no. 5, September.

Burns, P. and Whitehouse, O. (1995a) *Investment Criteria in Europe*, 3i European Enterprise Centre, Report no. 16, July.

Burns, P. and Whitehouse, O. (1995b) *Financing Enterprise in Europe 2*, 3i European Enterprise Centre, Report no. 17, October.

Cosh, A. and Hughes, A. (1994) 'Size, Financial Structure and Profitability: UK Companies in the 1980s', in A. Hughes and D.J. Storey (eds), *Finance and the Small Firm*, London: Routledge.

Cruickshank, D. (2000) *Review of Banking Services in the UK*, London: HMSO.

Dixon, P. (1991) 'Venture Capital and the Appraisal of Investments', *Omega*, vol. 19, no. 5.

DTI (1995) *Loan Guarantee Scheme*, URN 94/628.

DTI (1997) *Financing Your Business: A Guide to Sources of Finance and Advice*, URN 98/805.

DTI (1998) *Hire Purchase and Leasing*, URN 98/547.

HLB Kidson (2000) *Taking AIM: 4th Annual Survey*.

Hughes, A. (1992) 'The Problems of Finance for Smaller Businesses', Working Paper no. 15, Small Business Research Centre, University of Cambridge.

Jovanovic, B. (1982) 'Selection and the Evolution of Industry', *Econometrica*, vol. 50.

Macmillan, H. (1931) *Report of the Committee on Finance and Industry*, Cmd 3897, London: HMSO.

Murray, G. C. and Lott, J. (1995) 'Have UK Venture Capital Firms a Bias against Investment in New Technology Based Firms?', *Research Policy*, vol. 24.

Murray. G., (1996) 'Venture Capital', in P. Burns and J. Dewhurst (eds), *Small Business and Entrepreneurship*, Basingstoke: Macmillan – now Palgrave.

Sapienza, H. and Timmons, J.A. (1989) 'The Role of Venture Capitalists in New Ventures. What determines their Importance?', *Academy of Management Best Papers Proceedings*.

Stiglitz, J. and Weiss, A. (1981) 'Credit Rationing in Markets with Imperfect Information' *American Economic Review*, vol. 71.

Storey, D.J. (1998) *Understanding the Small Business Sector*, London: International Thompson Business Press.

Appendix: Sources of venture capital under £100 000

British Steel (Industry) Ltd
The Innovation Centre
217 Portobello Street
Sheffield S1 4DP
Tel: 0114 273 1612

Cambridge Research & Innovation Ltd
13 Station Road
Cambridge CB1 2JB
Tel: 01223 312856

Centreway Development Capital Ltd
Griffin House
9 Coventry Road
Coleshill
Birmingham B46 3BB
Tel: 01675 466796

Compass Investment Management Ltd
17-18 Dover Street
London W1X 4DQ
Tel: 0207 409 0014

Derbyshire Enterprise Board
95 Sheffield Road
Chesterfield
Derbyshire S41 7JH
Tel: 01246 207390

Donbac Ltd
Enterprise House
White Rose Way
Doncaster DN4 5ND
Tel: 01302 76100

Egan & Talbot Capital Ltd
Buckden Wood
Perry Road
Buckden
Huntingdon PE18 9XQ
Tel: 01480 812218

Enterprise Ventures Ltd
Enterprise House
17 Ribblesdale Place
Winckley Square
Preston PR1 3NA
Tel: 01772 203020

Equity Ventures Ltd
Du Pont House
Bristol Business Park
Bristol BS16 1QD
Tel: 01772 203020

Industrial Technology Securities Ltd
Surrey Technology Centre
Surrey Research Park
Guildford
Surrey GU2 5YG
Tel: 01483
457398

Lothian Enterprises Ltd
Geddes House
Kirkton North
Livingston EH54 6GU
Tel: 01506 415144

Midland Enterprise Fund for the South East
The Cadmus Organisation Ltd
Kings Business Centre
Reeds Lane
Sayers Common
West Sussex BN6 9LS
Tel: 01273 835455

Northern Enterprise Ltd
6th floor
Cale Cross House
156 Pilgrim Street
Newcastle upon Tyne NE1 6SU
Tel: 0191 233 1892

Seed Capital Ltd (Oxford Technology VCT)
The Magdalen Centre
The Oxford Science Park
Oxford OX4 4GA
Tel: 01865 784466

Transatlantic Capital Ltd
17 Devonshire Street
London W1N 2EY
Tel: 0207 436 1216

Yorkshire Fund Managers Ltd
St Martins House
210-212 Chapeltown Road
Leeds LS7 3HZ
Tel: 0113 294 5000

Industrial Development Board for Northern Ireland
Corporate Finance Division
IDB House
64 Chichester Street
Belfast BT1 4JX
Tel: 02890 233233

London Ventures (Fund Managers) Ltd
3rd floor
13-14 Golden Square
London W1R 3AG
Tel: 0207 434 2425

Loxko Venture Manbagers Ltd
6 Adam Street
London WC2N 6AA
Tel: 0207 240 5024

Midland Venture Fund Managers Ltd
The Square
Beeston
Nottingham NG9 2JG
Tel: 0115 967 8400

Scottish Enterprise
120 Bothwell Street
Glasgow G2 7JP
Tel: 0141 248 2700

South West Investment Group Ltd
Trevint House
Strangways Villas
Truro
Cornwall TR1 2PA
Tel: 01872 223883

Wales Fund Managers Ltd
50 Cathedral Road
Cardiff CF1 9LL
Tel: 02920 230490

chapter thirteen

The family firm

Contents

- The advantages of family
- Family business is big business
- A conflict of cultures
- Succession
- Points of conflict
- The introvert firm
- Resolving conflict
- Managing succession
- Summary

Learning outcomes

By the end of this chapter you should:

- Understand the significance of family firms in the business world;
- Appreciate the advantages and disadvantages of being part of a family firm;
- Appreciate the conflict of cultures between family and business;
- Have a framework for identifying points of conflict within the family firm, how they arise and how they might be resolved;
- Understand what is meant by an introvert firm and appreciate the dangers it faces;
- Have a framework to help understand the problems of succession within family firms;
- Have a framework for planning succession;
- Understand what goes into a family strategic plan and how it might be developed;
- Understand what goes into a succession plan and how it might be developed.

The advantages of family

Starting up a business on your own can be a stressful, lonely way to make money. Many people start up a business with friends – they are known and trusted and may well possess complimentary skills. So why not start up a business with the family? Trust is something that there is in abundance – particularly between husband and wife – and if all the family's income depends on the success of the venture then there is no doubting that the motivation to succeed will be strong, although this should be tempered with the recognition of the risk of having only one source of family income. There is the added advantage for husband and wife of giving each other support and friendship and working long hours may not be such a grind when with your partner. What is more, getting the whole family to help with the work brings an added resource to the firm – and one that may not have to be paid a wage.

Husband and wife teams, like Anita and Gordon Roddick of Body Shop, can work very successfully. For some couples being together all the time can help in their personal as well as business relationships; for others it might be a recipe for divorce and business failure. As with many issues relating to the family firm, there are few hard and fast rules. Conflict is most likely to arise in making decisions and here clear role definition and a separation between work and home are important. Based upon interviews with husband and wife teams in the USA, Nelton (1986) suggested that the successful teams shared the following characteristics:

● Marriage and children came first;
● The partners had enormous respect for each other;
● There was close communication between partners;
● Partners' talents and attitudes were complementary;
● Partners defined their individual responsibilities carefully;
● Partners competed with other companies, not each other;
● Partners kept their egos in check.

There is no theoretical justification for or clear evidence that family firms outperform non-family firms. Nevertheless, family firms have their advantages. Leach (1996) lists seven:

1 *Commitment*: family enthusiasm and family ties can develop added commitment and loyalty;
2 *Knowledge*: special ways of doing things in the business can be coveted and protected within the family;
3 *Flexibility in time, work and money*: putting work and time into the business when necessary and taking money out when the business can afford it rather than according to the dictate of a contract;
4 *Long-range planning*: because the firm is seen as the family's main store of value, something to be passed onto the next generation, family firms are better than others at taking a long-term view, although this may not involve formal planning processes;
5 *A stable culture*: relationships in family firms have had a long time to develop and the company's ethics and working practices are therefore stable and well established;
6 *Speedy decision-making*: like owner-managed companies, family firms can make decisions quickly because of the short lines of responsibility;
7 *Reliability and pride*: because of the commitment and the stability of their culture family firms can be very solid and reliable structures that, over time, build up good reputations with customers, reputations that the family guard with fierce pride;

> 'Inevitably when you are talking about family businesses there is a sense of generation. There has to be something to hand down, which is the greater shareholder argument of the long-term view. Other sorts of business may have different time horizons.'
>
> **Sir Adrian Cadbury,**
> *The Times* 8.07.00

> 'The continued strength of the Baxter's brand springs from the knowledge, involvement, passion and standards of the Baxter family. We determine the priorities and destiny of the company and so ensure that our family values are always reflected in all the products bearing the Baxter name.'
>
> **Audrey Baxter,**
> MD, **Baxter's Soups**
> *The Times* 8.07.00

Traditionally family businesses have been important in many primary sectors, such as farming. They also tend to thrive in areas such as hotels and restaurants, where high levels of personal service are required. The retail sector – butchers, bakers, florists, corner stores and so on – also boasts a large number of family firms. Family firms are also to be found in the cash generating food-processing industry. Finally there are many in the supply industries like transport and distributorships, especially in the motor sector.

Family business is big business

It is estimated that as many as 70 per cent of all UK businesses are family owned and they employ 50 per cent of the country's workforce (Institute for Small Business Affairs, 1999). In the European Union the proportion of family firms is claimed to be 85 per cent, whilst in the USA the proportion is as high as 90 per cent (Poutziouris and Chittenden, 1996). What is more, the stereotypical image of family living above the shop does not do the sector credit. They are not all small, lifestyle firms. Family-owned companies account for a substantial proportion of the value of the stockmarket. In the USA, family firms – where a family own more than a quarter of the shares – represent more than a third of the Fortune 500 (Leach, 1996). In Europe the pattern is similar. But most family firms – of any size – are privately owned.

> **Mars Inc.** is the seventh largest private company in the USA with income of over $15 billion a year from global brands such as Mars Bar, Milky Way and M&Ms. It is a second (arguably third) generation family firm – a family that is one of the richest in the world. Founded by **Forrest Mars Snr**, who died in 1999, it is now run by his sons Forrest Jr and John. Forrest Mars Snr was born into a confectionery making family in 1904. His father, Frank, ran a modestly successful business in Minnesota where he made candies overnight and his wife, Ethel, sold them from a trolley the next day. They had two main products, the Mar-O-Bar and Victoria Butter Creams, which became successful in 1923 when Woolworths started distributing it.
>
> Forrest Mars Snr claimed that the idea for the family's first really successful product, the Milky Way, came to him whilst sitting drinking a chocolate malt drink in a cafe and he suggested to his father that he should put it into a chocolate bar. Some time later, his father did just that, putting caramel on top of and chocolate around it. Milky Way was a huge success with sales of $800 000 in its first year. The family moved to Chicago and Frank built a mansion in Wisconsin. However, relations between father and son deteriorated as Forrest wanted further growth and expansion but Frank wanted to settle for an easy life.
>
> In 1932 Forrest left to set up a one-room chocolate business in Slough, England. He quickly produced a similar product to Milky Way, calling it a Mars Bar, using creamier milk chocolate and a sweeter toffee filling. The Mars Bar is a very British product, unknown in the USA. The company returned to the USA in the late 1930s with the hugely successful M&Ms, the candy 'that melts in your mouth, not in your hand'.
>
> *. . . to be continued*

Family firms have some of the strongest brands in business today. Mars, Lego and Levi Strauss are global brands and remain private, family companies. In Britain many family firms are household names – R. Griggs Group (maker of the famous Doc Martens boots, founded 1901), J. Barbour & Sons (maker of the very British waxed jackets, founded in 1894), Wilkin & Sons (maker of the famous Tiptree jams founded in 1885), Morgan Motor Company (maker of Morgan sports cars, founded in 1909 and the world's oldest privately owned car manufacturer) and Quad Electroacoustics (maker of distinctive hi-fi equipment, founded in 1936). However, until it merged with Schweppes in 1969, probably the best-known family firm in Britain was the chocolate and cocoa manufacturer J. Cadbury & Sons, founded in 1924.

Not only have these firms been around a long time, but also the values and beliefs on which they were established are well-known and respected. Familial brands build consumer trust over long periods and can be very valuable assets.

Indeed, many of the best-known brands today started out as family firms before becoming public companies. For example, the H J Heinz company was in family hands until 1946, when it went public. It was founded in 1888, although Henry J. Heinz started producing bottled condiments from 1869. Many companies still have links with the founding family. For example, the Ford Motor Company was launched by Henry Ford in a converted wagon factory in Detroit in 1903. His great grandson, William Ford Jr was appointed chairman in 1998. The Disney Corporation is the largest entertainment conglomerate in the world. The vice-chairman, Roy E. Disney, is a descendent of the original Disney family and is the main principle shareholder.

Cadbury merged with Schweppes in 1969, but the original family business was very much based on Quaker values and ideals. Founded by **John Cadbury** in 1824, the original shop sold drinking chocolate as a virtuous alternative to alcohol. In 1834 the firm started manufacturing drinking chocolate and cocoa.

John Cadbury's sons, George and Richard, saw the real expansion of the business. Whilst Richard concentrated on marketing, including the box designs for their chocolates, George concentrated on production. It was he who founded the now legendary Bournville factory and the picturesque village with its red-brick terraces, cottages, duck ponds and wide open park lands. Not only were workers given a fair day's pay, they were also rewarded with homes and education for their children.

Sir Adrian Cadbury, now sitting at the head of the chocolate-making family, has little to do with the company that was handed down from generation to generation for almost 200 years. However, he still believes that the closeness of family ties and the values that lie behind them are important. He even claims to sign his name in a strikingly similar way to the company's trademark name. While there is no longer a Cadbury on the executive board of Cadbury Schweppes – Dominic, Sir Adrian's brother was the last – Mathew, Sir Adrian's 41-year-old son, is a development director for Cadbury Schweppes in the USA.

The family firm has been the backbone of many continental European economies for decades. None more so than Italy where names like Agnelli, Pirelli and De Benedetti have long controlled large parts of Italy's industry. Because of the historically strong family networks, Italian owner-managers have been loath to surrender even part of the equity capital of their firms to investors and non-family managers have rarely received shares or share options.

But all this begs the question of what constitutes a family business. Essentially a family business is one that is owned or controlled by one family, although researchers have suggested many more precise definitions, for example:

1   An owner-managed enterprise with family members predominantly involved in its administration, operations and the determination of its destiny. Family members may include parents, children and grand-children; spouses; brothers, sisters and cousins (Poutziouris, 1994).
2   A company in which majority ownership (in terms of shares) or control lies in a single family and in which two or more family members are, or at some time were, directly involved in the business (Rosenblatt *et al.*, 1985).
3   For a quoted company, one in which 25 per cent of voting shares are controlled by the family (Nelton, 1986).

The search for a precise definition could be endless and rather fruitless. Probably the real answer is to ask the family. If family members are involved in the firm and feel a responsibility for it, then that is a good indication that it is a family business. They will probably say it is anyway. One of the overriding characteristics of the family business is the atmosphere of belonging and common purpose. Just as the small firm has the personality of the owner-manager imprinted on it, so the culture of the family is imprinted on the family firm. Rather than 'two arms, two legs and a giant ego', you have many arms, legs and egos. It is no wonder that the *Spectator* magazine once described the family business sector as 'an endless soap opera of patriarchs and matriarchs, black sheep and prodigal sons, hubris and nemesis'. And there you have the problem.

A conflict of cultures

At the heart of the family firm are its distinctive values and beliefs – its culture. Often the family culture can strengthen the business. For example, many successful family firms such as J. Cadbury & Sons and Wilkin & Sons were built around strong religious ethics whereby the success of the firm was shared with the workforce. In many ways the workforce becomes an extended family and relationships are cemented with trust and respect for the founding family. Families can display their values and beliefs in all sorts of quirky ways in the family firm. Sometimes these are good for the firm. They can bring clear values, beliefs and a focused direction. However, they can also bring a lack of professionalism, nepotism rather than meritocracy, rigidity and family conflict or feuding into the workplace. Any consultant who has worked with family firms realises how important it is to understand the family politics if they are to understand how the business operates.

Whilst family culture can be a tremendous asset for the firm, it can also create the potential for conflict. The problem arises when there are differences between

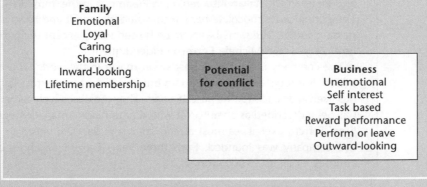

Figure 13.1 Family vs business cultures

the family and business cultures. Families exist primarily to take care and to nurture family members, whereas firms exist to profitably generate goods and services. Represented in Figure 13.1, the family culture is based on emotion emphasising loyalty, caring and sharing. It is inward-looking and lasts a lifetime. In contrast, business culture is unemotional, task-orientated and is based on self-interest. It is outward-looking, rewarding performance and penalising lack of performance. Conflict between the two cultures is unlikely at start-up but, as the firm grows and time passes, the potential for conflict increases.

The emotion-based family culture operates at a subconscious level. There are deep emotional ties that create love, trust and loyalty; but equally there can be disruptive influences like divorce, rivalry between brothers or conflict between son and father. Whilst families are

Wilkin & Sons is a family-owned business founded in 1885 and best known for its luxury Tiptree jams which sell to over 50 countries. The more esoteric jams such as 'Little Scarlet Strawberry' have attained almost a cult status among jam lovers.

The company is committed to sharing success with its workforce. At the company's 450 hectare estate at Tiptree in Essex, managers and directors test products as well as man the production lines when required. More than 100 of the 180 workforce live in houses owned by the firm. It has operated a non-contributory pension scheme for over a century. The firm has also created a trust which will eventually leave employees with a 51 per cent shareholding in the firm.

There is another ethical dimension to the firm. It has never borrowed and does not want to.

based on permanence and stability, entrepreneurial firms are based on opportunity and change. Even the positive influences of the family may be bad for the business, for example, when parental pride and loyalty gets in the way of objectivity and a son or daughter is appointed to a management position they do not have the skills to undertake. If there is a conflict of interest between the family

Ferrero Rocher is a truly European family firm. It was founded by two brothers Piera and Pietro in the Italian Alba region in Piedmont in the immediate post war years. They produced a chocolate bar which included nougat and hazel nuts and called it passa giadujot. The same basic recipe is used today except the current head of the firm, 74 year old **Michele Ferrero**, added liqueur.

The company is the fifth-largest sweet maker in the world with turnover of £2.4 billion. It is registered in Amsterdam but has 16 factories across Europe. The family has lived in Brussels for the past 25 years. They are obsessively secretive and Michele has been described as an autocrat with a paternalistic management style. Every 29 June, Ferrero executives must attend church in San Domenico to honour the day the company was founded. Each three years Ferrero organises a pilgrimage to Lourdes for all its 13 000 workers.

and the firm, for example in making the dividend payment that the family expects but the firm can ill afford, whose interest comes first? And the very closeness of the family can create an impenetrable barrier for the non-family manager who might feel 'passed-over' for promotion in favour of family or feel left out of the decision-making that seems to take place 'around the kitchen table'.

Family culture even influences the management style within a family firm. Research by Ram and Holliday (1993) suggests that family firms tend to adopt a style of 'negotiated paternalism'. Because of the relationships between family members, family businesses tend to use fewer formal management techniques. Family influence acts to dilute managerial power and discretion, with family members often able to negotiate their duties. In the researchers' opinion this can constrain operating efficiency and lead to management practices that are 'sub-optimal'.

What is more, business can influence the culture within the family. Indeed business can exact a toll on family life. The separation between the two can become very blurred in a family firm. Building a successful business can become

Mars Inc. is a very secretive company. The founder, **Forrest Mars Snr**, was a recluse and his sons shun public life. They also live and work with a frugality that is in stark contrast to many modern firms. The company is run according to a 24-page booklet which codifies Forrest Snr's management philosophy. These are called 'The five principles of Mars'. They are: Quality, Responsibility, Mutuality, Efficiency and Freedom.

All employees are known as 'Associates' and are on first name terms. Everyone from the top to the bottom have to punch their time-cards daily and receive a 10 per cent bonus for punctuality. There are no company perks such as cars, reserved parking or executive toilets. Indeed, no one even has a private office. Memos are against company policy. Meetings take place 'as needed'. Elaborate presentations are seen as a waste of time. All employees must do their own photocopying, make their own telephone calls and travel economy class on planes. John and Forrest Jr share a secretary with their sister, Jacqueline.

Moss Bros became a public company in 1950 after 100 years as a family concern. Founded in 1850 by Moses Moss, the great-grandfather of **Monty Moss** the current President of the company.

Originally Moses bought second-hand clothes, job lots and bespoke suits that customers did not collect. He filled the gaps in his stock with suits made in Savile Row during the quiet season. He would then sell-on his stocks throughout Britain. His two sons, George and Alfred, came into the business in 1897, when the Moss Bros name was formed. It was shortly after this that the brothers stumbled on a major element of their business – hiring clothes – when an eccentric stockbroker, turning to entertainment when his business failed, found he did not have a dress suit to wear because his own was in pawn and borrowed one from Alfred. Their reputation, initially was spread by word of mouth.

Alfred, the entrepreneurial one, built the business steadily until the 1930s when he began handing it over to George's son, Harry. Harry continued until the early 1970s with Alfred's son Basil and his own son, Monty eventually taking over as joint MDs.

There were always non-family members on the Board, but in 1970 the first of them, Harry Vanson, was appointed as joint MD and in 1976 became sole MD, with Basil as Chairman and Monty as Vice-Chairman. In 1988 they joined forces with Cecil Gee and Rowland Gee became MD. In effect, it became a two family business because Basil's son, Peter, also became Deputy Chairman and Monty's son, David, became Executive Director. Michael and Cecil Gee are also Board members.

an obsessive, single-minded occupation that drives family life into the shadows, creating tensions at home as well as at work. Married couples working together may feel unable ever to 'get away from the shop' and let the stress and tension of growing a business damage their personal relationship. Conflict at work – and there will be conflict in any growing business – may continue at home, feeding on itself and intensifying. A husband and wife team that divorce will find it difficult to continue working together. To survive, a family must learn to separate family and business life. Business and family issues need to be addressed directly, but in an open and balanced way that allows the business to be run properly whilst not disrupting family harmony. This is not always easy.

Succession

The old adage 'from clogs to clogs in three generations' is definitely true in relation to family firms. With each successive generation the survival rate diminishes. Poutziouris and Chittenden (1996) observe that:

Four out of five family businesses are managed by the first generation, which benefits from the entrepreneurial drive of the founder. However, less than one third of founders successfully pass ownership and management control of the family business to the second generation. Only 10 per cent of second generation family firms are transferred to third generation and less than 5 per cent ever reach beyond the third generation of family management.

However, not all owner-managers want to establish dynastic family firm. A large scale survey by Burns and Whitehouse (1996) found that only 32 per cent of British owner-managers wanted to pass their business on within the family, most (68 per cent) preferring to sell the firm, most commonly to a trade buyer, in order to make a capital gain. This contrasted strongly with Germany (57 per cent), Italy (62 per cent) and Spain (74 per cent) where most owner-managers wanted to keep the firm in the family. The same study showed that most owner-managers who inherited their firm wanted to pass it on to their children.

Figure 13.2 shows a life-cycle framework originally developed by Churchill and Hatten (1987) to aid the understanding of family business dynamics during the process of succession and transfer of power. The model suggests that changes in management, strategy and control can be planned and executed but are shaped by family relationships and driven by the inexorable human life-cycle. In the model the life-cycle of two generations is expressed as the level of influence a family member has on the strategic orientation and operations of the business, during the phases of family business development. Essentially it is a four-stage model that repeats, with increasing complexity as new generations join the firm.

Stage 1   *Owner-managed business* This is the early stage, beyond start-up, when the founder is in control but a son or daughter are introduced into the business on a permanent basis.

Stage 2   *Training and development of the new generation*   This is the stage where decisions are made, although not always formally, about passing the business on to the son or daughter and a process of training and development should be taking place to groom them for their role.

Stage 3   *Partnership* This is the stage when the son or daughter shows sufficient business acumen and expertise that the founder starts to loosen the reins of control, delegates authority and starts to share responsibility with them.

Stage 4   *Power transfer* This is the phase when strategic planning, management control and operational responsibility shifts from one generation to another. The succession process accelerates as the founder begins to retire and reduces their active participation in the business.

Points of conflict

Would that succession were usually so systematic and trouble-free. It is not. The problems arise in the areas marked as 'anomalies' in Figure 13.2. Although daughters are being brought increasingly into the family business, the most common relationship revolves around father and son. Many father–son relationships can work extremely well but psychologists tell us that this relationship has a unique potential for conflict. If you revisit the personal qualities likely to be present in the entrepreneurial founder, detailed in Chapter 2, you will realise that he is likely to have a very close emotional link with the business. He is likely to see it as an extension of himself, a symbol of his achievement, even an extension of his masculinity. He may guard power jealously and have problems with delegation. He may want to facilitate his son's succession but he may also want to control it. Subconsciously he may feel the need to be stronger than, and in control of, his son and succession may be seen as

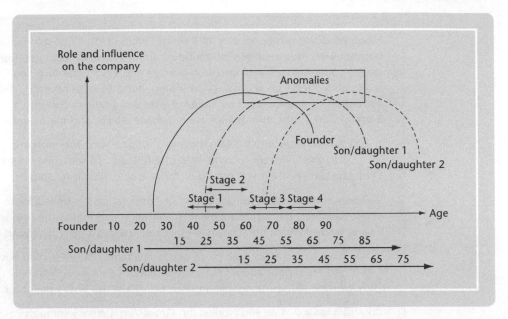

Figure 13.2   The family business life-cycle

a 'threat' to his masculinity. This can result in rivalry between father and son, each trying to be the dominant character.

From the son's perspective things are different. We are told that rebellion is natural in youth but, although it is tolerated and sometimes encouraged at home, at work it is something that is normally repressed. Even in its mildest form, this natural tendency will show itself in an increasing drive for independence from father. But if father is also the boss, there is potential for conflict, particularly if father is himself having problems delegating control. So the scene is set with a rebellious son, pressing for more power within the firm, seemingly opposed by a father who, at the same time, is saying that he wants to pass the business on to the son. To the son, the father may appear to be hanging on to power and he may begin to doubt whether father really will retire. In fact he may even begin to distrust his father, and that is the start of the end of the relationship. At the very least, the contradictory signals from the father are likely to lead to frustration in the son. What is more, for the son the option of leaving the business is problematic as it might be seen as disloyalty to the family.

With this high potential for conflict, it is a good idea to revisit Chapter 9 which gave us an insight into how conflict can be handled. Competing will simply intensify the conflict. Accommodating may result in the issues not being properly addressed. Worst of all is avoidance. Levinson (1983) describes how avoidance might show itself in the actions of the father. For example, the father may cultivate an atmosphere of ambiguity in decision making where rules and boundaries are unclear and he can 'meddle', in this way avoiding any overt conflict. Alternatively he may defer decisions until the last possible moment. Avoidance is often the approach adopted because addressing the business issues may lead to conflict which might in turn damage the father–son relationship. As we saw in Chapter 9, conflict is rarely best handled through avoidance, but rather through collaboration or compromise.

Noon Products was bought by W T Foods Group in 1999 but still remains a family business with four members of the board from the family business, four from the parent company and with one non-executive director. The firm produces Indian food for a range of customers including Birds Eye, Sainsbury's, Waitrose and Somerfield. It was founded by **Gulam Noon** and both his daughters, Zeenat and Zarmin, work in the firm as well as his brother, Akbar, and nephew, Nizar.

You have to work with the family in a professional way. The most important thing . . . is to give them the job and resist interfering . . . If someone doesn't come up to expectation, then you get rid of them, don't allow it to drag on.

Zeenat is responsible for packaging of temperature-controlled food. She is the eldest daughter, has a management qualification and joined the firm at the start, having worked with a hotel chain in India and just had a baby. She is on the Board.

You have to prove yourself more when its a family business. You have to show that you are serious about your job and about your career. You only get respect by working alongside people and not being just the boss's daughter.

Zarmin has a degree and worked for a travel firm before joining the business. She is director of Noon Restaurants, a separate enterprise.

It was quite a culture shock coming into the family business. My father lets you get on with it, but he likes to see the figures. You're not expected to go to him with small problems . . . unless you come up against a brick wall. But even then he'd prefer you to break through it yourself.

Family Business
The Stoy Centre for Family Business
vol. 8, issue 1, 2000

Leach (1996) claims that father–daughter relationships are less problematic:

Fathers seem more able to accept advice about the business and some criticism from daughters, and they often say that they would react to sons saying the same thing as if it were a personal attack.

He observes that fathers do not feel threatened by daughters, and daughters are more accommodating, being brought up to be more nurturing, attuned to emotional needs and giving priority to family harmony. Perhaps that is changing.

Nevertheless this may give us an insight into mother–son relationships in the family firm, about which there is little research. There is even less research into mother–daughter relationships. Indeed the assumed relationship in most of the literature is that of a patriarchal hierarchy within the family firm. We know next to nothing about the influences of an extended family, except in the context of ethnicity, or the development of new forms of families, such as those based upon gay relationships. Perhaps the future will see a redefinition of the term 'family firm'.

There can be yet another layer of complexity to the problems facing the family firm, this time caused by sibling rivalry. Sibling rivalry is normal, but some parents actively encourage it, particularly in the context of the family firm. If a number of sons and/or daughters work in the firm there may be rivalry between them as they vie for favour in the eyes of the father or mother. The custom of favouring elder sons with respect to inheritance, although in decline, still shows itself when it comes to succession in the family firm. Elder sons may be favoured at the expense of daughters or younger sons who may be more able. This can lead to the best talent leaving the family business or the brothers or sisters trying to carve out niches for themselves in the business to establish their independence. Even if the business is split equally between the children, there is the danger of sibling rivalry becoming institutionalised in the firm.

The introvert firm

All businesses must adapt and change to meet the demands of a changing marketplace, but there is a danger that family firms will become moribund and unable or unwilling to respond with each succeeding generation. Many firms do, of course, adapt. However some become increasingly introvert. They become inward-looking, unresponsive to messages from the marketplace and unreceptive to new ideas, they might even become unwilling to recruit managers from outside the firm or, worse still, from outside the family. How does this come about?

Families can become distracted from business for a number of reasons. Disagreement between family members might paralyse decision making within the firm. Avoidance behaviour in the extreme might lead to important business issues not being addressed. Damage done to the firm and relationships within it by the traumatic succession from one generation to another might leave it weak and, like the rabbit caught in the headlights of the car, traumatised. The past success of the firm which has led to increased prosperity for the family might itself cause problems. The family might start to regard the firm as their main store of wealth demanding regular dividends when the firm can ill-afford them, imposing restrictions on commercial decisions that reflect their risk aversion or vetoing capital investment decisions because it would drain cash flow. The family might also start to view the firm as a milk cow draining the cash away through expense

The family business of **J & B Wild** has had a stall in Manchester's New Smithfield Fish Market for 100 years. However, it has had to adapt and change in order to stay in business. Originally, it sold British white fish, made popular with the growth of fish and chip shops. Today British white fish is hard to find, fish and chip shops are in decline and the family has had to develop new products and find new customers just to survive.

Many years ago it started selling chicken, mainly to Indian restaurants in the area. It still sells fish, but most fish is now foreign, flown in from around the world. Most fish is now sold filleted. J & B Wild has developed a reputation for stocking a wide variety of 'exotic' fish which are sold mainly to Chinese restaurants. Fish has now become a food that is susceptible to fashions and fads and the family have to keep on top of market trends.

accounts, pensions, cars and other perks or 'jobs for the family'. Borrowings might be vetoed because the family do not want their main store of wealth and source of income to be exposed to any form of risk or the possibility that they might lose control. All of these things damage the business and can mean that it is not doing what it is supposed to do, that is, profitably generate goods and services.

This can be compounded by a sense of alienation felt by non-family members as they see cash being squandered, no decisions or bad decisions being made. The continuous conflict may make them feel uneasy and unsure about the future direction of the firm. They may feel forced to take sides when they do not wish to. They may feel that they are not part of the decision-making at all or that family considerations are always paramount. They may feel passed over for promotion in favour of less able family members. They might feel that there is no system for adequately rewarding them for the good work they do, for example, by taking some equity in the firm, because the family would not countenance losing control. Indeed the family might actively discourage or prohibit the employment of non-family managers.

Many of these issues come down to the business no longer having clear leadership. Second-generation firms might have a board comprising three brothers or sisters each with equal shareholdings and none with clear control. None of them might possess the entrepreneurial spirit of the founder. To compound the problem, they may all hate each other and be unable to agree on anything. To avoid this catastrophe family firms need ways of resolving family conflict and managing succession. They also need to reward and promote family employees strictly in line with their contribution to the firm and regularly and objectively evaluate the performance of all staff. Delegation outside the family should be taking place and being a member of the family should not be part of the criteria for promotion or appointment. In other words, family business management needs to be seen to be objective for the good of the firm and its family and non-family employees alike.

Resolving conflict

Arguably, the only real way to resolve conflict in the family firm is to resolve conflict in the family – a very tall order indeed. However, confining ourselves to business, the key to conflict resolution is communication and the appropriate style is one of collaboration or compromise. Admitting and, most importantly, understanding the nature and cause of the problem is a good first step. Understanding that many of the problems come from our genetic make-up should help to defuse the situation and make it less personal. Understanding how individuals naturally react to conflict (remember Thomas–Kilman conflict modes) can help explain why arguments happen. With a will, behaviours can be modified. With particularly difficult situations a third-party facilitator – a friend or professional mediator or counsellor – might help. However, the British are known for avoiding sensitive personal and family issues and difficulties.

Leach (1996) advocates the development of a family strategic plan which should be articulated in a written constitution that sets out the family's values and policies in relation to the business. He advocates a four stage process:

1 Addressing the critical issues relating to family involvement in the business. This involves looking critically at the business and the family and how they relate. How are conflicts between family and business interests to be resolved?

2 Establishing a family council to provide a forum in which members can air their views and participate in policy making. The council should develop ground rules as to how it should operate.

3 Drawing up a family constitution which involves developing a written statement of the family's values and beliefs and going on to develop policies and objectives. Does the family have any shared values and beliefs in relation to the business? What does the family want from the business? What is the involvement of family to be? Does the family wish to retain control of the firm? What should be the criteria for family entry into the firm? What is the management succession policy? Should family members who are active in the business be treated differently from those who are not? Who might own shares in the business and how might shares be disposed of? What should the dividend policy be? A checklist of what might go into a family constitution is shown in Table 13.1.

4 Monitoring the family's progress and maintaining regular communication within the family through regular council meetings.

Leach also advocates giving sons or daughters managerial autonomy within part of the business to help them grow and mature; separating out roles for other members of the family so as to minimise sibling rivalry. Many writers advocate the use of non-executive directors on the boards of family companies. They can

Everard Breweries is a family company that was founded in Leicestershire in 1849. It brews beers such as Tiger Best Bitter, Beacon Bitter and Everard Original from its Castle Acre site near Leicestershire and has a pub and hotel estate of over 150 units.

The fifth generation chairman is **Richard Everard**. He sees himself as the 'custodian' of the family assets in the business. The family objectives are the driving force behind the philosophy and resulting strategy of the firm. When he became chairman he sat down with the family and outlined their objectives and set about changing the business strategy to reflect them. Now the emphasis is on property and brewing accounts for only 30 per cent of turnover.

> We are fortunate in that we only ever had small families and only one surviving son per generation. After five generations, 90 per cent of the shares are held by only two family members . . . There is a rule that only one family member can have an executive position on the board in any one generation . . . We do not offer share options to attract senior people. That would be against our philosophy. . . I see my custodianship lasting another twenty years, but should anything happen to me I have left clear instructions on how the next generation should be trained for the position. This would include at least four years external training.

Family Business
The Stoy Centre for Family Business
vol. 7, issue 3, 1999

Table 13.1   The family constitution checklist

- Family values, beliefs and philosophy
- Family objectives in relation to the business
- Family involvement in the business – share ownership and disposal, voting and control
- Family involvement in the business – board membership, voting
- Family involvement in the business – selection of chairman and managing director
- Family involvement in the business – jobs and remuneration
- Family council meetings
- Procedures for changing the constitution

be the insurance against companies becoming too introvert. They can bring balance to board-room discussions and should be relied on to put the firm, not the family, first. In that sense they bring independence to meetings and can help resolve family squabbles. Alongside this they bring their own particular expertise and a new network of contacts.

Managing succession

The usual approach to managing succession is to ignore the issue and do nothing. It is almost as if owner-managers, particularly founders, are in denial about ever leaving the firm. It is a blind spot that they do not wish to discuss – a little like death. They are reluctant to relinquish power and control, they fear that doing so will somehow reflect on them, diminishing their status, identity and masculinity. Sometimes planning involves making unwelcome decisions that might upset the

Blackpool Pleasure Beach is a family business. **Geoffrey Thompson** has been Managing Director since 1976. Born in 1936 he is the grandson of the founder, William George Bean. His mother, Doris Thompson, born in 1903, is Chairman and still comes into the business every day, has lunch and signs cheques. All three children work in the business. The eldest is Amanda who is President of Stageworks Worldwide Productions, which presents stage and ice spectaculars at the pleasure beach.

Geoffrey is quite a workaholic but in 1997, at the age of 61, he had a stroke. Never daunted, he was soon back to work. Amanda says that her father has been a huge influence on her life and is concerned:

Daddy's working very hard again and he gets tired. Everyone asks him who's going to take over, but I know he wants to be in the company for ever . . . I've realised that nobody makes a decision without speaking to him first . . .I don't think daddy will ever come to terms with the fact that he might not be here for ever. But whatever happens, he's instilled his vision into all three of us that this will remain a family business.

The Sunday Times Magazine 23.07.00

family, particularly if it means selecting a successor from members of the family. Founders often fear retirement – the lack of activity, purpose, status, independence – and often typical entrepreneurs are so single-minded that they do not have other outside interests. However, if succession is not planned and managed it can be a traumatic and stressful event which might threaten the very existence of the firm.

Actually passing on the business within the family is just one of the options open to the founder. The other options are:

- *Trade sale* Competitors may be interested to buy the business as a going concern, generating cash or shares for the founder and the family. This may be attractive if cash is needed for retirement or other family reasons. It might also be just the right time to get a very good deal, for example because of consolidation in the industry. It might simply be that the business has become less attractive or more risky than when the founder set it up and there are better new opportunities for children.
- *Management buy-out* If there is a strong management team in the firm they might be interested to bid for the firm if they can arrange funding.
- *Management buy-in.* An external management team might be persuaded to bid for the firm, again, as a going concern.
- *Appoint a professional manager* With this option the family remain as shareholders and probably non-executive directors, receiving dividends and hoping to see the value of the business grow,
- *Appoint a caretaker manager* If the founder wishes to pass on the firm but the son or daughter is too young or inexperienced, they may appoint a caretaker manager to see the firm through until such time as they are ready to take on the role.
- *Liquidate* This is usually the least attractive option as the price for the assets will not reflect any goodwill.

If succession really is the chosen option it will need careful planning. Who should be the successor? Do they possess the necessary skills and temperament? If not, can they be developed through training and experience within the available time-frame? What are the financial, tax and pension consequences? The issues that need to be addressed may seem endless. To help approach the task systematically, Leach (1996) proposes the following approach:

1 Start planning early. The most successful successions are those that involve the next generation early in the process so as to allow them to grow into the role rather than coming as an unexpected 'event'.
2 Encourage inter-generational teamwork. It is important that all issues surrounding the succession are addressed and agreed by all the next generation, not just the chosen successor.
3 Develop a written succession plan. This is an action plan setting down what has to be done, by whom and when. It will include details of the founders reducing involvement and their successor's expanding role and responsibilities. It should also address the structure of the management team.
4 Involve the family and colleagues in your thinking and, when complete, show them the succession plan. This is about communication and getting commitment from everybody to the plan.

5 Take advantage of outside help. Succession has important financial, tax and pension consequences for the founder and the family. Consulting the firm's accountant and lawyer early in the process is vital.

6 Establish a training process. The plan should lay out how the successor is expected to develop the skills needed to take over the firm and over what time frame. This might involve education and training as well as job or work experience.

7 Plan for retirement. The owner-manager needs to be prepared financially and emotionally for retirements. Retirement will bring lots of free time and entrepreneurs, particularly, like to keep on the go.

8 Make retirement timely and unequivocal. When the timetable for succession is set, it is important to stick to it and not hang-on in the job. Sonnenfield (1988) characterised the founder as typically having four exit styles, the last two having a more positive effect on the business:

- *Monarchs*: who do not leave the business until they are forced out through ill-health, death or a palace revolt;
- *Generals*: who leave the business, but plot a return and quickly do so 'to save the business';
- *Ambassadors*: who leave the business quickly and gracefully, frequently to serve as post-retirement mentors;
- *Governors*: who rule for a limited term and turn to other activities then to gain fulfilment.

It could be that the future will see a decline in the importance of family businesses. The break-down of family networks, increasing demands for capital that families cannot supply, a booming stockmarket which makes obtaining a listing attractive – all these factors may mean that more and more companies are sold on. Certainly the survey by Burns and Whitehouse (1996) indicates this trend is underway in Britain. However, the high proportion of owner-managers still wishing to pass businesses on to the next generation contrasts strongly with the proportion actually succeeding in doing so.

Summary

Starting up as a family firm can be attractive because of the emotional support and helping hands that may not expect to be paid. As they grow, family firms can foster loyalty, responsibility, long-term commitment, not least to ethical standards, and a pride in 'the family tradition'. These virtues are often welded into a desire to transfer the firm from one generation to the next and to preserve it in difficult financial times. Seventy per cent of UK business can be described as family firms, many with household names like **Mars** and **Cadbury**. Many of today's best-known public companies started life as family firms and still have relationships with the founding family. Familial brands like **Baxter's Soups** build consumer loyalty over long periods and can be a very valuable asset.

At the heart of the family firm is the family culture – its values and beliefs. These can strengthen the business, for example the highly ethical convictions based on religious beliefs of **Cadbury** and **Wilkin & Sons**, maker of Tiptree Jams. They can be quite quirky, as in the case of **Mars.** They can be managed in an autocratic, paternalistic fashion like **Ferrero Rocher**.

There is, however, the potential for conflict because family culture is essentially based on emotion, emphasising loyalty, caring and sharing, whereas business culture is unemotional, task orientated and based on self-interest. The emotion-based family culture operate subconsciously and can get in the way of business. For example, family firms can suffer from nepotism and a lack of profession-alism. Managers who are not family members can feel alienated and isolated, believing that important decisions are being made without their involvement, 'over the kitchen table' rather than in the office. Family conflict and politics can result in the firm being neglected or business decisions being made for other than commercial reasons – the introvert firm which tries to ignore commercial reality. It can also mean that the firm is used as a milk cow for the family and loses its commercial edge. As we saw with **J & B Wild**, all firms need to change and adapt, but introvert firms sometimes do not see the need to do so.

Succession in the family firm is often problematic and can itself lead to conflict. Like Geoffrey Thompson of **Blackpool Pleasure Beach**, founders tend to ignore it until the last minute. Many of the problems stem from the entrepreneurial characteristics of the founder that make him reluctant to relinquish control of the business. Added to this there may be father–son rivalry as the son rebels or strives for independence within the firm. If there are more sons or daughters, then sibling rivalry can intensify the problem. As we saw with **Noon Products**, introducing the founder's children into the business needs to be handled with care.

Resolving conflict in a family business is often difficult. It requires accommodation or compromise. It might help to understand the nature and underlying cause of the conflict. But ultimately the best approach is to develop a family strategic plan and a family council to monitor it. Setting family objectives led **Everard Breweries** to change their business strategy to emphasise property more.

Succession can be managed. Planning needs to start early and needs to be intergenerational building in consultation with the firm's accountants and lawyers. A written succession plan should be developed which shows how the founder will exit and how the new generation will take over. It will detail any training and development needed and help the founder plan for retirement. Finally, when it is time to go, go!

● Essays and discussion topics

1 What are the advantages and disadvantages of starting up a business with your partner or spouse?
2 What are the advantages and disadvantages of being part of a family firm?
3 Familial brands build consumer trust over long periods and can be very valuable assets. Discuss.
4 Family firms are more common on continental Europe than in Britain. Why do you think this might be?
5 In the future family firms will decline in importance. Discuss.
6 Does it matter how you define a family firm?
7 How might family and business cultures clash?
8 Why are there so many examples of successful family firms which are based on strong religious or ethical bases?
9 What are the problems you might face in being in charge of running a family firm?

10 What are some of the underlying causes of conflict in a family and how might these show themselves in a family firm?

11 The family business sector is an endless soap opera of patriarchs and matriarchs, black sheep and prodigal sons, hubris and nemesis. Discuss.

12 What are the advantages and disadvantages of being an non-family employee in a family business?

13 What are the problems you might face in being the son or daughter of the founder employed in their firm?

14 How would you get on if you were working for your mother or father?

15 What is an introvert firm? How might a business avoid becoming one?

16 How can succession be managed?

17 What do you think would be a good training programme for a son or daughter intending to take over the running of the family firm?

18 In what circumstances might it be wise not to pass on the firm to a member of the family?

19 What should go into a succession plan?

20 What problems might an entrepreneur encounter in facing retirement?

Exercises and assignments

1 List the questions you would ask members of the family working in a family firm in order to highlight the advantages and problems of working there.

2 Based upon these questions, interview members of the family and write an essay highlighting the advantages and problems of working in the family firm.

3 List the questions you would ask the manager of a second or third-generation family firm in order to highlight the problems they encountered in taking over the firm.

4 Based upon these questions, interview the manager and write an essay highlighting the problems they encountered.

5 Write a specimen family constitution.

6 Find out what are the tax consequences of succession in the family firm.

Websites to visit

Visit the Stoy Centre for Family Business at www.fbn-i.org

References

Burns, P. and Whitehouse, O. (1996) *Family Ties*, 3i European Enterprise Centre, Special Report no. 10.

Churchill, N. and Hatten, K. (1987) 'Non-Market Transfers of Wealth and Power: A Research Framework for Family Business', *American Journal of Small Business*, Winter.

Institute for Small Business Affairs (1999) *All in the Family*, Policy and Research Issues, no. 1, August.

Leach, P. (1996) *The BDO Stoy Hayward Guide to the Family Business*, London: Kogan Page.

Levingson, H. (1983) 'Consulting with Family Business: What to Look Out For', *Organizational Dynamics*, Summer.

Nelton, S. (1986) *In Love and in Business*, New York: John Wiley & Sons.

Poutziouris, P. (1994) 'The Development of the Familia Business', in A. Gibb and M. Rebernick (eds), *Small Business Management in New Europe*, and Proceedings of 24th ESBS – September, Slovenia, in *New Europe*.

Poutziouris, P. and Chittenden, F. (1996) *Family Businesses or Business Families*, Institute for Small Business Affairs and National Westminster Bank Monograph 1.

Ram, M. and Holliday, R. (1993) 'Relative Merits: Family Culture and Kinship in Small Firms', *Sociology*, vol. 27, no. 4.

Rosenblatt, *et al.* (1985) *The Real World of the Small Business Owner*, San Francisco, CA: Jossey-Bass.

Sonnenfield, J. (1988) *The Hero's Farewell: What happens when CEOs Retire*, New York: Oxford University Press.

chapter fourteen

The exit

Contents

- Stagnate and die
- Failure
- The ingredients of failure
- Predicting failure
- Harvest
- Company valuation
- The never-ending cycle
- Summary

Learning outcomes

By the end of this chapter you should:

- Appreciate that the never-ending cycle of start-up and exit is part of the dynamic of the small sector that shows it is responding to changes in the market;
- Understand the ways an owner-manager can exit;
- Understand what constitutes business failure;
- Appreciate when a small firm is most at risk of failure and understand what contributes to it;
- Have a critical understanding of the process of failure;
- Appreciate the options open to the owner-manager in order to harvest their investment in their business and what needs to be done to get the best deal;
- Understand how company valuations are arrived at;
- Appreciate how small business management is different to large business management.

Stagnate and die

Most small firms are born to stagnate or die. As we saw in Chapter 1, in the UK most do not grow to any size – almost two-thirds of businesses comprise only one or two people, and often the second person is the spouse. Some 95 per cent of firms employ fewer than 10 employees and 99 per cent fewer than 50 employees. Half of businesses cease trading within three years of being set up, although, as pointed out, this does not necessarily mean that the closure has left creditors unpaid and it can be viewed in a positive light as part of the dynamism of the sector as it responds to changing opportunities in the marketplace. What is more, when the number of start-ups increases, the number of businesses ceasing to trade tends to do so as well. The pattern is broadly similar internationally, although the USA has an even higher closure rate (Bannock and Daley, 1994). A cynical observer might conclude that, in such a turbulent environment, mere survival is a badge of success.

The exit of an owner-manager can be a thing of sadness or joy, depending on how it is achieved. Ceasing to trade can be a sadness if creditors are left unpaid. For a sole trader this might lead to their personal bankruptcy (which can only be discharged by a court of law) as creditors pursue their debts by claiming their personal assets. Only a tiny number of business exits involve bankruptcy. For a limited company an inability to pay creditors can lead to insolvency and then liquidation, when a liquidator is appointed to dispose of the assets of the business, with their value going to the creditors. Statistically, total insolvencies are defined as all liquidations of insolvent companies plus all personal bankruptcies. These are what most people would agree to call business failures.

However, even with this definition there are problems of interpretation. It is not uncommon for a bank to foreclose on its debt, forcing a company into liquidation, knowing that it will secure repayment of its preferential debt at the expense of other creditors, and then to provide support for a 'new' company set up by the owner-manager undertaking exactly the same type of business. Is this a business failure?

The liquidation of a company, in itself, may be a natural way of bringing the business to an end. This is called a voluntary liquidation. If there are surplus assets then the company is not insolvent and the owner-manager may make a capital gain after creditors are paid. But perhaps the most attractive exit for an owner-manager is to sell the firm as a going concern. If they can achieve this they will reap the harvest of their years of investment in the business. But, even with a sale, definitions are not straight forward because it could be that the sale was prompted by the business making continuing losses which could ultimately have led to failure. Nevertheless, even this form of 'distress sale' may still yield a capital gain for the owner-manager.

Whilst in the USA business failure can be seen as a worthwhile experience for entrepreneurs, provided they are seen to learn from it, in the UK there is still a stigma attached to it. Being associated with a failed company can lead to problems when it comes to raising cash for another start-up. Bankers, in particular, need some convincing to persuade them to give an entrepreneur a second chance – particularly if they lost money on the first attempt.

The Iron Bed Company operates from two sites near Chichester, West Sussex, makes profits of £700 000 on turnover of £12 million and employs 180 people.

However, things were not always so successful. The founders, **Anne** and **Simon Notley** were unable to raise finance for the start-up because of their business track record. This included a failed pine shop and a business importing classic cars from the USA that collapsed in the early 1990s. The couple then ran a wind-surfing school for three years before setting up the company. But they had to invest £70 000 from the sale of their home because they could not raise a bank loan. Consequently, they spent their money very carefully, operating from disused chicken sheds and preferring to invest in promotion and marketing, including risqué newspaper advertisements.

Failure

Notwithstanding these definitional problems, in his review of the literature Storey (1998) identified a number of factors that influence the probability of business failure. These are not necessarily independent of each other. The factors he identified as having the strongest influence were:

- *Age of business*: simply reviewing the statistics tells you that young firms are more likely to fail than older firms. Half of firms cease trading within their first three years of existence. The longer a firm survives, the less likely it is to fail. One study estimated that a 1 per cent change in age leads to a 13 per cent improvement in the probability of survival (Evans, 1987).
- *Size of business*: similarly, the likelihood of failure is greater the smaller the firm. Size is, of course, related to age but it is easier to close a small rather than large firm. Also, as we saw in a previous chapter, large firms have more assets than smaller firms and are therefore better able to weather adversity in the short-term. The survey cited above estimated that a 1 per cent change in firm size leads to a 7 per cent improvement in the probability of survival.
- *Past growth*: firms that grow within a short period after start-up are less likely to fail than those that do not.
- *Sector*: failure rates vary from sector to sector with the construction and retail sectors showing the highest level of failures. Storey concludes, however, that the influence of sector is not as great as the first three factors above.

Storey also considered a number of factors which he concluded had a less certain influence on failure. These were:

- *Management*: most people would accept that the character and skills of the owner-manager as well as the team they draw around them influence the probability of either success or failure. Storey reviewed studies that tried to gauge the influence of work history (for example prior business ownership, management experience, unemployment), family background, personal characteristics (age, gender and ethnic background) and education but found the influences 'complex and difficult to predict' and failed to detect any patterns.
- *Economic conditions*: small firms are traditionally thought to be vulnerable to changes in economic activity with business failures expected to increase in times of recession. However, studies have failed to establish a clear relationship because of the influence of other factors such as previous levels of start-up.
- *Type of firm*: there is evidence that, unsurprisingly, franchises have a lower chance of failure than other businesses. More surprising, Storey concluded that limited companies are somewhat more risky than either self-proprietorships or partnerships, presumably due to their potential for unlimited personal liability.
- *Location*: there are clear regional variations in failure rates, however, these tend to correspond start-up rates with high rates of start-up going hand in hand with high levels of failure. The influence is therefore unclear.

E-commerce bring threats as well as opportunities to small firms. **The Good Book Guide** is a British mail-order bookseller set up in 1977. It is a family business run by **Peter Braithwaite** and employs some 60 people. Customers pay a subscription to receive a catalogue every month, in which some 80 reviewers write independent assessments of new books that the company offer for sale. The problem is that discount e-commerce rivals, such as Amazon.com, are starting to eat into their market. Subscriptions have fallen from a peak of 40 000 in 1995 to 35 000 in 1999, and book sales have seen a similar decline. Turnover in 1996 was down 10 per cent to £5.8 million.

The company's response was to set up its own website in 1997 but this was little more than an order taking facility. Since then the company has spent some £350 000 on a new IT system and £230 000 developing a website that is attractive and permits orders to be fed through the company's book despatch system (www.gbgonline.com). It now employs two full-time programmers. To combat the competition, it plans to highlight international delivery quoting delivery dates, price in different currencies as well as answering queries, online, about import duties. It also plans to create bulletin boards to help develop a community of interest.

The company has made losses in 1997 and 1998 and cash reserves have plummeted, making it necessary to use all the company's £400 000 overdraft facility. The danger is that the move to a free medium will encourage customers to use the book reviews but then shop around the www to find the cheapest price. Whilst The Good Book Guide did not want to discount, it now intends to introduce a loyalty discount.

- *Ownership*: the influence of ownership is less clear but it is suggested that larger firms with more than one plant are more likely to close a plant when facing difficult trading conditions than single-plant firms.
- *Business in receipt of state subsidies*: because state subsidy is often given to the weakest businesses, this influence is also difficult to verify.

Storey's review tells us little about the process of failure and therefore how it might be avoided. It implies that failure is mainly influenced by factors outside the owner-manager's control, many being the inevitable consequences of start-up. He points out that failure is endemic in the small business sector and that it has probably always been characterised by high levels. His overall conclusion – that 'the young are more likely to fail than the old, the very small are more likely to fail than their larger counterparts, and that, for young firms, probably the most powerful influence on their survival is whether or not they grow within a short period after start-up' – may be statistically accurate, but it is hardly of any use to owner-managers.

In an extensive review of some 50 articles and five books on the subject of small-business failure, Berryman (1983) focused more on the managerial causes of failure. He listed some 25 causes and categorised them under six headings:

1 *Accounting*: accounting problems such as debtor and stock control or inadequate records were sited most frequently in this review of the literature.

2   *Marketing*: marketing problems came a close second. These can be many and various from a lack of understanding of customer needs or identification of target customers to poor selling skills.

3   *Finance*: financing a firm that is failing is bound to be a problem. Cash flow will be poor and further finance may be unavailable. However, this is simply an obvious symptom of the problem rather than a root cause. Nevertheless, as many firms have found, undercapitalisation at start-up can be a significant factor in subsequent failure. Firms that are highly successful almost from start-up can face the danger of overtrading if they are undercapitalised.

4   *Other internal factors*: for example excessive drawings, nepotism or negligence.

5   *Behaviour of owner-manager*: Berryman lists such personal problems as inability to delegate, reluctance to seek help, excessive optimism, unawareness of the environment, inability to adapt to change and thinness of management talent as reasons for failure.

6   *External factors*: the effects of the economic environment or changes in the industry or market. Personal problems can also be significant.

Berryman notes that conclusions are difficult because of the lack of homogeneity of small firms. He also notes that many of the items in his list, particularly in categories 1 to 4, are symptoms rather than causes of failure. He categorised them simply as 'poor management' and concluded that this combines with the personality traits of the owner-manager and external factors to cause failure. However, his review still fails to help us understand the process of failure and, therefore, how it might be avoided.

The ingredients of failure

Building on the work of Berryman and using the model developed for business success in Chapter 10 (Figure 10.1), Figure 14.1 attempts to show the ingredients of business failure and can be used to understand how the process happens. Just as with business success, there is a recipe for business failure. Whilst the precise recipe varies from situation to situation, we know the ingredients of failure. It is a coincidence of a number of factors that is likely to lead to failure, as in a complex chemical reaction. The ingredients of failure comprise:

Entrepreneurial character

Referring back to Chapter 2, we recall that certain of the character traits of owner-managers and entrepreneurs can have very negative affects. For example, the strong internal locus of control can lead to 'control freak' behaviour such as meddling, an inability to delegate, a mistrust of subordinates or an unwillingness to part with equity in the business. Similarly, the strong need for public achievement might lead to unwise overspending on the trappings of corporate life, or the 'big project' that is too risky. The strong self-confidence can, *in extremis*, become 'delusional' behaviour evidenced by an excessive optimism, an exaggerated opinion of their business competence and an unwillingness to listen to advice or seek help. On top of this can be layered the problems associated with family firms. These combine to produce a potent set of behavioural ingredients which might become underlying causes of failure.

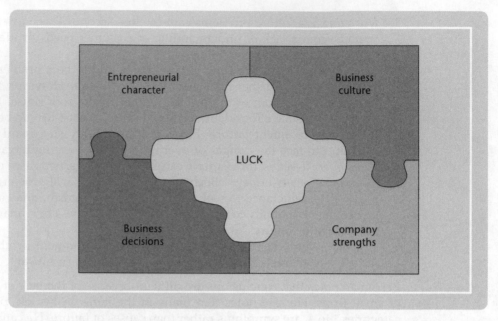

Figure 14.1 The ingredients of failure

In their empirical research of business failure, Larson and Clute (1979) listed eight personal characteristics to be found in owner-managers of failed firms. It is interesting how many of these factors are the negative sides of the character traits of entrepreneurs that we have already noted. The characteristics were:

- Exaggerated opinion of business competency based upon knowledge of some skill;
- Limited formal education;
- Inflexible to change and not innovative;
- Use of own personal tastes and opinions as the standard to follow;
- Decisions based upon intuition, emotion and non-objective factors;
- Past, not future-orientation;
- Limited reading in literature associated with the business;
- Resistant to advice from qualified sources but, paradoxically, accepts it from less-qualified.

Business decisions

By definition, bad business decisions are the opposite of good ones. They often stem from a lack of reliable information or an unwillingness or inability to understand it. For example, bad marketing decisions feature regularly in the literature on causes of failure and these often stem from a lack of understanding of what customers are really buying (benefits), who customers are (market segmentation) and why they do not buy from competitors (competitive advantage). This is basic marketing.

Some of the points when an entrepreneur is most likely to make bad management or personnel decisions are predicted by Greiner's growth model

(Chapter 9). These crises are predictable and the problems of dealing with them are anchored in the entrepreneurial character. Hence, for example, an unwillingness to bring in an outside manager may be related to the entrepreneur's unwillingness to delegate, or their unwillingness to give up equity (control) to attract a suitably experienced manager, or because of the mistrust of non-family managers. Many bad decisions stem from the character traits of entrepreneurs. For example, the decision to undertake the risky 'big project' that eventually brings the company down may have been influenced by the entrepreneur's need to demonstrate achievement and receive public applause and recognition.

One study analysed the events that threatened the survival of small firms and found that 38 per cent were marketing-related, 32 per cent finance-related, 14 per cent management-related, 13 per cent personnel-related, 10 per cent were 'acts of God' and 18 per cent had no associated crisis (Watkins, 1982).

Larson and Clute (1979) listed nine, what they called, 'managerial defects' of failed firms. Many of these we would call bad decisions, but some we would classify under 'weaknesses'. They were:

- Inability to identify target market or customers;
- Inability to delineate trading area;
- Inability to delegate;
- Belief that advertising is an expense, not an investment;
- Only rudimentary knowledge of pricing strategy;
- Immature understanding of distribution channels;
- No planning;
- Inability to motivate;
- Belief that the problem is somebody else's fault and a loan would solve everything.

Company weaknesses

Weaknesses and bad decisions are closely related, like chicken and egg. Many weaknesses stem from bad decisions in the past. For example, high gearing may be due to a decision not to dilute the equity of the firm by going to a venture capitalist. In this case the decision may again have stemmed from the character of the entrepreneur and their wish to retain control of the business. On the other

> Tech Board, a hard-board maker in Ebbw Vale, South Wales, was Britain's biggest venture capital backed start-up when it began trading in 1995. It was a £40 million project with £25 million of funding from a consortium of private equity houses, led by 3i. Its history in many ways reflects what has been happening to UK manufacturing since then. In 1998 it went into receivership and was rescued by Enron, the American energy and power firm. The new company, called **Imperial Board Products**, was sold in April 1999 to a management buy-out team. The purchase was funded by a combination of a loan from Enron, invoice discounting and some state aid. The management buy-out was highly geared and probably undercapitalised from the start. In August 2000 the firm went into liquidation.

hand, many bad decisions stem from poor information caused by inadequate systems.

A frequently cited weakness that is a contributory cause of failure is poor financial control – poor, infrequent information, lax debtor control and/or high stock holding. Poor financial control inevitably leads to the reappearance of Death Valley and a cash flow crisis. If you couple that with poor planning, then you have the potential for failure.

A major weakness cited by a number of studies is the typical overdependence of small firms on a small number of customers for too high a proportion of their sales (Cosh and Hughes, 1998). Another angle on this is the size of the product range. Some studies have shown that the wider the range, the lower the likelihood of failure (Reid, 1991).

External environment

Firms must cope with an ever-changing marketplace. Although direct effects cannot be proved statistically, small firms appear particularly vulnerable to macroeconomic variables – after all, they have less financial 'fat' than larger firms. Changes in overall consumer demand, interest rates and inflation can have a disproportionate effect on smaller firms. Many e-commerce start-ups that received first-round finance in 1999 failed to obtain second-round finance in 2000 because the market had changed so dramatically, forcing them to cease trading. There are also the 'acts of God' – the strike, the fire, the loss of the major customer – which a larger company might weather but the smaller firm cannot. Some external influences are clearly due to bad luck but some are due to bad judgement – the wrong place at the wrong time – and luck can have a disproportionate effect on smaller firms.

In reality the effect of the environment depends upon the time period, geographic area, and market sector in which the firm operates. Perhaps the most significant effect on smaller firms is the degree of competition within its industry and therefore Porter's Five Forces influence not only profitability, but, *in extremis*, the likelihood of failure. A small firm operating in a highly competitive market is more likely to fail than one operating in one with low levels of competition.

This model gives us an insight into the process of failure. It also reinforces many of the lessons of success. These four ingredients of failure interact together. Individually they are present in many firms, but it is only when they combine that the potential for failure is created. What makes the small firm different to the large one is the disproportionate importance of the influence of the owner-manager. Many bad business decisions stem from the entrepreneurial character. Many weaknesses stem from bad business decisions, which in turn may stem from the entrepreneurial character. However, the crisis that triggers the decline into failure is often brought about by some outside factor such as an unexpected change in the marketplace, customer tastes, competition or distribution channels. This may lead to further bad decisions being made by the owner-manager, for example a decision to overtrade or borrow too much. These, in turn, result in symptoms of failure such as running short of cash or declining profitability. The paradox is that the asset of the entrepreneurial character can become a liability in certain circumstances.

> ### ZedZed.com
>
> 'This is a story with an unhappy ending about my dot.com company **ZedZed.com**, a site for independent travellers, which went into liquidation in 2000. ZedZed.com was meant to be called ZigZag.com but that name had already gone. We raised £800 000, which was no mean achievement, but it wasn't enough. In February we encountered dot.com envy from our friends. In March we were winning awards and being asked to speak at conferences in Paris. In June we achieved 1800 user reviews per week. In August we were calling in the liquidators.
>
> Mistakes are always easier to see with the benefit of hindsight, and our worst error was to believe that internet businesses should be valued by the number of subscribers rather than the transactions that they make . . . Today you have to be profitable or else you are not going to get funded again. They say that internet speed is fast but three months is a short period of time to reverse your whole *raison d'être*.
>
> I think we did a lot right too. We built a site in six weeks on a very complicated back-end platform. We chose a content management system that would make us a serious force in the market, and we successfully leveraged that asset with larger organisations who might otherwise have ignored us. We devised a very successful low-cost user subscription campaign without the help of an expensive marketing agency like so many dot.coms. We kept our non-essential expenditure to a minimum, which allowed us to return 20 per cent of the initial subscription to investors. We employed 19 people on low salaries who genuinely loved their daily work. Being a chartered accountant, I knew where our financial position was on a daily basis and knew when the time had come to close the door.
>
> Setting up a dot.com business has been the most exciting, rewarding experience of my life, and of the lives of the team that I had around me. We did something new, different and useful to other people. Sadly for us and our investors, the capital markets have changed to such a degree that we have had to end our quest early. In doing so we are showing that there is sanity amid the madness. Don't pity the pioneers – envy us for our experience. Oh, and pay us well for them too!'
>
> **Edward Johnstone**
> Co-founder of **ZedZed.com**
> *Daily Telegraph* 17.08.00

Predicting failure

It is one thing to understand the process of failure, but it is quite another to try to predict it. Nevertheless many academics both in the UK and USA such as Beaver (1966), Altman (1968) and Taffler (1982) have tried to do this, mainly using financial ratios as relevant variables. Most studies have looked at large public companies because of the ready availability of this information. Financial information in smaller businesses tends to be less reliable, with the profit figure more easy to manipulate, less complete, since they do not have to disclose the same the amount of information as public companies, and less timely, since they do not face Stock Market pressures. However, it has been argued (Keasey and

Watson, 1991) that, because of these factors, if predictive models could be developed they would be extremely valuable, not only in terms of their predictive ability but also in terms of their information value or usefulness. This is not surprising given the problems of information asymmetry facing bankers in particular (see Chapter 12). For this reason trying to predict failure in small firms using models that employ publicly available information has attracted just as much interest as trying to pick winners.

Most of these studies use multiple discriminant analysis on a sample of failed and non-failed firms to select financial ratios that best discriminate between the two groups and then combine them into a simple number, or 'Z score', which indicates the likelihood of failure. Companies are matched by industry and size. Most studies then go on to test the predictive ability of the 'Z score' on a hold out sample which includes failed and non-failed firms. Studies have used the full range of ratios discussed in Chapter 10 – performance, profitability, asset efficiency, liquidity, gearing and risk – in an attempt to see which best predict failure. For example, one study looked at small firms in the construction and civil engineering sector. It tested 25 ratios and the final 'Z score' was calculated as shown below, with companies scoring below 0.36 having a high probability of failure:

$$Z = -0.143 + 1.608a + 0.001b + 0.461c + 0.352d - 0.007e$$

where:

a = net profit margin
b = debtor days
c = profit before tax divided by shareholder funds
d = profit before tax divided by current liabilities from the previous year
e = total sales over working capital from the previous year

In this study 72.9 per cent of the predictive ability came from the simple net profit margin ratio.

Studies like these have been criticised on many counts, not least because they look at symptoms rather than root causes of failure. In this respect the major practical problem with them is their timeliness. It is quite probable that by the time these symptoms manifest themselves in published accounts, the company will already have filed for bankruptcy. What is more, the effect of the external environment, particularly for smaller firms, is likely to be very high. For example, profit margins are likely to decline in most firms at times of recession and therefore any bank using this as a predictive tool might be tempted to foreclose on a large number of loans thus creating a self-fulfilling prophesy. One major UK clearing bank tested 'Z scores' extensively in the 1980s and decided not to use them.

Banks, of course, have a major piece of information at their fingertips that gives them an immediate insight into what is happening within the firm. This is the firm's bank account. From this banks can monitor cash inflows and outflows as well as balances and this can give them invaluable information about current performance long before it finds itself into published financial information. Notwithstanding this two major UK clearing banks started using an expert system called Lending Advisor in the 1990s to help them make lending decisions and monitor loans. This computer-based system combines 'hard' financial data with 'soft' judgmental data using weightings that can be adjusted to produce a lending 'recommendation'. The 'hard' financial data includes a range of historic as well as projected financial ratios. The 'soft' data includes a range of judgements about the management of the firm as well as its competitive advantage within its industry. In many ways the system simply attempts to make lending decisions more rational and consistent. The danger with it is that it masks the areas of judgement that are inevitably involved and focuses attention on the simple, final lending recommendation.

Harvest

The most attractive harvest option is probably to find a trade buyer, another company in the industry that understands the business. They are likely to place a higher value on the business than others because they can see ways of 'adding value' through the purchase, perhaps by synergy. In many cases they might be willing to pay cash, so the entrepreneur can walk away from the firm on the day of sale. David Bruce founded the Firkin chain of pubs in 1979 but sold it to Midsummer Leisure for £6.6 million nine years later when there were only nine pubs. Since then it has been sold and resold and now numbers many hundreds of pubs throughout the UK. David went on to do the same thing with the Hedgehog and Hogshead chain of pubs.

Another option may be a management buy-out – managers in the firm buying it from the founder. Although managers are unlikely to have the necessary capital, many venture capitalists, such as 3i, look very favourably on

In 1996 **Chris Hutt** sold **Unicorn Inns**, with its distinctive Newt & Cucumber brand, to the brewer Moorlands for £13.2 million. This was the culmination of almost five years work perfecting the Newt & Cucumber market offering, but always with an eye to the ultimate objective – an exit either through a trade sale or a stockmarket floatation. With this in mind Chris had developed the marketing plan we looked at earlier. But his experience of the trade told him that there were four critical success factors to achieve this goal of exiting:

● Finding suitable sites to roll out the Newt & Cucumber pub formula so that they could get to a suitable size to benefit from bulk purchase discounts and to be sufficiently attractive to potential buyers.

● Recruiting and motivating good pub management. To this end he put in place training programmes, appraisal systems and an attractive bonus package that rewarded managers who achieved targets in sales, margins, stockholdings and staffing costs (as percentage of sales) – four of the six key financial drivers.

● Putting in place strong financial controls – daily checks on cash takings and bankings (the fifth driver), weekly stocktaking and performance measurement against budget and the production of monthly management accounts.

● Promoting the brand, not only to customers, but also to the trade. To this end he started writing articles for the trade press and made every effort to get PR. For example, in 1992 Unicorn won the Multiple Operator of the year award.

Body Shop has come a long way from being set up by **Anita Roddick** in 1976 to become the multinational public company. It obtained a listing on the Unlisted Securities Market in the UK in 1984, offering shares at 95 pence, and it obtained a full listing in 1986. By the year ending 28 February 1991, turnover exceeded £100 million, profits £22 million and the share price 350 pence. Between 1984 and that date, against a *Financial Times* All Share Index of 100, its shares had risen from an index of 100 to 550. However, by mid-1995 the share price had fallen to 150 pence.

Increasingly the Roddicks were taking a back seat. Body Shop was attracting more competition from both newcomers and established retailers introducing 'natural' products. Because of the emergence of an aggressive US competitor called Bath and Body Works, it was forced into even more rapid expansion with a unfortunate effect on costs and profitability. It also faced criticism about the reality behind its ethical stance. In 1996 an attempted re-privatisation was abandoned because of the gearing implications. In 1998 a new Chief Executive was recruited with the Roddicks becoming co-chairmen. In 1999 the company withdrew from manufacturing. Profits and the share price have recovered. In 2000 **Anita and Gordon Roddick** resigned from Body Shop, multimillionaires.

management buy-outs and are keen to provide funds for them, provided the terms are right. However, managers are likely to know as much about the firm as the founder and can negotiate a tough deal. Indeed some management buy-outs fail because managers know the business too well and are unwilling to meet the asking price. What is more, it is possible that the owner might have to wait several years before the full balance of the sale price is paid.

A similar option is a management buy-in – a team of managers, often with experience in the industry buying the business. It is difficult to know where to turn to find managers interested in this sort of option, however, 3i does keep a confidential register of just such managers.

Finding a buyer, valuing the business and negotiating its sale are a daunting series of tasks that really should not be undertaken without professional advice and help. Many larger firms of accountants can help find buyers, just as they can help find companies to purchase, and they can act as a confidential 'front' in the search process. They are also likely to take a more objective view on company valuation than the entrepreneur and are essential in sorting out the detail of the deal, including the inevitable warranties and indemnities that will be requested by the purchaser. Finally there is the important consideration of taxation, where planning can considerably increase the money actually pocketed by the entrepreneur.

Owner-managers of sizeable companies can achieve personal liquidity and raise additional capital by 'going public' – floating the company on a stock exchange and selling shares in it. This is the route Anita and Gordon Roddick took with Body Shop, floating it first on the smaller Unlisted Securities Market (equivalent to AIM) and then obtaining a full stockmarket quotation. However, this option is problematic if the entrepreneur wishes to retire because the stockmarket's assessment of public share issues centres on the future potential of the firm, and if the float is simply intended to provide an exit for the entrepreneur, it is unlikely to be popular.

Most entrepreneurs want to sell-on their firm rather than to pass it on within their family (Burns and Whitehouse, 1996). However, few plan how to do it. Most rely instead on their instincts for sorting out an opportunistic deal at the last minute. And yet they are far more likely to achieve the best price for their business by planning ahead and building in to the business plan any steps that are needed to help with the harvest.

Company valuation

In practice, there are two basic ways of valuing a business:

1   *Market value of assets*: businesses that are asset-rich, such as a farm or a freehold retail premises, are often valued in this way. Tangible assets such as debtors, stocks, equipment, fixtures and fittings and particularly property are valued at their market rate. This might give a higher value than the second approach.
2   *Multiple of profits*: many firms, particularly those with few tangible assets, are valued based upon some multiple of annual profit. For example, if an appropriate multiple of profits were 5, a company making £100 000 per year would be valued at £0.5 million. If you look in the *Financial Times*, every public company has their price–earnings ratio quoted – that is, how many times the price of their shares is a multiple of their profits – the equivalent of a multiple of profits.

Companies can also be valued using a mix of both methods. Where there are tangible assets, such as property, these might be valued at market rates and then an element of 'goodwill' added based upon a multiple of profits.

The key question, of course, is what multiple of profits to use. Essentially what the buyer is interested in is the future profits the business will make and they are using current profits as a proxy measure. So, one factor to influence the multiple is the 'quality' of earnings. The longer the firm's track record of profitable trading, the higher the multiple. Another factor may be the quality of the management the owner will be leaving behind to continue running the firm. Can they do it without him? Different industry sectors tend to have different multiples that reflect the risk they are perceived as facing. The higher the perceived risk, the lower the multiple. Small, privately-held firms typically command a lower multiple than public companies in the same industry because there is a market for shares in a public company. Multiples in single figures are usual for small firms but at the end of the day it depends how much the buyer wants the firm. If it has strategic importance, for example enabling it to get into a key overseas market, it can easily pay well over any normal market valuation.

One outside factor is the rate of interest. Higher interest rates usually mean lower multiples. Since the purchase of a business often necessitates a buyer borrowing funds, the gearing of the purchased firm, in its final form, can be a factor. If borrowings are high, as they often are in management buy-outs, the company is vulnerable to changes in profitability as it will have high, fixed

Freeserve was floated on the stockmarket in 1999 with a valuation of £1.5 billion, despite having traded for only about a year and not having made any profit. This valuation was based upon the two elements to its business; firstly, as an internet access provider, competing against companies such as Demon Internet. Disks are distributed through its parent, Dixons, and through direct advertising. It does not charge any fee for this service but gets its revenues from a small share of the call charges. It also 'owns' the customer. In 1999 this generated 60 per cent of Freeserve's turnover. This revenue depends on the number of users, the amount of time users spend online and the share of the call charges it is able to negotiate. With so few overheads the gross margin here is almost 100 per cent. However, the absence of any real assets and untested customer loyalty in a market which is becoming increasingly competitive as more and more consumer brands offer the same free service make this part of the business worth probably less than £50 million.

The real value of Freeserve lies in the second part of the business, the portal, which converts visitors to the site into consumers spending time and money. Here Freeserve competes against other consumer portals ranging from Amazon.com. to Yahoo! This aspect generated only 40 per cent of revenues in 1999, but investors were asked to judge the potential of the business. American portals bring in between $1 and $4 of commerce per user, per month.

The US firm Altavista, for example, brought in $166 million in e-commerce and advertising in 1998 from some 11 million customers ($15 per customer). By comparison, Freeserve in 1999 had only 2 million customers bringing in only $1.5 million ($0.75 per customer). This was the potential that investors in Freeserve were valuing.

interest charges. If the return on total assets falls below the rate of interest, it can be in trouble and the higher the borrowing, the greater the trouble. This is what happened to the heavily borrowed small firms in the early 1990s when interest rates soared at the same time as profits tumbled.

The valuation of dot.com businesses has proved extremely problematic. Many needed large amounts of finance at start-up and beyond. Even those that became public companies quickly in their life, like Freeserve, still do not trade profitably. Because this is a new industry, valuation is extremely difficult and the market tends to value what it perceives as the potential these businesses have, rewarding those first into the market because of the perceived 'first-mover advantage.' Indicators of potential for a dot.com business may be the number of click-throughs, customers or members it has but increasingly investors are looking for the potential to turn this into real profit. Customers have proved reluctant to pay for many internet services and customer loyalty seems a very transient affair. Many business formats have simply not worked and B2C trading will probably not take off until more broadband connections are available. It is little wonder that the very high valuations put on many of these businesses in 1999 – in the heyday of 'dot.com frenzy' – came crashing down in 2000 as investors realised that it could take a long time for the potential to turn into real dividends. In the mean time the firms realised that Death Valley really can seem to go on forever and financial control in a start-up really is about cash-flow management.

The never-ending cycle

The never-ending cycle of start-up and exit is part of the dynamic of the small firm sector as firms respond to the ever-changing marketplace. It is one of the reasons why governments all over the world now recognise that small firms have a vital and increasingly important part to play in the economy of the twenty-first century. In this environment survival is a badge of success. And behind every success, and indeed failure, there is a person and a human interest story to tell. Successfully managing growth is a Herculean task. Is it any wonder that so few owner-managers decide to try it? Those who do and succeed really are the super-heroes of the modern world.

Which brings us back to where we started this book – the entrepreneurs themselves. These individuals and their values, beliefs and actions really are the distinguishing feature of small firms, not size *per se*. The family element simply adds complexity. They shape how the firm develops and the decisions it makes. They are influenced by a whole range of factors – they are both born and made, shaped by their background and experiences. And they are not always rational. Their spider's-web approach to management, using informal influence to get their way, has parallels in the business networks they develop and their relationship approach to marketing. For them the job of doing business is a social affair, a core part of their life. They are adept at resolving the conflict that is a constant part of their life. They have a particular hands-on approach to management – they like to manage by doing – and a short-term, incremental approach to decision-making. Strategy often emerges as they assess how they are doing – a reactive, adaptive and ultimately flexible approach to the uncertainty of the entrepreneurial environment. And the risk of failure and the implications for them and their family is a key factor influencing business decisions. Nevertheless they find ways of creating and making the most of the opportunities created by change. They innovate, albeit not in the classical Schumpeterian way. Table 14.1 tries to summarise the main distinguishing characteristics of the small firm.

Table 14.1 Distinguishing characteristics of entrepreneurial small firms

Distinguishing characteristics	⬛ Influence of entrepreneur dominates
	⬛ Influence of family can be important
	⬛ Operates in a highly uncertain, risky environment
Approach to environment	⬛ Sees opportunities and pursues them
	⬛ Uses innovation to create competitive advantage
	⬛ Short-term, incremental approach to decision-making
	⬛ Flexible, adaptive, emergent approach to strategy
	⬛ Personal implications of failure important influence
Approach to management	⬛ Relationship-based approach to all aspects of business
	⬛ Adept at handling risk, uncertainty and ambiguity
	⬛ Good at resolving conflict
	⬛ Action-orientated – a hands-on approach
	⬛ Uses informal influence in managing people
	⬛ Prefers informal, spider's-web organisation
	⬛ Develops personal business networks
	⬛ Personal relationship approach to marketing
	⬛ Strongly intuitive, but self-reliant and confident
	⬛ Evolves as business grows

Because of these factors, small firms really are fundamentally different to large ones, where the interests of shareholders are normally assumed to be of major importance and the influence of any one individual is far less. What is more, just as every individual in the world is different, so too is every small firm. Not only are small firms a heterogeneous group, individual firms adapt and change as they grow and develop to meet the changing needs of the market place. And, although the stage models of growth help us towards an understanding of the dynamics of growth, this makes it difficult to generalise about the distinguishing characteristics of small firms. Table 14.1, therefore contains many very broad generalisations that must be treated with caution. However, it does explain why small firms and entrepreneurs are worthy of separate study. Small firms are not just scaled-down versions of large ones, they are interesting, exciting and unpredictable. And the entrepreneurs that run them really are the superheroes of the twenty-first century.

Summary

Most firms are born to stagnate or die – not to grow to any size. There are three sorts of exit:

- *Cessation of trade* – where the business just winds up without creditors being owed any money. Most exits are of this form.
- *Failure* – which involves liquidation of insolvent companies and personal bankruptcy.
- *Harvest* – which involves selling the business on as a going concern.

In the USA investors see failure as part of the entrepreneurial learning process. However, in the UK, as **Ann** and **Simon Notley** found when they started up **The Iron Bed Company**, it is not always viewed in the same way and can cause entrepreneurs problems when it comes to raising cash for future ventures. The main factors influencing the statistical likelihood of failure are age and size of business, past growth and sector. The main managerial causes of failure involve poor management (accounting, marketing, financing and other factors), behavioural characteristics of the owner-manager and external factors. Companies like **The Good Book Guide** may face difficulties outside their control but it does not necessarily lead to failure.

The recipe for failure involves a coincidence of four factors which interact like a complex chemical reaction. These are:

- *Entrepreneurial character* – particularly 'control freak' behaviour, delusional behaviour and the need for achievement;
- *Business decisions* – such as inability to delegate or the 'big project';
- *Company weaknesses* – accounting controls and overdependence on a small number of customers are common. As with **Imperial Board Products**, lack of adequate finance is another common problem;
- *External environment* – for example, Porter's Five Forces measures the degree of competition in the industry.

Many weaknesses stem from bad business decisions, which in turn may stem from some inherent character traits of the entrepreneur. Often events in the external environment trigger the chemical reaction that causes the decline into failure. Luck plays a part but, as with **ZedZed.com**, it is not always clear what is luck or bad judgement.

The harvest involves selling the business as a going concern either to a trade buyer, a management buy-out or management buy-in. As with **Unicorn Inns**, this needs careful planning and professional advice. Another option to raise liquidity may be 'going public', but the entrepreneur will find it difficult to exit in the short term. What is more, as Anita Roddick and **Body Shop** found, the Stock Market can exert strong short-term pressures that constrain the actions of management.

Company valuation is not a science. It depends on what a buyer is willing to pay, and therefore how important the purchase is to them. There are two commonly used methods of valuation – market value of assets and a multiple of profit. Multiples depend on the quality of earnings, the quality of management, the industry sector and the general economic climate. Few private companies command a multiple into double figures.

The never ending cycle of start-up and exit is part of the dynamic of the small-firm sector that shows it is responding to the changing demands of the market place. However, behind every exit there is a personal story, as we saw with **ZedZed.com**.

Small firms have three distinguishing characteristics – the uncertain, risky environment they operate in and the central influence of the entrepreneurs and their families. Their approach to this environment is opportunity-driven, innovative, involving short-term incremental decisions and strategies that are flexible, adaptive and emerge from previous action. Ultimately they are concerned about the personal implications of failure. Their approach to management is hands-on, informal and relationship-based. They are adept at handling risk, uncertainty and ambiguity and good at resolving conflict. They develop networks and are good at relationship marketing.

● Essays and discussion topics

1 Why do most small firms stagnate or die?
2 Is it good that so many small firms cease trading?
3 What constitutes failure in business?
4 What do you think of Storey's conclusion about failure; that 'the young are more likely to fail than the old, the very small are more likely to fail than their larger counterparts, and that, for young firms, probably the most powerful influence on their survival is whether or not they grow within a short period after start-up'?
5 How do you distinguish between causes and symptoms in business failure?
6 If you are trying to predict failure does it matter if you measure symptoms rather than causes?
7 Do entrepreneurs make their own luck?
8 The entrepreneurial character is as much a liability as an asset. Discuss.
9 You cannot distinguish between bad business decisions and business weaknesses. Discuss.
10 Running a growing small firm is one perpetual crisis. Discuss.
11 What do you think of Edward Johnstone's comments about ZedZed.com going into receivership?

12 What are the pros and cons of selling a business rather than passing it on within the family?
13 There is no such thing as company valuation, only a willing buyer and a willing seller negotiating a price. Discuss.
14 Are there any lessons from product/service pricing (Chapter 5) for company valuation?
15 Dot.com business valuations are just fantastical. Discuss.
16 How are small firms different to large ones?

● Exercises and assignments

1 Analyse the options for The Good Book Guide. What do you think of its chances of success?
2 Check the current valuation of Freeserve in the financial press. Investigate how this valuation might be justified.
3 Find a business that has recently failed and try to fit the circumstances of its failure into the framework of the failure model shown in Figure 14.1.
4 Using desk research, write a case study of a failed business.

● References

Altman, E.I. (1968) *Financial Ratio's Discriminant Analysis and the Prediction of Corporate Bankruptcy*, vol. 23, no. 24, September.

Bannock, G. and Daley, M. (1994) *Small Business Statistics*, London: PCP.

Beaver, W.H. (1966) *Financial Ratios as Predictors of Failure*, Journal of Accounting Research, Supplement on Empirical Research in Accounting, pp. 71–111.

Berryman, J. (1983) 'Small Business Failure and Bankruptcy: A Survey of the Literature', *European Small Business Journal*, vol. 1, no. 4.

Burns, P. and Whitehouse, O. (1996) *Family Ties*, 3i European Enterprise Centre, Special Report no. 10.

Cosh, A. and Hughes, A. (eds) (1998) *Enterprise Britain: Growth Innovation and Public Policy in the Small and Medium Sized Enterprise Sector 1994-97*, Cambridge: ESRC Centre for Business Research.

Evans, D. (1987) 'The Relationship between Firm Growth, Size and Age', *Journal of Industrial Economics*, pp. 567–82.

Keasey, K. and Watson, R. (1991) *The State of the Art of Small Firm Failure Prediction: Achievements and Prognosis*, International Small Business Journal, vol. 9.

Larson, C. and Clute, R. (1979) 'The Failure Syndrome', *American Journal of Small Business*, vol. iv, no. 2, October.

Love, N. and D'Silva, K. (2001) *A Model for Predicting Business Performance in SMEs: Theory and Empirical Evidence*, Paper presented at the British Accounting Association Conference, March 26–27, University of Exeter, England.

Reid, G.C. (1991) 'Staying in Business', *International Journal of Industrial Organisation*, vol. 9.

Storey, D.J. (1998) *Understanding the Small Business Sector*, London: International Thomson Business Press.

Taffler, R.J. (1982) *Forecasting Company Failure in the UK using Discriminant Analysis and Failure Ratio Data*, Journal of Royal Statistical Society, vol. 145, part 3.

Watkins, D. (1982) 'Management Development and the Owner-manager', in Webb, Quince and Watkins (eds), *Small Business Research*, Aldershot: Gower.

Entrepreneurship exercises

1 The dream

If you think you would like to run your own business, work through the following exercises to see if you really have what it takes. Read Chapter 2 first.

1 Answer the following questions to see if you are the type of person to succeed.

		Yes	No
(1)	Do you work hard at things that interest you?	☐	☐
(2)	Are you a self-starter, somebody who does not need pushing?	☐	☐
(3)	Are you the sort of person who frequently has new ideas?	☐	☐
(4)	Do these ideas usually get implemented?	☐	☐
(5)	Are you willing to put in the extra hours to get thing done?	☐	☐
(6)	Have you a supportive family that does not object to you putting in those extra hours?	☐	☐
(7)	Do you usually do your own thing rather than follow the crowd?	☐	☐
(8)	Do you set yourself goals and gain satisfaction from achieving them?	☐	☐
(9)	When things go wrong do you press on regardless if you believe in what you are doing?	☐	☐
(10)	Are you fairly stable – not too many ups and downs?	☐	☐
(11)	When you don't get your own way, do you shrug it off, not bear a grudge and just get on with life?	☐	☐
(12)	Can you motivate others to work with you?	☐	☐
(13)	Are you willing to take measured risks?	☐	☐
(14)	Can you live with uncertainty about the future?	☐	☐
(15)	Are you willing to try your hand at most things?	☐	☐
(16)	Do others consider you a fairly good all rounder?	☐	☐

If you answered 'yes' to all these questions you have the makings of a successful entrepreneur. But are you really sure you answered the questions honestly? Why not ask someone close to you to rate you in these areas.

2 List the advantages and disadvantages of:

- Employment
- Self-employment

3 List the reasons you want to set-up your own business. Are they good enough to motivate you to succeed?

4 List the reasons why you should not set up your own business. Can they be overcome or, if not, are you prepared to live with the risk?

5 Try estimating your current monthly personal and domestic costs using the checklist below:

- Rent/mortgage
- Community charge
- Utilities (electricity, gas, water, telephone)
- Other monthly standing orders (for HP, insurance, subscriptions etc.)
- Food
- Clothing
- Travel (including any vehicle costs, if you own one)
- Entertainment

Now try estimating what these might be if you were to economise. Can you survive on this? Would you be willing to survive on this? When you undertake the start-up exercise that follows make sure that you have sufficient CASH (drawings or salary) each month to meet these personal and domestic costs. Carry this forward to the cash flow forecast.

2 Start-up

This 16-part start-up exercise can be undertaken as one exercise or as relevant chapters of the book are completed:

Exercises	Chapter	Topics
1–3	4	Business ideas
4–9	5	Feasibility: customer and benefit analysis, market research, break-even, resources
10–11	6	Profit and cash flow evaluation
12–15	8	Business plan
16	12	Obtaining finance

1 Follow this four-step guide to generating ideas for a start-up, adapted from Timmons.[1] The aim is to generate as many ideas as possible so while generating ideas it is important not to evaluate them or get bogged down in the detail of how they may or may not work.

Step 1 *List ideas.* Think of unmet market needs, changes in technology or legislation or demographics, ideas you have seen in other regions or countries that you have not seen here, knowledge and information gaps.

Step 2 *Expand the list.* Think about your personal interests, experiences, desired lifestyle, values and what you feel you are likely to do well or would like to do.

Step 3 *Get feedback on the list from at least three people who know you.* Knowing you, they might be able to add to the list by interpreting it slightly differently.

Step 4 *Jot down insights, observations and conclusions about your ideas and personal preferences.*

---

1 Timmons, J. A. (1999) *New Venture Creation: Entrepreneurship for the 21st Century*, Singapore: McGraw-Hill International.

2 Using the list generated from this exercise, evaluate each idea against the following eight criteria, using a score of 1 (very poor or very unattractive) to 5 (very high or very attractive).

- *Attractiveness of idea* – Would you enjoy doing it?
- *Ability to undertake* – Do you have the skills needed to do it?
- *Practicality* – Is it something that really can be done?
- *Potential market demand* – Will customers buy it?
- *Ability to combat competition* – Is there competition and can you combat it in some way?
- *Ability to differentiate* – Can you differentiate it in some way that can be sustained over a long period?
- *Price potential* – Can you avoid competing simply on price?
- *Resource availability* – Do you think you have, or can get, the resources you need to start-up this business?

The top scoring three or four ideas might be worth exploring further.

3 List the critical factors that you would need to make certain were right in taking the top scoring three or four ideas from the previous exercise further. Evaluate the ideas and select the one you want to take further. Be aware that the one you select may still prove not to be commercially viable and you may have to return to this list to research another idea.

4 Consider the features and benefits of the product or service you have decided to research further:

- List the features.
- Alongside this, list the benefits that the customer derives from those features.
- Alongside that, list the proof you might offer the customer to convince them the benefit is real.

For example:

Shop stays open late ⇨ Flexibility in shopping time ⇨ Come and see
New car suspension ⇨ Greater ride comfort ⇨ Test drive

5 Undertake appropriate desk and field research to find out as much as you can about the market that you wish to enter. Write a brief report giving:

- Estimates of the size and growth of the market.
- Details of competitors – names, strengths and weaknesses.
- An evaluation of the degree of competition in the market, using the Competitive Analysis Checklist, below.
- An evaluation of your business strengths and weaknesses.
- The basis for your competitive advantage over competitors.

Competitive Analysis Checklist

	High	Medium	Low
Competitive rivalry	☐	☐	☐
Power of customers	☐	☐	☐
Power of buyers	☐	☐	☐
Ease of entry to market	☐	☐	☐
Threat of substitutes	☐	☐	☐
Overall evaluation	☐	☐	☐

6 Write a brief report giving details of:

- The target market you are aiming to sell to.
- The marketing strategy you aim to adopt, giving details of any basis for differentiating your product or service and the marketing you aim to adopt.
- The selling price you have decided to set for your product or service, giving details of the variable cost per unit and the average cost per unit (given your estimated sales volume) that you face along with the 'going rate' in the market.
- Any particular launch strategy.

7 Using the break-even worksheet on the next page, work out the break-even point for your business idea. Do you think you can achieve this level of sales?

8 List any equipment you might need for the start-up. Find out the cost of this equipment. Can it be borrowed? Can it be leased or hired? If so, find out the costs.

9 For the product or service you have selected, team up with two other students, one as a customer another as an observer and conduct a role playing sales interview lasting 15 minutes with the customer. Make certain each of you understands the role you are playing. Plan your interview using the outline contained in Chapter 5. When it is finished, get the observer to give you feed-back on how you performed. Make certain you understand the implications, not only for your own selling skills, but also for the benefits offered by your product or service.

10 Refer back to the break-even worksheet and from it prepare a profit statement.

11 From this estimated profit statement prepare a cash flow forecast, using the pro forma cash flow forecast provided on the next page.

12 Undertake a SLEPT analysis on the business idea.

13 Undertake a SWOT analysis on yourself in terms of your ability to run your own firm.

14 Write a mission statement for your business that reflects what business you are in and what you want it to become.

15 Using as a model the specimen business plan in the Appendix to Chapter 8 that is closest to your business (retail, service or manufacture); prepare a business plan for your own business idea, using the pro forma on the following pages.

16 Prepare a schedule showing the amount of finance you need to start the business, the uses to which it will be put and the proposed sources – lease, HP, factoring, overdraft, loans (long vs short-term), venture capital. How do you think a financier will view your proposition? Do you have security to offer? Can the amount of finance you need be reduced in any way?

Break-even worksheet

Sales:	£	(A)
Less direct (variable) costs:		
materials	£	
direct wages	£	
other	£	
Total direct costs:	£ _____	
Gross profit/contribution:	£	(B)
Fixed costs (overheads):		
wages/salaries (including taxes)	£	
rent	£	
heat/light/power	£	
advertising	£	
insurance	£	
transport/travel	£	
telephone	£	
stationery/postage	£	
repairs/renewals	£	
depreciation	£	
local taxes	£	
other _____	£	
other _____	£	
Total fixed costs	£ _____	(C)
Net profit	£	
Less drawings or dividends	£ _____	
Profit retained in the business	£ _____	

$$\text{Break-even point} = \frac{(C) \times (A)}{(B)}$$

Cash flow forecast

Month:												

SALES

Volume:												
Value:												

RECEIPTS

Sales – cash												
Sales – debtors												
Capital introduced												
Grants, loans etc												
Total (A)												

PAYMENTS

Materials												
Wages/salaries												
Rent												
Heat/light/power												
Advertising												
Insurance												
Transport/travel												
Telephone												
Stationery/postage												
Repairs/renewals												
Local taxes												
Other _____												
Other _____												
Capital purchases												
Loan repayments												
Drawings/dividends												
Total (B)												

CASH BALANCES

Cash flow (A)−(B)												
Opening balance												
Closing balance												

Business plan

Business name and address:

Proprietor's name and address:

Business form:

Business activity

Aims:

Objectives:

Market size and growth:

Competitors:

Names	Strengths	Weaknesses

Your business:

Strengths	Weaknesses

Competitive advantages:

Proposed customers:

Advertising and promotions strategy:

Pricing strategy:

Premises

Equipment

Key people and job functions:

Background details of key people:

Financial highlights

12 months to:

Turnover:

Profit:

Break-even:

Funding requirement:

Source of funds:

Forecast profit and loss account

Business:

Period: **£000**

Sales: (excluding VAT)		£	*(A)*
Less direct (variable) costs:			
materials	£		
direct wages Overtime	£		
other	£		
Total direct costs		£	
Gross profit/contribution:		£	*(B)*
Fixed costs (overheads):			
wages/salaries (including taxes)	£		
rent	£		
heat/light/power	£		
advertising	£		
insurance	£		
transport/travel	£		
telephone	£		
stationery/postage	£		
repairs/renewals	£		
depreciation	£		
local taxes	£		
other Professional fees	£		
other	£		
Total fixed costs		£	*(C)*
Net profit		£	
Less Interest			
Net profit after interest			
Less: Tax			
Profit retained in the business		£	

$$\textbf{Breakeven point} = \frac{(C) \times (A)}{(B)}$$

Cash flow forecast

Month:												
SALES												
Volume:												
Value:												
RECEIPTS												
Sales – cash												
Sales – debtors												
Capital introduced												
Grants, loans etc												
Total (A)												
PAYMENTS												
Materials												
Wages/salaries												
Rent												
Heat/light/power												
Advertising												
Insurance												
Transport/travel												
Telephone												
Stationery/postage												
Repairs/renewals												
Local taxes												
Other _____												
Other _____												
Capital purchases												
Loan repayments												
Drawings/dividends												
Total (B)												
CASH BALANCES												
Cash flow (A)−(B)												
Opening balance												
Closing balance												

3 Growth audit

This 10-part start-up exercise can be undertaken as one exercise or as relevant chapters of the book are completed:

Exercises	Chapter	Topics
1–2	9	Personal qualities of the owner-manager The management team
3–6	10	The product-market offering The competitive environment Financial performance
7–10	11	Evaluation of growth options

For a selected small firm:

1 Using Growth Audit Checklist 1 as a guide, evaluate the personal qualities of the owner-manager and their ability to handle growth and take the firm forward.
2 Using Growth Audit Checklist 2 as a guide, evaluate the management team and their ability to handle growth and take the firm forward.
3 Using Growth Audit Checklist 3 as a guide, evaluate the product-market offerings of the firm and the opportunities for growth. Use the checklist for each product-market offering. Represent the product-market portfolio in a Boston matrix.
4 Using Growth Audit Checklist 4 as a guide, evaluate the competitive environment and competitors facing the firm and evaluate how they might develop sustainable competitive advantage.
5 Using Growth Audit Checklist 5 as a guide, undertake a financial analysis of the firm and draw up your conclusions about how it is performing. If you are able to obtain projected or budgeted financial statements, repeat the analysis.
6 Analyse the results from steps 1 to 5 and summarise in the form of a SWOT analysis.
7 Break down the total budgeted sales for next year into the four categories of the Product/Market Matrix:

£ Sales		£ Sales
Existing	Product Development	
Market Development	Diversification	
Total sales:		

8 Critically analyse how the firm proposes to achieve the increase in sales:

- List the ways the company intends to achieve greater market penetration.
- Detail why the company is going into new markets and how it is going to do so.
- Give details of any new product(s) it intends to sell and why existing customers are expected to buy.
- Give details of and the rationale for any diversification. Explain how it will go about diversifying.
- Give details of and the rationale for any mergers and acquisitions. Explain how it will go about making the acquisition or merger.

9 In the light of the SWOT Analysis, and after discussion with management, evaluate the growth strategy the firm is following. How would you rate the chances that the firm will meet its sales target?
10 Write up your findings in the form of a report. Indicate any other growth opportunities that the firm might face. Evaluate the financing options for all opportunities.

Small Business Audit Checklist 1

Personal qualities of the owner-manager

- Why is the owner-manager in business?
  - are they push or pull factors?

- Is the owner-manager entrepreneurial?
  - are they opportunistic, innovative, self-confident and self-motivated, proactive with vision and flair and a willingness to take risks?

- Are they willing to make, and emotionally strong enough to endure, sacrifices and personal hardship for the sake of the business?

- What are the entrepreneurs long term objectives?
  - is it capital gain, regular income, need for achievement, contribution to society, provide employment, produce something that is needed, build something that will outlive them, achieve status, have fun?

- Does the entrepreneur really want the firm to grow?

- Does the entrepreneur have the ability to change the way they manage the firm as it grows?
  - will they be able to delegate but control and coordinate?

- Does the entrepreneur have the ability to become a leader?
  - do they have vision and ideas, have the ability to undertake long-term strategic planning, communicate effectively, have the potential to create the right culture in the firm and will they be able to monitor and control performance effectively?

- What style of leadership will they adopt?
  - is it appropriate for the group they manage, the tasks they undertake and the situation they are in?

- Are they able to cope with crises effectively?

- Can they build a management team?

- Can they build an effective board of directors?

Small Business Audit Checklist 2
The management team

- Is there a management team in place?
- Does it have an adequate mix of outside experience?
- Do they have the right skills mix?
- Is there a proper organisation structure?
- Is it appropriate for the degree of task complexity?
- Are there any gaps in the structure?
- Is authority delegated to the management team?
- Are there proper controls in place to monitor their performance?
- Is there an appropriate culture in place?
  - influenced by appropriate organisational and cognitive processes and behaviours?
- Are they a cohesive team?
  - do they have the right mix of Belbin team roles?
- Are there any gaps in the team profile?
- How does this show itself in the way they operate?
- Do the team handle conflict in an effective manner?
- Is the management team cohesive?
- Is the management team motivated to succeed?
  - are they personally motivated, are there appropriate incentives in place?
- Is there a concern for staff within the firm?
- Is staff turnover generally low?
- Is the level of absenteeism, for illness or accident, average for the industry?
- Do staff see themselves as part of the firm, with adequate remuneration and career paths?
- Are there skill gaps in the firm?
- Do staff generally receive adequate training?
- Do staff understand the vision or mission of the firm and do they 'buy-into' it?
- Are management and staff motivated to succeed?

Small Business Audit Checklist 3

The product-market offering

● Can the firm identify the target market segments they are selling to?

● Are customer needs understood?

● Are the benefits offered by the products/services understood?

● How loyal are customers?

● How frequent are customer complaints and are they properly followed up?

● Does the firm understand where each product-market offering is in its life-cycle?

● Does the position for the firm mirror that of the industry?

● Is the portfolio of product-market offerings balanced?

● Are new product-market offerings planned to replace those coming to the end of their life?

● Does the firm understand the value chain for each of its product-market offerings?

● Does the firm have any bench-mark information on how it compares or how its product-market offerings compare to those of competitors?

● Does the firm follow a definite generic marketing strategy for each product-market offering?

● Can it command leadership in this area?

● Does the firm understand its core competencies?

● Does the firm command operational excellence, product leadership or customer intimacy?

● Does strategy emphasise something that makes the firm as unique as possible and delivers as much value to the customer as possible?

● Does the strategy reflect the position of each product-market offering in its life cycle?

● If cost is important for any product-market offering, does the firm understand the economies of scale it faces and can it command cost leadership?

● If differentiation is important, does the product-market offering have a strong brand?

● If focus is important, does the firm undertake frequent and thorough market research, and does it has strong customer relations?

Small Business Audit Checklist 4

The competitive environment

- Does the firm regularly undertake market research?

- Does the firm regularly monitor trends in the industry or sector?

- Are there any trends in the market or industry that are likely to particularly affect the firm?

- How competitive does Porter's Five Forces analysis show the firm's industry to be?

- Relative to this, how well is the firm performing?

- Does the firm have any views about future trends (SLEPT) that might affect it?

- Does it have a strategic response to these trends?

- Does the firm have information on competitors?
  - size, profitability and operating methods?
  - bench-mark performance for efficiency, quality and so on?
  - marketing strategies of competitors?

- Can the firm identify which competitors are successful and why?

- Does the firm know of any important changes that competitors will be making in the future?
  - marketing mix?
  - new markets or market segments?
  - new or developed products?

- What is the basis for the firm's competitive advantage?

- How sustainable is this?

Small Business Audit Checklist 5

Financial performance

Performance

Return on shareholders funds (%) $\dfrac{\text{Net profit (after interest)}}{\text{Shareholders funds}}$

Return on total assets (%) $\dfrac{\text{Operating profit (before interest)}}{\text{Total assets}}$

Profitability

Net margin (%) $\dfrac{\text{Net profit}}{\text{Sales}}$

Gross margin (%) $\dfrac{\text{Gross profit}}{\text{Sales}}$

Cost of materials (%) $\dfrac{\text{Cost of materials}}{\text{Sales}}$

Cost of labour (%) $\dfrac{\text{Cost of labour}}{\text{Sales}}$

Overhead cost (%) $\dfrac{\text{Overhead costs}}{\text{Sales}}$

Asset efficiency

Capital/Net asset turnover $\dfrac{\text{Sales}}{\text{Net assets}}$

Debtor turnover $\dfrac{\text{Sales}}{\text{Debtors}}$

Stock turnover $\dfrac{\text{Sales}}{\text{Stock}}$

Fixed asset turnover $\dfrac{\text{Sales}}{\text{Fixed assets}}$

Liquidity

Current ratio $\dfrac{\text{Current assets}}{\text{Current liabilities}}$

Quick ratio $\dfrac{\text{Current assets excluding stock}}{\text{Current liabilities}}$

Gearing

Gearing ratio (%) $\dfrac{\text{All loans + overdrafts}}{\text{Shareholders funds}}$

Short-term debt ratio (%) $\dfrac{\text{Short-term loans + overdrafts}}{\text{All loans + overdraft}}$

Interest cover $\dfrac{\text{Trading profit}}{\text{Interest}}$

Risk

Margin of safety $\dfrac{\text{Sales} - \text{Break-even sales}}{\text{Sales}}$

Selected further reading

Economists' perspective on small business

Binks, M. and Vale. P. (1990) *Entrepreneurship and Economic Change*, Maidenhead: McGraw-Hill.
Cosh, A. and Hughes, A. (eds) (1998) *Enterprise Britain: Growth Innovation and Public Policy in the Small and Medium-Sized Enterprise Sector 1994–97*, Cambridge: ESRC Centre for Business Research.
Schumacher, E.F. (1974) *Small is Beautiful: A Study of Economics as if People Mattered*, London: Abacus.
Storey, D.J. (1998) *Understanding the Small Business Sector*, London: International Thomson Business Press.

Entreprepreneurship

Bolton, B. and Thompson. J. (2000) *Entrepreneurs: Talent, Temperament, Technique,* Oxford: Butterworth-Heinemann.
Chell, E. (2001) *Entrepreneurship: Globalisation, Innovation and Development,* London: Thomson Learning.
Chell, E., Haworth, J. and Brearly, S. (1991) *The Entrepreneurial Personality*, London: Routledge.
Drucker, P.F. (1985) *Innovation and Entrepreneurship: Practice and Principles*, London: Heinemann.
Kuratco, D.F. and Hodgetts, R.M. (2001) *Entrepreneurship: A Contemporary Approach* (5th edn), Orlando: Harcourt College Publishers.
Morrison, A. (ed.) (1998) *Entrepreneurship: An International Perspective*, Oxford: Butterworth-Heinemann.

Entrepreneurship and small firms

Baty, G. (1990) *Entrepreneurship in the Nineties,* New Jersey: Prentice Hall.
Burns, P. and Dewhurst, J. (eds) (1996) *Small Business and Entrepreneurship*, Basingstoke: Macmillan – now Palgrave.
Cannon, T. (1991) *Enterprise: Creation, Development and Growth,* Oxford: Butterworth-Heinemann.
Deakins, D. (1996) *Entrepreneurs and Small Firms,* London: McGraw-Hill.
Harrison, J. and Taylor, B. (1996) *Supergrowth Companies: Entrepreneurs in Action*, Oxford: Butterworth-Heinemann.
Kuratko, D.F. and Welsch, H.P. (2001) *Strategic Entrepreneurial Growth*, Orlando: Harcourt College Publishers.

Entrepreneurial marketing

Carson, D., Cromie, S., McGowan, P. and Hill, J. (1995) *Marketing and Entrepreneurship in SMEs,* London: Prentice Hall.
Chaston, I. (2000) *Entrepreneurial Marketing: Competing by Challenging Convention,* Basingstoke: Macmillan – now Palgrave.

Family firms

Leach, P. (1996) *The BDO Stoy Hayward Guide to the Family Business*, London: Kogan Page.

How-to-do-it texts: Start-up

Barrow, C. (2000) *Essence of Small Business*, London: FT Prentice.
Hodgetts, R.M. and Kuratko, D.F. (2001) *Effective Small Business Management* (7th edn), Orlando: Harcourt College Publishers.
Murphy, M. (1996) *Small Business Management*, Financial Times Management.
Stokes, D. (1998) *Small Business Management: A Case Study Approach,* London: Letts Educational.
Timmons, J.A. (1999) *New Venture Creation: Entrepreneurship for the 21st Century*, Singapore: McGraw-Hill International.

How-to-do-it texts: Growth

Dewhurst, J. and Burns, P. (1993) *Small Business Management*, Basingstoke: Macmillan – now Palgrave.
Timmons, J.A. (1999) *New Venture Creation: Entrepreneurship for the 21st Century*, Singapore: McGraw-Hill International.
Vyakarnham, S. and Leppard, J. (1999) *A Marketing Action Plan for the Growing Business,* (2nd edn), London: Kogan Page.

Selected websites

General interest small business

Department for Education and Employment *Highlights* for small business: www.business-info.org.uk/highlights
Entrepreneur Magazine (US): www.entrepreneurmag.com
Sunday Times Enterprise Network: www.enterprisenetwork.co.uk
Wall Street Journal (US): www.startup.wsj.com

Government help, support and information

Business and Innovation Centre: www.bbic.co.uk
Department for Education and Employment *Resources* for small business: www.business-info.org.uk/resources
Department for Education and Employment Business Online Forums: www.businessdfee.gov.uk
Department of Trade and Industry: www.dti.gov.uk
US Small Business Administration: www.sbaonline.sba.gov

Case studies and articles

Entrepreneur Magazine (US): www.entrepreneurmag.com
Fast Company (US): www.fastcompany.com
The Sunday Times Enterprise Network: www.enterprisenetwork.co.uk
Wall Street Journal (US): www.startup.wsj.com

Start-up help

Barclays Bank: www.smallbusiness.barclays.co.uk
British Franchise Association: www.british-franchise.org
Business Incubators: www.ukbi.co.uk
Business Links: www.businesslink.co.uk
LivewireYoung Entrepreneurs: www.shell-livewire.org
Master Planner: www.masterplanner.co.uk
National Federation of Enterprise Agencies: www.smallbusinessadvice.org.uk
NatWest Bank: www.natwest.co.uk
Small Business Service: www.businessadviceonline.gov.uk
3i: www.3i.com

Web start-up help

Business Incubator: www.business-incubator.com
Business and Innovation Centre: www.bbic.co.ukBarclays Bank: www.businesspark.barclays.com/ebusiness
Information Society Initiative (ISI) Programme for Business: www.isi.gov.uk
Sage: www.sage.com
Virgin Biznet: www.virginbiz.net

Growth help

Business Links: www.businesslink.co.uk
Forum for Private Business: www.fpb.co.uk
Small Business Service: www.businessadviceonline.gov.uk
3i: www.3i.com
Trade Partners UK: www.tradepartners.gov.uk

Family business

Stoy Centre for Family Business: www.fbn-i.org

Downloadable business tools, including business plans

Barclays Bank: www.smallbusiness.barclays.co.uk
Department for Education and Employment *Resources* for small business: www.business-info.org.uk/resources
Master Planner: www.masterplanner.co.uk
NatWest Bank: www.natwest.co.uk
Wall Street Journal (US): www.startup.wsj.com

Business and management information

Barclays Bank business opportunities profiles service: www.smallbusiness.barclays.co.uk
Bnet: www.bnet.co.uk
Enterprise Zone: wwwenterprisezone.org.uk
Start-ups: www.startups.co.uk

Finance

Barclays Bank: www.smallbusiness.barclays.co.uk
Business Angels: www.businessangels.co.uk
Department for Trade and Industry: www.dti.gov.uk
First Tuesday Club: www.firsttueday.com
HSBC: www.banking.hsbc.co.uk
Lloyds TSB: www.lloydstsb.co.uk
NatWest Bank: www.natwest.co.uk
3i: www.3i.com

Small business research and researchers

Centre for Entrepreneurial Leadership (US): www.celee.edu
Institute for Small Business Affairs: www.ourworld.compuserve.com/homepage/haleassoc
Small Business Research Portal: www.smallbusinessportal.co.uk
SME-Learning newsletter: www.sme-learning.com

Recommended journals

Since small firms are the most common form of business, it is not surprising that most of the academic journals in business, management and economics will contain articles about them. The easiest way to find academic articles on a topic related to small firms is to use a web-based search-engine. Your library will advise you on the most appropriate one to use.

However, this is an academic topic in its own right and, of course, many of the issues facing small firms are interdisciplinary in nature. There are a number of journals that are specifically concerned with entrepreneurship and small business; here are some of them:

Entrepreneurship and Regional Development
Entrepreneurship, Theory and Practice
European Venture Capital Journal
International Journal of Entrepreneurial Behaviour and Research
International Journal of Entrepreneurship and Innovation
International Small Business Journal
Journal of Business Venturing
Journal of Small Business and Enterprise Development
Journal of Small Business Management
Small Business Economics

Index